Contents

How to use this book

The American Express Pocket Guide to Mexico is an encyclopaedia of travel information, organized in the sections listed on the previous page. There is also a comprehensive index and gazetteer (pages 213–224), and there are full-colour maps at the end of the book.

For easy reference, the Mexico *A–Z* is, as far as possible, arranged alphabetically. For the organization of the book as a whole, see *Contents*. For places that do not have separate entries in the *A–Z*, see the *Index*.

Abbreviations

As far as possible only standard abbreviations have been used. These include days of the week and months, points of the compass, street names (see ***Addresses*** in *Planning*/***On-the-spot information***), C for century, and measurements.

Cross-references

Whenever a place or section title is printed in *sans serif italics* (for example *Acapulco* or *Basic information*) in the text, this indicates that you can turn to the appropriate heading in the book for further information. Cross-references in this typeface refer either to sections in the book – *Basic information* or *Planning*, for example – or to individual entries in the *A–Z* section, such as *Mexico City* or *Uxmal*. For convenient reference, use the headings printed at the top corner of the page (see, for example, *Basic information* on pages 7–8, *Mexico City* on pages 120–140, or *Uxmal* on pages 188–189).

Bold italics are used to identify sub-sections. For instance: 'see ***Calendar of events*** in *Planning*' will refer you to page 38; in the entry for ***Events*** in *San Cristóbal de las Casas* (on page 167), readers are referred to ***Places nearby*** for the fiestas in surrounding villages, which are described in the same section (i.e. *San Cristóbal de las Casas*).

How entries are organized

Tehuacán
Map 13F8. Puebla. 283km (177 miles) SE of Mexico City on RF 150. Population: 65,000. Served by air, train (on Mexico City–Oaxaca line) and bus.

'Tehuacán' is a household word in Mexico, meaning any kind of sparkling mineral water, and reasonably so, as the town is by far the largest producer in the country. It is also a fairly pleasant resort for liverish and infirm Mexicans, who come to take the mildly radioactive waters. Travellers often stop for a night on the way from Mexico City to *Oaxaca*.

The health-giving waters can be sampled free of charge at a fake Aladdin's cave by the Peñafiel bottling plant. Other worthwhile sights in town include the church of **El Carmen** (*Reforma Norte*) with its dazzling *faïence* dome, and the **Museo del Valle de Tehuacán** (*Calle 1 Norte*). Exhibits prove that this valley was where the cultivation of maize began 7,000yrs ago, a vital stage in the development of Mesoamerican civilizations from hunter-gatherers to settled villages.

Bold type is used in the text primarily for emphasis, to draw attention to something of special interest or importance. It is also used to pick out places – churches or minor museums, for example – that do not have separate descriptions of their own.

Map references

Each of the colour maps at the end of the book is divided into a grid of squares which are identified vertically by letters (A, B, C, D, etc.) and horizontally by numbers (1, 2, 3, 4, etc.). A map reference identifies the page and square in which the town or place of interest can be found – thus *Guanajuato* is located in the square identified as Map **11**C5.

Price categories

Price categories are denoted by the symbols □ ▮□ ▮▮□ ▮▮▮ and ▮▮▮▮ which signify cheap, inexpensive, moderately priced, expensive and very expensive, respectively. In the cases of hotels and restaurants these correspond approximately with the following actual price ranges, which give a guideline at the time of printing. Although actual prices will inevitably increase, in most cases the relative price category – for example, cheap or expensive – will be likely to remain more or less the same.

Prices in Mexico City and the major resorts are usually at least 50 percent higher than elsewhere.

Price categories	Corresponding to approximate prices for **hotels** *double room with bath (single rooms are not much cheaper)*	for **restaurants** *meal for one with service, tax and house wine*
□ cheap	under $500	under $250
▮□ inexpensive	$500–1,000	$250–500
▮▮□ moderate	$1,000–1,500	$500–1,000
▮▮▮ expensive	$1,500–3,500	$1,000–2,000
▮▮▮▮ very expensive	over $3,500	over $2,000

Bold blue type for entry headings.

Blue italics for address, practical information and symbols, encapsulating standard information and special recommendations. For list of symbols see page 6.

Black text for description.

Sans serif italics used for cross-references to other entries.

Bold type used for emphasis.

Entries for hotels, restaurants, Shops, etc. follow the same organization, and are sometimes printed across a narrow measure.

In hotels, symbols indicating special facilities appear at the end of the entry.

Holiday Inn
3.5km (2¼ miles) N of Puerto Vallarta ☎ (322) 2-1700 ▮▮▮▮
230
The Holiday Inn provides dependable fun for all the family, including paragliding for the more adventurous. Set on a quiet beach away from the town, but there are diversions enough to keep everybody busy.

Key to symbols

- Telephone
- Telex
- Not to be missed
- Worth a detour
- Good value (in its class)
- Tourist information
- Car parking
- Hotel
- Simple (hotel)
- Luxury (hotel)
- Cheap
- Inexpensive
- Moderately priced
- Expensive
- Very expensive
- Number of rooms
- Rooms with private bathroom
- Air conditioning
- Residential terms available
- American Express
- Carte Blanche
- Diners Club
- MasterCard
- Visa
- Secure garage
- Own restaurant
- Meal obligatory
- Quiet hotel
- Lift
- Facilities for the disabled
- TV in each room
- Telephone in each room
- Dogs not allowed
- Garden
- Outstanding views
- Swimming pool
- Good beach nearby
- Tennis court(s)
- Golf course
- Riding facilities
- Fishing facilities
- Conference facilities
- Restaurant
- Simple (restaurant)
- Luxury (restaurant)
- A la carte available
- Set (fixed price) menu available
- Good for wines
- Open-air dining available
- Building of architectural interest
- Church/cathedral
- Entrance free
- Entrance fee payable
- Entrance expensive
- Photography not permitted
- Guided tour available
- Guided tour compulsory
- Cafeteria
- Special interest for children
- Bar
- Disco dancing
- Casino/gambling
- Live music
- Dancing

Before you go

Documents required

Foreigners entering Mexico as tourists must hold a passport and, unless on a trip of less than three days solely to a border area, a tourist card. Tourist cards are issued free at Mexican embassies, consulates and tourist offices; they are also obtainable at land frontiers, but it saves time to get them in advance. Valid for 90 or 180 days, they are good for one entry only unless you specifically apply for a multiple-entry card. Children under 15 do not need a card if travelling with their parents; up to the age of 18 they will need a document signed by parents and a lawyer giving them permission to travel, if they are not with their parents.

Vaccination certificates are not needed, but many doctors nonetheless recommend tetanus, typhoid, cholera and hepatitis injections.

Any valid national or international driving licence is acceptable in Mexico. In addition you will need the vehicle registration certificate (to obtain a car permit at the border) and either proof of ownership or signed authorization from the owner. It is also necessary to take out Mexican insurance, either beforehand or at the border; the more expensive 'juridical insurance' also acts as a kind of bail bond, and can save the holder from imprisonment after an accident.

Travel and medical insurance

It is advisable for all travellers in Mexico to insure possessions fully against loss, damage or theft. Medical insurance is indispensable, and should also cover you for possible repatriation expenses. Flight and holiday cancellation insurance may be worth considering.

Money

Mexican currency is decimal, based on the peso ($), which contains 100 centavos (c). Coins are the 20c (used for public telephones), 50c, $1, $5, $10, $20 and $50; these last two are very similar. Bank notes are $50, $100, $500, $1,000, $5,000 and $10,000; the larger bills can be difficult to change.

At the time of writing, any amount of foreign currency in cash or travellers cheques can be taken in or out of Mexico. There are however limitations on the amount of pesos that can be reconverted when leaving. Check before leaving.

Travellers cheques in dollars issued by American Express, Thomas Cook, Barclays and Citibank are widely recognized. Make sure you read the instructions included with your travellers cheques. It is important to note separately the serial numbers of your cheques and the telephone number to call in case of loss. Specialist travellers cheque companies provide extensive local refund facilities through their own offices or agents; American Express, through their offices (listed individually in the *A–Z*) or through any Avis agency, is the quickest.

American Express, MasterCard, Visa, Diners Club and Carte Blanche are accepted in the more expensive hotels, restaurants and shops, and also by airlines and car rental agencies. Elsewhere it is unwise to rely on credit cards.

Personal cheques can be cashed at banks and at some hotels, and are accepted in many shops, hotels and restaurants. It is wise to carry enough cash to cover all eventualities.

Customs

Tourists are allowed to import reasonable quantities of anything clearly intended for personal use (except drugs, weapons or pornography). In addition, travellers over the age of 18 may import duty-free:

Tobacco goods 200 cigarettes *or* 50 cigars *or* 250g tobacco.
Alcoholic drinks 1 litre spirits *and* 1 litre wine.
Perfume 500g/600cc/17½fl oz.
Other goods Goods to the value of $1,000.

When returning, regulations for nationals vary with each country. Make sure you have receipts for purchases made in Mexico, and for any expensive or new items you took with you.

It is forbidden to export from Mexico any genuine archaeological remains and certain classes of antiques. Temporary restrictions on export of gold and silver items are currently in force.

Getting there

By air: Mexico City is well served by a variety of international airlines. In addition, the cities and resorts of Acapulco, Cancún, Cozumel, Guadalajara, La Paz, Manzanillo, Mazatlán, Mérida, Monterrey, Puerto Vallarta and Zihuatanejo receive regular flights from US cities and some charter or holiday package flights. Schedules and fares vary, and it is worth shopping around for cheap excursion fares. Travellers from the southern USA can save money by bussing to the nearest major Mexican border city, and from there flying to Mexico City.

Reservations to the USA from Mexico need to be reconfirmed 72hrs in advance; failure to do this can result in the loss of seats.

By train: Mexico City is served by trains from the border cities of Mexicali, Nogales, Ciudad Juarez, Piedras Negras, Nuevo Laredo and Matamoros. There is no direct link with the US rail network. The trip is even cheaper than the bus, but is also slower and less punctual. Accommodations are reasonable on express trains, especially on the Nuevo Laredo 'Aztec Eagle'. A sleeping compartment costs surprisingly little more than the ordinary fare; early reservations through a travel agent or at the Mexico City Buenavista station are advisable.

By bus: Buses are a more reliable method of transport than trains. There are frequent and cheap deluxe buses from all frontier cities to the capital. The longest journey is from Tijuana (42hrs), the shortest from Matamoros (14hrs). Advance reservations can be made at Greyhound offices in the USA or through travel agents. There are no return tickets, and return reservations are best made on arrival at Mexico City.

By car: The major routes from the US border to Mexico City, with approximate driving times, are described in *Planning*. Since night driving in Mexico is not advisable, at least one overnight stop will be necessary. See also ***Getting around by car***, below.

By ship: From ports on both US seaboards, a variety of cruises leave for Mexican resorts, with Mazatlán, Acapulco, Puerto Vallarta, Cabo San Lucas and Zihuatanejo as the most popular destinations. Prices are not unreasonable bearing in mind the excellent accommodation, food and entertainment offered. Special packages are the best deal, including air fares from Europe or from inland US cities. From Europe, there are no regular sailings to Mexico, although some around-the-world cruises stop at Veracruz.

Climate

There is no longer a recognized tourist season, as inclement weather is rare, but in general the coastal resorts are especially pleasant during the winter (Dec–April) and inland areas during the early summer. The rainy season has lost its former clockwork regularity, but lasts approximately from June–Sept, when in non-desert areas it rains for an hour or so in the afternoon.

The central inland areas enjoy something like 'eternal spring' weather, with daytime temperatures nearly always between 19–29°C (66–84°F). The central W coast averages 20–27°C (68–80°F) during the winter and stabilizes at the upper end of the range in the summer; in late autumn there are occasional hurricanes. The whole of the SE of the country, except for the Chiapas highlands, is always hot, sometimes semi-tropical, and, especially on the Gulf coast and in the rainy season, extremely humid. Temperatures above 33°C (91°F) are common. The N is uniformly sunny and dry, with no noticeable seasons; daytime temperatures are around 25°C (77°F). Baja California is mostly desert, and in the summer temperatures often soar beyond 40°C (104°F).

See also ***When and where to go*** in *Planning*.

Clothes

In most of the country casual informality is the rule, although men should pack one tie just in case. Shorts are not worn except at beach resorts. In the larger cities, a lightweight suit for men and a short evening dress for women are advisable for dining out in the evening.

For visiting the hotter regions do not wear artificial fabrics, which become uncomfortable, especially in areas of high humidity. It is important to have a good pair of walking shoes with non-slip soles for clambering over ruins. In native areas, women are advised to cover their legs and upper arms, since scanty cosmopolitan fashions are regarded as indecent.

Poste restante

Correspondence marked *a/c Lista de Correos* (c/o General Delivery) may be sent to the main post office in any town; proof of identity is required to pick it up. An alternative is to have mail sent to hotels where you will be staying, marked with the approximate date of arrival. American Express also accept mail for their clients. The addition of formalities such as 'Esq.' to an address can cause confusion.

Getting around

Unless driving your own car, a judicious combination of the various means of transport available combines economy with flexibility.

When walking in the country, do not venture out alone, because of the risk of mishaps such as falls.

Flying

Mexico has two major internal airlines, Mexicana and AeroMexico, linking all major cities and resorts to Mexico City. If proceeding between minor destinations, it is usually necessary to change planes in Mexico City or one of the larger provincial capitals. Planes are modern and safe, although timekeeping is lax. Excursion fares and package deals are available on some routes. Fares are cheap – typically three times as much as a deluxe bus.

In addition, there are a variety of feeder and regional airlines, some of them using excitingly antique planes. Schedules and routes change constantly – hotels can provide up-to-date information.

Between airports and the city they serve, there is invariably a bus or taxi service with a fixed tariff.

Railway services

Trains are even cheaper than buses, but are slower and less reliable. They rarely arrive on time, and such details as water supplies and air conditioning tend to be neglected. The trains from the US border to Mexico City are better than those s of the capital – whatever anyone says about it being a wonderful experience, these latter are best avoided. The only train trip which is not better made by other means is the ride across the mountains from Los Mochis on the Pacific coast to Chihuahua (see *Chihuahua* in the *A–Z*).

Buses

Along every main road in Mexico, a bus passes every few minutes, and even on the humblest dirt track at least twice a day. The routes are operated by hundreds of rival companies.

There are several categories of bus, from super-deluxe down to shambling third-class country buses. Tourists should always travel in the highest category available – the price difference is minimal, and the benefits great; prices are in any case subsidized and therefore very low. Tickets are sold at bus stations and should be obtained as long in advance as possible; there are no return fares. Some hotels will send out a messenger to collect tickets.

All except express buses will stop more or less anywhere to pick up or set down – just stand by the side of the road and wave. The bus stations in most towns are near to but not in the centre; ask taxi drivers to take you to the *central camionera*.

Buses within major towns are very cheap but dirty and crowded, and follow unpredictable routes. Some knowledge of Spanish and local geography is necessary before venturing onto these.

Taxis

Taxis are a convenient and cheap way to get around in cities and towns. Prices are low, especially when the driver uses the meter; if there is one in the taxi, its use is compulsory, the only exception being the special tourist cabs, which have bilingual drivers. If no taxi appears when needed, ask for the nearest *sitio* (taxi-rank), and either telephone or go there. In towns where taxis have no meters, there is usually a fixed system of tariffs, and only if actually going outside the town limits is it necessary to bargain in advance over the price. Many taxi drivers (as all over the world) are dishonest and truculent. Do not let yourself be intimidated, and complain to the local tourist office about any abuses. One surprising detail is that many taxi drivers have only the most elementary knowledge of their city, and moreover are unable to read maps. If in doubt, wait for a helpful and knowledgeable driver.

In the capital and other large cities, a collective taxi system (*peseros*) operates up and down main avenues, charging a set fee. These are preferable to buses and the Mexico City Metro; as with the buses, they have their eventual destination written somewhere on the front.

Getting around by car

Driving in Mexico is without doubt more dangerous than in the USA or Europe, and accidents are frequent. However, it is the most convenient way to see much of the country, and if you are aware of the hazards, it is easier to avoid them.

Many drivers are irresponsible and undisciplined, changing lanes and stopping without looking or indicating. Some roads are well maintained, but even on motorways, potholes and rocks can be a nasty surprise. An additional hazard on minor roads are the *topes* (sleeping policemen), which are poorly marked and can easily destroy a car's suspension. Many cars and buses have faulty lights, if any, and Mexicans often drive at night unlit in any case. Kamikaze cyclists, lunatic bus drivers, and wandering drunks, children and livestock present further problems: driving at night is especially dangerous.

In the cities, traffic jams are bad, and traffic lights often disregarded; parking is always a problem. Priority goes to the largest or fastest car on roundabouts and at intersections, and to the first car to flash its lights on minor roads.

Mexican road signs more or less follow the international pattern, but are often hard to see, being set high on the walls of corner buildings. A large **E** indicates that parking is available. If the **E** has a line through it, parking is illegal. The sign *caseta de cobro* means toll-booth – it is always worth taking the toll-roads (*cuota*) in preference to the older free (*libre*) roads, for they are faster and better maintained.

Mexican motoring laws are randomly enforced, often regrettably with the aim of securing a small bribe for the policeman involved. It is usually advisable to pay up, especially if the alternative is a trip to the police station, but do not be afraid to bargain. Speed limits are not observed, but foreigners are advised to comply if only for safety's sake. Cars illegally (or in some cases legally) parked are sometimes towed away, or have their licence plates removed by the police. In either case, it is a nightmare to recover them and involves considerable time and expense. It is necessary to take a taxi to the nearest police station (*delegación*), and hope that the car has not been lost or sold. See also ***Emergency information*** on page 17.

Renting a car

Rates for car rental are low, and any valid driving licence is acceptable; some agencies impose a minimum age limit of 25. It is always necessary to check such details as lights, brakes, steering, oil, water, spare tyre, etc. – do not accept a vehicle in less than perfect condition. To avoid complications, a credit card is the best method of payment. Advance reservation can be done from home through large agencies such as Hertz, Avis or Budget. Do not be too surprised if the car you reserved is not the one you get, but do refuse to pay extra. Insurance is arranged through the rental company, and should be regarded as compulsory even if it may seem optional.

Mopeds and bicycles can be rented at resorts. Two-wheel transport is unfortunately regarded as fair game by many drivers, so avoid traffic.

Boat services
Apart from various ferry services across river estuaries and to inshore islands, the only useful boat services within Mexico, although unpleasant, are from the mainland to Baja California. Schedules vary, and should be checked at a travel agent; some are daily, none less than twice weekly. Routes are Mazatlán – La Paz, Los Mochis – La Paz, Puerto Vallarta – Cabo San Lucas, and Guaymas – Santa Rosalia. Reservations for cars or for a cabin should be made as far ahead as possible. Local air services however are quicker and not much more expensive.

Maps
Lack of accurate base information makes all Mexican maps unreliable to some extent; erratic road-building programmes, for example, are often shown as completed long before the event. The maps at the end of this book compare favourably with most. The free maps distributed by tourist offices are accurate only for main roads, and the only reliable street guide to the whole of Mexico City is published by ROJI and sold on newsstands.

On-the-spot information

Public Holidays
Jan 1; Constitution Day, Feb 5; Benito Juarez Day, Mar 21; Labour Day, May 1; Battle of Puebla Day, May 5; First day of Congress (*Informe*), Sept 1; Independence Day, Sept 16; Columbus Day (*Día de la Raza*), Oct 12; Anniversary of the 1910 Revolution, Nov 20; Day of the Virgin of Guadalupe, Dec 12; Dec 25.

Banks and offices always close, but most restaurants and some shops remain open. Banks and offices may also close unpredictably to celebrate local holidays.

Time zones
Most of Mexico remains on Central Time all year around, 6hrs behind GMT and 7hrs behind BST. The states of Baja California Sur, Sonora, Nayarit and Sinaloa, in the NW, are on Mountain Time, 7hrs behind GMT and 8hrs behind BST. Baja California Norte is on Pacific Time, 8hrs behind the UK all year around as it is also the only state to operate Daylight Saving Time.

Banks and currency exchange
Money and travellers cheques are best exchanged at banks, open Mon – Fri 9am – 1.30pm. Exchange bureaux at international airports remain open for longer hours, but it saves time to arrive in Mexico with enough pesos to pay for a taxi to your hotel. Most hotels will change money at the official rate, although some may try to make a profit. Cash advances on credit cards are available at the discretion of the local bank or agent. American Express offer various cheque-cashing facilities by prior arrangement. The exchange rate on credit card purchases is entirely up to the company: when inflation is high in Mexico this is usually (but not always) to your advantage.

Credit cards and travellers cheques are not much use in remote areas of countryside. At some lesser establishments, attempts are made to impose a surcharge on credit card users; if possible, refuse to pay, and make sure that credit card bills cannot subsequently be altered.

Shopping and business hours

Hours are not always as advertized, and are subject to long and irregular breaks. Offices generally open by 10am, and then close down for lunch between 2–4pm or longer; however evening closing can be as late as 7.30pm. Shops are open between 10am–7pm, closing for lunch only in smaller towns. On Saturday and Sunday there is more variation, with some shops closing for the entire weekend and others opening normally.

Rush hours

Rush hours affect all major cities and towns and as a rule coincide with the start and finish of shopping and business hours, but are getting longer all the time. Public transport becomes unpleasantly crowded and traffic grinds to a halt.

Post and telephone services

Mexican mail is cheap but slow and erratic. Never post letters in street post boxes, which can go weeks without being emptied, but leave them at post offices (*oficina de correos*) or at hotel desks. Post offices open Mon–Fri 9am–7pm, Sat 9am–1pm. Sending packages abroad is reasonably secure, but do not send objects of value. However, to send a package from abroad into Mexico is to guarantee loss or at least damage, and is never worth doing.

International and national telegrams are best sent via a hotel desk. International telegrams may also be sent from the central telegraph office in Mexico City (*Balderas 14, ZP1*). It is not possible to transfer charges.

In all cities there are numerous telephone booths, where local calls can be made for the minute sum of 20c (insert the coin before dialling). Long-distance calls are often most easily made through the operator (☎ *02*) transferring the charge (*por cobrar*). The international operator (☎ *09*) speaks English.

Direct dialling throughout Mexico and to much of the world is now also usually possible. For calls outside the local area, dial the national code (*91*) followed by the exchange code (given in brackets throughout this book). The service to the USA is more efficient than that within Mexico, but it is expensive, and it is actually cheaper to call home on transferred charges. All towns and cities have long-distance call offices (*cabina de larga distancia*), but there is often a long queue, and it is better to make calls through hotel switchboards.

Addresses

The prefix *Avenida* or *Calle* (street) is usually omitted, and the street known simply by its name. Common suffixes are *Nte* or *Norte* (N), *Sur* (S), *Pte* or *Poniente* (W) and *Ote* or *Oriente* (E). The road along a seafront is usually referred to as the *Malecón* (waterside), whatever its real name, and the same applies to the main square, always called the *Zócalo*, for a complex reason explained in *Mexico City/Sights*. Addresses without numbers often have the suffix *s/n* (*sin numero*).

Public lavatories

Away from airports and railway stations, public lavatories are few and far between and decidedly unsavoury. Hotels and restaurants will usually oblige passers-by in need, but even in smarter establishments standards of hygiene can be low. Men's toilets are signposted *hombres*, *caballeros* or *señores*: women's *damas*, *mujeres* or *señoras*. It is advisable to carry tissues with you.

Electric current
Electric current has now been standardized at 110v 60 cycles AC – the same as the USA. Travellers may need transformers and socket adaptors for the flat two-pin plugs in general use; check before you go.

Laws and regulations
Few tourists ever get into trouble with the Mexican law, and in many cases those that do are treated leniently. However, Mexican law regards alleged offenders as guilty until proved innocent. They can be jailed for up to 72hrs without being charged, and are allowed only one telephone call in that time. This must be used to secure legal assistance, either via a consul or a friend. In any case, the consul should be contacted.

Nude swimming is against the law, and Mexican public opinion is strongly against the practice. For most minor motoring offences, an on-the-spot fine or bribe will settle matters; tourists are usually let off with a caution. In the case of a major accident, everyone involved is normally jailed while the police sort things out. Tourists with juridical insurance (see ***Before you go***, above) will be released more quickly.

In the case of drug offences, tourists are treated, if anything, more harshly than Mexicans. Consular officials are unable to help, and long sentences are handed out. The drugs world is full of violent, ruthless criminals and covert police agents. If searched by the police, insist on turning out your own pockets, for cases of 'planting' are not unknown.

Customs and etiquette
Mexican time-keeping is both art and science: it is always difficult for foreigners to get used to Mexicans' idea of time, which is imprecise and elastic. It is socially disastrous, for example, to arrive punctually at a function or party, and meetings generally start about 1hr after the stated time. To make it clear that you are going to arrive at a certain hour, a useful phrase is *hora inglesa* (English time). The Mexican counter to this is the word *ahorita* (a diminutive of 'now') which in practice can mean anything from half an hour later to infinity. Lateness also is no indicator of discourtesy.

Most visitors will be unaccustomed to the degree of open friendliness shown by Mexicans. Men frequently greet each other with great bear-like hugs (*abrazos*), while indiscriminate kissing and hand-shaking is *de rigueur* at social gatherings. This courtesy does break down when it comes to standing in line, when the principle of survival of the fittest rules. In crowds, women will occasionally be pestered, but although irritating, there is seldom any malicious intent.

Although there are some signs of change, Mexican society is strongly male-dominated at all levels. Foreign women accustomed to more equal treatment would do better to be amused rather than be irritated at the courteous but patronizing behaviour of men.

Tipping
The general rule for tourists is to leave a tip if in doubt. Taxi drivers are the only exception, although it is usual to leave any small change. At restaurants a tip of 10–15% is expected,

although if there is a service charge, less will be adequate. Tipping at hotels is less common: make sure that any tips you leave actually get to the people who made your stay pleasant. It is also customary to tip car watchers, porters, petrol station attendants, theatre ushers and so on; the current price of a beer will be sufficiently generous. Somewhat larger sums are given to hairdressers, manicurists and tourist guides.

The line between a tip and a bribe (*mordida*) can become blurred. Customs officials, bureaucrats, traffic police and reservations clerks can all become more helpful if primed with a few hundred pesos.

Disabled travellers
Mexico has not become disability-conscious, and only the adventurous should consider a trip here. They are certain to experience discomfort, inconvenience and incomprehension.

Local publications
In Mexico City, a daily English-language newspaper, *The Mexico City Daily News*, is published; it is sold in all resorts and major cities. In addition to this, various free magazines and handouts are available at the desks of good hotels.

Tourist police
In Mexico City, special tourist police are on patrol in central areas. They are helpful and friendly, and many speak various foreign languages.

Useful addresses

Tourist information
Ministry of Tourism Juarez 92, ZP1, Mexico City ☎(5) 250–0123. A prompt and efficient desk and telephone service.

American Express Travel Service Hamburgo 75, ZP6, Mexico City ☎(5) 553–3599. A valuable source of information for travellers in need of help or advice.

Details of tourist offices and American Express Travel Service branches in other major cities are given in the *A–Z*.

Main post office (oficina de correos)
Correo Mayor, Tacuba and Ruiz Alarcón, ZP1, Mexico City. Open Mon–Fri 8am–midnight, Sat–Sun 8am–8pm. International telegrams: Balderas 14, ZP1, Mexico City. Open 8am–midnight.

Airlines
The two major Mexican airlines have numerous offices in all major towns. The following central reservation services are manned by English-speaking booking agents.
AeroMexico ☎(5) 553–1577
Mexicana ☎(5) 585–2666

Tour operators
American Express Hamburgo 75, ZP6, Mexico City ☎(5) 511–0309. Otherwise best arranged through hotels.

Car rental
Central telephone reservations for all Mexico (English spoken):
Avis ☎(5) 578–1044
Budget ☎(5) 566–6800
Hertz ☎(5) 566–0099

Motoring organization

AMA (Asociación Mèxicana Automovilista) Orizaba 7, ZP7, Mexico City ☎(5) 511–5940. Maps and touring information; some reciprocal arrangements with foreign motoring organizations; check before departure.

Major places of worship

Details of services in English are given daily in the *Mexico City Daily News*.

Embassies and consulates in Mexico City

Australia Reforma 195, ZP5 ☎(5) 566–3055
Austria Campos Elíseos 305, ZP5 ☎(5) 540–3415
Belgium Musset 41, ZP5 ☎(5) 254–3828
Canada Schiller 529, ZP5 ☎(5) 254–3288
Denmark Campos Elíseos 170, ZP5 ☎(5) 250–8577
Finland Ávila Camacho 1 (9th floor), ZP10 ☎(5) 557–8811
France Havre 15, ZP6 ☎(5) 533–1360
Germany, West Lord Byron 737, ZP5 ☎(5) 545–6655
Greece Reforma 284, ZP6 ☎(5) 528–5935
Israel Sierra Madre 215, ZP10 ☎(5) 540–6341
Italy Palmas 1994, ZP10 ☎(5) 596–3655
Japan Reforma 395, ZP5 ☎(5) 553–6744
Netherlands Ávila Camacho 1, ZP10 ☎(5) 557–9588
Norway Virreyes 1460, ZP10 ☎(5) 540–5220
Spain Parque Vía Reforma 2105, ZP10 ☎(5) 596–1833; consular office at Edgar Allan Poe 91, ZP5 ☎(5) 531–6158
Sweden Ávila Camacho 1 (6th floor) ZP10 ☎(5) 540–6393
Switzerland Hamburgo 66, ZP6 ☎(5) 533–0735
UK Río Lerma 75, ZP5 ☎(5) 511–4880
USA Reforma 305, ZP5 ☎(5) 553–3333

Conversion tables

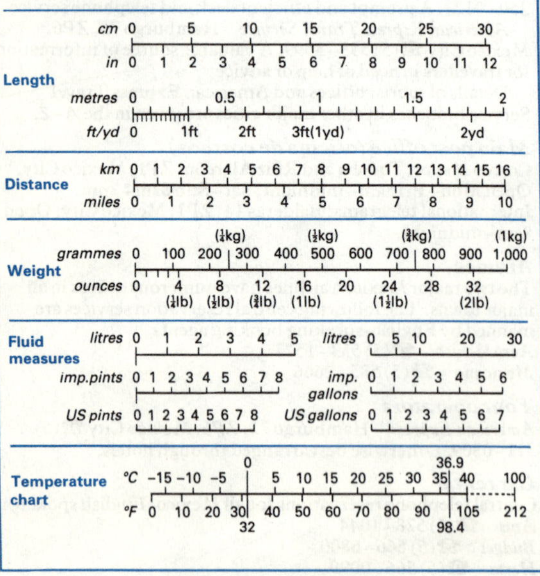

Emergency information

Emergency services

Police ☎06
Ambulance ☎(5) 557–5758/9/60 (Mexico City Red Cross)
Fire ☎(5) 736–3700 (Mexico City)
Lost persons ☎(5) 658–1111 (Mexico City)
A 20c coin is needed for telephone booths. Outside Mexico City, the police or hotels will help.

Hospitals with emergency departments

American British Cowdray Calle Sur and Observatorio, ZP18, Mexico City ☎(5) 277–5000, or for emergencies ☎(5) 515–8359. Outside the capital, ask at hotel desks or look in the telephone directory Yellow Pages under *Sanatorios*.

Other medical emergencies

Look in the telephone directory Yellow Pages for *Médicos* (doctors) or *Dentistas* (dentists). Hotel desks will help.

Late-night pharmacies

These are not easy to find, but those that exist are advertized in the Yellow Pages under *Farmacias–Servicio de 24 horas*.

Motoring accidents

—*Do not* call the police unless strictly necessary.
—*Do not stop* if you see an accident. Witnesses of accidents are frequently jailed to prevent them from disappearing. If questioned by the police, deny any involvement.
—If the car is rented, call the number given in the rental agreement.
—*Do not* admit any liability, or incriminate yourself.
—*Try* and persuade witnesses to stay and give evidence.
—If the other driver is insured, exchange details.
—Contact your insurance company as soon as possible.

There are no roadside phones on the open road; if in need of help, it is necessary to stop a passing motorist.

Car breakdowns

A fleet of special repair trucks known as the 'Green Angels' patrols main roads. The service is free, except for mechanical parts. In the event of a breakdown, pull off the road and raise the bonnet. Otherwise, call the number in the car rental agreement, or ask a passing motorist to alert the nearest garage with towing service, listed in the telephone directory Yellow Pages under *Automóviles–talleres de reparación*.

Lost passport

Contact your consulate, who will issue emergency documents.

Lost travellers cheques

Follow the instructions provided with your travellers cheques, or contact the nearest office of the issuing company. Contact your consulate or American Express in emergencies.

Emergency phrases

Help! *¡Ayúdame!*
There has been an accident. *Ha habido un accidente.*
Where is the nearest telephone/hospital? *¿Dónde está el teléfono/hospital el mas cercano?*
Call a doctor/ambulance! *¡Llame a un médico/ambulancia!*
Call the police! *¡Llame a la policía!*

Introduction

Most visitors to Mexico arrive well equipped with preconceptions: some, incredible though it seems to those who know the country, still expect to find a land of big-hatted *bandidos* snoozing in the sun under a cactus, rising only to wash down red-hot chilis with tequila. The Mexico they find both embraces and defies preconceptions. It is hard to generalize about a country where Indians barely out of the Stone Age follow their old way of life in the jungle, while in the next clearing the latest computerized technology extracts oil to fuel industries in the world's largest city. Extremes are common: wealth and poverty, beauty and squalor, baking deserts and glacial mountains, friendly efficiency and surly incompetence. In the words of a popular car-sticker: *Mexico, ámalo o déjalo* – 'Mexico, love it or leave it'.

Most visitors love it, and it is no surprise that Mexico is today a prime tourist destination. Fortunately, it is so vast in size that tourist invasions can easily be accommodated. There is plenty for everybody – hundreds of miles of palm-shaded beaches, awesome ruins of great lost civilizations, charming colonial towns and the cosmopolitan pleasures of luxury travel.

The modern tourist can spend a vacation in Mexico without speaking a word of Spanish. This, however, is to cut oneself off from perhaps the greatest attraction of all – the Mexicans themselves, a complex people who have inherited a long, often painful, but unique and fascinating history.

The Mexicans

The traumatic birth of Mexico occurred in 1521 with the bloody fall of Aztec Tenochtitlán to the Spanish Conquistadors. The nation's infancy before independence consisted of the following three centuries of harsh Spanish exploitation and dominance of the native peoples. Even now, despite revolutions, social changes and much bloodshed, inequalities survive from this period, transmuted into modern economic terms, and their reform is a continuing national priority. Events and themes from all three eras of its history – Pre-Hispanic, colonial, and independence – have left their mark on today's Mexico. Only in recent years have these disparate elements been forged into the strong sense of national identity which is now apparent. Nor is the process complete; millions of non-Spanish-speaking natives would be amazed to hear themselves described as Mexican, and are only marginally integrated into national life.

They are the direct descendants of the ancient Aztecs, the Maya and other peoples whose civilizations were so rapidly overthrown and destroyed by the Conquistadors. One of history's great tragedies is the wholesale destruction by the Conquistadors of Pre-Hispanic cultural achievements. The sad legacy of this catastrophe is that, with the exception of the Aztecs, very little is known of Pre-Hispanic history, music or daily life; the few painted scrolls (*códices*) that do survive have more or less defied translation. However, even the archaeological evidence leaves no doubt that socially and culturally Pre-Hispanic societies were in many ways more advanced than their European counterparts. In 1521 Tenochtitlán was the largest city in the world, controlling a domain the size of modern France. Given that neither the wheel nor metal implements were in everyday use, this achievement seems all the more striking.

Despite their backwardness in some respects, it is difficult to understand how such powerful and brilliant civilizations could have been defeated by a mere handful of adventurers. The likely explanations are complex. Aztec society, for instance, was so hierarchical and preoccupied with the observance of intricate religious ceremonies and dictates that it was unable to respond imaginatively to an entirely new threat. It has been pointed out that if the Aztec warriors had concentrated on killing the intruders, rather than trying to capture them for sacrifice, their victory would have been certain. Spanish technological superiority – guns, horses and swords – also played a part, as did the Aztecs' superstitious fear that their invaders might be gods. More important still was the effect of new European diseases.

Within months of the fall of Tenochtitlán the other societies of Mesoamerica had undergone a similar fate. Their priests and rulers were executed, their ancient legends, theology and customs outlawed as witchcraft, while the people suffered compulsory conversion to Christianity, and virtual enslavement. For many years it was widely believed that the Indians had no souls, and they were regarded as beasts of burden. Despite this, one can still trace a strong Pre-Hispanic influence not only in the native areas but in everyday Mexican life. A good example is the prevailing attitude to death. Mexicans are fatalistic at the best of times, but for fiestas such as the Day of the Dead the notion of death is embraced with macabre enjoyment and relish; this derives directly from Pre-Hispanic religions, which glorified death and sacrifice.

After the Conquest, the country was divided up into vast Spanish-owned haciendas (estates) and into the domains of monasteries, while numerous grid-plan towns were laid out. These were the three principal tools of colonization. The economic relationship of New Spain with its mother country was entirely one-way: it was a place for Spaniards to come and get rich before retiring to Spain. It was the growing number of Mexican-born Spaniards who eventually caused the upheavals of the early 19thC which led to independence, rather than the unfortunate Indians, whose position was not greatly improved. Ironically, the trouble started because the Creoles (as they were known) wished to be treated as full and equal citizens of the Spanish Crown; the idea of independence came only later.

The new republic came into existence in 1821, but modern Mexican history is usually regarded as beginning in 1917, when the Revolution ended with the enactment of the Constitution of Querétaro. The events of the following turbulent century explain and define subsequent themes in Mexican affairs. The most important theme emerging in the 19thC is that of land reform; the failure of drastic land reform by Benito Juarez in the 1850s was one of the main causes of the 1910 Revolution. This was compounded by the subsequent ruler, Porfirio Díaz, who neglected agriculture while laying the foundations of modern industrial Mexico. The first successful reforms were not carried out until 1934, under President Lázaro Cárdenas. The situation, still confused and unsatisfactory in much of the country, leads to occasional social unrest. Mexico's ruling party, the PRI (Party of Institutional Revolution) has in theory been strongly committed to land reform ever since its foundation in 1927; the practical difficulties however, are daunting, and industrial growth is a more tempting short-term priority.

Modern Mexico

Mexico is an interesting example of that apparent contradiction, the one-party democracy; it has been ruled continuously by the PRI since 1927. Opposition parties do exist, but for a variety of reasons never gain significant electoral success; to be effective, dissent must be expressed within the framework of the PRI. Other important centres of power include the trade unions, the Roman Catholic Church, the armed forces and private industry. The role of the army in politics has been limited ever since the Revolution, and Mexico commits relatively little to arms expenditure. Apart from minor internal problems, the only military threat to Mexico is the possibility that trouble in Central America might spill over its southern borders. Like the army, the Church is constitutionally hemmed in, but nevertheless exercises a strong hold on the loyalty and imagination of working people. The emblem of the country's patron saint, the Virgin of Guadalupe, has been used as a battle symbol in popular uprisings ever since 1810, and her image is to be seen in every home, factory and vehicle across the land. The power of the Church in Mexico is dormant, like the snow-capped volcanoes towering over Mexico City. Not so the trade unions, who are officially a part of the PRI, and are in a strong position to enforce the demands of organized labour, often indeed against the wishes of the government.

As well as the large nationalized industries, where the PRI and the unions are dominant, there are large private industrial groupings in Mexico. They are concentrated in the North, and suffer considerable difficulties from the taxation, expropriations and barriers to investment imposed by the government in the South. It has been said frequently of late that Mexico is turning into two countries: the socialist South, and a free-enterprise North. While there is little danger of an actual split, the differences are accentuated by the growing cultural identification of the North with the USA. Here and in the southern USA a new Anglo-Hispanic society seems to be emerging, encouraged by the massive flow of people across the frontier, both legal and illegal. Many Mexicans regard the flow of illegal emigration northwards as Mexico's answer to the land loss to the USA of 1848 – an invasion without armies.

The modern industrial boom in Mexico was made possible by the discovery of huge oil reserves. Ironically, this good fortune was a significant factor in bringing about the financial crisis of 1982, when Mexico's foreign debts were for a short time the largest in the world. The combined evils of falling oil prices, excessive public expenditure, protectionism and runaway inflation led to a drastic drop in the value of the peso. Things were not helped by a disillusion with politicians and public officials, widely perceived as being corrupt and inefficient. It remains to be seen whether President Miguel de la Madrid, elected in 1982, can reunite the nation and regain international confidence; there are, however, grounds for cautious optimism.

Other more long-term problems facing Mexico are those common to all developing nations: over-population, explosive urban growth, inadequate control over polluting industries, destruction of agricultural and natural environments, and the depletion of resources. The important position which Mexico has assumed as the 15th industrial power in the world and as influential spokesman for the developing nations would be greatly strengthened if effective solutions to all of these daunting problems were to emerge over the next few years.

Time chart

c.30000BC The first men to enter the Americas cross the Bering Straits from Siberia and spread S in search of game.

c.2500BC Cultivation of corn, enabling evolution to more settled societies.

The Pre-Classic era (c.1500–c.200BC)

c.1000BC Flowering of Olmec civilization in SE of Mexico. Trade and war carry their culture and religion throughout Mesoamerica.

c.800BC Under Olmec influence, the peasant communities of the Valley of Mexico grow more sophisticated, developing the Tlatilco culture.

c.700BC The Izapa culture develops in the jungles of modern Guatemala under Olmec influence.

c.400BC The violent destruction of the Olmec capital of La Venta and the gradual disappearance of the Olmecs. Some possibly migrate to Monte Albán in the Valley of Oaxaca, where a powerful Pre-Zapotec culture is emerging.

The Classic era (c.200BC–c.AD900)

An age characterized by the blossoming of various minor Pre-Classic cultures into major urban civilizations. The two most important are the Teotihuacán culture of the Valley of Mexico and the brilliant Mayan culture, which starts in the jungles of Central America and spreads to the Yucatán.

c.300AD The highly centralized Teotihuacán state reaches the apogee of its power, with trading colonies as far S as modern Guatemala. Its influence has been traced in all other areas of civilization: the Totonacs of the Gulf, the Zapotecs of Oaxaca, the cultures of the W and even the Maya farther S.

c.600–c.900 The collapse of Teotihuacán and the end of its predominance. Civil unrest, soil exhaustion, plague, drought and barbarian invasion from the N all play a part. During the next 300yrs the same forces lead to the collapse of all the Classic civilizations.

The Post-Classic era (c.900–1521)

Repeated barbarian invasion from the N and the adoption of civilized ways by the invaders lead to the growth of new cultures. The most important of these is the civilization of the warlike Toltecs, who dominate the Valley of Mexico from their capital of Tula. In the SE, the outstandingly artistic Mixtecs supplant the Zapotecs.

c.980 Invasion of the Yucatán peninsula by Toltecs, and spread of the cult of Quetzalcoatl, the Plumed Serpent. This leads to the birth of a new Toltec-Maya culture known as the Itzá.

1168 Tula destroyed by further waves of marauders from the N, followed by the dispersal of the Toltecs. Coincidentally, it is also in this year that the Aztec (or Mexica) tribe are supposed to have left their unknown island home in search of a new capital, which would be pointed out to them by their gods.

1345 After nearly two centuries of wandering, the Aztecs settle in their city in Tenochtitlán in the swamps of the Valley of Mexico. It rapidly becomes the centre of a powerful trading empire, exacting tribute from coast to coast and from as far S as the Valley of Oaxaca.

1492	Christopher Columbus discovers the New World.
1512–18	Spanish explorers reconnoitre the coast of the Yucatán and the Gulf of Mexico.
1519	Hernan Cortés lands near modern Veracruz on April 21, with artillery, horses and some 500 soldiers. He capitalizes on resentment of the Aztecs to recruit first the local Totonacs and later, after some resistance, the Tlaxcalans in his march on Tenochtitlán. Cortés enters the city peacefully on Nov 12, but imprisons the Emperor Montezuma. Resistance is tempered by the widespread belief among the Aztecs that he is the reincarnation of the god Quetzalcoatl.
1520	Cortés leaves Tenochtitlán to defeat a rival expedition led by Diego Velasquez, and on returning finds his garrison under Aztec attack. He manages to reunite his forces, but after a month the Spaniards are forced to flee; in the bitter fight to escape, many are killed and much treasure is lost.
1521	After a three-month siege, Cortés regains Tenochtitlán from the Aztecs, decimated by famine and new European diseases. The city is razed and its people massacred or enslaved. The conquest of Central Mexico quickly follows.
	***The colonial era** (1521–1821)*
1522	Cortés appointed ruler of 'New Spain' by Carlos V. The reconstruction of Tenochtitlán starts, under the new name of Mexico.
1524	Franciscan monks arrive to start the task of evangelizing the native peoples, followed by the Dominicans. New Spain is soon covered with monasteries and missions.
1598	With the colonization of New Mexico complete, all of modern Mexico and much of the southern USA is now under Spanish rule. The native population is used as slave labour on the vast estates and in the mines. For two centuries, there is little change in the status quo, and the Spanish settlers grow rich and keep the native population in subjugation.
1808	Napoleon Bonaparte's invasion of Spain sparks off a rebellion of Creoles (Mexican-born Spaniards) against Spanish rule, which is crushed.
1810	Inspired by the American War of Independence and the French Revolution, a group of Creoles plots another rebellion, led by Father Miguel Hidalgo, a priest, and Ignacio Allende, an officer in the royalist army. On Sept 16, Hidalgo delivers his famous *grito* (call to arms) at Dolores Hidalgo. Guanajuato and San Miguel are soon taken and sacked, and the uprising spreads.
1811	Royalist forces defeat Hidalgo, who is executed. José María Morelos continues the struggle.
1813	Morelos declares Mexico's independence at the Congress of Chilpancingo.
1815	Morelos is defeated and executed.
1821	The former royalist officer, Agustín Iturbide, proclaims the Constitution of Iguala, offering peace to Spain and freedom to all. On Aug 24, the Treaty of Córdoba is signed, confirming Mexican independence.

The era of interventions (1821–1914)

1822	Iturbide proclaims himself Emperor of Mexico.
1823	Iturbide is forced to resign, and is eventually executed by soldiers of the ambitious young general Santa Anna.
1824	A new constitution declares Mexico a federal republic, under the presidency of the former soldier Guadalupe Victoria.
1829	A small Spanish army arrives on the coast of the Gulf, intending to repeat Cortés' success, but is defeated at Tampico by Santa Anna.
1831	Santa Anna becomes President.
1836	American colonists in Texas rebel; after an initial Mexican success at the Alamo, Santa Anna is captured at the Battle of San Jacinto and forced to recognize Texan independence.
1838	As a result of indignities suffered by French citizens in Mexico, the French mount a brief punitive expedition, during the course of which Santa Anna loses a leg.
1845	Texas joins the USA; Mexico declares war.
1847	Mexico City occupied by American troops.
1848	Near bankruptcy, Mexico is forced to concede the states of Arizona, New Mexico and California to the USA.
1855	Final fall of Santa Anna, followed by the election of President Comonfort, committed to change Mexican society by reducing the power of the Church and the military.
1858	Comonfort overthrown by conservatives. A civil war between conservatives and reformist liberals ensues.
1861	The liberal Benito Juarez triumphs, and becomes Mexico's first Indian president. He is at once faced with a massive foreign debt, and suspension of payments leads to a military intervention by Spain, Great Britain and France.
1862	Alarmed by France's warlike stance, the Spanish and the British withdraw their troops. On May 5, a French army is defeated at Puebla.
1863	A reinforced French army takes Mexico City, and the Imperial Crown of Mexico is given to Maximilian, a cousin of the French Emperor Napoleon III.
1866	French troops withdraw to face the Prussian threat in Europe. Benito Juarez is able to resume government.
1867	Maximilian captured and executed at Querétaro.
1872	Death of Juarez.
1876	Juarez's popular general Porfirio Díaz takes over, apparently committed to democratic rule. However, he amends the constitution and rules for 36yrs, with one short break (1880–84). He encourages foreign investment, and brings peace, solvency and an industrial infrastructure to the country. Despite these successes, agriculture is neglected, and the lower classes see none of the wealth.
1910–11	Díaz overthrown by the idealistic reformer Francisco Madero, aided by the revolutionary armies of Emiliano Zapata in the S and Pancho Villa in the N.

1913 Madero proves unable to carry out the promised land reforms and is murdered by General Huerta, who proclaims himself President. He is at once opposed by the 'Constitutionalist' armies of Zapata, Villa, Venustiano Carranza and Alvaro Obregón.

1914 Brief American intervention in Veracruz on the side of the Constitutionalists. Huerta defeated, and Venustiano Carranza becomes President. War breaks out between the victors, with Zapata and Villa returning to banditry.

The modern era

1917 The Constitution of Querétaro is enacted, strongly anti-clerical and promising labour and land reforms.

1920 Carranza assassinated. Obregón assumes the presidency, and instigates only limited reforms.

1927 Popular religious uprising led by the 'Cristeros' ('Christians') is savagely repressed by the anti-clerical government of Plutarco Calles.

1934 The first large-scale land reforms are carried out by President Lázaro Cárdenas.

1938 Nationalization of the oil industry.

1942 Mexico enters World War II on the side of the Allies but takes little part.

1946 Election of President Miguel Alemán. Redistribution of land continues, accompanied by rapid industrial growth.

1968 Some social unrest. Suppression of student protest: 'Tlatelolco massacre' in Mexico City.

1982 In response to flight of capital funds and increasing foreign debt, President López Portillo nationalizes the banks and institutes exchange control. His successor, de la Madrid, establishes a programme of economic austerity.

Some suggestions for further reading

In this small selection, asterisks after authors' names indicate that some of their other works are also of interest.

Fiction Carlos Castaneda (*), *Journey to Ixtlán*; Carlos Fuentes (*), *Burnt Waters*; Graham Greene, *The Power and the Glory*; D.H. Lawrence, *The Plumed Serpent*; Malcolm Lowry, *Under the Volcano*.

Travel writing Frances Calderón de la Barca, *Life in Mexico*; Charles Flandrau, *Viva Mexico*; Aldous Huxley, *Travels in the Mexique Bay*; D.H. Lawrence, *Mornings in Mexico*.

History Henry Bamford Parkes, *A History of Mexico*; Bernal Díaz, *The Conquest of New Spain*.

Art and archaeology Ignacio Bernal (*), *Mexico Before Cortés: Art History and Legend*; Nigel Davies (*), *The Kingdoms of Ancient Mexico*; Pedro Rojas, *The Art and Architecture of Mexico*; Jacques Soustelle (*), *Arts of Ancient Mexico*; Katherine Tyler Burchwood, *The Origin and Legacy of Mexican Art*.

Anthropology Oscar Lewis (*), *The Children of Sánchez*; W. & C. Madsen, *A Guide to Mexican Witchcraft*; Frances Toor, *A Treasury of Mexican Folkways*.

Modern Mexico Octavio Paz (*), *The Labyrinth of Solitude*.

Art and architecture

It may not often seem so to the traveller, but the similarities and continuity between the various Mesoamerican civilizations are much more important than the differences. The common trends which emerge from the 2,500yrs of Pre-Hispanic history are clear, based largely on archaeological evidence. The cities which formed the base for societies were in fact ceremonial centres for the complex religions; these religions dominated all artistic achievement, and governed also aspects of everyday life. The rulers were priest-kings, and beneath them society was strictly hierarchical, a system which hampered social, artistic and technological evolution. Despite knowledge of metalworking techniques for decorative purposes, Mesoamerican civilization remained essentially Stone Age in character, a remarkable fact given its brilliant achievements. Similarly, although the wheel was used in children's toys, it was never utilized for transport, and even the largest pyramids were constructed with nothing more than manpower.

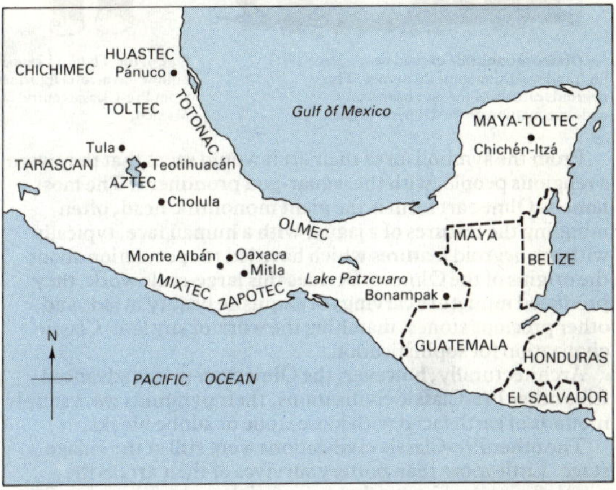

There are three main periods: the Pre-Classic era (*c.*1500–*c.*200BC), when urban culture developed; the Classic period (*c.*200BC–*c.*AD900), the golden age of powerful theocratic civilizations; and the Post-Classic era (*c.*900–1521), a more troubled and militaristic age, although not deficient in artistic achievement. There are also six distinct areas, of which three are of major importance: the Valley of Mexico; the Valley of Oaxaca; and the SE, including the Yucatán peninsula and most of modern Guatemala. Farther from the influence of the great cities are the two coasts of Central Mexico, and the northern states of modern Mexico.

The Pre-Classic era

The brilliant Olmecs from the Gulf coast dominate Pre-Classic art. Little is known of their origins or language, but they were certainly the first Mesoamerican people to build pyramid bases for temples, to work precious stones, to carve large stone altars, sculptures and steles (low-relief tablets), and to evolve a calendar system.

A miniature in serpentine of the **Olmec jaguar god**.

An **Olmec monolithic carved head**, 15m (49ft) high and weighing some 20 tonnes. The negroid features of the face have led to wide speculation on the Olmecs' origins.

One of the *Tlatilco Venuses*, hollow terra-cotta figurines from Pre-Classic central Mexico.

From the symbolism of their art it would seem that they were a religious people, with the jaguar-god prominent. The most famous Olmec art form is the giant monolithic head, often mingling the features of a jaguar with a human face, typically with the negroid features which have led to speculation about the origins of the Olmecs. Besides this large-scale work, they produced miniature carvings of exquisite beauty in jade and other precious stones, matching the work of any later Classic civilization for sophistication.

Architecturally, however, the Olmecs were less advanced. Like other Pre-Classic civilizations, their pyramids were simply mounds of earth faced with loose stone or adobe blocks.

The other Pre-Classic civilizations were still at the village stage. Little more than pottery survives of their art, as they generally worked in perishable materials and not in stone. Some of this pottery, although technically crude, does show imagination and even humour – especially fine are the *Tlatilco Venuses*, plump but graceful ladies from the Valley of Mexico now in the Museo Nacional de Antropología in Mexico City. Pre-Classic pottery deals with all aspects of daily life but rarely with religion, which was yet to assume the all-embracing importance seen in later cultures.

The Pre-Classic pottery style developed furthest along the W coast, in modern Colima and Nayarit, where figurines of great realism were produced. However, these cultures of the W remained essentially Pre-Classic in character throughout the Classic era, despite some adoption of techniques such as stone-working, and this style is known as 'Evolved Pre-Classic'.

The Classic era

Teotihuacán

The main Classic civilization of the Valley of Mexico was based at an enormous ceremonial centre outside Mexico City. Traces of its artistic influence are found throughout Mesoamerica.

The architecture of Teotihuacán itself is on a massive scale. The main pyramids have stepped sloping sides, but many of the surrounding buildings are constructed on the *talud y tablero* principle of stepped terraces, with stucco reliefs, murals, and carved heads of gods and animals, all showing a high level of craftsmanship. The murals are not preoccupied with the violence and sacrifice associated with later cultures. The religious symbolism, rather, revolves around the rain-god Tlaloc and the peaceful plumed serpent-god, later known as Quetzalcoatl.

Early Teotihuacán pottery resembles Pre-Classic work; later on, however, the figurines become more individualized and are often wearing tall feather head-dresses. Functional pottery vessels become fine and delicate, decorated with fresco painting or with intricate inlaid glazing; the predominant colours are red and green, with designs for the most part resembling those of the mural paintings.

Perhaps the finest artistic products of Teotihuacán are the beautifully inlaid masks of stone, using such precious materials as jade, mother-of-pearl and garnet, which were probably used as death masks. Their restrained and powerful creativity place them among the highest achievements of Mesoamerican art.

The Zapotecs

From their great hilltop city at Monte Albán, the Zapotecs dominated the Valley of Oaxaca during the Classic era. Their art and architecture show the influence of Teotihuacán, of the Olmecs, and of the Maya.

The architecture is austere and well-ordered, making skilful use of columns to create large internal spaces. The famous low-relief panels of Monte Albán are probably of Pre-Zapotec origin, and show Olmec influence; the Zapotec calendar glyphs (symbols) on them were added at a later date. These glyphs are found on steles and on murals throughout the Zapotec area, for the calendar was central to their religion. The best Zapotec murals are found in tombs and resemble those of Teotihuacán in both subject matter and style.

The Zapotecs were superb potters; even functional items were decorated with intricately modelled or incised motifs. More interesting still are the ornamental and ritual vessels which were developed into a unique and accomplished art form. They are incorrectly known as funerary urns; although usually found in tombs their actual purpose is not known. A typical urn has only a small receptacle and is in the form of a god, sometimes the rain-god Tlaloc (known here as Cocijo) whose clothing, jewellery and head-dresses are shown in superb detail. These urns are by far the most intricate product of Mesoamerican ceramic art.

The Maya

The Mayan culture was spread over a large area, including the Yucatán peninsula and much of the Central American rain-forests, and although its development was parallel to the other Classic civilizations, it was more directly derived from the Olmec culture. The Maya built well over a hundred large ceremonial centres, and were by far the most advanced Mesoamerican culture in terms of mathematics, astronomy, calendrical computation, and architecture.

Architecture, their greatest art, developed regional variations over the large area of Mayan culture. There are three main building types: the pyramid, usually steeper than those of Central Mexico, with a stone temple and soaring roof-comb at

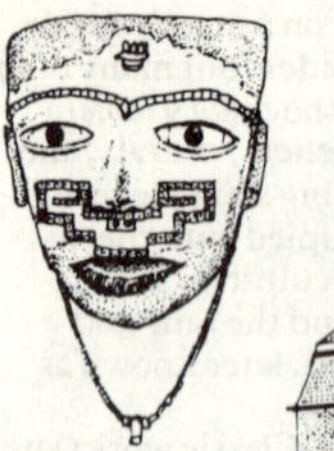

Left **Teotihuacán funerary mask**, inlaid with jade.
Right **Zapotec ceramic urn** in the form of a goddess.
Below **Temple of the Inscriptions** at the Mayan city of **Palenque**, unusual in having a burial chamber inside.

the summit; the palace, consisting of chambers around courts; and the ball-court, for playing a sacred game. The original Mayan style is called the 'Petén', after the region of modern Guatemala in which the civilization reached its greatest peak, and is characterized by especially steep pyramids, low-relief decoration on all wall surfaces, and extensive use of corbel vaulting and the 'Mayan arch', with sloping sides and a lintel. It is also in the Petén area that the finest sculptured steles are to be found.

Simultaneously, in the Yucatán, the 'Puuc' style was developing. It had more elaborate facades, decorated with stone and stucco masks; palaces often had two storeys, with great monumental doorways. If this was the Mayan Baroque, then the later 'Chenes' and 'Río Bec' styles of the South were the Mayan Churrigueresque. The graceful proportions of the 'Puuc' are completely lost under great masses of ornamentation, in a way strangely reminiscent of 17thC Mexican churches.

Of other Mayan art forms, the *códices*, painted scrolls with hieroglyphic writing, were almost all destroyed by the Spaniards, while wood-carving and weaving have also disappeared. Like the Olmecs, they were skilled jade workers, and also engraved bones. Functional pottery was decorated with stylized painted and appliquéd motifs. In some areas the art of figurine modelling reached great heights of realism, thus going against the predominance of symbolism and ritualism; the finest of these come from the island of Jaina off the coast of Campeche. The same realistic tendency is found in some mural painting; the famous murals of Bonampak, in particular, must rank among the world's great works of art.

The Gulf coast

After the dispersal of the Olmecs the Gulf area lost its importance. During Classic times, it was occupied by a people referred to as the Totonacs, although it is not known whether they spoke the Totonac language now used in this area. Farther north lived the Huastecs, an isolated branch of the Maya.

The Totonac pyramids were unique in their construction, using rows of niches in place of the usual vertical panels. They were also accomplished potters, but their most notable art forms were the strange 'yokes', 'palmate stones' and 'votive axes', of smooth, sculpted stone with incised designs; no convincing explanation has been given for their use, and the names are purely speculative. The designs show a consummate blend of realism and abstraction.

The Post-Classic era

The Toltecs

After the decline or collapse of all the great Classic civilizations, the Toltecs were one of the first invading tribes to settle in the Valley of Mexico. Although they assumed many of the civilized customs and the religion of their predecessors, the emphasis of Toltec culture was always more violent, militaristic and secular.

Toltec architecture is less impressive than that of Teotihuacán, but in comparison is innovative in its complex planning and use of columns. The decoration of the buildings – murals, carvings and low-reliefs – is highly accomplished. Typical themes are eagles and jaguars representing the two military orders, human sacrifice, processions of warriors, and plumed serpents; this last symbolizes here a more malevolent aspect of Quetzalcoatl, as one who demanded continual human sacrifice. The dominant image in their sculpture is the warrior, of which the best examples are the four enormous *atlantes* (spear-throwers) on the Temple of the Morning Star at their capital of Tula. Another typical form is the *chac-mool*, a reclining figure with a receptacle for sacrificial offerings. Examples have been found all over Mesoamerica, indicating widespread Toltec influence.

The Toltecs were among the first to start the working of precious metals, and were probably skilled engravers of jade and precious and semi-precious stones; however, little of their jewellery has been found. Toltec pottery, with the exception of some very fine hollow figurines of the gods, is functional and uninteresting.

The Maya-Toltecs

After the fall of Tula in 1168, a group, probably of Toltec origin, known as the Itzá, emigrated to the Yucatán peninsula. Their new skills and knowledge were the impetus for a revival of the declining Mayan culture. Although they came as conquerors, the 'Itzá Renaissance' which resulted is a genuine fusion of Mayan and Toltec traditions. All the main themes of Toltec architecture are present, and the decoration is similarly military; use of such Mayan techniques as the arch and corbel vaulting has the effect of freeing planning constraints. The actual workmanship leaves no doubt that the craftsmen were Maya, working under the control of a ruling Itzá warrior-class.

The Maya-Toltec civilization was in some respects uninteresting – the murals, for example, although energetic and vivid, do not rival those of the Classic Maya, and very little of note has been found in the way of pottery. Metalworking, on the other hand, became highly advanced; especially fine are the *repoussé* gold discs found at the bottom of the sacred well at Chichén Itzá. Maya-Toltec culture fell into decadence about a century before the arrival of the Spaniards, and subsequent artistic production was negligible.

The Mixtecs

At the same time as the 'Itzá Renaissance', a mountain tribe called the Mixtecs was establishing dominance over the Zapotecs in the Valley of Oaxaca, and over a large area to the north including much of the modern state of Puebla. The achievements of Mixtec craftsmen were without equal in such fields as metalwork, pottery, carving, and hieroglyphic scroll painting (*códices*). The best finds of Mixtec work come from the tombs of Monte Albán, where the treasures include jade and crystal statues, mosaics of semi-precious stones, and exquisite *cire-perdue* gold-and-silver jewellery moulded around wax.

Mixtec architecture is known for large areas of geometric decoration, using thousands of small carved stones. The later Zapotecs adopted this technique under Mixtec direction for the famous palaces of Mitla.

Mixtec polychrome pottery was so highly prized that it is found all over Mesoamerica. It has elegant and restrained forms, with stylized religious themes for decoration.

The Tarascans

In the west of Mexico, the Pre-Classic styles followed an independent evolution throughout the Classic period, reaching a level of considerable sophistication. In the Post-Classic era, there was a minor flowering of the Tarascan culture in the area around Lake Patzcuaro. Although only semi-urbanized, the Tarascans became expert metalworkers and potters rivalled only by the Mixtecs. The art of the feather mosaic was also developed here, and these works were highly valued by the Aztecs; unfortunately no examples survive.

A Toltec *chac-mool* at **Chichén Itzá**; the figure holds a bowl for sacrificial offerings.

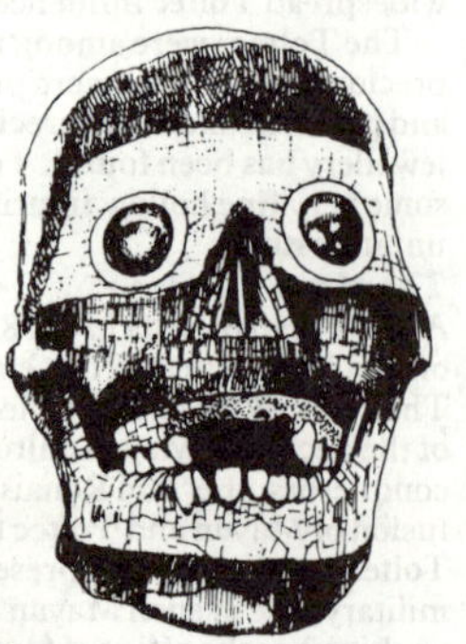

This **mask of the Aztec god of darkness, Tezcatlipoca,** was made from the skull of a sacrificial victim, and inlaid with turquoise and other semi-precious stones.

Left One of the **Mayan temples** in the older part of the city of **Chichén Itzá**. The Spaniards called it **La Iglesia** ('The church'), although its true purpose remains unknown. The carvings include masks and key patterns.

The Aztecs

In the early 15thC, a semi-barbaric Nahua tribe known as the Mexica became socially and politically dominant in the Valley of Mexico. The influence on the Aztecs of their predecessors, the Toltecs, was strong, as was that of their neighbours such as the Mixtecs. All of these elements they combined in a new and dynamic way, but sadly, of all the cultures thriving at the time of the Conquest, Aztec art suffered the greatest destruction at the hands of the Spanish.

The general appearance of their architecture was massive and sombre, with palaces and very steep pyramids similar to the early 'Puuc' Mayan style, although larger. The decoration, with the insistent themes of war and sacrifice, is more reminiscent of the Toltecs. Aztec religious beliefs were highly complex, since whenever they conquered a people their gods were assimilated into the pantheon. The sculptures that have survived show great inventiveness in depicting the gods, sometimes realistic, at other times symbolically abstract, but never over-decorated; gruesome subjects are frequent, since human sacrifice was more practised by the Aztecs than by any other people. Only with recent discoveries at the Templo Mayor in Mexico City has the extent of Aztec skill in such arts as jewellery, pottery and engraving become apparent.

Post-Conquest architecture

Following the Spanish Conquest of 1521, the architectural traditions of millennia disappeared almost without trace. An era of ecclesiastical building began with styles influenced by developments in Europe, especially Spain. Throughout the colonial period, secular building, derivative of church building in style, remained of secondary importance. The evolution of Mexican architecture was not however a mere imitation of the Spanish. The cultural relationship of the two countries was a complex interaction, producing a separate mode of Mexican architectural expression, which reached its highest point with the dramatic flowering of the Mexican 'Ultra-Baroque' or Churrigueresque in the 18thC. The naming of the different styles is a matter of continuous debate, with each academic school discerning different periods and devising particular names for them. This is further complicated by the fact that many churches include elements of various styles incorporated over a long period of building.

The first colonial architecture (1521–80)

Immediately after the Conquest, the four orders of friars (Augustinian, Dominican, Franciscan and Jesuit) began the task of building monasteries to act as centres for the conversion of the native peoples. Each of the orders had its own characteristics, but the basic pattern was constant: a simple basilical church, looking onto a walled forecourt or 'atrium'. The monastery, with its chambers grouped around a two-storey cloister, would be beside the church, with the main door also on the atrium. A third element, unique to Mexico, is the open chapel or *posa* on one side of the atrium, used for outdoor ceremonies involving unbaptized Indians. In the centre of the atrium was usually a carved stone cross, early examples of which often show Pre-Hispanic decorative motifs.

The earlier monasteries are in a simple Spanish Romanesque style, with some Gothic touches added to fortifications. The Renaissance eventually came to Mexico in a form far removed from the classical purity of the Italian High Renaissance. Both in Spain and Mexico, the Renaissance inspired the development of the Plateresque style, which retained elements of the Gothic and the Mudejar (Islamic) styles. Typical of the Plateresque are flat surfaces decorated with medallions, simple classical orders with minor variations, and restrained ornamentation. The influence of the Gothic is commonly seen in pointed crenellations, and more occasionally in pointed arches. The Islamic influence is confined to such features as exquisitely carved and fitted woodwork, and flat, rich areas of geometric ornamentation. Despite these other elements, the Plateresque is essentially a product of the Renaissance.

***Mexican Baroque** (1580–1730)*

Towards the end of the 16thC the first phase of monastery building came to an end, and work started on the great three-nave cathedrals, such as those at Mexico City and Puebla. At the same time, the growth of the Baroque in Spain was being felt in Mexico. The first phase of Mexican Baroque architecture, however, neglects the dynamic organization of space typical of its European original, and consists of little more than a decorative fashion for enrichment of facades and altar screens with Plateresque ornamentation. The classical orders are more or less preserved, although a certain liberty of proportion becomes apparent.

The development of Mexican Baroque from the late 17thC is associated with the use of the two architectural elements whose names are used to describe the periods of their popularity. The first to appear is the 'Solomonic' column, either twisted or helical, with a Corinthian capital. This phase, corresponding to the European High Baroque, is characterized by rich Renaissance-inspired decoration.

The second phase is the Churrigueresque.

***Churrigueresque** (1730–80)*

This period is variously known as the age of the *estipite* (after the characteristic architectural element), Mexican Churrigueresque, or Ultra Baroque. The *estipite* is a complex form of pilaster, with a classical capital and a curious collection of parts, including square and circular blocks with medallions, and an inverted obelisk base. Ironically, the Spanish architect de Churriguera, after whom the style is named, was not known for his use of this form.

The most important feature of the Churrigueresque style is the amazing profusion and richness of ornament, which often submerges structural elements in a stone froth of foliage, statues, medallions, garlands and cherubs. Especially striking is the polychromatic tile decoration of the Puebla Churrigueresque. The artistic and religious passion of the Mexican craftsmen who elaborated the style is arguably the most impressive phenomenon in the history of Mexican architecture.

***Neoclassical and the Porfiriato** (1780–1910)*

The intensity of the Churrigueresque was short-lived, and it was succeeded by the rational calmness of the Neoclassical, arriving in Mexico 50yrs after its European emergence. The final prosperous years of the colonial era saw the erection of fine Neoclassical buildings by architects trained at the Academy of San Carlos (opened 1781).

After independence was achieved in 1821, the turbulent conditions and poverty of the country precluded significant building projects. Only when stability and prosperity returned under Porfirio Diaz (1876–1911) was there a revival of

Loreto Chapel, San Luis Potosí, built *c.*1700 with the Solomonic columns of the Mexican Baroque.

Palacio de Bellas Artes, Mexico City. First designed in 1900, this Italianate palace shows the grandeur and eclecticism of style of *Porfiriato* architecture.

architecture. Typical of the *Porfiriato* period were grandiose public buildings in an eclectic variety of cosmopolitan styles, ranging from Italianate Art Nouveau (Palacio de Bellas Artes, in Mexico City) to Spanish/Islamic Gothic (the main post office, also in the capital). The emphasis lay on following European trends to prove that Mexico was a modern, advanced nation. The Revolution of 1910, however, put another halt to building.

Modern architecture

When building resumed in the 1920s, the styles more or less reflected contemporary fashions in the USA and Europe. There were attempts to create a Mexican neo-colonial style, and even a native or Pre-Hispanic-inspired style, but the functionalism of steel and reinforced concrete won the day for large-scale projects and housing. The work of the muralists (see below) gave a distinctly Mexican flavour to public buildings, but only recently has it been possible to speak of Mexico as having a separate architectural identity.

At its best, this is represented by buildings such as the Museo Nacional de Antropología in Mexico City, or the great pyramid hotels at the beach resorts. Here one can see bold treatment of volume, mass and light, imaginative use of local materials, and an integration of interior and exterior space. The style is eclectic, but among others, motifs from Mexico's architectural past are apparent. Mexican architects lead the world in the use of very lightweight concrete shell structures; these graceful parabolic forms are frequently used to roof large single spaces such as churches.

Post-Conquest painting and sculpture

During the early colonial period almost all sculpture and painting dealt with religious subjects. At first the artists were all Spanish immigrants, such as Cristóbal de Villalpando; as time passed, professionally trained Mexican-born Spaniards, and even some Indians, emerged, among them Cabrera, Ibarra, Alcibar and Tinoco. Mexican painting followed Spanish fashions even more slavishly than did Mexican architecture. The Mexican Baroque, with its emphasis on chiaroscuro and formal elaboration, reached its height in the early 18thC; a reaction of simplification followed.

In 1781 was founded the first art school in Mexico City, the Progressive Academy of San Carlos, an event which proved to be a landmark in the development of Mexican art; famous academicians included Manuel Tolsa, Jerónimo Gil and José María Vasquez. Even so, it was only after Independence that Mexican art began to reflect immediate reality. The most famous painter of this period is José María Velasco, whose grandiose landscapes, now national treasures, contrast nature's immensity with the beauty of man's creation. After the upheavals of the 1910 Revolution, artistic endeavour was concentrated on mural painting (see below).

Mexico City today is one of the most artistically active capitals of Latin America, and a visit to the permanent collection of the Museo de Arte Moderno will give a good idea of the current scene. In the new and excellent Museo Nacional de Arte the entire broad sweep of Mexican artistic history is shown.

The muralists

Throughout Pre-Hispanic and colonial times, religious buildings were decorated with large, colourful murals. The tradition disappeared after Independence in 1821, but was revived by the new 1910 Revolution government, who began the practice of commissioning murals for public buildings. The intention was to capture the hearts of the largely illiterate population, while encouraging a new sense of national identity and an appreciation of the indigenous artistic heritage. As a result the murals can seem rather didactic, with titles such as *Workers United* and *Pan-American Unity*; despite this, the boldness and imagination of the artists usually transcends the subject matter. Today the mural is Mexico's finest and most distinctive national art form, and remains a potent tool of mass communication.

The three great muralists were Diego Rivera (1886–1957), Clemente Orozco (1883–1949) and David Siqueiros (1898–1974). Rivera was perhaps the most politicized of the three; he felt strongly that his art should reject foreign influence and create a new national symbolism. The result was a heady blend of historical mysticism, with pagan, native, Christian and Marxist themes. Rivera's greatest murals are in the Palacio de Cortés (in Cuernavaca), the Palacio Nacional and the El Prado hotel (both in Mexico City).

Clemente Orozco was based in Guadalajara; his work relies more on creating a sense of dynamic movement, where Rivera was statically decorative. Among his best work are murals at the Casa de Azulejos and the Museum of National History in Mexico City, and in public buildings throughout Guadalajara. Siqueiros was more innovative, experimenting with new paints, multiple perspectives, and with abstraction; he remained committed to social reform throughout his life, and even spent some time in prison as a result. His best-known works are at the Poliforum Siqueiros in Mexico City.

Later muralists have generally tended to produce more commonplace work, painting to order for bureaucrats and politicians and rarely emerging from the shadow of the great masters. Honourable exceptions include Rufino Tamayo, who decorated the Museo Nacional de Antropología, and Juan O'Gorman, whose wall mosaics combine art and architecture in an exciting and unique way, relying heavily on Pre-Hispanic symbolism. The walls of the University City library in the capital are his largest and most interesting work.

Music and dance

The Mexicans have music and dance in their blood. Nowhere is the richness and diversity of their cultural origins more apparent; in many areas, the native people have retained their songs and dances almost unchanged since Pre-Hispanic times, with stringed instruments added to the traditional drums, flutes and percussion instruments. One of the main reasons why so much native music has survived is the early missionaries' policy of encouraging the Indians to perform their traditional dances for the honour of the new God. In remote areas this custom has survived, and ancient war and fertility dances are still performed in front of churches on fiesta days. Other dances were invented by the missionaries to educate their flocks; a good example is the *moros y cristianos* dance which illustrates the early wars in Spain between the Moors and the Christians. The strongest influence on the music, of course, is that of Spain, but African rhythms predominate in some coastal areas, while in the north of the country the influence of the United States is noticeable.

The best way for the visitor to experience the full range of regional dances is to see a performance by the Ballet Folklórico, either in Mexico City or on tour. Numerous varied and well-choreographed dances are performed in the correct costumes, including stately flamenco-inspired dances from Spain and, at the other end of the spectrum, the Yaqui Deer Dance from the north of Mexico, in which dancers enact the hunting and killing of a deer.

Perhaps the most impressive of all the native dances still performed is that of the *Voladores*, the flying pole dance, originating from the eastern coast. The brightly costumed dancers whirl down through space, spiralling around a tall tree trunk to which they are tied by a long rope. Like all of the native dances, it has its origins in religious ceremonial which is now little understood; the Spanish missionaries believed it to be nothing more than a dangerous game.

It is still possible to see native dances performed in some villages, where they play an important part in the strange mixture of paganism and Catholicism that is the usual native religion. Sadly, however, these customs are slowly dying out, and it is hard to tell whether they will exist for much longer outside the dance companies and the widespread hotel-organized displays.

Less likely to die out is the cheerful sound of *mariachi* music, originating in the state of Jalisco and now common all over Mexico. *Mariachis* are professional musicians, available for hire, who dress in silver-studded black uniforms and accompany their songs with guitars, violins and trumpets. Traditionally, they are employed by young men to serenade their loved ones or for special occasions such as weddings or birthdays. Today the two main centres for *mariachis* are the Plaza Garibaldi in Mexico City and the Plaza de los Mariachis in Guadalajara, where they congregate and play songs while awaiting customers, the songs varying from the hauntingly sad to the bright and brassy.

Serenading in the small hours was once banned by a mayor of Mexico City, but was reinstated by his successor to massive public acclaim within hours of his taking office. However customs change, the Mexicans will never lose their love of music and dance.

Orientation map

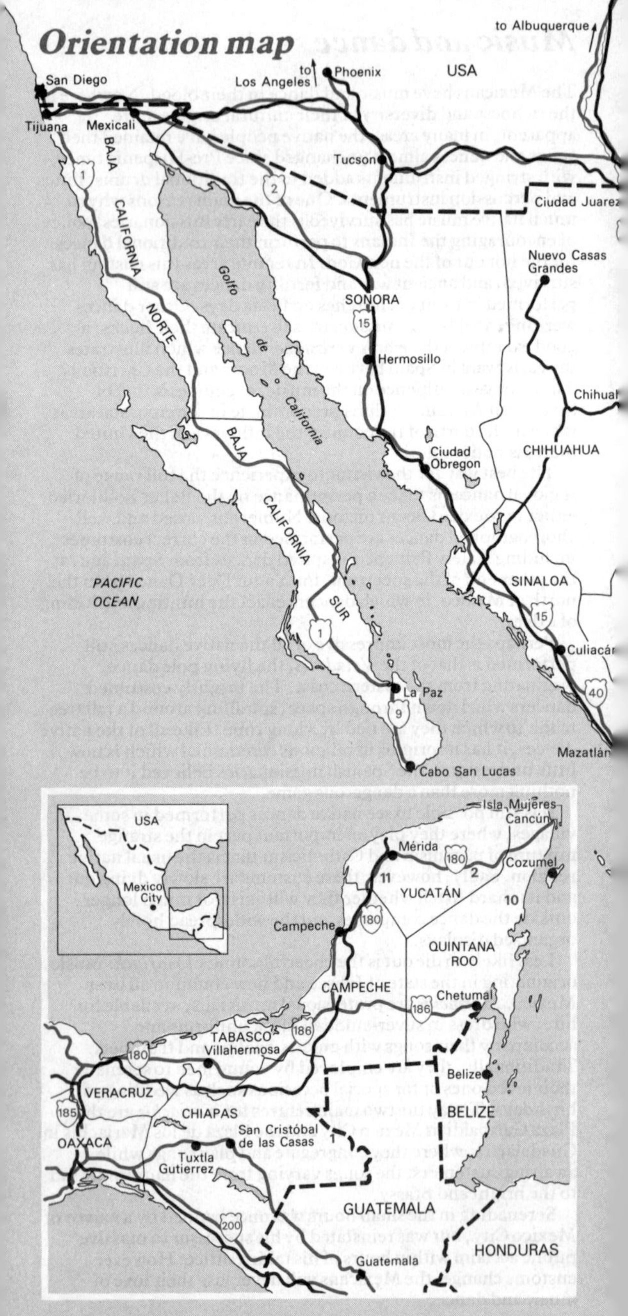

Major archaeological sites
1 Bonampak and Yaxchilán
2 Chichén Itzá
3 El Tajín
4 Malinalco
5 Mitla
6 Monte Albán
7 Palenque
8 Teotihuacán
9 Tula
10 Tulum
11 Uxmal
12 Xochicalco
13 Zempoala
National boundaries
State boundaries
International airport
Principal roads
Principal railway lines
National highways
20
Dallas
Paso
Río Grande
Río Bravo del Norte
Houston
San Antonio
Pan-American Highway
Ojinaga
Ciudad Acuña
Piedras Negras
Corpus Christi
Nuevo Laredo
COAHUILA
Reynosa
Matamoros
Monterrey
Torreón
Saltillo
NUEVO LEÓN
URANGO
Golfo de Mexico
Durango
ZACATECAS
SAN LUIS POTOSÍ
Ciudad Victoria
TAMAULIPAS
Zacatecas
San Luis Potosí
Tampico
NAYARIT
Aguascalientes
Tepic
León
QUERÉTARO
Guadalajara
San Miguel de Allende
Tuxpan
Puerto Vallarta
Guanajuato
Querétaro
GUANAJUATO
HIDALGO
Pachuca
JALISCO
ESTADO DE MEXICO
Jalapa
Morelia
Mexico City
TLAXCALA
Tlaxcala
Veracruz
Manzanillo
MICHOACÁN
Toluca
Puebla
COLIMA
Cuernavaca
MORELOS
PUEBLA
VERACRU
Taxco
Ixtapa
Zihuatanejo
GUERRERO
Oaxaca
Acapulco
OAXACA
Puerto Escondido
Puerto Angel
N
0 100 200 300 400 500 600 km
0 100 200 300 400 miles
16
45
49
40
57
85
101
54
5
70
180
80
90
130
200
15
140
37
95
190

Calendar of events

Every Mexican town has up to four or five of its own annual fiestas, typically celebrated with fireworks, processions, dancing, bullfights, religious services and heavy intake of alcohol. These are some of the better known and nationally celebrated fiestas. See also ***Public Holidays*** in *Basic information* and ***Events*** throughout the *A–Z*.

January

New Year's Day. Especially good at *Mitla*, with all-night Zapotec dancing around bonfires.

Jan 6. Day of the Kings. Native dancing at *Malinalco* with pilgrimage to nearby Chalma.

Jan 17. San Antonio Abad. In country areas animals are blessed outside churches.

Jan 18. Santa Prisca religious fiesta. See *Taxco*.

February

Carnival week (dates vary). Fairs, flower shows, masquerades, street theatre, cultural events. The best are at *Mazatlán*, *Mérida* and *Veracruz*; other good ones are at *Acapulco*, *Cuernavaca*, Huejotzingo (see *Puebla*), *Tampico* and *Tepoztlán*.

Feb 2. Candelmas (Candalería). Best are the colourful semi-aquatic celebrations at Tlacotalpán (see *Veracruz*).

Easter

Holy Week universally celebrated, with parades and Passion Plays; best are at *Patzcuaro*, *Taxco* and *San Cristóbal de las Casas*.

April

Apr 1–7. *San Cristóbal de las Casas*. Large Indian fair, attended by Indians from all over Chiapas.

Apr 15. *Fortín de las Flores*. Flower festival.

Apr 15–30. *Aguascalientes*. Fiesta de San Marco.

May

May 1. Labour Day parades in all major cities.

May 3. Holy Cross (Santa Cruz). *Valle de Bravo*. Dancing.

May 5. *Acapulco* and *Puebla* have best fiestas to celebrate Battle of Puebla.

May 15. San Isidro (patron saint of animals). Oxen widely are decorated with flowers and ribbons, and blessed.

June

June 1. Navy Day. Parades at ports.

Corpus Christi (Thurs, date varies). Ritual blessing of children. Totonac flying pole dance at Papantla (see *Poza Rica*).

July

July 1. *Guanajuato*. Fiesta begins.

Oaxaca. Guelaguetza fiesta (date varies). Indian dances.

August

Aug 8. Paracho (see *Uruapan*). Fiesta with pagan flavour.

Mid-Aug, for one week. Santa Clara de Cobre (see *Patzcuaro*). Copper fair.

Aug 15. Assumption (Asunción). Religious processions – in state of Tlaxcala over carpets of flowers.

Aug 27–31. *Zacatecas*. Fiesta de la Morísima, including Dance of the Moors and Christians.

Aug 28. San Agustín. *Puebla* has the best fiesta.

September

Sept 6–9. Virgen de los Remedios. *Cholula*. Native dancing.

Sept 15. Independence Day. In every Zocalo the mayor gives the *grito* (revolutionary call to arms). Celebrations last all night and next day; best at *Dolores Hidalgo* and *Mexico City* (military parade next day).

Sept 29. San Miguel. *San Miguel de Allende*. Lively fiesta.

October

Guadalajara. Arts festival.

Oct 12. Columbus Day (Día de la Raza). Parades through *Guadalajara* and nearby Zapopán.

November

Nov 1. Day of the Dead (Día de los Muertos). Candlelit vigils in cemeteries, most notably at Janitzio (see *Patzcuaro*), Mixquic (see *Amecameca*) and San Gabriel Chilac (see *Tehuacán*).

December

Dec 12. Virgen de Guadalupe. Largest and most fervent worship of Mexico's patron saint is at *Mexico City* shrine.

Dec 16. Start of Christmas celebrations with *posadas* (processions, followed by parties); all the usual fiesta events.

When and where to go

A 'grand tour' of Mexico, with a brief but adequate visit to each of the cities and sights described in this book, would probably occupy the best part of a year. Problems in deciding how to spend a vacation of a few weeks in Mexico are therefore best faced before departure. The traveller who needs most advice is the one arriving in Mexico City by air, wishing to see a good cross-section of the sights – some ruins, a colonial monument or two, a few Indian markets, with maybe a day or so on the beach to round it all off.

Without doubt, the most rewarding and complete tour possible within the length of an ordinary vacation is a three-week journey through the southeast. In its fullest form, it would involve leaving Mexico City through the state of Puebla, progressing through Oaxaca and Chiapas up to the Yucatán peninsula, and returning to Mexico City on the Gulf route, passing through Veracruz. Although it is demanding, this tour would certainly show the very best of every facet of Mexico, and should be given careful consideration by any undecided traveller.

On this or on any of the numerous other possible itineraries, the internal air network and the convenient system of one-way car rentals can be used to shorten or to link the various tours. The non-motorized tourist will find all the suggestions in the following pages accessible by public transport, although some of the minor attractions between cities are less worth the effort of stopping off to see. For those whose intention is to fly straight to one of the resorts, of which Mexico has a superb range, a separate survey compares their attractions and characters and the advantages of their locations.

There is no longer any definite tourist season in Mexico, and there are few areas where it is disagreeable for much of the year. The resorts are especially pleasant during the winter (Dec–April) and are crowded then and over public holiday weekends. But the advent of air conditioning has taken the sting out of the hot summers and made the resorts into all-year destinations; only in Baja California is it so hot that some resort hotels close in summer.

The central and western uplands – Mexico City and the colonial towns – are more visited during the pleasant summer months, although the winters are mild. Certain cities, such as Cuernavaca, Guadalajara and Taxco, are blessed with 'eternal spring'. Nights are cool throughout the year, and the other blemish is the rainy season (June–Sept), when the blue skies are covered for an hour's rain in the afternoon. Mountain climbing and off-road expeditions are therefore best left until the dry season.

The southeastern states are popular throughout the year, although the heat and humidity build up to very uncomfortable levels in places during the heavy rainy season. Semi-tropical temperatures persist throughout the year, and the only areas with noticeable winters are inland from the SE coast, especially the Chiapas highlands, where the climate is similar to that of Mexico City.

Northern Mexico is sunny and dry throughout the year, with little seasonal variation. There is only a short and light rainy season, and it is rarely cool. In most of Baja California, which is largely desert, it hardly ever rains, and it can become unbearably hot in the summer.

Area planners and tours

Mexico divides naturally into the following touring areas, which are described with Mexico City as the focal point, but with suggestions also for linking tours without returning to the capital. The main N to S highways are also described, with possible detours and the best places to stop overnight en route. Places printed in italics are described in the *A–Z*.

Areas: Mexico City and places nearby

Mexico City, where most visits to Mexico begin and end, is the obvious point of reference for touring the country. To see the sights of the city, three days is a minimum, including the best part of one at the Museo Nacional de Antropología. For a more exhaustive visit ten days is a realistic length, in which case it is advisable to break it up with some day-trips or longer excursions, to avoid big-city exhaustion. Within easy one-day range are a galaxy of fascinating attractions: Pre-Columbian ruins, colonial monuments, markets, and places of natural beauty. Below are some suggestions to help in planning your visit. Those unwilling to drive, or pressed for time, will find the hotel-organized bus tours a good way to cover a lot of ground quickly. Of the various companies operating, a reliable one is **Linea Gris** (*Londres 166, ZP6* ☎ *(5) 533–1665*).

Route 1: Mexico City–Teotihuacán day-trip

Leave the city along Insurgentes Norte, out past the Plaza de las Tres Culturas at Tlatelolco, where the Aztec ruins and the colonial church are worth a brief visit. On the outskirts of the city, E of Insurgentes, stands the country's holiest shrine, the Basilica de la Virgen de Guadalupe. The large new church and its colonial predecessor merit a good hour, with a short walk up to the chapels on the hill behind.

Continue N along Insurgentes and follow the signs for Pirámides Cuota; a small toll is payable on this road. The pyramids of *Teotihuacán*, about 40mins' drive away, are probably the most impressive ruins in Mexico. Expect to spend at least 3hrs exploring them, climbing the great Pyramid of the Sun, and seeing the small museum. If you stay on in the evening, see the son-et-lumiére.

On the way back to the capital the road passes the clearly signposted monastery of Acolmán. An hour spent here provides a good introduction to colonial art and to the architecture of the numerous monasteries, which acted as control points for the Spanish. Try to miss the rush hour when you return to the city – Insurgentes is blocked solid between 5–7pm.

Route 2: Mexico City–Tepotzotlán–Tula day-trip

Take the Querétaro toll road (RF 57) N from the city. After 35km (22 miles), follow the signs to *Tepotzotlán*, a small town about 3km (2 miles) W of the road. The church is one of the most remarkable examples of the Mexican Churrigueresque style, and in the adjoining monastery there is a good collection of colonial art. Return to the main road until you see the signs for *Tula*, some 20mins to the NE along a good road. This, the legendary capital of the Toltecs, is guarded by the great statues of warriors, staring impassively over the hills and through the centuries.

To make a full day's excursion, continue E along small roads via Mixquiahuala to join RF 85 at Actopán (see *Pachuca*),

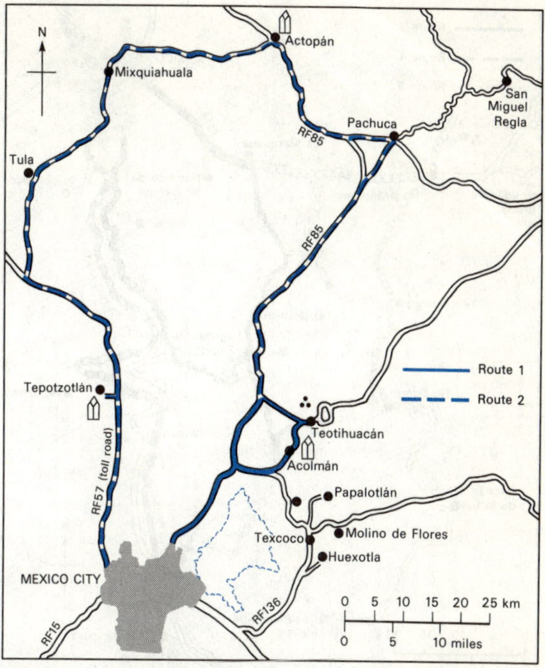

another monastery, with especially fine murals in the open chapel.

Return to Mexico City via *Pachuca*; the road passes near the pyramids of *Teotihuacán*, and, if it is late enough, this could be a good opportunity to see the son-et-lumière show, which starts at 7pm every night of the week bar one, which varies (check whether it is on before leaving).

A good place to spend the night near Pachuca is at the old hacienda of San Miguel Regla, 20mins N; a weekend of riding and swimming here makes an excellent break from the tiring business of tourism.

Route 3: Mexico City–Malinalco day-trip

Leave Mexico City W along Reforma, which soon becomes the RF 15 for Toluca. Turn S at La Marquesa and take the curving road down through the pine forests to the ruins of *Malinalco*, a small Aztec site on a mountain eyrie. The walk up to the ruins, allowing time to explore them, will take two hours.

Leave by the road E to the village of Chalma, which pilgrims transform into a colourful spectacle of religious fervour every Sunday. From here head N to Santa Marta, where a turn E passes by the lakes of Zempoala, surrounded by forests, and a good place for a picnic and a stroll. This road eventually joins the old free road from Cuernavaca to Mexico City, now the RF 95. Mexico City is entered from the S, a good chance for those staying in the centre to see the sights in this quarter. Most noteworthy are the University City, with its bold modern architecture, and the Museo Diego Rivera.

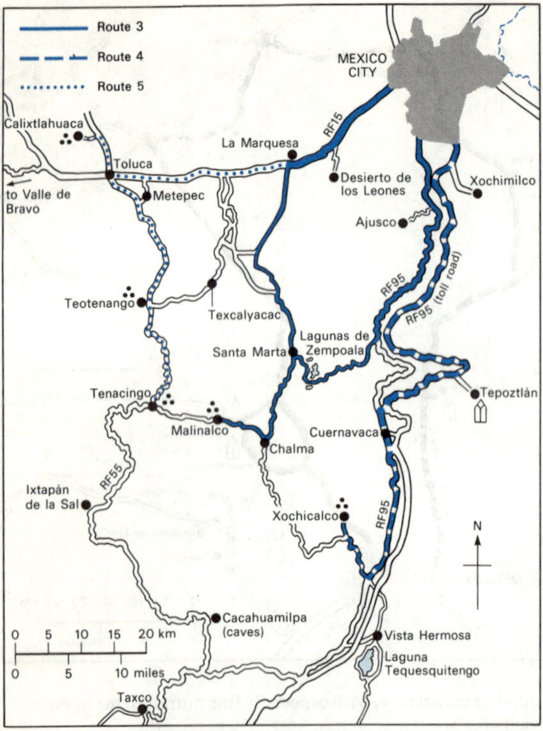

Route 4: Mexico City – Tepoztlán – Cuernavaca day-trip

Leave Mexico City as early as possible, taking the Cuernavaca toll road, RF 95. After 76km (46 miles), follow the signs for *Tepoztlán*, a charming little town built around a large monastery. A hearty breakfast at one of the little restaurants near the Zocalo is a good idea, since the famous Pre-Columbian remains are an hour's stiff climb away, high above the valley in volcanic crags.

For lunch, head into *Cuernavaca* – a real treat would be Las Mañanitas, Mexico's best-known restaurant, but it is necessary to book days ahead. The sights of Cuernavaca would easily fill an afternoon, starting with the Palacio de Cortés on the Zocalo. If you already know the city, a good alternative is the extensive site of *Xochicalco*, 45mins' drive southwest.

Cuernavaca has several charming hotels for weekenders: reserve about a year ahead for the rooms at Las Mañanitas, and two weeks or so for the others. To stay nearer to Xochicalco, the only place is the old hacienda of Vistahermosa, near the shores of Lake Tequesquitengo.

Route 5: Mexico City – Toluca day-trip

The road to Toluca, the RF 15, is a continuation of Reforma, heading W out of town. It is about one hour's drive to *Toluca*, where the Friday market is the only real tourist draw.

After loading up with native arts and crafts, head N along RF 55 to the ruins of Calixtlahuaca, just W of the road after 8km (5 miles). The circular pyramid here is of great antiquity and is the only one of its kind near Mexico City.

Take RF 55 back through Toluca and S towards Taxco. Places of interest include the pottery village of Metepec and, near Tenango, the impressive ruins of Teotenango, where there is also a small museum.

If you are not going back to Mexico City direct (via Texcalyacac) or via Toluca, the RF 55 continues S to Tenacingo, from where a rough road leads to the hilltop site of *Malinalco* (see ***Mexico City–Malinalco day-trip***, above).

A good weekend spot near Toluca is the sports resort of *Valle de Bravo*, 1½hrs due W, signposted along a good but narrow and twisting road.

Other day-trips from Mexico City

When the major destinations have all been visited, there remain a multitude of lesser sights, sometimes even more fascinating and always more of an adventure to visit. Described under the ***Sights nearby*** sections of *Amecameca, Cuautla* and *Texcoco* are enough minor attractions to make a separate day-trip of each. Colonial monasteries are well represented, and especially worthwhile are the little-known Pre-Columbian remains at Chalcatzingo, E of *Cuautla*. The best place to stay near Cuautla is at the Hacienda Cocoyoc, on the way to Cuernavaca: so long as there are no conferences scheduled, it is an excellent weekend haunt, but reserve a week ahead. There are no hotels at either Amecameca or Texcoco.

Area: The state of Puebla

A day-trip to Puebla from Mexico City is possible but tiring, and it is better to stay in one of the area's excellent hotels for a few nights, making excursions into the surrounding countryside and shopping and sightseeing at leisure. Puebla is on the way to the Gulf of Mexico and to the state of Oaxaca, so a stay there can make an interesting prelude to either of these longer trips.

Four-day excursion from Mexico City to Puebla

Day 1 Leave Mexico City along Zaragoza, which becomes RF 190, the toll road to Puebla. The drive takes about 2hrs, passing through rolling woody countryside – but watch out for the lunatic bus drivers who use this road as a race-track. In the afternoon, start on the sights of *Puebla*.

Day 2 It will take another energetic day to finish seeing the city's main attractions. There are several interesting museums, and such jewels of ecclesiastical architecture as the chapel of Santo Domingo.

Day 3 Leave Puebla heading SSW along RF 190, stopping after about 30mins at Atlixco for the sombre and impressive monastery. Turn back towards Puebla; at Acatepec there is a dazzling example of a Puebla tile-decorated Baroque church, and, just beyond, a road N leads to Cholula. Follow this to Tonantzintla, where there is another Puebla-style church, and to *Cholula* itself, where the exploration of the Great Pyramid and the myriad churches on top of the other pyramids will easily occupy the rest of the day.

Day 4 Leave Puebla NW along the old free road to Mexico City, RF 190 (the *Libre*). The first stop is after about 30mins at Huejotzingo, where a huge and grim fortified monastery

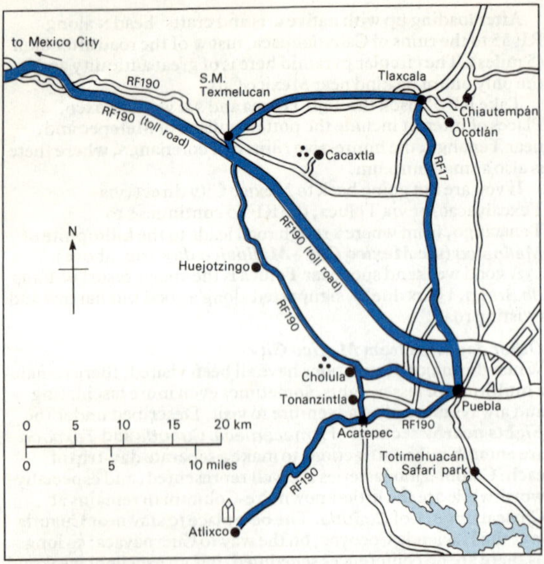

dominates the town. Continuing N, follow the signs to *Tlaxcala* over the Mexico toll road. It is a charming little town, neglected by tourists despite possessing such attractions as the remarkable monastery of San Francisco, whose church has the finest Mudejar timber roof in the Americas. On the way back to Puebla down RF 17, a well-signposted detour leads to the ruins of Cacaxtla; the standard of the recently discovered mural paintings is higher here than at any other Pre-Columbian site in the country.

Almost every village in this area has a pretty little church with an orange tiled dome. None are of special note, but the leisurely traveller will not pass them all by.

Area: Guerrero
Excursion to Taxco and Acapulco

Allow 5 days minimum.
From Mexico City, it is possible to travel either via *Cuernavaca* or *Toluca* to reach Taxco. However, except at holiday weekends or unless there are sights near Toluca you wish to see, it is better to use the Cuernavaca free road, RF 95. Allow about 3½hrs' driving time.

If there is no hurry, an interesting detour leaves RF 95, 24km (16 miles) S of Cuernavaca; it passes by the ruins of *Xochicalco*, then arrives at the large network of caves of Cacahuamilpa, where a visit takes around an hour. From here to the enchanting colonial silver town of *Taxco* is another hour's drive; the last stretch of road is twisting and more safely driven during daylight. Two or three days spent staying at one of Taxco's delightful colonial inns and exploring the churches and the silver shops will seem all too short.

From Taxco down to the coast at Acapulco is at least 4hrs' drive, and again, it is advisable not to drive it at night; the region between Taxco and Acapulco is poor, and in some areas away from the main road family vendettas and the drug trade lead to disturbances. As a precaution, do not stop on the road, except at army checkpoints.

The joys of *Acapulco*, with its dusk-till-dawn nightlife, beautiful beaches and myriad water-sports, may well be all that is needed to round off the vacation. In this case, a good plan is to make the trip down to Acapulco in a rented car which can then be left there, leaving you free to fly back to the capital.

Excursion to Zihuatanejo

Those who find Acapulco too hectic are bound to find satisfaction at the twin resorts of *Zihuatanejo* and *Ixtapa*, some 4hrs' drive N up the coast. Here all tastes are catered for, with the gleaming new white towers of Ixtapa and the unspoiled fishing-village charm of Zihuatanejo. It is also possible to fly back to Mexico City from here, leaving the rented car at the airport.

Acapulco to the southeast and the Yucatán

The quickest way to reach the touring areas of Oaxaca, Chiapas and the Yucatán is to take the coastal road, RF 200. It takes a full day's drive to reach the small fishing village of *Puerto Escondido*, and another half day from here to the city of *Oaxaca*. Before leaving, check that all of the bridges along the road are in operation: during the rainy season, there can sometimes be delays caused by flooding.

Area: The Bajío

A week or so exploring the cities in the hills N of Mexico City makes an interesting expedition from the capital, giving an insight into the little-known colonial period of Mexican history. It also makes a good diversion for travellers on a leisurely trip back to the USA.

Excursion to the colonial cities

Allow 5 days minimum.
Leave Mexico City on the toll motorway RF 57 to Querétaro. Possible stops along the way include the major sights of *Tula*

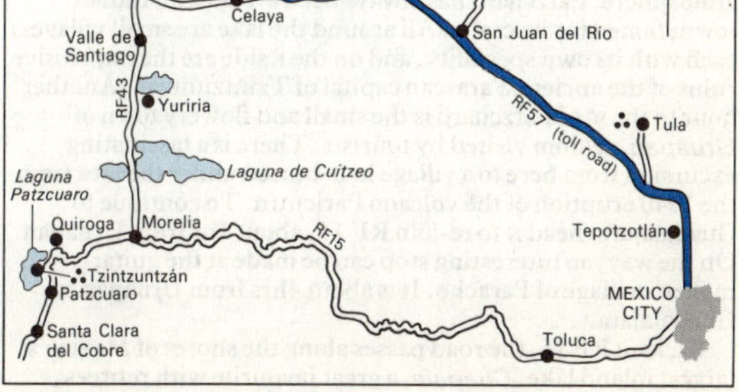

and *Tepotzotlán*, usually seen on day-trips from the capital. The town of *San Juan del Río* is also worth a visit, if only to buy the semi-precious stones for which it is famous. Near San Juan are several country resort hotels, popular with weekenders from Mexico City and Querétaro.

The first main city is *Querétaro*, some 2½hrs from the capital. It has a well-preserved colonial centre, but due to industrial development has lost much of its charm. The hotels are reasonable, but it is more agreeable to press on the further 63km (42 miles) to *San Miguel de Allende*, a place of almost legendary attractions, where hundreds of foreign writers and retirees have chosen to make their homes. Unless you have friends here, two days is enough to explore the town.

The next destination is the university town of *Guanajuato*, just an hour's drive farther west. On the way, stop at *Dolores Hidalgo*, a small town which was the starting point for Mexico's 19thC war of independence. Guanajuato is one of the best preserved of the colonial silver cities, well provided with small inns in ancient buildings that make it a pleasure to stay there. On the outskirts of town, towards Dolores Hidalgo, is one of Mexico's finest churches, La Valenciana, by a disused silver mine of the same name. Allow three days to savour at leisure the atmosphere of Guanajuato, and to visit such attractions as the gruesome mummies up at the Panteón, and the Teatro Juarez. It is necessary to reserve hotels some weeks ahead during the cultural festivals which Guanajuato hosts during the spring.

From here, you can return to Mexico City via the lesser colonial cities of Irapuato, Salamanca and *Celaya*, along RF 57. To lengthen the tour by another week or so, head S towards *Morelia* and *Patzcuaro* via Valle de Santiago (see ***Area: Western Central Mexico***, below) and Yuriria.

Area: Western Central Mexico

Mexico City to Guadalajara

Allow 9hrs' driving time.

Leave Mexico City W along RF 15 via *Toluca*. The first possible night's stop is at the spa town of San José Purua (see *Morelia*), where the infirm can take the health-giving waters. It is more interesting to continue a further 45mins to *Morelia*, about halfway to Guadalajara, and a colonial city of great charm with some fine historic buildings, although less well-known than its rivals to the north.

At this point a 3hr detour is possible. Less than one hour's drive to the W of Morelia is the town of *Patzcuaro*, on the lake of the same name. Unlike Morelia, which has a Spanish atmosphere, Patzcuaro has always been a Tarascan Indian town, famed for its crafts. All around the lake are small villages, each with its own speciality, and on the E side are the impressive ruins of the ancient Tarascan capital of Tzintzuntzán. Another hour to the W of Patzcuaro is the small and flowery town of *Uruapan*, seldom visited by tourists. There is a fascinating excursion from here to a village half-buried under the lava from the 1940 eruption of the volcano Paricutín. To continue to Guadalajara, head N to re-join RF 15, about 1hr from Uruapan. On the way, an interesting stop can be made at the guitar-maker's village of Paracho. It is about 4hrs from Uruapan to Guadalajara.

Back on RF 15, the road passes along the shores of Mexico's largest inland lake, *Chapala*, a great favourite with retirees.

Here there are reasonable hotels, where the unhurried can dally for a day or two.

To see the sights of *Guadalajara*, two days is an absolute minimum, although to enjoy its gracious atmosphere and excellent hotels and restaurants four days would be more realistic. Beyond Guadalajara, RF 15 continues on up the coast towards *Tijuana* and the US border, described below under ***The Pacific Highway*** route from north–south.

Guadalajara to the Pacific coastal resorts

Guadalajara is half a day's drive from the important resorts of *Puerto Vallarta* (RF 15 and RF 200) and *Manzanillo* (RF 54). If heading for Manzanillo, try to spend a night on the way at *Colima*, where there are two interesting museums, one of vintage cars, the other of local archaeology. It is a pleasant city in a beautiful position off the main tourist path.

Guadalajara to Mexico City via the Bajío

Leave Guadalajara on RF 80 for *San Luis Potosí*, joining RF 45 at Lagos de Moreno. A slightly tortuous route (RF 45, RF 110, RF 51 and RF 57) brings you to Mexico City via the famous colonial cities of *Guanajuato*, *San Miguel de Allende* and *Querétaro*. Five days would hardly be too long to do them all justice.

Area: The Gulf

The journey from the capital down to the semi-tropical Gulf passes through beautiful mountain country. There is plenty to see on the way and, depending on the time available, a choice of routes, each with its own attractions.

Routes from Mexico City to the Gulf

The quick way The quickest way to reach the Gulf coast from Mexico City is to take the *Puebla* toll road, RF 190, and then RF 150 to *Veracruz*, Mexico's oldest port. It is an easy day's drive (allow 8hrs' driving time), but if you have more time an agreeable place to spend a night is the small town of *Fortín de Las Flores*, under the shadow of the towering *Orizaba* volcano.

Via Jalapa and Zempoala A pleasant alternative route (allow 7hrs' driving time) is to take RF 140 from *Puebla*, which passes through the town of *Jalapa* and near the ruins of *Zempoala*.

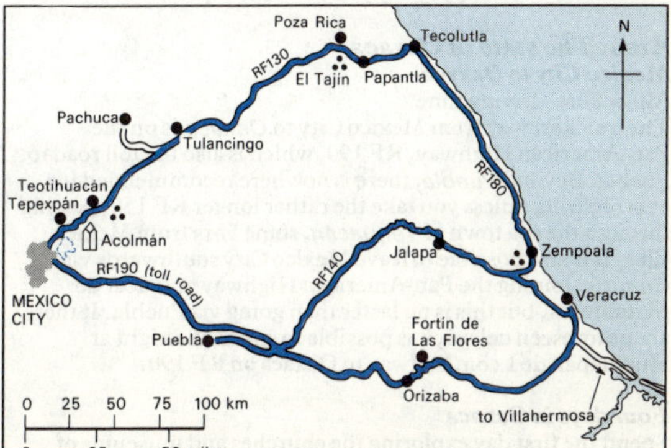

The archaeological museum at Jalapa is worth an hour of anyone's time. An overnight stop may be necessary if you are to do justice to the ruins at Zempoala; adequate hotels are available in Jalapa.

Via Teotihuacán and El Tajín Instead of leaving Mexico City on the Puebla road, head out on RF 130 via the pyramids of *Teotihuacán* and towards the Gulf coast via the town of *Poza Rica*. Spend the night here, leaving early in the morning for the fascinating Totonac ruins of *El Tajín*, S off RF 130. At the nearby village of Papantla, visitors may be lucky enough to see the famous Totonac flying pole dance, performed for fiestas and sometimes on Sundays. Farther down the coast, a good place for a beachside lunch of grilled fish is at Tecolutla, just off the road to the east. Allow 10hrs' driving time for this excursion; if time permits, the ruins of Zempoala, (see *Veracruz*), some 10km (6 miles) inland towards Jalapa on RF 140, are worthwhile.

Veracruz to the Yucatán peninsula
Allow 18hrs' driving time on RF 180.
The farthest that can be driven within a day from *Veracruz* is to the disagreeable city of *Villahermosa*. With a few brief halts at the pretty little towns along the road, such as Tlacotalpan, an alternative first night is at *Coatzacoalcos*, no better than Villahermosa, although it is probably better to press on to the latter, since despite its disadvantages it has two of the best archaeological museums in Mexico. Within 1½hrs NW of Villahermosa are the recently excavated Mayan ruins of Comalcalco, well worth a detour if time permits.

From Villahermosa, RF 180 continues along the coast to *Campeche*, via *Ciudad Carmen* and several ferry crossings, and is not recommended. The inland road, RF 186, is much quicker, and passes by the beautiful Mayan ruins of *Palenque*, well signposted to the S and about 2hrs from Villahermosa. There are good hotels at the village near the ruins, and an overnight stop allows the best part of a day to see the ruins and explore the surrounding jungle.

Beyond here, the fortified port of *Campeche*, on the Yucatán peninsula, is the next place to spend the night, about half a day's drive on RF 186 and RF 261 (see ***Area: The Yucatán peninsula***, below). Those not travelling by car should resist the temptation to take the train from Palenque to Campeche and Mérida, for it is an appallingly unpleasant experience.

Area: The state of Oaxaca
Mexico City to Oaxaca
Allow 8hrs' driving time.
The quickest way from Mexico City to *Oaxaca* is on the Pan-American Highway, RF 190, which is also the toll road to Puebla. Beyond *Puebla*, there is nowhere recommended for overnighting unless you take the rather longer RF 150, passing through the spa town of *Tehuacán*, some 5hrs from Mexico City. It is also possible to leave Mexico City southwards via *Cuautla*, joining the Pan-American Highway at Izúcar de Matamoros, but this is no faster than going via Puebla. If there are unforeseen delays, it is possible to spend the night at Huajuapán de León, halfway to Oaxaca on RF 190.

Four days in Oaxaca
Spend the first day exploring the churches and museums of *Oaxaca* itself. A morning visit to the enormous ruined Zapotec

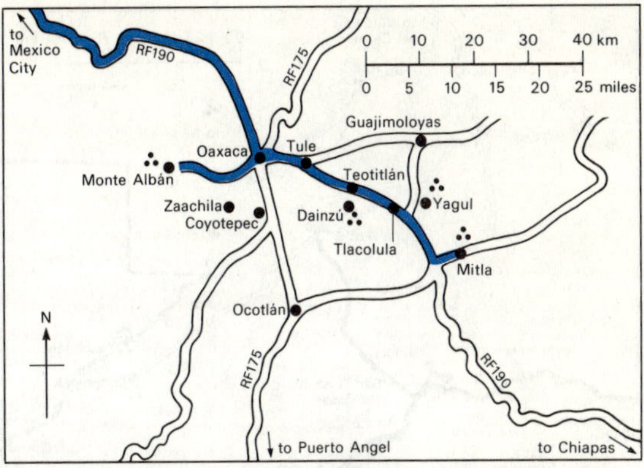

city of *Monte Albán*, and an afternoon in the villages to the S of Oaxaca (Zaachila and Coyotepec are especially worthwhile) will then occupy another day. Between Oaxaca and the Mixtec site of *Mitla*, 30mins SE on RF 190, are sufficient places of interest to occupy a whole day: they include the ruins of Dainzú and Yagul, not to mention the largest tree in the world at Tule. See *Mitla* itself the next day – the intricately adorned palaces deserve no less than refreshed and alert visitors. After a morning at Mitla, return to *Oaxaca*, and pass the afternoon in the fascinating markets and shops, where the arts and crafts of the Indian population make irresistible presents and souvenirs. The Mercado Juarez, on Sat, is best.

Oaxaca to Chiapas and the Yucatán peninsula

Allow 11hrs' driving time to Villahermosa.
To get from Oaxaca to the Yucatán peninsula, the quickest way is on RF 190 E to Juchitán, then N on RF 185 to *Coatzacoalcos* and along the coastal RF 180 to *Villahermosa* (see ***Area: The Gulf***, above). This route has the disadvantage that there is nowhere pleasant on the way to spend the night, although there are passable hotels at *Tehuantepec*, *Coatzacoalcos* and *Villahermosa*. It is more agreeable to make the hard day's drive from Oaxaca to *Tuxtla Gutierrez* on RF 190, and then, after a night's stop at Tuxtla, it is only 3½hrs N to Villahermosa on RF 195. Beyond Tuxtla on RF 190 lies the fascinating state of Chiapas; see ***Area: Chiapas***, below.

Area: Chiapas

Although it is possible to go directly from *Oaxaca* to the major sites and resorts of the Yucatán, the fascinating and little-known state of Chiapas can easily be included in any tour of southeastern Mexico – even to most Mexicans, it is a strange foreign country.

Six-day visit to Chiapas

Day 1 Spend the previous night at the state's administrative capital of *Tuxtla Gutierrez*, which can be reached by air from Mexico City or by road on RF 190. The zoo and small regional museum are the only attractions here, so set out early for *San Cristóbal de las Casas*, the highland colonial city at the heart of native Indian lands. The drive takes 2hrs, but a detour to the

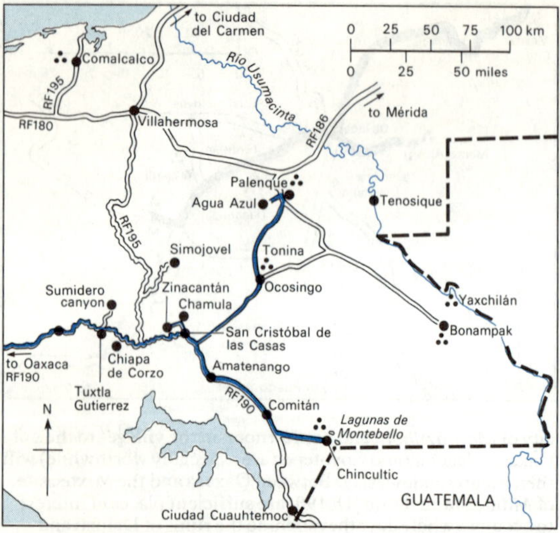

amazing Sumidero canyon and a brief halt at the interesting little town of Chiapa de Corzo (see *Tuxtla Gutierrez*) are well worthwhile.

Day 2 Exploration of San Cristóbal and its colourful Indian market.

Day 3 Expedition down the Pan-American Highway towards Guatemala. About 2hrs from San Cristóbal are the Mayan ruins of Chincultic, and the famous *Lagunas de Montebello*, each one a different colour and all surrounded by beautiful virgin forests.

Day 4 Visits to the villages around *San Cristóbal de las Casas* – two of the most interesting are Chamula and Zinacantán. Market day in all of the villages is Sunday.

Day 5 Excursion by small plane to the jungle sites of *Bonampak and Yaxchilán* to see the superb Mayan murals; hotels will make arrangements.

Day 6 Leave San Cristóbal on the minor road heading N towards Palenque, after first checking on its condition. Near the village of Ocosingo, the fine ruins of Tonina (see *Palenque*) have only recently been excavated. Those not travelling by car may wish to save time and an arduous bus trip by travelling to Palenque in a small plane: the trip is not expensive and the views are spectacular.

Area: The Yucatán peninsula

The region has both the best beaches and the most grandiose and inspiring ruins in all North America, making it an important tourist destination in its own right and an ideal place for a 2–3 week vacation. Many visitors fly direct to one of the resorts, such as *Cancún* or *Cozumel*, and from there make brief excursions to the ruins, organized by the hotels.

Two-week tour of the Yucatán

This suggested tour of the Yucatán is for travellers arriving by road along RF 186 from *Villahermosa*. The same loop can be followed by flying to *Campeche*, *Mérida* or one of the resorts, and there renting a car.

Leave Villahermosa early in the morning, arriving at the old fortified port of *Campeche* in time for a late lunch of seafood down on the waterfront. Spend the rest of the afternoon exploring the city, and leave the next morning for *Mérida* along the long road, RF 261, which passes near five major archaeological sites. Stop first at Edzna (see *Campeche*), then drive straight on to *Uxmal*, where there are good hotels near the ruins; the visit will take at least the rest of the day. The next day, head back a short distance to the lesser known but worthwhile ruins of Kabah, Sayil and Labna, and from there on to Mérida via Oxkutscab and Muna.

Book in for a two-night stay at *Mérida*, and spend an entire day sightseeing and shopping in town, with a visit on the second afternoon to the nearby site of Dzibilchantún, 30mins' drive north. The next day and night should both be spent at *Chichén Itzá*, the most important site on the peninsula; again, there are good hotels near the ruins.

From Chichén Itzá, another half-day's drive will bring you to the Caribbean coast at Puerto Juarez, near to the island resorts of *Cancún*, *Cozumel* and *Isla Mujeres*. Two or three days of relaxation may be welcome at whichever of the three takes your fancy.

Suitably refreshed, the next cultural attraction is the seaside Mayan city of *Tulum*, on RF 307 heading S. A good place to spend the night near here is at the solitary hotel by the ruins of Cobá, an hour inland from Tulum.

From here, head down to the strange city of *Chetumal* for interesting duty-free shopping and some reasonable hotels. It is also on the border with the former British colony of Belize. From Chetumal W to the nearest hotel is a long day's drive, either to *Campeche* to complete the loop, or on to the hotels at the ruins of *Palenque*, towards *Villahermosa* on RF 186. If there is time, stop on the way at the ruins of Kohunlich, 30mins out of Chetumal.

Area: North–South highways

Most of northern Mexico consists of great expanses of mountains and deserts, with the towns many hours' hard drive apart. With careful planning of overnight stops, however, the long N to S drives can become more of a pleasure and less of an ordeal.

The Pacific Highway (RF 15): Tijuana to Mexico City

Allow 36hrs' driving time.
The longest but probably the most interesting of the main N–S roads, linking San Diego in the USA with Guadalajara and Mexico City. After the seedy but lively border city of *Tijuana* there is nowhere of great interest until the resort port of *Guaymas*, although there are adequate hotels at Caborca and *Hermosillo*. From Hermosillo, an interesting excursion down to the coast at Bahía Kino is recommended for those whose vacation is restricted to this part of Mexico. At Guaymas and at the neighbouring tourist development of San Carlos the beaches and fishing are excellent, while the hotels are improving rapidly.

The next interesting place to stay is *Alamos*, a well-preserved colonial mining town 30mins' drive off the main road between the dull city of *Ciudad Obregón* and *Los Mochis*. The latter is only 1hr from Alamos and, although of little interest itself, is the Pacific terminus of the amazing Chihuahua-Pacific Railway which crosses some of Mexico's wildest mountain country (see *Chihuahua*). An excursion of a few days by train is highly recommended; leave your car at a hotel car park.

After Los Mochis, *Mazatlán*, the next stop, is a bustling port that is fast growing in importance as a beach resort. It is an easy day's drive from here to Mexico's second city of *Guadalajara*, and then another day to the capital. For details of where to stop or to make detours from the road between Guadalajara and Mexico City, see ***Area: Western Central Mexico***, above.

Detour from the Pacific Highway: the coast road RF 200

At the town of *Tepic*, between Mazatlán and Guadalajara, the Pacific Highway turns inland, and the coastal road becomes the RF 200 linking some of Mexico's largest resorts: *Puerto Vallarta*, *Manzanillo*, *Zihuatanejo and Ixtapa*, and *Acapulco*. The RF 95 then links Acapulco with Mexico City by way of *Cuernavaca*. Parts of the RF 200 are poorly maintained, so check conditions ahead before leaving any town.

The Pacific Highway: short excursions into Mexico

For those based near the border in the USA, a good short vacation is to drive down RF 15 to one of the ports and to take a ferry across the Sea of Cortés to *Baja California*, where RF 1 runs the length of the peninsula back up to the US border. Ferries leave from *Guaymas*, *Los Mochis*, *Mazatlán* and *Puerto Vallarta* (but the Mazatlán–La Paz ferry has a poor reputation for cleanliness and punctuality).

A good two-week vacation plan would be to go down to *Los Mochis*, with overnight stops at *Guaymas* and *Alamos*. After an excursion up into the mountains it is then a short trip over to La Paz. For details of where to go around La Paz and of the drive up to *Tijuana*, see *Baja California* in the *A–Z*.

RF 45: Ciudad Juarez to Mexico City

Allow 25hrs' driving time.

Beyond the large industrial border city of *Ciudad Juarez*, the first possible overnight stop is at the pleasant city of *Chihuahua*; if time permits, an interesting detour is to the ruins of Casas Grandes (see *Chihuahua*) SW of Juarez. This will add at least 5hrs' driving time, so it may be necessary to spend the night at the hotel in the village of Nuevo Casas Grandes before continuing. From *Chihuahua*, interesting excursions up into the wild mountains of the Sierra Madre are possible on the Chihuahua-Pacific Railway, leaving your car in Chihuahua at a hotel car park.

The next place of interest to stop for the night is the colonial mining town of *Parral*; then comes *Durango*, a centre of the 'western' movie industry. It would however be possible to reach the charming city of *Zacatecas* within a day from Chihuahua; even those just passing through should stop to see its remarkable Churrigueresque cathedral, one of the finest Churrigueresque buildings in Mexico.

From Zacatecas, Mexico City is another hard day's drive. Probably the quickest way is to cut across to *San Luis Potosí*, and then on down RF 57 via *Querétaro*. For the less hurried, there are several possibilities for interesting detours and stopovers. The first detour is to the ruins of Chicomoztoc, 45mins' drive S of *Zacatecas* on RF 54. About halfway from

Zacatecas to Mexico City on RF 45 is the colonial city of *Guanajuato*, 15mins E of RF 45 on RF 110. For ideas on exploring this area more fully, see ***Area: The Bajío***, above.

The Pan-American Highway (RF 85): Nuevo Laredo to Mexico City
Allow 20hrs' driving time.
A more interesting and arduous drive than RF 57, which runs parallel all the way: those wishing to reach Mexico City quickly should cut across to RF 57 at *Saltillo*, by-passing Monterrey.

Monterrey is the first major city on RF 85, a large industrial city with some minor places of interest, but near to several spots of great natural beauty, such as the Mesa Chipinque plateau just W of the city. Beyond Monterrey the road becomes more twisting and difficult. The best place to spend another night on the road is at *Ciudad Valles*, from where it is an easy day's drive to the capital. After Valles, the only possibility for a stopover is *Pachuca*, less than 2hrs from Mexico City; worthwhile sights along the road include the monasteries of Ixmiquilpán and Actopán, both reached before Pachuca.

The Piedras Negras Highway (RF 57): Piedras Negras to Mexico City
Allow 18hrs' driving time.
A fast and reasonably maintained route from Eagle Pass on the US border to Mexico City, with possible overnight stops at *Saltillo*, Matehuala, *San Luis Potosí* and *Querétaro*. There are no major tourist attractions on this road.

The east-west highway (RF 40 and RF 15)
Allow 20hrs' driving time.
The first opportunity for southbound travellers to cut right across the country between the main N to S highways: it passes through the major cities of *Matamoros*, *Monterrey*, *Saltillo*, *Torreón* and *Durango*, reaching the Pacific coast on RF 15 near the port and resort of *Mazatlán*. At all of these there are reasonable hotels, but only Monterrey, Durango and Mazatlán are of sufficient interest to merit more than a short stopover. The last part of the road before the coast, passing through magnificent mountains, demands special caution.

The resorts

Acapulco

Of Mexico's resorts, the name with the greatest hold on the imagination is *Acapulco*, conjuring up visions of film-stars, yachts and dollars. Acapulco is certainly the most visited of the resorts, and does boast more than its share of celebrities. The attractions are many, chief of them being the nightlife, but including also excellent fishing, water-sports and hotels. For these reasons Acapulco is the standard against which other Mexican resorts are usually compared – which is not to say that it wins on all counts; it is a big city, and its jet-set sophistication is too hectic to suit everyone's idea of a restful break.

The new resorts: Cancún and Ixtapa
In the early 1970s, as Mexico's increasing popularity filled its resorts to bursting point, two virgin beaches were chosen by computer as the sites for the country's new luxury pleasure machines. This bold experiment quickly paid off, and doors are now open to visitors at the futuristic hotels of *Cancún*, on the

Caribbean coast, and *Ixtapa*, N of Acapulco on the Pacific. Of the two, Cancún has enjoyed a more rapid rise to fame and boasts more extensive facilities; the out-of-hotel nightlife at both is still developing. The immediate neighbour of Ixtapa, the still largely unspoiled fishing village of *Zihuatanejo*, means that a vacation spent there can offer assured variety. Cancún, on the other hand, offers the chance to visit the superb Mayan ruined cities of the Yucatán.

The Caribbean islands: Cozumel and Isla Mujeres
Not far from Cancún are two other island resorts, *Cozumel* and *Isla Mujeres*, neither having the jet-set appeal or luxury hotels of their younger sister. Cozumel caters principally for underwater sports enthusiasts, but is also a good choice for the middle-budget sun-worshipper. Mujeres is more for the 'have guitar, will travel' crowd, who are untroubled by lack of air conditioning and care little for sophisticated pleasures.

Unspoiled paradises: San Blas, Puerto Angel and Puerto Escondido
Other resorts in the Isla Mujeres class, undeveloped but more or less geared to the demands of the international traveller on a budget, include *San Blas*, on the Pacific coast near *Tepic*, and, farther S, the twin fishing villages of *Puerto Escondido* and Puerto Angel, similarly 'Robinson Crusoe' in atmosphere and within easy reach of *Oaxaca*. Although Angel and Escondido have small airports, most people arrive at these places overland.

Pacific resorts: Puerto Vallarta, Manzanillo and Mazatlán
Unlike Zihuatanejo, which acquired a luxury neighbour in Ixtapa, the fishing village of *Puerto Vallarta* has itself developed into one of Mexico's most sophisticated and luxurious resorts, while losing little of its charm in the process. Most of its foreign clientele arrive by air, as they do at *Manzanillo*, some 4hrs' drive down the coast, where family fun and good fishing are the order of the day. The same is true of *Mazatlán*, farther N, although an important difference is that more people use their own cars to get here from the USA. At both of the latter there are good hotels, and although neither could yet be characterized as a luxury resort, the general trend is in that direction.

Baja California and the Sea of Cortés: Guaymas and Cabo San Lucas
Future tourist development in this area of Mexico appears probable given the proximity of the USA. On the mainland, *Guaymas* and its satellite San Carlos have good hotels but are still more geared to deep-sea fishing than to beach vacations. Over the Sea of Cortés, the *Baja California* peninsula seems more likely to experience a boom. Already there is a good clutch of luxury hotels around Cabo San Lucas on the southern extremity. The other Baja resorts however are small and resemble Guaymas in their emphasis on fishing.

The peninsula's attractions do not yet include much in the way of non-hotel restaurants and nightlife, apart from the cities of La Paz, *Ensenada* and *Tijuana*. Although Tijuana does have a beach, it is not really a resort. Ensenada, on the other hand, just an hour from the USA, is growing in importance; as well as its fishing, there are good beaches and more than adequate hotels and restaurants. No plans yet exist, but the Cancún of the 21stC will probably not be far from here.

Where to stay

Mexican hotels will be a pleasant surprise for those revisiting the country after a long absence. Massive financial investment and a new generation of professional managers have more or less eliminated the comically dreadful establishments of popular tourist lore.

Prices

Hotel prices are lower than in the USA and Europe, although higher up the price scale the difference is much less, and the situation is always changing. Tariffs are fixed by the Tourism Secretariat, who also publish erratic one to five-star ratings. Remember also that 15% tax is added to all hotel bills, but that tips are at your discretion. The single traveller will usually have to pay 80% or even 100% of the double rate.

Reservations

The resorts and popular inland vacation spots fill up completely during holiday weekends. At all times it is advisable to make reservations at least two weeks ahead, and for Acapulco, months are better than weeks to secure the hotel of your choice. Some establishments will still accept telephone reservations, but this gives the traveller no security; it is better therefore to reserve ahead through a travel agent, who can wire a deposit. Be sure to take the hotel confirmation with you, for in the event of overbooking they are obliged to find you suitable alternative accommodation. Unless hotels are advised of a likely late arrival, rooms will not be held beyond 6pm.

Categories of accommodation

Most luxury hotels in Mexico are controlled by international hotel chains, and, in addition to the standard high-quality rooms and service, many offer shops, travel agents, sports facilities, social programmes and organized excursions. Staff often speak good English. In the resorts, some hotels try to insist on the American Meal Plan (full board); in theory they are not allowed to do this, but in some cases there is nothing to do except change hotels.

Medium-priced hotels usually offer restaurants, showers with rooms, air conditioning where it is necessary, and at least one staff member who speaks English. Cities such as Cuernavaca, Guanajuato, Morelia, San Miguel Allende and Taxco boast some old colonial inns in 16th–17thC town houses.

In all of Mexico's cities it is possible to find amazingly cheap accommodation, usually around the main square. Always check the room before signing in, for some are totally unacceptable, and standards vary wildly from week to week. Telephone reservations are unheard of, English rarely spoken, and anything but cash is usually greeted with a puzzled stare.

American-style motels line the main highways around most Mexican cities, especially in the north. In this guide a selection in the moderate to expensive price range has been included. One word of caution, however: the seedier-looking motels often function to some extent as brothels.

Finally, in the main coastal resorts it is possible to find self-contained flats and bungalows on condominium rental or time-sharing arrangements. They are moderate to expensive in price, and arrangements should be made through a travel agent before departure for Mexico.

Food and drink

Mexican cuisine reflects the national character, being a rich and unique blend of indigenous and Spanish traditions, with wide regional variations. The red-hot chili dishes of popular imagination are more of a Texan phenomenon, and bear little relation to the exquisitely subtle use of spices and flavours that characterizes genuine Mexican cooking.

Restaurants

Recommendations in this book concentrate, although not exclusively, on restaurants offering authentic Mexican cuisine. There are usually plenty of cheaper restaurants around a town's Zocalo or waterfront (*malecón*), but their standards can vary from day to day and the best idea is to walk around and see where the locals are eating. With a few creditable exceptions (mostly in Mexico City) hotel restaurants are pricier and less interesting.

It is always worth ringing beforehand to see if reservations are advisable; telephone reservations are usually accepted, and the table is held for about 10mins after the stated time. Adequate notice for most places is the morning of the same day.

Restaurant prices are always considerably lower than in the USA or Europe; even luxury restaurants are up to 50% cheaper, although imported wines can erode the advantage. A tax, currently 15%, is added to all bills, and a 10–15% tip is customary. Fixed-price menus are rare in the evening, but at lunchtime excellent value '*comida corrida*' lunches are more common.

Most restaurants open around 12.30pm and close when the last diner is persuaded to leave, usually around midnight. Mexicans eat their lunch between 2–4pm, but it often goes on for hours and overlaps with early evening diners. The most popular hour for dinner is 9.30–10.30pm. Hotel restaurants have more rigid hours, usually 12.30–2.30pm and 7.30–10.30pm.

Food

Some of Mexico's regional dishes have become so famous that they are now served all over the country. No vacation would be complete without sampling, for example, *guajalote con mole* (turkey in *mole* sauce). The sauce, first invented in Puebla, is often known as *mole poblano*; it is very complicated, made from up to 40 different ingredients, of which one is unsweetened raw chocolate. Also originating in Puebla is the stuffed chili dish called *chiles en nogada*, served only around the time of the independence celebrations (Sept) with a topping in the national colours.

Tortillas

For thousands of years, the main staple of Mexican cooking has been the *tortilla*, a maize pancake. One of the most characteristic sounds of the countryside is the rhythmic slapping of housewives beating out the day's *tortillas* at dawn. They are served with every meal and are the basis of numerous snacks and dishes, the two most famous being *tacos* and *enchiladas*, both of which consist of rolled *tortillas*, filled with whatever takes the chef's fancy, and served with a spicy sauce. The ubiquitous *enchiladas Suizas*, filled with chicken in a rich cream and cheese sauce, have little to do with Switzerland.

Other *tortilla* snacks include *tostadas*, *gorditas*, *flautas* and many others. If you buy them off street stalls, be sure not to eat the greenery, and choose a clean-looking vendor and stall. The other well-known Mexican snacks, *tamales*, also use the same maize dough as *tortillas*, but are made with a handful of it, stuffed with meat, and then steamed in a corn husk.

Meat dishes
The best meat dishes come from the N of Mexico, the style of cooking known as *norteño*. Large juicy steaks are the speciality of the cattle ranching state of Chihuahua, but the drier and more barren states of the NW concentrate on kid (*cabrito*) dishes, usually served with wheat *tortillas*. A favourite meat dish now found all over the country is *carne asada a la Tampiqueña*, well-beaten strips of steak served grilled with a selection of beans, vegetables, and *guacamole* (avocado paste). Mexican barbecued meat (*barbacoa*) is cooked for many hours in an underground pit.

Seafood
It is wise to eat seafood only at coastal cities and in the smarter inland restaurants. The freshest and best seafood is served at the humble beachside huts that line all popular beaches.

For starters, a good choice is the deliciously chewy *ceviche* fish cocktail, made from uncooked fish pickled in lime juice; a variation on this is *ceviche de pulpo* (squid). To follow, the most famous of Mexican fish dishes is the *huachinango a la veracruzana* (red snapper Veracruz-style); the delicately flavoured fish is served in an aromatic red sauce of garlic, spices and mild chilis. Lobster, giant shrimps, and crayfish are the basis of other interesting dishes. More exotic and unfamiliar will be the turtle (*tortuga*) stews and game fish steaks.

Desserts
Puddings are the only disappointment of Mexican cooking. Most are excessively sweet and sticky concoctions of milk, eggs and sugar. It is better to go for one of the exotic tropical fruits, such as *papaya* (paw-paw), mango, or pomegranate. In the smarter restaurants, ice creams (*nieves* or *helados*) are delicious.

Drink
Mexico's most famous alcoholic offering to a grateful world is of course tequila, the ambrosial firewater made from distilled cactus juice. Many prefer it straight with salt and lemon, but the Cointreau-laced margarita cocktail is a less dramatic assault on the taste buds. For a smooth tasting and well-aged tequila, ask for 'Commemorativo'. Also made from cactus, and similar to tequila, is mescal, famous (or infamous) for the dead worm at the bottom of the bottle. The poor relation of these two is pulque, a sort of milky, yeasty cactus beer favoured by peasants for achieving cheap oblivion; although full of protein and vitamins, most foreigners find it unpalatable.

Like many other countries, Mexico is claimed to have the best beer in the world. There are two varieties, dark (*oscura*), and light (*clara*); good *oscuras* are Negra Modelo and Tres Equis, and among the *claras* are Bohemia and Carta Blanca.

Local wines are less reliable, but producers have been learning from the dramatic recent improvement in both quality and quantity of Californian wines.

Brandy (of sorts) and excellent rum are also produced in Mexico, together with a plethora of strange and sticky regional liqueurs. Before trying them, remember that alcohol can have up to three times its normal intoxicating effect at the altitude of Mexico City.

Coffee and tea

The most typically Mexican way to drink coffee is *café de olla*, brewed for hours with cinnamon and sugar added. If you want coffee with milk, ask for it *con crema* (with cream), and not *con leche*, which will bring a concoction of warm milk and instant coffee. Ordinary breakfast coffee is called *café americano*, and is served black. *Espresso* and *cappucino* are often available.

For a cup of tea, ask for *té negro* (black tea) to produce the desired result, but more interesting are the local herbal teas. After a large dinner try some aromatic *té manzanilla*.

Food and health

Some travellers to Mexico experience mild stomach upsets, usually due simply to change of diet, in which case symptoms disappear after a few days. A few simple precautions are:

— At high altitudes, where the digestion works slowly, avoid excesses of food or alcohol.
— Avoid tap water or anything that may have been washed in it. Water purification tablets are only of limited use.
— Peel all fruit. Avoid water melons since their juices are likely to be contaminated.
— All meat, especially pork, should be well cooked.
— Avoid roadside snacks until you are well used to Mexican food (up to a month after arrival).
— Avoid unpasteurized milk.

Shopping

It is a restrained visitor indeed who can leave this nirvana of shopping without at least doubling the weight of his luggage. In tourist centres, shopping hours are often extended beyond the standard 10am–7.30pm. Most shops close on Sunday and in city commercial districts sometimes also on Saturday afternoons; large suburban shopping centres often close on Monday instead of Sunday.

How to shop

The most important rule is to watch out for inferior shoddy imitations; this applies to almost anything you might wish to buy. The other rule (except in department stores) is to bargain: a little simulated lack of interest, or a willingness to pay in cash, will work wonders. Where there are no marked prices, and in markets, aim for at least 25% off the asking price. As a general rule, the more English a trader speaks, the higher his prices.

What to look for

Folk arts and crafts

Regional specialities from all over Mexico are often available in major tourist centres, with no price increase from the place of origin; the state-run FONART stores provide a good starting-point. Remember that it is illegal to export genuine Pre-Columbian items.

Old traditions live on in hand-woven textiles, often using Pre-Columbian patterns and techniques. Beware of garish imitations in the N especially, although *Saltillo* is known for *sarapes* (ponchos), rugs and *rebozos* (shawls). Traditions are stronger W of the capital around *Chapala*, *Morelia* and

Patzcuaro. The states of Chiapas and Oaxaca in the SE produce fine weaving and embroidery; the heavily decorated *huipils* (blouses) are particularly eyecatching. As a general rule, do not wear native costume in the areas of origin out of respect.

The native gifts for proportion and decoration also live on in ceramics. Best-known are the towns of Metepec (see *Toluca*), *Puebla* and Tlaquepaque (see *Guadalajara*). In Metepec are produced the brightly coloured 'Trees of Life' which adorn homes all over Mexico. Tableware can chip easily with heavy use, an exception being the striking black pottery (which is slightly radioactive) from the villages near *Oaxaca*.

Other good buys are leather goods from all over Mexico; hammocks from the Yucatán; native paintings on tree bark (*amate*) from the state of Mexico; lacquerware from *Uruapan* and guitars from nearby Paracho; semi-precious stones from *San Juan del Río* and La Magdalena (see *Guadalajara*); and copper from Santa Clara del Cobre (see *Patzcuaro*).

Silver and jewellery

The main centre for the production of silver jewellery in Mexico is the pretty little colonial town of *Taxco*, high in the mountains of Guerrero. The standards of design and workmanship are very high, with modern and Pre-Columbian motifs combining into an original and pleasing effect; more conventional pieces are also on sale. It is a good idea to check the hallmark (it should read 925), and the strength of any moving parts such as hinges. Silver is also sold in Mexico City and other major tourist centres; the Tane chain is known for its exquisite designs and high prices, and branches can be found in some luxury hotels and in Mexico City's Zona Rosa. In the state of Oaxaca can be found some interesting gold jewellery based on the Pre-Columbian treasures found in the tombs of Monte Albán.

Casual clothing

At *Acapulco*, *Cancún*, *Puerto Vallarta* and other major resorts, numerous boutiques offer a good selection of casual but elegant resort wear, many of the embroidered patterns on the women's clothing being based on original native costumes. A must for men is one of the *guayabera* pleated shirts, originating from the Yucatán peninsula. They are acceptable as semi-formal wear throughout the country, and are cool and comfortable.

In *Mexico City*, fashions are sophisticated and cosmopolitan, and prices are low. The quality of the goods is however often rather poor: fabrics, stitching and dyes are not of the best, and watch out especially for non-colour-fast dyes in the brighter hues. The same is true of the shoes, which look an excellent bargain but can soon cause disappointment.

Nightlife

In most of Mexico, the best nightclubs and discotheques are to be found at the luxury hotels, and only in Acapulco and Mexico City is there a good selection of independent establishments. In large cities and resorts, a free information sheet in English details the various events and spectacles on offer. At the coastal resorts, at the cheap and cheerful beach discos which come and go with alarming rapidity, it can be great fun dancing barefoot on the sand until dawn. Foreigners should avoid the rougher bars or *cantinas*, especially those which do not admit women.

Mexico A–Z

The opening hours of Mexican museums are erratic by any standards; late opening, early closing and unscheduled lunch breaks should never come as a surprise. As a general rule, Monday is the closing day, and opening hours are from 10am–6pm; this will be referred to in the text as 'standard hours', and significant variations will be noted. When a museum closes for lunch, this will also be specified; again, hours are variable, but 1–3.30pm is typical.

Entry fees for all sights are invariably very low, and it is helpful to have some small change handy. In some cases, a separate small charge is made for allowing photography. Tripod photography is forbidden.

Sights and places of interest

A selection of major sights with cross-references to the *A–Z*.

Archaeological sites

Bonampak and Yaxchilán
Cacaxtla
 See *Tlaxcala*
Calixtlahuaca
 See *Toluca*
Casas Grandes
 See *Chihuahua*
Chalcatzingo
 See *Cuautla*
Chichén Itzá
Cholula
Cobá
 See *Tulum*
Dzibilchaltún
 See *Mérida*
Edzna
 See *Campeche*
El Tajín
Kabah
 See *Uxmal*
Labna
 See *Uxmal*
Malinalco
Mitla
Monte Albán
Palenque
La Quemada
 See *Zacatecas*
Sayil
 See *Uxmal*
Templo Mayor
 See *Mexico City*
Teotenango
 See *Toluca*
Teotihuacán
Tula
Tulum
Uxmal
Xochicalco
Yagul
 See *Oaxaca*
Zempoala
 See *Veracruz*

Places with notable colonial architecture

Acolmán
 See *Teotihuacán*
Alamos
Campeche
Guadalajara
Guanajuato
Jalapa (Xalapa)
Mérida
Morelia
Oaxaca
Patzcuaro
Puebla
Querétaro
San Miguel de Allende
Taxco
Tepotzotlán
Tlaxcala
Zacatecas

Museums

Castillo de Chapultepec, *Mexico City*
Museo Antropológico, *Colima*
Museo Arqueológico, *Jalapa*
Museo Arqueológico, *Mérida*
Museo del Estado, *Guadalajara*
Museo Diego Rivera, *Mexico City*
Museo Nacional de Antropología, *Mexico City*
Museo Nacional de Arte, *Mexico City*
Museo Rufino Tamayo, *Oaxaca*
Museo Tabasco, *Villahermosa*
Museo Zaragoza, *Colima*
Na-Bolom Centro de Estudios Científicos, *San Cristóbal de las Casas*
Parque la Venta, *Villahermosa*

Resorts

Acapulco
Cabo San Lucas
 See *Baja California*
Cancún
Cozumel
Isla Mujeres
Manzanillo
Mazatlán
Puerto Angel
 See *Puerto Escondido*
Puerto Escondido
Puerto Vallarta
San Blas
Zihuatanejo and Ixtapa

Acapulco ★

Map 7I8. Guerrero. 417km (260 miles) S of Mexico City on RF 95. Population: 850,000. Served by air (international airport 30km/19 miles E) and bus. Car rental: Avis, Costera Miguel Alemán 711 ☎ (748) 4-1342; Hertz, Costera Miguel Alemán 1945 ☎ (748) 4-1361, and at airport ☎ (748) 9-1353 i Costera Miguel Alemán 187 ☎ (748) 2-6007/5-1178, and Costera Miguel Alemán 54 ☎ (748) 4-6656. UK Consul: Hotel Las Brisas ☎ (748) 4-6605. US Consul: Costera Miguel Alemán 552-06 ☎ (748) 2-1906. American Express Travel Service: Costera Miguel Alemán 709-1 ☎ (748) 4-6375.

The very name of Acapulco conjures up an image of sun, sand, sea, sex and the international jet-set. Its reputation was formed in the 1950s, when exotic vacations were available only to the jewel-studded few, but nowadays, with 4 million visitors annually, it is no longer as exclusive as it was. Since the less you wear, the better your disguise, anyone you meet nowadays on Acapulco's beaches may be a celebrity; but real celebrities are quite thin on the ground, most preferring to stay in their private villas up in the hills.

In the wake of this explosion in popularity, the Mexican government has been spending freely in the last few years to re-glamorize Acapulco, cleaning up around its tacky edges, enforcing strict planning controls, and clamping down on the unscrupulous. It was about time, too, although Acapulco's claim to be one of the world's premier resorts was never in serious doubt.

Deep-sea fishing, paragliding, surfing or golf are just ways to fill the days while waiting for night-time. For like no other place in the world, Acapulco comes alive at dusk. Around the bay, the mountains become dark shadows before the starry tropical sky. The lights of high-rise hotels and cars along the Costera gleam and wink, reflecting in the calm ocean like a giant funfair. Suddenly, there are people everywhere, strolling, strutting, preening, sitting and tapping their feet to the disco beat wafting on the breeze.

It is even rumoured that there are some visitors who have never seen Acapulco in daylight, when it is both beautiful and dramatic. For even the most determinedly blasé, the blue sky, green mountains plunging down to the sea, tropical flowers and palm trees, and sheltered bay with its perfect beaches and great crescent of white towers, will prove irresistible.

Events For details of weekly events, see the free information sheets distributed at all hotels. The large hotels all organize various entertainments and fiestas. There are also weekly bullfights, and frequent performances of the Ballet Folklórico at the Centro Acapulco.

Before Lent, Acapulco Carnival (hotels are even fuller than usual).

On Dec 12, feast of the Virgin, particularly lively in Acapulco.

Sights and places of interest

The town

Acapulco has an interesting history but one of which little physical evidence remains. It was one of the first Spanish ports, rapidly becoming the main entry point for precious cargoes on their way from the Far East and South America to Spain. These made the overland journey to Veracruz via Mexico City on horses and mules. The only relic of those days is the pentagonal **Fuerte San Diego** (*500m/550yds E of the Zocalo on*

the waterfront, closed Tues), built in the 18thC to protect the port.

The **Zocalo** itself is surrounded by small shops and cafés, with a rather bizarre Neo-Byzantine cathedral, but the real focus of interest is the **Costera Miguel Alemán**, the waterfront boulevard, where nearly all the smart hotels, restaurants and shops are located. It is usually known just as the 'Costera', and, quite simply, the Costera *is* Acapulco.

La Quebrada ★

Due W of the Zocalo, by the Mirador Hotel, there are some jagged cliffs around a narrow inlet. Every day, and sometimes at night, the most daring *acapulqueños* dive into the shallow and turbulent waters from a height of 40m (130ft). It needs split-second judgment and nerves of steel. Especially dramatic after dark, when they dive in pairs, holding flaming torches. Divers and spectators alike can regain breath at the nearby **Mirador Calinda** hotel.

Other sights

Leave the children at the **Dolphinarium** (*Playa Condesa* *shows noon, 2pm, 6pm, 8pm*) and visit the large new cultural centre, the **Centro Acapulco** (see ***Nightlife***). Part of the complex is the **Museo de Acapulco** (*open standard hours*), which has two rooms of Pre-Columbian finds, and one of local crafts that are also for sale.

The **Laguna Coyuca** ☆ (*behind Playa Pie de la Cuesta*), a brackish jungle lagoon with facilities for boating and fishing as well as swimming, is pure adventure fantasy – only man-eating crocodiles are missing!

Out past the airport is the **Laguna Tres Palos**, larger and wilder.

Hotels

Acapulco Plaza
Costera 22 (748) 4-4242
1,002 AE CB VISA

Location: At centre of the bay. Operated by Holiday Inn, this is the largest, most central of the luxury hotels, with attractive split-level rooms, special activities for children and six restaurants.

Las Brisas
Carretera Escénica 5255
(748) 4-1650 016837
300 AE CB VISA

Location: 13km (8 miles) S on airport road. An all-pink dream village, hewn out of the cliffs and hills overlooking the bay. At the centre is a 17thC fortress, surrounded by small clusters of pink villas and blue swimming pools. Even the new roller skating rink and the fleet of jeeps (at guests' disposal) are pink. With several good bars and restaurants, and every conceivable facility, this is one of the world's great resort hotels.

Condesa del Mar
Costera, at Playa Condesa
(748) 4-2355 500
AE CB VISA

Location: Near centre of the bay. In the evening, bands play in the lively, bustling lobby, which is a riot of flowers and fountains.

There are wonderful views of the bay, even from the swimming pool, which has its own excellent restaurant. There are reciprocal arrangements with the El Presidente and Tortuga hotels.

Continental
Costera s/n (748) 4-0909
435

Location: At centre of the bay. This Hyatt hotel is cheaper but nearly as luxurious as the ***Acapulco Plaza*** (see above). A vast pool surrounds a 'tropical' island with a restaurant and bar. There's a good variety of water-sports, and the usual bars and restaurants.

Holiday Inn
Costera 1260 (748) 4-0410
016844 358

Location: On a busy part of the beach. A tall cylindrical tower on Condesa beach; the equal of its most luxurious rivals but with lower prices and good package deals for families.

Hyatt Regency
Costera 666 (748) 4-2888
693

Location: On E of the bay, near the naval base. Very large and often still full. Good value in summer, when meals are not obligatory. The bars and restaurants are worth a visit, and sports and excursions are well organized.

Paraíso Marriott
Costera, at Playa Hornos
(748) 2-4140/2-4741
442

Location: Near centre of the bay.

Good social programme and water-sports, but small pool and beach. Delicious seafood at the **Supper Club**.

Pierre Marqués
Playa Revolcadero (748)
4-2000 320

Location: 16km (10 miles) s on airport road. The 'honeymoon package' is especially good value, but it is also an elegant family hotel, and a favourite with golfers and tennis players. There are reciprocal arrangements with the adjacent ***Princess*** (see below), now under the same highly professional management.

Princess
Playa Revolcadero (748)
4-3100 016857 777

Location: 18km (11 miles) s on airport road. A dramatic Aztec pyramid construction, smothered by tropical blooms. A variety of restaurants and bars, air conditioned tennis courts, four swimming pools and a lively nightlife all work to make this a memorable holiday experience. (See ***Pierre Marqués***, above.)

Villa Vera Raquet Club
Lomas del Mar 35 (748)
4-0333 92

Location: Near centre of the bay. The restaurant and discotheque are among the best in town, and usually attract a sprinkling of celebrities. Facilities include a fleet of self-drive jeeps, cable-TV and excellent tennis courts. Glamorous luxury for affluent sophisticates, at suitably exclusive prices. Children are not allowed.

Restaurants

In addition to the numerous restaurants in the hotels mentioned above, the following independent restaurants can be recommended.

Armando's Taj Mahal
Carretera Escénica 39 (748)
4-1233

A gleaming white Indian extravaganza. Indian, Mexican and exotic seafood specialities amid opulent surroundings.

Blackbeard's *(Barbas Negras)*
Playa Condesa (748) 4-2549

Piratical atmosphere: fun for lunch, romantic for dinner. Good steak and lobster. Dance barefoot or take a dip between courses.

Bohío
Roca Sola 17 ☎ *(748) 4-3454*
A quiet retreat from Acapulco's high-speed hustle. Good seafood.

Carlos 'n' Charlies
Costera 999 ☎ *(748) 4-0039*
Closed Tues.
Arrive early, as reservations are not accepted and long queues can form – although celebrities and the very rich can walk straight in. The menu is long and jokey, the waiters laid-back and the food excellent.

Embarcadero
Costera 25 ☎ *(748) 4-8787*
A strange mixture of Polynesian fantasy and 'elegant dockside' decor – waiters dressed as stevedores, and desert island monkeys and parrots. Food includes steaks and some Mexican-Chinese inventions.

Kycho
Costera 5080 ☎ *(748) 4-4422*
An elegant Mediterranean-style restaurant in the discotheque area, specializing in seafood and steaks. Play backgammon at the bar before dining.

Las Madeiras
Carretera Escénica 39 ☎ *(748) 4-4378*
Ultra-fashionable, so reserve several days ahead. Luxurious decor with low lights, glinting silver, dark polished wood and leather. Superb international cuisine.

Normandie
Costera and Malespina ☎ *(748) 2-3868/5-1916*
Excellent, sophisticated French cooking. Very smart.

Picalagua
Juarez 19 ☎ *(748) 2-2142*
Simple decor but outstanding seafood, including shark, crab, turtle, or a delicious *cerviche de pulpo* (pickled octopus in lime-flavoured marinade).

Sunset Bar
Costera 115 ☎ *(748) 4-4777*
A gourmet beachside grill next to the **UBQ** disco (see ***Nightlife***). Informal jet-set elegance (no blue jeans).

Villa Demo
Av. del Prado 6 ☎ *(748) 4-2040*
The best Italian restaurant in town, with fine gardens and shaded terraces.

Yes
Playa del Moro ☎ *(748) 4-8873* to
Terrific for an inexpensive beachside lunch; candlelit dinners and cocktails are moderately priced.

Nightlife

In truth, beaches all over Mexico can rival those here; it is after dark that Acapulco becomes the undoubted queen of Mexican resorts.

The hotels offer a variety of shows, discos, *dîners dansants* and nightclubs. But the real fun lies away from the hotels, and each year, a different and new place becomes the top spot, where everyone has to be seen at least once a week. This can only be discovered by listening on the grapevine, as the news will only reach the guidebooks a year later. But the other six nights can be spent in adequate style at the older favourites.

Discos open around 10pm (but never really get going until midnight) and stay open for as long as the dancers can stand the pace, which is often until dawn. Many of the discos have pure oxygen added to the atmosphere, which has the result of reducing the effects of tiredness and alcohol – but only until you step outside. Dress is outrageous and elegant, so leave the jeans at home. There are, unfortunately, often long queues outside popular establishments, and if so, the best chance of getting in is to look wilder and more glamorous than the opposition. Be warned that reservation policies vary from week to week.

For information in English on plays and films ☎ *(748) 4-7050.*

Centro Acapulco
Plaza Mexicana ☎ *(748) 4–7050* IIII ⚲ ● ♫ ≡ AE CB ⊕ ◉ VISA
One night of any visit to Acapulco should be spent in this complex, which houses theatres, cinemas, restaurants and bars, and is always busy with activity ranging from serious cultural events, like the **Ballet Folklórico**, to the **Disco Centro**, where there is enough space-age technology to reach the moon, and a distinctive atmosphere created by a strange mixture of lasers and mock Aztec deities.

Bars
Of the various gay bars, the most welcoming and entertaining (for non-gays too) is **9** (*Deportes 110*). A more conventional singles bar is **Plus 1** (*Costera 182* ☎ *(748) 4–6430*), slightly down-market of the others. At **Boccaccio's** (*Costera 5040* ☎ *(740) 4–1900*), there is more of an organized party atmosphere, with beauty contests and other entertainments.

Discos
A good place to start is at **'UBQ'** – the **Ultimate in Beauty and Quality** (*Costera 115* ☎ *(748) 4–4777*) – where the music is loud and the drinks very cold. Perhaps the best lightshow is at **Magic** (*Costera and Yucatán* ☎ *(748) 4–8815*), although another top contender is **Baby'O**, out at the end of the Costera (*Horacio Nelson* ☎ *(748) 4–7474*), where a jacuzzi, a barber's shop and a breakfast room help to keep revellers beautiful and well nourished. Acapulco's first deluxe disco was **Armando's LeClub** (*Costera 2230* ☎ *(748) 4–1233*), but for a really big concentration of celebrities it is now better to try **Le Jardin** (*Yanez Pinzón 10* ☎ *(748) 4–8295*), owned by the ***Villa Vera Racquet Club*** (see ***Hotels***).

Shopping
Acapulco specialities include Taxco silver, leatherware and fashionable resort gear. The easiest way to shop in Acapulco is simply to lie on the beach, where anything from stuffed parrots to Rolex watches can be bought from enterprising young hustlers. Prices, however, can be high unless you are good at bargaining. In the hotel shops, by comparison, prices are fixed and the selection is greater. The best hotels for shopping in are the ***Princess*** and ***Las Brisas*** (see ***Hotels***).

More dedicated shoppers will wish to visit the gleaming new shopping mall at the **Centro Acapulco**, where there are numerous flashy boutiques. Silver is an especially good buy here. Similar but smaller centres are the **Flamboyant** and **El Patio**, both near the Hyatt Regency hotel.

In the streets around the Zocalo are the smaller, older shops where bargains can be had, while Av. Hidalgo also has its share of smarter establishments. But for real bargains, visit the markets and craft centres. Start at the government-run **FONART** store (*Costera 267*) for crafts from all over Mexico. More local specialities can be seen and bought at the **Museo de Acapulco** (*Costera 4834, by the Centro Acapulco*). Try also the small craft section at the **Acapulco market** (*two blocks behind the waterfront Customs House*) and the **Pueblito** (*Costera, at Reyes Católicos*).

Sports and activities
Acapulco today may be challenged by the new, purpose-built resorts at *Ixtapa* and *Cancún*, which offer a different, perhaps less worldly range of pleasures. But for sheer variety of outdoor activites, from any water-sport you care to imagine to excellent golf, it has no rival.

Beaches
The 50 or so beaches around Acapulco fall in and out of fashion with bewildering rapidity, so if you want to keep up with the jet-set, be prepared to move fast and listen to the nightclub grapevine. A variety of water-sports is available at all beaches in the bay, and chairs, parasols and thatched huts can be rented. Many of the larger hotels come right down onto the beaches; with reasonable discretion, anyone willing to tip the attendants can use the pools and terraces. Anything from a three-course meal to a Cuba Libre can be purchased at the beachside restaurants.

All beaches are public and free, but the price of services varies with what the vendor can get away with and the time of day. Beach vendors can be a nuisance, although, for the idle, they take the walking out of souvenir hunting.

La Condesa, central on the bay by the ***Condesa del Mar*** hotel and a social centre for daytime action, is the most crowded and expensive of the beaches, and probably the most fun. Avoid the gay section if your preferences lie elsewhere. East from the Condesa del Mar, **Hornos** is a good beach for the late afternoon and a game of mini-golf.

Caleta and **Caletilla** face **La Roqueta Island** on the western peninsula. Both are well protected little bays, especially popular in the mornings, and good for those on a moderate budget. Boats leave every few minutes for the island, where a pleasant beach is inhabited by some notoriously alcoholic donkeys. Take a boat with a glass bottom and see the underwater **shrine of the Virgin of Guadalupe** ☆

12km (7 miles) NW of town is **Pie de la Cuesta**, with both the most dangerous swimming and the most colourful sunsets. Come here to catch the last of the sun, and to drink a long cocktail. The waters are infested with sharks and manta rays – keep out.

Heading W from the Condesa del Mar along the airport road lie several beaches. **Icacos**, long, uncrowded, with usually calm waters, stretches from the Hotel Presidente out towards the Las Brisas peninsula. Above **Pichilingue**, round to the E of the peninsula in Puerto Marqués Bay, are the villas of the rich, powerful and famous. **Puerto Marqués**, one of the high-fashion beaches, has good swimming and innumerable diversions. **Revolcadero** ☆ is the next beach around and is overlooked by two of the most exclusive hotels, but has large waves and a strong undertow.

Water-sports

Every conceivable water-sport may be sampled in Acapulco, from deep-sea fishing to the exhilarating thrill of paragliding. Surfing is discouraged on the more popular beaches near the centre.

Yacht cruises

Tickets are available at hotel desks for half-day yacht cruises. With a good party atmosphere, they are a painless way to explore.

Places nearby

The coastal road SE towards Puerto Escondido is usually in fair condition, but bridges occasionally disappear during the rainy season, so it is wise to inquire before leaving. The coast is known as the 'Costa Chica' (Little Coast), as opposed to the 'Costa Grande' (Big Coast) from Acapulco NW to Zihuatanejo.

Shortly after the airport, African faces, reflecting descent from escaped African slaves, appear; at the largest of the coastal villages, **Cuajinicuilapa** (240km/150 miles), African customs have survived almost unchanged. Farther on, at **Pinotepa Nacional** (286km/179 miles), African blood has mixed with the local Chatino and Mixtec strains. The usual fiestas of the religious calendar are a fascinating medley of cultures.

From Pinotepa, either head N for *Oaxaca* or continue towards the resorts of *Puerto Escondido* and Puerto Angel. Hotels along the way are rudimentary; at Pinotepa there is one small, nameless inn with no telephone. But beautiful deserted beaches all the way more than compensate. Those with scuba gear who are prepared to sleep under the stars should take the track from Cuajinicuilapa to **Punta Maldonaldo**, famous for its countless species of brightly coloured tropical fish.

Aguascalientes

Map 11B4. Capital of Aguascalientes. 252km (158 miles) NE of Guadalajara on RF 70 and RF 54. Altitude: 1,890m (6,200ft). Population: 285,000. Served by air, rail (on Querétaro-Torreón line) and bus. Car rental: Budget ☎ (491) 6-4350 i Circunvalación Y. Mahatma Gandhi ☎ (491) 6-0123.

A colonial silver city in a rich agricultural area, surrounded by the thermal springs after which it is named. There are few colonial buildings left, but the fine climate and agreeable tree-shaded parks make it a pleasant stopover for the traveller. Local embroidery is very reasonably priced, and well worth investigating. The city was founded in 1575, and was built over a labyrinth of Pre-Columbian tunnels and chambers. Their origin is unknown, and they are not open to the public.

Events From Apr 20–May 1 and July 27–Aug 5, local festivals. Flower battles, fireworks and bullfights. The highlight is Apr 25, St Mark's Day.

Aug 15, native dancing in front of the cathedral.

Sights and places of interest

Zocalo

The 18thC Baroque **cathedral** on the main square has interesting colonial paintings in the nave, of which the best known is the *Adoration of the Magi* by José Alzibar. Opposite is the **Palacio de Gobierno**, another Baroque building, with 20thC murals in the courtyard. Not far away, at Zaragoza 505, is the small **Museo de la Ciudad** (Museum of the City).

Sights nearby

Hotels will arrange visits to the nearby **Peñelas Hacienda**, said to produce the fiercest fighting bulls in Mexico. Impromptu visitors are not encouraged.

H **Francia** (*Plaza Principal 113* ☎ *(491) 5–6080*) has large pleasant rooms, and **Paris** (*Plaza Principal 129* ☎ *(491) 5–1121*) has a *fin de siècle* atmosphere. A recommended motel is **Medrano** (*José Maria Chavez 904* ☎ *(491) 5–5500*).

Akumal ☆

Map 9G13. Quintana Roo. 460km (288 miles) E of Mérida on RF 307 and RF 180; 240km (150 miles) N of Chetumal on RF 307.

A one-hotel luxury resort on the palm-shaded beaches of Quintana Roo, that is Mexico's first underwater national park.

Underwater Museum

On shore if entered from land. Usually open, no regular hours.

An interest in skin-diving is indispensable – even most of the museum is underwater. On dry land you can see the smaller and more perishable relics retrieved from wrecked galleons far out under the waves. Larger pieces, such as great cannons and anchors, covered in barnacles and coral, have simply been towed in under the lee of the shore. Visits to the wrecks, and to submerged Mayan ruins, can be arranged at the hotel; a guide is advisable. There are good facilities for scuba novices, but it takes a few days to learn.

Sights nearby

Xel-há ☆

10km (6 miles) S.

Rent equipment at Akumal for a visit to this amazing natural aquarium. The water in the lagoons and underwater caves is crystal clear, and the fish are numerous, unafraid and psychedelic. Beautiful visual effects are caused by cold, fresh streams flowing into the warm and salty sea.

H Club Akumal (*Reservations: Mexico City* ☎ *(5) 250–4111* AE CB Ⓓ ◉ VISA).

Alamos ☆

Map 3D5. Sonora. 121km (76 miles) SE of Ciudad Obregón on RF 15 for 66km (41 miles), then turn off E; 210km (131 miles) N of Los Mochis on RF 15 for 158km (99 miles), then turn off E. Population: 6,500. Served by bus.

A worthwhile half-day excursion off the coast road between *Ciudad Obregón* and *Los Mochis*, and deserving an even longer stay. Several foreign artists and retired people restored the magnificent Baroque and Moorish-style houses on the outskirts, and now live here. Thanks to their efforts, the town has been designated a national monument, and the newest building in town is well over a century old. Alamos formerly was the capital of all western Mexico and rivalled Taxco in silver production but, stricken by droughts, Indian uprisings, and the 1910 Revolution, its population dwindled. Now it is only a tenth of what it was in the days when the town gloried in the name of *Pueblo Real de la Limpia Concepción de Los Alamos.*

The area is also renowned as the home of the Mexican Jumping Bean, which can be bought in the Zocalo. It makes an unrewarding pet, for the movement is only caused by a parasite in the bean.

Event On Dec 8, fiesta.

Sights and places of interest

Zocalo (*Plaza de Armas*)

A small cobbled square of great charm, arcaded on three sides. On the fourth is the church of **Nuestra Señora de la Concepción** (1784), which replaced an earlier Jesuit Mission burned by rebellious Mayo Indians. The narrow streets around the square are full of impressive mansions built during the prosperous 18thC.

Casa de los Tesoros (*House of the Treasures*) 🏛
Obregón 10.

The best known of the restored residences, about two blocks from the main square. It is a low building with a colonnaded inner courtyard, and now houses a hotel. It is worth dropping by for a meal or coffee in order to enjoy the colonial interior and furniture.

H **Casa de los Tesoros** 🏛 (*Obregón 10* ☎ *(642) 8–0010*) is a fine colonial inn – reserve well ahead; **Los Portales** (*Plaza Principales* ☎ *(642) 8–0111*) is also recommended.

Amecameca

Map 12E7. State of Mexico. 59km (37 miles) s of Mexico City on RF 115 and RF 90. Altitude: 2,470m (8,100ft). Population: 24,000. Served by rail (on Mexico City–Cuautla line) and bus.

A small market town which, together with a visit to some interesting nearby villages and a stroll on the lower slopes of *Popocatepetl*, makes an excellent day-trip from Mexico City. There is a Sunday market, with a small local crafts section.

Events In Feb or Mar, Ash Wednesday celebrations at Amecameca (see below).

On July 25, fêting of St James when masked performers dance at Chalco; on Dec 8, similar celebration of Immaculate Conception at Ozumba.

On night of Nov 1, macabre festivities culminating in ritual burning of cardboard skeletons at Mixquic (11km/7 miles from Chalco, by the road w to Xochimilco).

The town

After a brief visit to the 16thC monastery by the main square, climb the hill to the church of **Nuestro Señor del Sacromonte**, overlooking the town. Here there stands an ancient **statue of Christ**, venerated by pilgrims at the lively fiesta on Ash Wednesday. The views of the valley and of the great volcano behind are magnificent.

Sights nearby

Monasteries to the south

Stop first at **Ozumba**, 10km (6 miles) s, to see the 16thC murals in the monastery. They show Cortés humbly welcoming the first missionaries to arrive in New Spain. See also *Cuautla*.

Monasteries to the north

The town of **Tlalmanalco**, 10km (6 miles) N, has a 16thC monastery with an interesting Plateresque open chapel. Another 27km (17 miles) brings you to **Chalco**, an important Pre-Columbian town, not yet archaeologically explored. The monastery and church here are again worth a quick visit, and it is then only 7km (4½ miles) to the Mexico City-Puebla free road.

Baja California

Maps 2&3. In NW Mexico. Distance from Tijuana–Cabo San Lucas: 1,678km (1,049 miles). Population of peninsula: 1,650,000. Airports: Cabo San Lucas, Ensenada, Mexicali, La Paz, Tijuana. Car ferries: Cabo San Lucas–Puerto Vallarta, La Paz–Mazatlán, La Paz–Los Mochis, Rosalia–Guaymas.

Baja is a spine of wild mountains and barren plains, jutting S through the Pacific under the wide dome of the desert sky. Until recently, the only signs of human life on the peninsula were little fishing villages at oases on the coasts and abandoned mission churches amid drifting sands. The pleasures of Baja were primarily for the adventurous, preferably those equipped with small planes.

In 1973 a road was opened from N to S and, gradually, Californians began to drive down, attracted by the fishing and the solitude of the great spaces. Luxury resort hotels soon followed, and regional tourist planners today entertain high hopes that Baja will become the playground of the SW United States. If only a fraction of the hordes who visit Tijuana could be lured on down, those hopes would be more than satisfied.

Little is known of the history of Baja before the Conquest, although there is evidence that there may have been as many as 50,000 inhabitants. Recently, cave paintings of unknown origin have been discovered high in the central mountains; the hardy can hire mules and guides at **San Ignacio** to visit them. Various attempts by the Spaniards to settle on Baja were unsuccessful due to the hostile climate and inhabitants. Cortés himself nearly lost his life while in search of a mythical treasure of pearls, and it was not until the 17thC that Jesuits managed to establish permanent settlements.

During the Mexican-American War, Baja was occupied by US troops who were eventually expelled. Two further attempts by Americans to colonize Baja followed, both under the guise of creating an independent state. One Richard Walker went so far as to invade La Paz in 1853 with a few of his friends. After a short time he was bundled off home, and soon met an untimely death in Central America after trying a similar gambit there. In 1910, a certain Richard Ferris kindly offered to name his proposed new republic *Porfiria*, in return for the gift of the peninsula from the Mexican dictator, Don Porfirio Díaz. This scheme also came to nothing.

See also separate entries for *Tijuana*, *Ensenada* and *Mexicali*.

The north-south road

From Ensenada to La Paz

The drive down Baja takes you through some of the most desolate and beautiful moon-like landscapes in the world. Although no longer a major adventure, it is demanding both on car and driver and should not be undertaken at night. Fill your tank at any opportunity, and carry food, water and spares. Distances given are from *Ensenada*.

The first stop is at **San Quintin**, 185km (115 miles) S then 1km (½ mile) W, a fishing village in a fertile agricultural oasis. The road beyond skirts the Pacific for 58km (36 miles), then veers sharply left through a boulder-strewn cactus desert. A turning on the left at 465km (291 miles) leads 70km (44 miles) E to the **Bahía de los Angeles**. Here there is excellent fishing but primitive accommodation; boat rental is possible, but you will need your own gear.

Guerrero Negro, 574km (359 miles), is back on the Pacific coast. The town comes to life in early spring when schools of whales congregate in the nearby bays to mate; hordes of nature lovers assemble and rent boats and planes to watch them. It is a fascinating occasion, although not without hazards in a small boat. Oil discoveries, however, may not only change the town but threaten the habitat of the whales.

The next landmark is **San Ignacio**, 717km (448 miles), a mission village in an oasis of date palms. Here arrangements can be made to visit the cave paintings of the interior (ask at the ***El Presidente*** hotel – see below). Various tracks lead W to rudimentary fishing establishments along the coast. The main road continues E, reaching the Sea of Cortés at **Santa Rosalia**, 790km (494 miles). From this old copper mining town, a ferry leaves daily for *Guaymas* on the mainland.

Before **La Paz**, 1,342km (839 miles), are the pretty little oasis towns of **Mulege**, 853km (533 miles), and then **Loreto**, 987km (617 miles). The latter, once the capital of all Baja, is now just a small port built around a large old mission building.

Hotels

Guerrero Negro (*574km/359 miles from Ensenada. Map 2C3*).

El Presidente
Reservations: Mexico City (5) 395-0333 to 25

Location: Near saltmines, which are worth a visit. Expeditions to watch the mating whales can be arranged in season.

Loreto (*987km/617 miles from Ensenada. Map 3D4*).

El Presidente
Reservations: Mexico City (5) 395-0333 250

Location: In an attractive small resort. Attractions include expeditions to painted caves in the interior, and a strange underground discotheque.

The **Flying Sportsman Lodge** (*no telephone*), a small sports resort, has its own private airstrip.

Mulege (*853km/533 miles from Ensenada. Map 2D3*).

Serenidad
No telephone to 35

Location: In a pleasant small resort. You can rent equipment and receive instruction in underwater sports, and there is organized social life.

San Ignacio (*717km/448 miles from Ensenada. Map 2D3*).

El Presidente
Reservations: Mexico City (5) 395-0333 to 30

Location: In centre of a small town in a steep valley. Expeditions are

arranged to the nearby cave paintings in the interior. The hotel itself is a haven for the weary traveller.
[symbols]

San Quintin (*185km/115 miles from Ensenada. Map 2B2*).

[H] **El Presidente** (*reservations: Mexico City ☎ (5) 395–0333* [symbols]) is a colonial-style mini-resort.

La Paz

Map 3E4. Baja California Sur. 1,350km (844 miles) s of Ensenada on RF 1. Population: 100,000. Served by air (international airport 13km/8 miles s), sea (from Mazatlán and Los Mochis ☎ (682) 2–0109) and bus. Car rental: Avis, El Presidente hotel ☎ (682) 2–2345 Tx 052234, and at airport ☎ (682) 2–1813 i Plaza Constitución, on 5 de Mayo ☎ (682) 2–1190.

La Paz became the capital of Baja California Sur in 1830. Since the arrival of the road, it has become a sizeable modern city and feels like a boom town, for the whole state is a duty-free area, although prices are not always attractive to foreign visitors.

Fishing is the single main tourist attraction, and boats and gear can be rented through any hotel. For the less predatory, other water-sports are available, although the emphasis on commercial tourism is shifting S to Cabo San Lucas (see below). In the evening, La Paz is a place for strolling up and down the waterfront, where the best seafood restaurants are found. Over a fish steak and ice-cold beer, watch the **Sea of Cortés** pass through all shades of red and orange to inky black.

[H] The following hotels, all having [symbols] among other facilities, are recommended: **Los Arcos** (*A. Obregón 498 Sur ☎ (682) 2–2744* [symbol]) is a pleasant colonial-style inn on the waterfront; **Gran Hotel Baja** (*Calle Rangel ☎ (682) 2–3900* [symbol] *to* [symbol]) is the largest and best hotel in town; **La Posada** ✿ (*Reforma, at Playa Sur ☎ (682) 2–0663* [symbol]) is an exclusive small inn with one of the best restaurants; **El Presidente** (*at Playa Caimancito, 5km/3 miles N on Pichilingue road ☎ (682) 2–6544* [symbol]) is a pleasant new beach hotel, with a reasonable restaurant offering a good weekly Mexican grill (the day varies).

[R] **Estrella del Mar** (*Malecón* [symbols]) serves game-fish steaks and other seafood specialities; **El Taste** (*Malecón and Juarez, past Los Arcos hotel* [symbols]) has cheerful decor, good seafood and steaks.

South from La Paz

Beyond La Paz, the peninsula widens out to its squared end, 120km (75 miles) to the S, the area where most intensive touristic development has taken place. A reasonable paved road runs around, closing the loop at a point 27km (17 miles) S of La Paz. 189km (118 miles) from La Paz, the road again reaches the coast at **San José del Cabo**, a small fishing port rapidly developing as a tourist destination, with a fiesta on Mar 19.

Cabo San Lucas, 33km (21 miles) farther SW, stands on the dramatic southern tip of the peninsula. Here luxury hotels are springing up like dragon's teeth, gleaming white temples of sun-worship. The best beaches are not the crowded ones by the hotels, but deserted little coves out by the cliffs, some of which can only be reached by boat; glass-bottomed launches which tour the cliffs will take you there and pick you up later. These tours, which should on no account be missed, cruise out past pelicans and basking seals to the naturally formed **Arch of Cortés** ☆ where the waters of the Pacific and the Sea of Cortés meet in a churning witches' cauldron under the ragged rocks.

Hotels

South of La Paz, many hotels insist on American-plan accommodation (meals obligatory) during the summer; until a few restaurants open, however, this is not too irksome a restriction. Food can be disappointing, as the supply of fresh food is erratic. Nightlife is also centred on the hotels.

Cabo San Lucas (*Map 3F4*).

Cabo San Lucas
No telephone 100
Location: Facing main beach. This deluxe modern version of a Spanish mission hotel has fine seven-room villas and its own airstrip. Water-sports are available.

Finisterra
(684) 3–0100 to 58
Location: At the very end of the promontory. This hotel is built on a high clifftop, with spectacular views overlooking the swirling waters of the cape.

Hyatt Baja
(684) 3–0044 125
Location: On beach towards the promontory. This luxurious adobe-built terraced village offers water-sports and has all imaginable facilities.

Twin Dolphin
(684) 3–0140 50
Location: On main beach. Elegant rooms, an Oriental garden and water-sports are among this hotel's many attractions.

San José del Cabo (*Map 3F4*).

Las Cruces Palmilla
No telephone 45 *Closed in summer.*
Location: On coast near San José. An exclusive fishing resort with its own airstrip; the architecture is Neo-Moorish.

El Presidente San José
(684) 2–0211 to 250
Location: 1km (½ mile) N of San José. A beach resort hotel on the shores of an enchanted lagoon, particularly suitable for families. Water-sports are available for adults.

Bonampak (and Yaxchilán) ★

Map 9H12. Chiapas. 130km (81 miles) SE of Palenque by jungle track (impassable during heavy rains). Served by air taxi from Palenque, Tuxtla, San Cristóbal de las Casas (40 mins) and Villahermosa.

This can be either one amazing day's excursion by light plane, or, for those with explorer's blood in their veins, a long arduous trek through the jungle. As well as **Bonampak** and **Yaxchilán**, two of the best of the ruined Mayan cities, it is also easy to visit the nearby villages of the primitive Lacandon people, who have barely emerged from the Stone Age.

The best place to seek advice on overland routes and guides is at the **Na-Bolom Centre** at *San Cristóbal de las Casas*, or at the tourist office at *Palenque*. It is possible to reach Bonampak from Palenque by jeep, but beyond there the journey can be dangerous, and is not recommended for the inexperienced.

Sights and places of interest

The Painted Temple of Bonampak ★

The plane will land right beside the ruins, which stand on high ground near the river Lacanja. From the strip, walk straight into a large open space, surrounded by palaces and temples, with a large stele in the middle, showing a priest-king, and, to the N, a monumental stairway.

At the top of this stairway, on the right, is the famous **Painted Temple**. Its murals are now sadly deteriorating because of the breathing and flash guns of visitors, and methods of protection are being discussed. Perhaps more than any other Mayan work of art, these vivid paintings give an idea of the way of life of this mysterious civilization.

There are three rooms. In the central one are scenes of war, with warriors wearing leopardskins sacrificing their prisoners. The left-hand room shows a religious ceremony; richly dressed priests perform dances, and may well be praying for the victory depicted in the central room. In the right-hand room is the victory banquet, with musicians, acrobats and dancers, and anxious servants tending to their masters' every need. The guide will almost certainly claim that this is the Sistine Chapel of the Americas, an unfelicitous phrase which will probably outlive the murals.

Up on the hill behind the main group of buildings are other temples, half-smothered by green tendrils. In one of them, you may come across one of the Lacandon Indians, who may try to hitch a lift in the plane, perhaps to the site of Yaxchilán, 15mins' flight away.

Yaxchilán ★

Yaxchilán stands on the banks of the wide, sluggish river Usumacinta, whose yellow-grey waters wind through the jungle, marking the border between Mexico and Guatemala. It lies halfway between Tikal, in the Peten area of Guatemala, and *Palenque*. The buildings, a blend of Peten and classic Mayan styles, rival in beauty and interest any other site in Mesoamerica. It is the most remote of Mexico's major tourist attractions. Unless oil is found in the area, no road will be built, condemning Yaxchilán to many more years of decay. Resident archaeologists are fighting to prevent the giant temples from crumbling further, but, unlike the more manicured sites, Yaxchilán seems alive with whispering ghosts. If the one extravagance of your trip is the flight here, it will have been both worthwhile and memorable.

Sights nearby

Ten minutes' flight away are the small townships of **Lacanjá** and **Najá**. They are inhabited by the Lacandon Indians, distinguished by their uncut black hair and costume of simple cotton smocks. Only a few hundred of these shy and peaceful people survive, and their way of life is so threatened that they should not be regarded as a tourist attraction; prospective visitors should first seek advice at the **Na-Bolom Centre** in *San Cristóbal de las Casas*.

Campeche ☆

Map 9G12. Capital of Campeche. 219km (137 miles) sw of Mérida on RF 180. Population: 120,000. Served by air, rail (on Coatzacoalcos–Mérida line) and bus. Car rental: Hertz, Prolongación 59 s/n ☎ (981) 6-4855

i Baluarte San Carlos, Av. Ruiz Cortines 61 ☎ (981) 6-5593.

An old and interesting city, well worth including in a tour of the Yucatán peninsula, where Hernandez de Córdoba first set foot on Mexican soil in 1517, and in 1540 a permanent settlement was founded by Francisco de Montejo. The fortified port is bounded on three sides by forests, the historical source of its wealth, where the Conquistadors discovered precious woods. Logwood was the most important: a costly red dye was made from it and exported as far afield as England, where it was used to colour soldiers' coats.

Wealthy Campeche was a glittering target for the pirates of

the Caribbean, and was looted and burned on frequent occasions. Surprisingly, it was only at the end of the 17thC that the massive fortifications were built. The maritime attacks then ceased, but as late as the 19thC the walls remained a useful defence against devastating armies of rebellious Mayan peasants.

Campeche does not look only to the past, but is a thriving industrial and agricultural centre. Oil is the predominant industry. Fishing for shrimps is also important; they form the basis of many of Campeche's distinctive seafood recipes. The city is also likely to become a major centre for tourism, as access to nearby beaches and Mayan cities has improved.

Sights and places of interest

Los Baluartes (*The forts*) ☆

All but one of the eight forts remain, as do the two main gates to the city and some of the walls. Originally there were 2km (1¼ miles) of walls, which took 2yrs to build using slave labour from nearby villages. An official guide may be hired at the **Baluarte San Carlos,** where the tourist office is located. This is the most important of the forts. On its roof are ancient cannons, while underneath is a rabbit warren of passages linking it to other forts and to the cathedral.

In the **Baluarte San Miguel** is a museum containing pirate relics and arms, together with portraits of the more villainous raiders and a model of the city as it used to be. The moat is said to have been filled with crocodiles, but this may be untrue, as it was also said to have been filled with quick-lime. At the smaller **Baluarte de San Soledad** is an excellent **museum of archaeology** (▬ *open Mon–Sat 9am–2pm, 3–9pm, Sun 9am–noon*), boasting a collection of pottery from the island of Jaina, just along the coast.

Catedral de San Bartolomé ✝

On the Zocalo.

Completed in 1546, this is the oldest church on the peninsula. The typically Spanish architecture lacks the distinctive Mexican flavour of later churches. The *Stations of the Cross* were painted by native craftsmen under Spanish direction, hence the Mayan look of the faces.

Sights nearby

Becal

99km (62 miles) NE on RF 180.

A village where the renowned Campechano hats are manufactured in a large, damp cave, then seasoned for a year before being sold.

Bolonchén de Rejón

110km (69 miles) NE on the road to Uxmal.

The name of this village means 'Nine Wells' – which is indeed what you will find there. Hire a guide to visit the large network of caverns nearby. These are typical of the peninsula, which is honeycombed with similar geological formations. The enormous *cenotes* or wells near almost all the major ruins are formed by the collapse of caves near the surface.

Edzna ☆ 🏛

33km (21 miles) E on the long road to Mérida, then 19km (12 miles) S ▬

A 7thC Mayan city, the largest accessible ruin in the state. It has an unusual five-storey **pyramid** decorated with fine carvings.

See also *Uxmal*.

[H] **López** ✿ (*Calle 12 no.189* ☎ *(981) 6–3334* ▮□ ⚌) is a family hotel with a good restaurant; **Baluartes** (*Ruiz Cortines s/n* ☎ *(981) 6–3911* ▮▮▮ ⚌ ≈) and **El Presidente** 🏛 (*Ruiz Cortines 51* ☎ *(981) 6–2233* ▮▮▮ ⚌ AE CB ◐ ◉ VISA ≈) are also recommended.

Hotel nearby

(40km/25 miles S on Champoton road).

Siho Playa 🏛

☎ *(981) 6–2989* ▮▮▮ 🛏 *80* ▤ 🚗 ⚌ AE CB ◐ ◉ VISA

An isolated luxury resort with fishing, water-sports and tours of archaeological zones. The decor is neo-colonial, the atmosphere relaxed.

R Reached by taxi, **El Refugio de Lorenzillo** (*Av. 7 de Agosto 49* *(981) 6–1111*) serves fresh seafood amid piratical decor.

Cancún ★

Map 9F13. Quintana Roo. 319km (199 miles) E of Mérida on RF 180. Population: 50,000. Served by air (international airport 26km/16 miles S) and bus. Car rental: Avis and Hertz, at airport (988) 4–1633 i Super Manz. 4, Ret 8A, Lote 12 (988) 3–0123. US Consul (988) 3–0178. American Express Travel Service: Hotel América Loc. 4 (988) 3–1999.

The name means 'crock of gold' in the Mayan tongue, but only a few years ago there was nothing here but a long golden-white sandbar, stretching out through coral reefs into the luminous blue sea. Tourist gold must have seemed a long way off when the spot was selected by computer for development into a super-resort for the 21stC jet-set, and there was widespread criticism as construction began during the 1970s. But already the bold experiment has paid off. Sun-worshippers from all over the world jet in to sample the unique blend of underwater, beachside and night-time delights. From the air the curving sweep of great hotels looks almost surreal in its beauty, a sculpture of white concrete, palm trees and limpid blue pools.

Cancún is serviced entirely by a purpose-built city, **Ciudad Cancún** (Cancún City), on the mainland, linked to the island resort area by a causeway. It is becoming a conference and convention centre of world renown, even hosting international government summits; the gleaming new Convention Centre stands at the point where the island curves sharply S, past the **Laguna Nichupte** where the shopping centres are located. The most popular public beach is the **Chac-mool**, in every respect the equal of the hotel beaches, while the prices of services such as chairs, sports and food are a little lower. At the S end of the island are some recently discovered **Mayan ruins**, most easily accessible by boat.

Those on a budget are advised to stay at one of the commercial hotels in Cancún City, which is linked by a bus service to the entire length of the island. Buses also run N as far as **Punta Sam** and **Puerto Juarez**, from where ferries depart for *Isla Mujeres*.

Hotels

Camino Real
Punta Cancún (988) 3–0100 249

Location: At E corner of the island. This beautifully designed total pleasure resort has its own beach and lagoon. All water-sports are available and boats can be rented. There's even a bar in the pool.

Club Mediterranée
Punta Nizus (988) 3–0439 300

Location: 19km (12 miles) from Cancún City, on a secluded peninsula at SE tip of the island. The main attractions of this well-designed, Mayan-style village are water-sports and a lively, organized social scene. There are superb facilities, including shops. Golf can be arranged. Non-residents (even travel writers) are rigorously excluded.

Sheraton
Paseo Kukulkán ☎ *(988) 3–1988* Tx *73339*
Location: The southernmost hotel on the island. A fun-machine designed like a Mayan pyramid, next to some genuine archaeological remains. A worthy rival to the ***Camino Real***, with the added bonus of a jacuzzi suite.

Villas Tacul
☎ *(988) 3–0349* *27*
Location: On N *coast.* Attractively decorated private villas which are just as luxurious but much quieter than the resort hotels.

Numerous other hotels, all having and water-sports, shopping and arrangements for golf, include **Aristos** (*Playa Chacmool* ☎ *(988) 3–0011* Tx *07300*); **Calinda Quality Inn** (☎ *(988) 3–1600*); **El Presidente** (☎ *(988) 3–0200*).

In downtown Cancún City is **Plaza de Sol** (*Yaxchilán 31* ☎ *(988) 3–0888*).

Restaurants

Cancún 1900 (*Convention Centre* ☎ *(988) 3–0048*) serves international cuisine in a quasi-historical atmosphere; **Carlos 'n' Charlie's** (*in hotel zone* ☎ *(988) 3–0846*), has an amusing menu, waiters and clientele; **Mauna Loa** (*opposite Convention Centre* ☎ *(988) 3–0693/5* *to*) is a Polynesian fun-palace with bars and discos that stay open late; **Maxime** (*Pez Velador 8, in hotel zone* ☎ *(988) 3–0438*) is noted for elegant, formal, international cuisine; **Soberanis** (*Coba 5, Cancún City* ☎ *(988) 3–0782*) is only a taxi ride from the hotel zone, with pleasingly simple decor and serving delicious seafood.

These restaurants face stiff competition from the hotels, where cuisine is usually excellent – and meals are sometimes charged for automatically in any case.

Nightlife

Hotel desks distribute a free guide to the various entertainments, Mexican fiesta nights and beach parties offered by the hotels. They are usually open to all comers, either free or at low cost, but drinks and food are expensive.

Nightlife, at present, is centred on the hotels, but will probably diversify in future years, as at other resorts. Start each evening in a different hotel bar, watching the sunset over a Tequila Sunrise. You will probably have to return to your hotel for dinner, and can then explore the discos; there are good ones at the ***Camino Real*** and ***El Presidente*** hotels (see ***Hotels***) and also at the **Verano Beat** hotel. Cancún closes down early by cosmopolitan standards, and all is quiet by 2am. But dining and dancing at the restaurants in the **Convention Centre** – one of the few alternatives to the hotels – continues until late.

Shopping

The island's two shopping centres, the **El Parian** and **Caribe**, are at the Laguna Nichupte. Specialities include elegant resort wear, souvenirs, jewellery and craft items from all over Mexico. Although Cancún is a duty-free zone, prices are high.

Sports and activities

Golf Cancún has one of the best golf courses in the world, the **Pok-ta-Pok**, designed by Robert Trent-Jones. Equipment can be rented at the club house, just before the Convention Centre and facing onto the Laguna Cancún.

Water-sports The large hotels all make their own arrangements for guests. Waterskiing, deep-sea fishing, boat rental and other facilities are also available at the **Cancún Yacht Club**, on your left after leaving the mainland.

The best snorkelling and scuba-diving are at the S end of the island; equipment rental and other arrangements are best handled through your hotel. The promontory past the Camino Real hotel is also worth exploring, although the water can be rough. Real enthusiasts should head S to *Akumal* and *Cozumel*.

Places nearby

Isla Mujeres, reached by boat from Punta Sam N of the city, makes a good day's excursion. There are hotel tours (the only convenient way) S to *Akumal* and *Tulum*, but a visit S to *Cozumel* from Puerto Morelos, down the coast, will be rushed without an overnight stop.

There are also daily air tours to all of these places, and to *Chichén Itzá* and *Palenque*, which can be arranged through your hotel. The view of Cancún from the air is breathtaking.

Celaya

Map 11C5. Guanajuato. 45km (28 miles) W of Querétaro on RF 45 and RF 57. Altitude: 1,800m (5,900ft). Population: 114,000. Served by rail (on Mexico City-San Luis Potosí line) and bus.

A typical town of the Bajío (see *Planning*), clean and agreeable, with well-kept parks. At the centre of town is the **Jardín Municipal** (Municipal Garden), with the modern colonnaded local government building on one side. Behind it is the old **Plaza de Armas**, with a famous **Independence monument** designed by Celaya's best-known son, the architect, poet, sculptor and painter, Francisco Tresguerras (1759–1833), whose work can be seen all over the town.

Celaya is famous for its sweetmeats, especially *cajeta*, made from caramel and milk and flavoured with cinnamon. Make sure you try the *crepas con cajeta* (cajeta pancakes) at one of the restaurants.

Events On July 16 and Aug 15, religious fiestas.

In Dec, ceremonial candlelit processions before Christmas. Carol singing and receiving of gifts.

Sights and places of interest

Convent and church of San Francisco 🏛 †
Guadalupe Victoria and Doblado.
Tresguerras is buried here in the small chapel. The buildings were started in the 17thC, but Tresguerras was responsible for their reconstruction, and the ornate high altar and entire facade of the church are attributed to him.

Templo de Carmen 🏛 †
Obregón and Madero.
This elegant and very un-Mexican Neoclassical church is Tresguerras' most famous work. The *Last Judgment* and other murals in the chapel are also by him.

[H] **Mary** (*López Mateos and Zaragoza* ☎ *(461) 2-0450*) has a locked garage for guests' cars; **Motel Campestre** (*Pan-American Highway km264* ☎ *(461) 2-0929*) is a convenient stopover.

Chapala

Map 10D3. Jalisco. 53km (33 miles) S of Guadalajara. Population: 15,000. Served by bus from Guadalajara.

The towns and villages on the shores of Mexico's largest inland lake, 28 by 82km (18 by 51 miles), are a favourite haunt of weekenders from Guadalajara. They are also a haven for writers, painters and retired people, many attracted from the

USA by the sunshine and because dollars stretch further in Mexico; some, unable to leave as a result of the 1982 bank nationalization and the seizure of all dollar assets held in the country, are now less fond of their adopted country. But Chapala is still a pleasant place – especially if you can leave after the weekend. The water level and cleanliness of the lake may be threatened by local industry.

Sights and places of interest

The town

The first stop should be the **Chapala Society Headquarters**, in the centre, where free and copious information is available about anything from chess partners to the best fishing spots on the lake. Those unlucky with rod and hook can choose from a large number of small restaurants along the lakeside, which serve fresh whitefish from its rather muddy waters. The atmosphere along here is lively, particularly at weekends, with numerous vendors and *mariachis* from Guadalajara.

The lake

Leaving Chapala westwards and passing along the lake, the main places are described in sequence below.

Ajijic (8km/3 miles), a colonial pueblo with a sizeable artistic community, has several art galleries and shops selling local crafts. People here still speak in hushed tones of the 'Night of the Long Knives' in 1965, when respectable citizens, deciding to take the law into their own hands, ran out of town any excessively Bohemian or insufficiently free-spending foreign elements. In 1926, the all-time great bohemian, D.H. Lawrence, stayed here when he wrote *The Plumed Serpent*.

Farther around the lake, **Cosala**, with its thermal baths and a regular geyser, is followed by **Jocotepec** (6km/4 miles from Ajijic), worth a visit on Sunday for its market – bargain for woven *sarapes* (ponchos).

[H] **Chula Vista** (*3km/2 miles W towards Ajijic* ☎ *(376) 5–2313*) is a pleasant country hotel; **Posada Ajijic** (*16 de Septiembre 2, Ajijic*) has good views of the lake, and the best restaurant in town; **Real de Chapala** (*Paseo del Prado 20, Chapala* ☎ *(376) 5–2416*) is very popular at weekends with water-sports *aficionados*.

[R] Many excellent restaurants in Chapala cater to the expatriate community. For the local speciality of whitefish, start at **Campestre del Lago** and **La Terraza** on the lakefront.

Chetumal

Map 9H13. Capital of Quintana Roo. On the border of Belize, 571km (357 miles) E of Villahermosa on RF 186; 379km (237 miles) S of Puerto Juarez on RF 307. Population: 50,000. Served by air (from Mexico City and Mérida) and bus i *Obregón 457* ☎ *(983) 2–2103.*

Chetumal is a bizarre place, a small, dusty, modern town, surrounded on three sides by tropical jungle, baking under a blazing sun. Yet every other shop seems to sell cameras, videos, hi-fi and jewellery, or Dutch cheese, English tea and other incongruous delicacies – for the state of Quintana Roo is a duty-free zone, although prices aren't necessarily low.

Chetumal makes a good base for hunting or archaeological expeditions into the jungle. Ask at the tourist office for advice on the condition of jungle tracks leading to the countless Mayan ruins, or on where to hire a guide. Visits can also be made to neighbouring **Belize**, formerly British Honduras.

Places of interest nearby

Bacalar

40km (25 miles) N.

A small village on the road to Tulum, on the shores of a turquoise jungle lagoon with banks thick with mangrove trees. Near the village is a ruined

18thC **fortress**, built as a defence against buccaneers. It changed hands several times during the Mayan revolt of the 19thC, finally falling to the Mexicans in 1901. Just 5km (3 miles) to the N is a large natural well, the **Cenote Azul**.

Kohunlich ☆
60km (38 miles) W, then 9km ($5\frac{1}{2}$ miles) S on a track.
Excavations are still in progress at this recently uncovered Mayan site on the road to Francisco Escarcega. Near the entrance is a large **pyramid**, from the top of which the whole of the site can be seen. The most interesting buildings are grouped around the central terrace. The **Temple of the Masks** is especially notable, the features of the masks suggesting a strong Olmec influence.

[H] Advance reservation is needed at **Continental Caribe** (*Héroes 171* ☎ *(983) 2-1100* to), and the modern **El Presidente** (*Chapultepec and Héroes* ☎ *(983) 2-1273*).

Chichén Itzá ★
Map 9G13. Yucatán. 119km (74 miles) E of Mérida on RF 180. Served by air taxi (from Cancún and Mérida) and bus.

This is the best-known of the Mayan ruined cities, forming the high point of any visit to the Yucatán peninsula. Founded in the 5thC AD, it was taken over some five centuries later by the invading Toltecs. It became the centre of the new, flourishing Mayan-Toltec civilization, and grew into a vast ceremonial complex covering some 10sq.km (4sq. miles). Then, 100yrs before the arrival of the Spaniards, the great city was suddenly abandoned, and the inhabitants returned to the simple rural life which their descendants still lead today. About 30 of the structures have now been uncovered and restored.

As well as the main ruins described below, there are literally hundreds of jungle-bound temples and pyramids for the energetic explorer; a small boy plus a small fee will ensure that you do not get lost.

Those with time to spend the night at a hotel in Chichén will find the **Caracol Observatory** impressive and eerie under starlight. It is worth rising at dawn for the view of the ceremonial complex from the **Castillo Pyramid** in the mellow light, evocative of the far-off days when the sun rose over a great bustling metropolis.

Valladolid (see *Mérida*), a little farther E, has several inexpensive hotels.

The ruins

El Castillo and environs
N of the highway

Most important and impressive of the ruins is the great terraced pyramid known as **El Castillo** (The Castle), which provides striking evidence of Mayan skill in engineering and arithmetic. On the days of equinox only, the great carved heads of serpents at the foot of the stair look as if they have shadow bodies, undulating up the side of the balustrade to the summit. The pyramid has 365 steps, one for each day of the year, leading to the **Temple of Quetzalcoatl** (The Plumed Serpent) at the summit. Similarly, the terrace sections correspond to the 18 months of the Mayan 'year', and the side panels to the 52yrs of the Mayan 'century'. Inside the temple, at the summit, is a **stone throne**, carved as a jaguar, before which is a *chac-mool*, a reclining figure upon which offerings were placed.

The other buildings of the central complex can be seen from the pyramid. The sacred **ball-court**, the largest and finest in Mesoamerica, has walls decorated with low-reliefs showing sacrificial rites. Nearby is the **Temple of the Jaguar Warriors**, where frescoes show the Toltec conquest of the peninsula. Immediately to the right stands the **Group of the Thousand Columns**, each carved like a plumed serpent.

The **sacred cenote** (well), some 300m (330yds) N along a causeway, is 60m (200ft) in diameter and 20m (65ft) deep. In troubled times, sacrificial victims laden with precious ornaments were thrown down here to appease the gods. Divers have recovered many gold and jade objects, but unknown treasure remains under the thick, dark mud. Most of the victims were apparently young girls, and it was considered an honour to be chosen.

Old Chichén ☆
s of the highway.
First on the left is a smaller *cenote*, which was used only for the water supply; it is one of the older ruins, and dates from before the Toltec invasion.

More important than human sacrifice to the original Mayan people were precise astronomical observations for their complex calendar. The round building at the centre of Old Chichén is a sophisticated observatory, known as **El Caracol** (The Snail) because of its spiral staircase, rare in Mayan architecture. The windows are placed so as to record the longest and shortest days of the year, and openings in the roof were used for accurate night-time observations.

In the same group of buildings is a small version of the Castillo, used by the Toltecs to store bones. Other nearby buildings were known to the Spaniards as the Abbey, the Church and the Nunnery – names which have nothing to do with the actual uses of the buildings, about which little is known.

Sight nearby
Balancanché ☆
8km (5 miles) E of the ruins *Tours are erratic, leaving every hour or so during daylight.*
Those continuing E by car should visit this huge network of caverns, reached by a well-signposted track. Some of the caves were used by the Toltecs as sanctuaries, and offerings and incense burners have lain undisturbed for more than 1,000yrs. The caves are cold and slippery underfoot, so take suitable clothing and footwear.

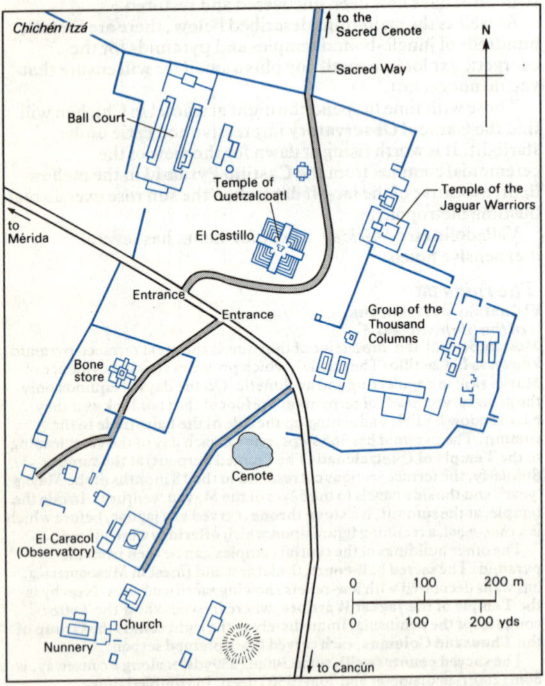

H **Hacienda Chichén** (*near the ruins; reservations* ☎ *Mérida: (992) 1-9212*), a 17thC hacienda; **Mayaland** (*by the ruins; reservations* ☎ *Mérida: (992) 1-9212*), a colonial-style hotel; **Misión Chichén** (*2km/1¼ miles from the ruins; reservations* ☎ *Mérida: (992) 3-9500*); **Villa Archaeologica** (*near the ruins; reservations* ☎ *Mexico City: (5) 514-4995*), a pleasant Club Mediterranée inn with a good archaeological library.

R Good lunches for day visitors are served at the ***Hacienda Chichén*** and ***Mayaland*** hotels (see above).

Chihuahua

Map 4C6. Capital of Chihuahua. 376km (235 miles) s of Ciudad Juarez on RF 45. Altitude: 1,430m (4,690ft). Population: 470,000. Served by air (international airport 16km/10 miles NE), rail (on Ciudad Juarez–Mexico City line, and terminal of Los Mochis line) and bus. Car rental: Avis, Hotel El Presidente ☎ (141) 2–2288, and at airport ☎ (141) 3–0032; Hertz, Díaz Ordaz 220 ☎ (141) 2–5100
i Venustiano Carranza 505 ☎ (141) 2–6363.

Although usually associated with miniature dogs, Chihuahua is also the name of Mexico's largest state, larger than the British Isles, and of that state's capital city. The latter, pleasant and prosperous, is situated on a wide plain to the E of the Sierra Madre mountains and is surrounded by timber forests and cattle ranches. It was founded in 1709, its original wealth coming from nearby silver mines, few of which are now in operation. Although not in itself a major tourist attraction, many pass through and spend a night or two here, for it is located on a main N–S highway, and is a terminus of the amazing **Chihuahua-Pacific railway** (see below).

Sights and places of interest

The city centre

Downtown Chihuahua is spread around three main plazas, Constitución, Zaragoza, and Hidalgo, all within a few blocks of each other. Start at Constitución, with a visit to the 18thC Baroque **cathedral**. The carvings of the twelve apostles on the facade are especially fine; the interior, rather surprisingly, is in the classical Doric style.

Leaving the plaza and keeping the 20thC municipal palace to the right, Plaza Hidalgo is reached in about 5mins. In the middle stands a large **monument to Father Miguel Hidalgo**, who was executed near here in 1811 after the initial failure of his rebellion against Spanish rule. On one side of the square is the building, now the **Palacio Federal**, where Hidalgo and his fellow conspirator Ignacio Allende were imprisoned. Opposite is the **Palacio del Gobierno**, partly built as a Jesuit college in 1711. The rebels were shot on the patio here; the scene is shown in vivid 20thC murals, together with several other bloody episodes from Chihuahua's past.

Two blocks to the N, on the Plaza Zaragoza, is the church of **San Francisco**, where Hidalgo's headless body was kept until 1823. Only then, following the success of the revolution he had launched, could the body be buried together with the missing head.

Pancho Villa's house (*Casa Pancho Villa*)
Calle 10 no.3012 Open standard hours, but closed on Sun not Mon.

During the uprising of 1910, the notorious bandit and revolutionary, Pancho Villa, was based in Chihuahua. Here he raised the *División del Norte* army, whose victories helped to secure the downfall of the dictator, Porfirio Díaz. To visit his home, leave Constitución on Independencia, after eight blocks turn right into Ochoa and carry on until you reach Calle 10. One of Villa's several rival widows has turned it into a shrine to his memory. Exhibits include his clothing and guns, and even the bullet-riddled car in which he was assassinated in 1923.

Sight nearby

Casas Grandes

Map 3C5. 353km (221 miles) NW on RF 45 and RF 10, and on Los Mochis–Ciudad Juarez railway line.

An important archaeological site, which makes the long detour worthwhile for the energetic traveller. The city covers 6sq.km (2½ sq. miles), and was built by the American Oasis Culture around AD1000, and abandoned 200yrs later. Little is known of the builders, and the site is only partially restored, but ruins and landscape are impressive.

The **Rodeway Inn** motel in Nuevo Casas Grandes (☎ *(168) 4–1048*) is a convenient motel and will arrange trips into the Sierra Madre and to other nearby archaeological sites.

[H] Chihuahua is well provided with hotels in all categories. A selection is: **El Presidente** (*Libertad 9* ☎ *(141) 6–0606* to), central; **Tierra Blanca** (*Niños Héroes and Camargo* ☎ *(141) 5–0000*), a central motel; **Victoria** (*Juarez and Colón* ☎ *(141) 2–8893*), a pleasant hotel 15mins' walk from the centre.

[R] Chihuahua is renowned for steaks. The juiciest are at **La Calesa** (*Juarez 3300* ☎ *(141) 2–8555*) and the ***El Presidente*** hotel (see above).

Other good restaurants within a taxi ride from the centre are: **El Bandido** (*Av. de Las Américas 1303* ☎ *(141) 3–9492* to), with Wild West decor; **Los Parador de Tony Vega** (*Juarez 3316* ☎ *(141) 5–1333*), for steaks and international cuisine.

Places nearby

The Sierra Tarahumara ★ Chihuahua is the natural starting point for expeditions to these wild, grandiose mountains of the **Sierra Madre**, to the W. While it is possible to penetrate this region in a rugged vehicle, there are no reliable maps, and the roads are poor even when they exist as shown. Much of the area has not yet been properly explored.

The best way therefore to visit it is via that 20thC miracle of engineering, the **Chihuahua-Pacific railway ★** This affords breathtaking views of soaring, jagged mountains and vertiginous canyons, while the astonishing number of bridges and tunnels is announced by the train attendant. The train takes some 14hrs to reach steamy *Los Mochis*, down on the Pacific coast. There are several places to stop on the way, with reasonable hotels (but only average food) near the railway.

Each hotel organizes its own expeditions to canyons, waterfalls, Tarahumara Indian villages, and other regional attractions. Most exciting of these is the four-day expedition by mule down the Copper Canyon from **El Divisadero**, although this is not for the faint-hearted. The **Copper Canyon** (Barranca del Cobre) is in fact a series of linked canyons, in some places four times the size of the Grand Canyon in the USA.

[H] **Cabañas Cañón del Cobre**

Near Estación Creel 23 Reservations: Hotel Santa Anita, Gabriel Leyva and Hidalgo, Los Mochis ☎ (681) 2–0046

Location: 28km (18 miles) from Estación Creel (buses meet all trains). No electricity or telephone, but this simple, comfortable hotel, set in beautiful walking country, is the best place to stay in the mountains. There are daily expeditions taking in a nearby waterfall, a 16thC mission, caves, a lake and the canyons, and there are occasional performances of Tarahumara music. Full board compulsory.

[H] **Cabañas Divisadero**

El Divisadero 34 Reservations: Aldama 407-C, Chihuahua ☎ (141) 2–3362.

Location: 2 mins' walk from El Divisadero railway station. The hotel offers breathtaking views of the Copper Canyons, and Tarahumara guides are available for walking expeditions. There are cheerful sing-songs every night. Full board compulsory.

Y

[H] Misión Cerocahui
Near Bahuichivo 28 Reservations: Hotel Santa Anita, Gabriel Leyva and Hidalgo, Los Mochis ☎ (681) 2–0046.
***Location:** 7km (4½ miles) from Bahuichivo railway station (buses meet all trains).* Comfortable accommodation without frills (no electricity or telephone) in a peaceful little mission village. There are daily expeditions to the canyons. Full board compulsory.

Chilpancingo

Map 7H8. Capital of Guerrero. 280km (174 miles) S of Mexico City on RF 95; 133km (83 miles) N of Acapulco on RF 95. Population: 30,000. Served by bus.

No more than a small agricultural town, yet the capital of the enormous state of Guerrero, which includes Acapulco. If you stop for a snack, see the murals in the **Palacio de Gobierno** on the Zocalo, commemorating, among other things, the first-ever Mexican Congress, held in the town in 1813.

Places of interest nearby

The countryside around offers two rewarding trips for the energetic and independent traveller. There is no commercial organization of these excursions, and until recently the area had a reputation for minor banditry; although this is now under control, keep to the routes suggested.

Juxtlahuaca caves ☆
49km (31 miles) SE via RF 95 and E turning for Colotlipa.
From Colotlipa you can engage the guide necessary for the final 8km (5 miles) along a hill track to the enormous and stunning caves. Besides stalactites, underground lakes and waterfalls, there are **Olmec cave paintings** dating from around 1000BC, possibly the oldest on the continent. Take flashlights and warm clothing.

Mexcala and river Balsas
50km (31 miles) N on RF 95.
The bridge over the river is the starting point for an exhilarating raft trip through gorges and white water to **Ciudad Altamirano**, a day away. A bus or truck should be available there to bring you back to civilization; check at Mexcala. The guide will return with the raft. Allow two days.

[H] Posada Meléndez (*Juarez 50 ☎ (747) 2–3718*).

Cholula

Map 12E7. Puebla. 12km (8 miles) W of Puebla on RF 150. Altitude: 2,150m (7,052ft). Population: 21,000. Served by train (on Puebla–Izúcar line) and bus.

Formerly one of the greatest Pre-Columbian cities, the small town of Cholula now has two claims to fame: that the **Great Pyramid** is the world's largest structure, and that there is a church for every day of the year.

Recently, it has become the host town to the **University of the Americas**, which offers courses to foreign students. (*For details, write to University of the Americas, PO Box 507, Puebla.*)

Events On Feb 2 and Sept 8, lively fiestas.

Sights and places of interest

The churches
If truth be told, there are no more than 100 churches, most of them sited on small hills that were once pyramids. Start with the 18thC **Nuestra**

Señora de los Remedios, on the ***Great Pyramid***, from where the myriad tiled domes and towers of the others can be seen rising above the houses of the town. Down on the main square, visit the **Capilla Real**, built in 1540; its 49 small domes and *mudejar* timberwork give it the air of a mosque. Also on the square is the monastery of **San Gabriel**, with a large 16thC Gothic-vaulted church. From here, you can carry on visiting churches until the sun goes down or until you tire.

The Great Pyramid ☆

The 500m-sq. (⅓ mile) pyramid is now just a great mound crowned with an 18thC church (see above), but offers to the visitor a honeycomb of archaeologists' **tunnels**; some 10km (6 miles) of them were dug to examine all the superimposed structures. It was the Pre-Columbian system to add a new layer every 52yrs, and models of all the different stages are on display at the small **museum** (*open 10am–5pm*) behind the pyramid. There is some dispute over the origins of the ancient Cholulans, with Olmec, Toltec and Mixtec influences all discernible. What is certain is that the city's long history came to an abrupt end in 1519, when the advancing Cortés, fearing an ambush, ordered its destruction and the massacre of its inhabitants.

[H] Villa Arqueológica

2 Poniente no.601 ☎ (22) 47–1966. Reservations: Mexico City ☎ (7) 511–1284 40

***Location:** Next to the Great Pyramid.* A colonial-style Club Mediterranée inn which makes a good base for exploring the Puebla area by car.

Ciudad del Carmen

Map 8H11. Campeche. 168km (105 miles) NE of Villahermosa on RF 180; 211km (132 miles) SE of Campeche on RF 180. Population: 60,000. Served by air, ferry (irregular sailings 7am–7pm linking the coast road) and bus.

An adventurous, more leisurely alternative to the inland road from Villahermosa to Campeche is the coastal road via Ciudad del Carmen. In fact, the route is not all road; there are four ferries on the way, so check before leaving that all are running.

Carmen is on the W end of the **Isla del Carmen**, a thin ribbon of sand across the mouth of the Laguna de Terminos. Once a haunt of pirates, it is now a shrimp-fishing centre. The oil boom too has left its generally ugly mark.

The waters of the lagoon teem with shark, barracuda, tarpon and other fish. Ask at your hotel for information on boats and guides for hire. Some are based at **Isla Aguada**, on the far side of the first northbound ferry.

The city and environs

Start with a walk along the waterfront, passing fishermen mending their nets, small shipyards, a naval station, and much photogenic quayside bustle. Out to sea, bobbing at anchor, are hundreds of shrimpers, many now disused because of the oil boom.

To the N of the city are beaches, now rather oil-covered but still worthwhile for collectors of shells. To the S is the fishermen's district where fresh shrimps and cold local beer can be enjoyed at waterfront cafés.

The roads to and from Carmen pass deserted white-sand beaches, bordered by coconut groves. From the ferries you can usually see Mayan Indians paddling their tree-trunk canoes.

[H] **Isla del Carmen** (*Calle 20 no.11 ☎ (938) 2–1246*); **Lli-re** (*Calle 32 no.25 ☎ (938) 2–0589*).

[R] Try **Carmelo** (*Calle 26A and Calle 35 ☎ (938) 2–1178*) for seafood specialities, or **Los Flamboyanes** (*Calle 26 no.153*) for international cuisine.

Ciudad Juarez

Map 4B6. Chihuahua. 375km (233 miles) N of Chihuahua on RF 45. Population: 700,000. Served by air (international airport 17km/11 miles S), train (terminus of lines from Chihuahua and Los Mochis) and bus. Car rental: Avis, Av. 16 de Septiembre no.999 ☎ (161) 4–0019; Hertz, at airport ☎ (161) 4–0511 i Av. Malencón y Francisco Villa ☎ (161) 2–5007. US Consul: Av. López Mateos 924 ☎ (161) 3–4048.

For many people arriving over the Rio Grande from El Paso this is the first taste of Mexico. It is the largest and most interesting of the border cities, with some good hotels and Mexican restaurants, two bullrings and several markets for Mexican crafts, although it has been badly hit by the recent recession. It is of course more Americanized than other Mexican cities; in particular, there are enough dental clinics for a city three times the size, catering for the one-day visitors who come over for a bullfight and for some cut-price dental work.

Events On Aug 10, feast of San Lorenzo.

On Dec 4, feast of Santa Barbara. The city fills with crowds of fun-seekers, and there are bullfights, fireworks and performances of folk-dances.

Sights and places of interest

The oldest building, dating, like the town, from 1659, is the shrine of **Nuestra Señora de Guadalupe** on the Zocalo, with massive adobe walls and hand-carved wooden beams.

From 1864–66, while the French troops of Emperor Maximilian were occupying Mexico City, President Benito Juarez governed Mexico from the house at Av. 16 de Septiembre no.527, which is open to visitors (*standard hours*). Like the city, the **Cultural Centre** on the Zocalo is named after President Juarez. It has examples of folk arts, archaeological remains from Casas Grandes, (see *Chihuahua*), and historical items including mementoes of the 1910 Revolution, when the city was stormed twice by the bandit revolutionary Pancho Villa.

[H] The best hotels are near the Pronaf commercial and shopping centre on the NW edge of town: **Fiesta Real** 🏛 (*Centro Pronaf ☎ (161) 3–0047*); **Plaza Continental** (*Lerdo Sur 112 ☎ (161) 2–2610* 65), in a downtown location; **Plaza Juarez** (*Centro Pronaf ☎ (161) 3–1310*).

[R] There are more than 100 restaurants here, but none of them are outstandingly good. Two possibilities are: **Flamboyán** (*Lincoln 137 ☎ (161) 3–5300*), and **La Fogata** (*Triunfo de la República 2323 ☎ (161) 3–0040*), where you can get your teeth into a vast Chihuahua steak.

Ciudad Obregón

Map 3D4. Sonora. 263km (163 miles) S of Hermosillo on RF 15; 225km (139 miles) N of Los Mochis on RF 15. Population: 210,000. Served by air, train (on Guadalajara–Nogales line) and bus.

A dusty modern city with little to offer the tourist. There are reasonable hotels and restaurants for passing travellers, and some stay longer for the hunting and fishing up in the Sierra Madre.

Places of interest nearby

Indian villages

Around Obregón and Navojoa, 67km (42 miles) S, are the various villages of the **Yaqui and Mayo Indians**. Until quite recently they were wild and rebellious, but now live more or less at peace with Spanish-speaking society; indeed, their culture and customs are slowly disappearing under the assault of the Coca-Cola civilization. They have been much visited recently by travellers searching fruitlessly for the Yaqui sorcerer Don Juan, the subject of Carlos Castaneda's series of books; remarkable works though they are, they have little to do with the harsh realities of life in a subsistence economy in the bleak deserts and mountains of Sonora. It is sometimes possible to visit native festivals, but they are of more significance to anthropologists than to tourists. One of the more accessible takes place between May 10–20 at **Etchojoa**, 20km (12 miles) SW of Navojoa, with the 'stag dance' by men wearing deer masks.

H **Motel Costa de Oro** (*Miguel Alemán and Allende* ☎ *(641) 4–1775*); **Valle Grande** (*Miguel Alemán and Tetabiate* ☎ *(641) 4–0940*).

Ciudad Valles

Map 12B7. San Luis Potosí. 475km (295 miles) N of Mexico City on RF 45 and RF 85. Population: 66,000. Served by train (on San Luis Potosí–Tampico line) and bus.

A town of little intrinsic interest which serves as a useful stopping point for motorists, with some pleasant hotels. On the outskirts there is a small **Museo Regional Huasteco** (*S on RF 85, open standard hours*) with Huastec antiquities from nearby sites.

Occasionally, it is possible to see the extraordinary **Huastec flying pole dance** ☆ in one of the villages to the S; the tourist office or your hotel will advise.

Places of interest nearby

Tamazunchale

107km (67 miles) S on RF 85.

Known affectionately as 'Thomas and Charlie' to the thousands of Americans who used to pass through when it was on the main N–S road. On Sundays, the Huastec Indians pour in from all around to the market. It is an animated and attractive scene, and you may pick up some native embroidery at bargain prices.

Xilitla

83km (52 miles) S; turn W after 72km (45 miles) on RF 85.

A large and interesting Huastec village set in richly tropical country, and built around the remains of a Spanish monastery. Some of the women still wear the traditional embroidered costume. The fiesta is on Aug 27.

H Most hotels here cater for the passing motorist. **Casa Grande** (*Carretera Mexico–Laredo 85* ☎ *(138) 2–0066*); **Valles** (*Carretera Mexico–Laredo 36* ☎ *(138) 2–0050*).

Hotels nearby

There are several resort hotels nearby where you can break the journey for a sporting country weekend. The best of these is **Quinta Covadonga** (*15km/9 miles towards Mexico City on RF 85* ☎ *(138) 2–0608*), a quiet hotel with vast grounds providing many sporting facilities including a golf course.

R **España** (*Hidalgo 442* ☎ *(138) 2–1045*) is open 24hrs a day and offers Spanish cuisine.

Ciudad Victoria

Map 5E8. Capital of Tamaulipas. 287km (179 miles) SE of Monterrey on RF 85. Population: 150,000. Served by air, train (on Monterrey–Tampico line) and bus **i** *Carrera Torres 708* ☎ *(131) 2–1111.*

The first major city on the way S from *Matamoros*, offering more to huntsmen and anglers than to culture-seekers, although the **cathedral** and **Palacio de Gobierno** on the Zocalo are worth a glance.

H There are no luxury hotels, but reasonable accommodation can be found at: **Everest** (*Cristóbal Colón Norte 126* ☎ *(131) 2-4050*); **Panorámico** (*Guatemala and Bolívar* ☎ *(131) 2-3130*), a motel; **Sierra Gorda** (*Av. Hidalgo Oriente* ☎ *(131) 2-2280/1*), located downtown.

Sports and activities

Keen anglers need go no farther – start with catfish in the rivers near town, and graduate to bass in the large reservoirs nearby. The best known of these is the **Presa Vicente Guerrero**, 20km (12 miles) N; it was stocked with half a million bass in 1970, and offers basic lakeside accommodation. Game and fowl shooting are also available around the lake.

At **Soto la Marina**, 120km (74 miles) E, there is good river fishing, and 30km (19 miles) farther at **La Pesca**, on the coast, excellent sea fishing.

The tourist office and hotels will help with finding guides for hunting and fishing.

Coatzacoalcos (and Minatitlán)

Map 8H10. Veracruz. 172km (107 miles) W of Villahermosa on RF 180; 311km (193 miles) SE of Veracruz on RF 180. Population: 250,000. Served by air, train (on Veracruz–Mérida line) and bus. Car rental: Avis, Hotel Coatzacoalcos ☎ (921) 2-1637.

Important regional centres which form a staging post on many journeys, yet few travellers stay longer than they have to in these booming industrial twin towns. The port of Coatzacoalcos has plenty of sleazy low-life, but its large red-light districts, beloved of sailors and oilmen, are not recommended for tourists. It is also to be the Gulf terminus of a new rail link across the Isthmus of Tehuantepec, which is scheduled to start full operation in 1988 with the ambitious target of putting the Panama Canal out of business.

H **Club Terranova**
7.5km (4 miles) towards Minatitlán ☎ (921) 2-5100 100
AE CB Φ MC VISA

An exclusive luxury resort especially favoured by tired oil executives.

H There are many ordinary commercial hotels, but two reasonable ones are: **Margón** (*Zaragoza 302* ☎ *(921) 2-0572*); **Valgrande** (*Hidalgo 207* ☎ *(921) 2-1624*), which serves excellent seafood.

Colima ☆

Map 10E2. Capital of Colima. 220km (136 miles) SW of Guadalajara on RF 54. Population: 90,000. Served by air, train (on Guadalajara–Manzanillo line) and bus. Car rental: Hertz, Independencia 51 ☎ (331) 2-6600 i Av. Juarez 111 ☎ (331) 2-4360.

A pleasant, semi-tropical city of gardens and 18thC buildings aired by fresh mountain breezes from the great Nevado de Colima, the mountain which dominates the town and the surrounding fertile plain. Although a rewarding place to spend a day or two, it is neglected by tourists, who are eager to get to the fun zones of the coast. Perhaps they are also worried by the town's own volcano, the **Volcán de Colima**, which some vulcanologists predict will produce a major eruption within 50yrs.

Events On Feb 2, fiesta in honour of the Virgin. The local peasants have a fierce devotion to her: celebrations begin a week beforehand and culminate with religious dances, fireworks and long religious ceremonies. Only a week or so later, amateur bullfighters can try their luck in the main bullring; an exciting spectacle, but participation is only for the brave (or foolish).

Sights and places of interest

Museo Antropológico (*Anthropological Museum*) ☆
27 de Septiembre, 6 blocks N of the Zocalo ▣ *Open standard hours, closed for lunch.*

A small and well laid out museum containing finely detailed ceramic figurines, sculptures and everyday objects that combine to give a clear impression of life in Pre-Conquest Colima. Of special charm are the figures of the small pot-bellied dogs esteemed a great culinary delicacy.

Museo Zaragoza (*Zaragoza Vintage Car Museum*) ☆
Belisario Dominguez 80, 6 blocks E of the Zocalo ▣ *Open standard hours, closed for lunch.*

A surprising place to find one of the best collections anywhere of antique American cars, all in working order. There are many more being restored at the **Zaragoza family ranch** outside town, which real enthusiasts may be allowed to visit (*ask at the museum*).

Places of interest nearby

From Colima, a good paved road leads 9km (5½ miles) N to the small crafts village of **Comala**, famous for its wrought-iron work and painted furniture. For the more adventurous, there is magnificent walking on the foothills of the volcano, reached along an unpaved road from the N outskirts of Colima.

[H] **Los Candiles** (*Blvd. Camino Real 399* ☎ *(331) 2–3212* ▮▮□ ⚌ ≈) is a motel with a good restaurant; **Villa del Rey** ✿ (*Blvd. Camino Real km 1* ☎ *(331) 2–2917* ▮▮□ *to* ▮▮▮□ ⚌ ≈) has a tranquil atmosphere. A fairly ordinary hotel located near the Zocalo is **Casino** (*Portal Morelos 11* ☎ *(331) 2–1406* ▮□).

Córdoba

Map 13E9. Veracruz. 129km (81 miles) SW of Veracruz on RF 150. Population: 110,000. Served by train (on Puebla–Veracruz line) and bus.

It was in Córdoba that the last Spanish Viceroy signed a treaty acknowledging Mexican independence on August 24 1821, thus furnishing this attractive colonial town with what is still its main claim to fame. On the main square, opposite the **Hotel Zevallos**, where the treaty was signed, there is a **monument to General Iturbide**, who signed for the new nation.

Event On Aug 24, fiesta to commemorate the treaty.

[H] **Hotel Zevallos** (*Av. 1 no. 111* ☎ *(271) 2–2722* ▮□), overlooking the Zocalo, is of historical interest – the Charter of Independence from Spain was signed here in 1821. **Palacio** (*Av. 3 and Calle 2* ☎ *(271) 2–2188* ▮▮□ ⚌) has a central location and provides free car-maintenance for guests.

[R] Try the restaurants in the arcade under the ***Hotel Zevallos*** (see above), especially the **Parroquía** (▮▮□).

Cozumel, Isla de ☆

Map 9G13. Quintana Roo. Island 45km (28 miles) at longest, 18km (11 miles) at widest. 2½hrs S of Puerto Morelos and Cancún; 1hr E of Playa del Carmen – check ferry times at Chetumal or Mérida. Population: 11,000. Served by air (international airport 3km/2 miles S of San Miguel) and ferry. Car rental: Avis, Hotel El Presidente ☎ (987) 2–0322, and at airport ☎ (987) 2–0099 ***i*** *Malecón, near Zocalo ☎ (987) 2–0357. American Express Travel Service: Barbachano, Hotel Cozumel Caribe ☎ (987) 2–0100.*

Island resorts have always had a special mystique and appeal, and Cozumel has been a magnet to visitors for well over

1,000yrs, although there was a slight gap of about four centuries after the Conquest when it became no more than a refuge for pirates. The second tourist boom began after World War II, when US servicemen stationed here during hostilities began to return. They spent their days under the crystal-clear waters around the reefs, and their nights in hammocks on the beach. The resort, having the advantage of the fine airfield left by the Americans, grew rapidly and is now regarded by many as the skin-diving capital of the world. Unfortunately, a large Mayan city – the main evidence of the first tourist boom – disappeared for ever, bulldozed under the runway. There are still dozens of small overgrown ruins dotted around the interior, which can be visited with a guide and a rented jeep. Not many people bother; the interior is not as spectacular as the coast.

The island is almost completely flat, and is covered by thick and thorny scrub inhabited by stinging insects; the beaches are idyllic. Although the diving fraternity sets the tone and the atmosphere, there are many others who just come to relax and bake in the sun. The new super-resort up the coast at *Cancún* has creamed off the most frenetic pleasure-seekers, not to mention the financial investment, so Cozumel looks set to carry on at its own casual, friendly pace for the foreseeable future, none of which worries the locals or regulars.

Sights and places of interest

The island's only town is **San Miguel**, where life is concentrated along the seafront and around the Zocalo, a pleasant place to sit in the evening at a café and discuss the day's adventures chasing multi-coloured fish in and out of sunken shipwrecks. All around the plaza and pier are the diving shops, who also arrange lessons and guides for novices.

The major resort hotels lie along the white-sand beaches both ways from town – the better beaches are to the N (see ***Hotels***). 9km (5½ miles) S of town is the **Laguna Chancanab** which is being developed as a diving centre, and 6km (4 miles) farther is the popular beach of **San Francisco**. Buy freshly grilled fish at the beach restaurants here, then rent snorkel equipment to go out and see tomorrow's lunch.

To get to the places outside town, either take a taxi – they are numerous and cheap – or rent a car or, as many prefer, a motorbike; there are now about 100km (62 miles) of paved road, so a day's exploration can be fun. Another good way to see the island is to take one of the day-cruises organized by the hotels.

Hotels

La Ceiba
Playa Paraíso, s Zone ☎ *(987) 2-0379* 112

Diving tuition is provided here, and there is a good restaurant. The rooms in the new 11-storey tower are best. Scuba divers will enjoy the 'adventure trail' that starts from the beach.

Cozumel Caribe
Playa Santa Pilar ☎ *(987) 2-0100* 220

All the modern, well-furnished rooms enjoy balcony views of Cozumel's fine beaches. There is a good water-sports programme.

El Cozumeleño
Playa Santa Pilar, N Zone ☎ *(987) 2-0050* 100

This hotel provides a sophisticated if incongruous Parisian atmosphere, and is on a pleasant beach. One of the more luxurious retreats on the island, with touches of luxury and enough facilities to keep guests occupied day and night.

Galápago Inn
Costera 8W km 1.5 ☎ *(987) 2-0366/2-0627* 20

Very much geared towards diving. Has a good seafood restaurant which becomes very lively in the evening.

Mayan Plaza
Playa Santa Pilar (987) 2–0411 94

N of town on a beautiful secluded beach, with elegant Mayan-style decor.

El Presidente
Playa San Francisco, s Zone (987) 2–0322 200

The first luxury hotel on Cozumel, next to Palancar reef, with excellent diving and evening entertainment.

Sol Caribe
Playa Paraíso, s Zone (987) 2–0700 220

An enormous Mayan-style pleasure-pyramid, a stunning piece of modern architecture, which has its own diving instructor and shop, and a popular disco.

Hotel nearby

Pez Maya

Pez Maya
Only accessible by plane from Cozumel. For details contact the Mayan Plaza hotel (987) 2–0411 20 (two-person villas)

One of the world's great luxury resorts. Although known for its fishing it is perfect also for sybaritic lazing and pleasure seeking. By far the most expensive hotel on the peninsula, but well worth it for the solitude, the fantasy Mayan decor, and the impeccable service. For those seeking a real break, the lack of telephones is a major attraction. The hotel has equipment for every conceivable water-sport.

Other hotels are: **Mara** (*N Zone (987) 2–0105*); **La Perta** (*s Zone (987) 2–0188*); **Villa Blanca** (*s Zone (987) 2–0865*).

Restaurants

The tourist department is trying to abolish the hotels' mandatory meal plans, and good restaurants are opening all the time. The speciality of the island is seafood. Credit cards are not widely accepted, so take cash.

Beachcomber
Laguna Opens at sunset.

A romantic beach location providing international and exotic food.

Carlos and Charlie's and Jimmy Kitchen
On the waterfront (987) 2–0191

Excellent food for a fun-loving crowd.

Casa Denis
Calle 19 and Sur 13, near the Zocalo

Exotic Yucatán cuisine is served in a beautiful tree-shaded courtyard. Cozumel's best restaurant; make a reservation through your hotel or call in the day before.

Pepes
Av. 5 Sur (987) 2–0701 to

In a central position near the Zocalo, this is a must for delicious Mexican creations.

Soberanis
Calle 1 and Sur 5, near the Zocalo (987) 2–0246

For the best seafood try this simply decorated establishment, a no-frills restaurant with a good and varied menu.

Nightlife

No longer do the resort hotels have a monopoly on the after-hours entertainment, although each hotel has a 'Mexican fiesta night' open to everyone (*free magazines give details*).

Nightspots in Cozumel include the following: **Hipopótamo** (*s end of town on beach*), a popular spot; **Morgans** (*near the Zocalo*), an elegant place to dine as well as dance; **Scaramouche** (*on the waterfront*), a competitor for Hipopótamo.

Cuautla

Map 12E7. Morelos. 47km (32 miles) E of Cuernavaca on RF 138; 102km (63 miles) S of Mexico City on RF 90 and RF 15. Population: 21,000. Served by train (on Mexico City–Izúcar line) and bus.

Some years ago, Cuautla was being promoted as an alternative to *Cuernavaca* for weekenders and tourists. It never caught on, and frankly there is little of interest here apart from a few hotels and some sulphur baths. What it does have to offer, however, is its position in the middle of one of the most fascinating areas of Mexico: it makes an ideal centre for excursions, less tiring than either Cuernavaca or Mexico City.

Monasteries to the north

Leave Cuautla by the road N to Amecameca, and after 6km (4 miles) turn E for **Yecapixtla** (15km/10 miles), where there is a fine 16thC monastery with a Gothic vaulted church and a carved stone pulpit. The same road continues to **Ocuitico** (16km/10 miles) and **Tetela** (23km/14 miles), each with small monasteries. The one at Tetela is less interesting, but at Ocuitico there is an imposing arcaded bell tower and a pretty cloister.

From here, return to the Amecameca road. Turn N, then after 4km (2½ miles) turn W, which brings you shortly to **Atlatlahuacán**. Here again, a monastery dominates the village, as at **Totolapán**, some 5km (3 miles) beyond. From here, the road passes through some magnificent countryside, with soaring craggy rocks rising steeply over the plains, and joins the new Mexico City–Oaxtepec highway at the pottery village of **Tlayacapan**. The large monastery here is usually closed and is falling into disrepair, but the splendid church is open.

It is then another 9km (5½ miles) to **Oaxtepec**, a small, pretty town that has become a vacation centre for the Mexican Social Security Institute; it is very crowded at weekends, when the facilities are open to visitors. 4km (2½ miles) from here, rejoin the Cuautla–Cuernavaca road at Cocoyoc (see ***Hotels***, below). Cuautla is 7km (4½ miles) E, while 10km (6 miles) W lies a fortress-like monastery, with some well-preserved open chapels, at **Yautepec**.

Monasteries to the south

Leave Cuautla on RF 190 for Izúcar de Matamoros, and after 21km (13 miles) turn N at the Amayuca crossroads to **Zacualpan**, a further 8km (5 miles). The monastery church here is noteworthy for its ornately-carved and gilded 19thC altar and for the earlier murals in the cloister. Returning to Amayuca, cross straight over RF 190, heading S. After 2km (1¼ miles), turn E for **Chalcatzingo** ☆ where there is a monastery, but more important, some fascinating and little-known ruins; ask in the Zocalo for a guide to lead you the final 1km (½ mile) along a track. The guardian of the site will give you a rough map, locating the various relief paintings and carvings spread about the steep hillside. The oldest may have been here over 2,500yrs; the masterpiece depicts graphically the horror on the faces of the victims of a sea monster.

Beyond the Chalcatzingo turning, the road continues S to **Jonacatepec** (2km/1¼ miles), with a 16thC monastery, and, after 12km (8 miles), **Tepalcingo**, with a fine Churrigueresque church.

H Prices are much lower than in *Cuernavaca*, but the atmosphere is rather run-down. The **Vasco** (*San Martín 40* ☎ *(735) 2-1400*) has well-furnished rooms with fans in the modern wing and its own sulphurous thermal spring.

Hotel nearby

Cocoyoc (*7km/4½ miles NW of Cuautla*).

Hacienda Cocoyoc
On Cuernavaca road ☎ *(735) 2-2000* 184

By far the best hotel in the area. A well-restored, magnificent old hacienda which makes a restful base, provided that you avoid holiday weekends and check beforehand that no conferences are scheduled.

Cuernavaca

Map 12E6. Capital of Morelos. 85km (53 miles) s of Mexico City on RF 95. Altitude: 1,532m. (5,026ft). Population: 700,000. Served by train (on Mexico–Balsas line) and bus. Car rental: Hertz, Plan de Ayala 300 ☎ (731) 4–3800 i Morelos 205-A ☎ (731) 2–1815, and Jardín Juarez 7–108 ☎ (731) 4–5425.

Renowned for its perfect climate and flower-filled gardens, Cuernavaca has attracted foreigners and weekenders ever since the Aztec lords sought retreat here. Cortés himself started building a retirement home here in 1532, but died before he could occupy it.

For all that, it can be a disappointing place for the modern tourist to visit, for most of the gardens have high walls, and the sights are too spread out to stroll around. To enjoy Cuernavaca, it is best to stay in one of the hotels with a large and pleasant garden, and to set aside plenty of time for leisurely excursions. Better still is to stay with friends or relatives – it is surprising how many visitors can think of somebody they know in this city of expatriates.

The name Cuernavaca means 'cow-horn' in Spanish, but that is only because the Conquistadors were unable to get their tongue round the Aztec name *Cuauhahuac*. Throughout the colonial period it remained a peaceful and prosperous town, but in the 1910 Revolution became the scene of savage massacres and lootings, as the local rebel Emiliano Zapata and his peasant army took a terrible revenge on the rich Spanish landowners. His strange mixture of idealism and blood-lust eventually proved too much even for his fellow rebels, and he was assassinated in the countryside towards Cuautla in 1919; but in those poor villages of Morelos where he lived, he is now a popular hero, and the name Zapata can sometimes be seen newly scrawled on a wall in protest at the restored prosperity of Cuernavaca.

Events At beginning of Lent, carnival. Processions, fireworks and bullfights.

In spring, flower festival in the Borda Gardens.

On Nov 1, Night of the Dead in the Borda Gardens.

Sights and places of interest

Borda Gardens
5mins w of the Zocalo 📷 *Open 10am–6pm.*

These quiet gardens were laid out in the 18thC by a rich Taxco mineowner, after whom they are named. Deep in the park is his grandiose **palace**, now gently decaying, and over in the corner is a small **museum** of contemporary art.

Cathedral †
Opposite the Borda Gardens, on Morelos and Hidalgo.

The sober and massive cathedral was founded in 1529 by Cortés, and was originally conceived as part of a Franciscan monastery. This was a staging post for Japan-bound missionaries, and inside the cathedral are remains of murals depicting 16thC mission life in the Far East. Also of note are some striking new abstract stained-glass windows. Every Sunday morning, there is a *mariachi* Mass with guitar accompaniment; check the time at the tourist office, and arrive early, since it is always crowded.

Hotel Casino de la Selva
Leandro Valle 1001 ☎ (731) 2–4705.

Known less as a hotel than as the home of some vast **murals** painted by David Siqueiros in the 1920s, mainly concerned with social injustice and as artistically bold as they are politically aggressive.

The hotel is also the starting point for guided tours (📷 *times irregular*) of some of Cuernavaca's more beautiful houses and gardens.

Palacio de Cortés
Zocalo Open Fri–Tues 10am–6pm. Closed Wed, Thurs.
An impressive, fortress-like building, originally the headquarters of Cortés' large estates and now the state museum. It stands on the SE corner of the laurel-shaded Zocalo, which is exceptional in Mexico for having no kind of church on it. The most important exhibits are the huge **murals** by Diego Rivera. They show nothing less than the history of Mexico, with the emphasis on scenes of mayhem and the exploitation of the Indians by the Conquistadors; the other displays, of antique weapons, armour, and instruments of torture, may help one to see Rivera's point. From the rear of the first floor loggia can be seen the peak of *Popocatepetl* shining white in the sun. After your visit, sit at one of the outdoor cafés in the Zocalo, made up of three squares, and with luck a strolling *mariachi* band will come and play a tune.

Pyramid of Teopanzolco
Calle Río Balsas Open 10am–6pm.
It was not until 1910, when heavy shelling of the nearby railway station shook off the top-soil, that these remains of a small Aztec ceremonial centre were discovered. On examination, it was found that the main pyramid was built over an earlier structure, and the main staircase of the first construction has been exposed and restored. Parts of the old temple walls remain on top of the pyramid.

Salto de San Antonio
1.5km (1 mile) NW of the Zocalo, at end of Calzada.
The surroundings of this impressive waterfall have been tidied up and landscaped, and there is a small souvenir market nearby. A popular picnic spot at weekends.

Hotels

Cuernavaca undoubtedly has one of the best selections of good, characterful hotels to be found anywhere in Mexico.

Casa de Piedra
Plan de Ayala 629 (731) 5-6100 24
Despite its forbidding exterior there are delightful rooms and gardens inside. Fires are lit in every room in cold weather. Good restaurant.

Casino de la Selva
Leandro Valle 1001 (731) 2-4705/4700 to 300
An enormous hotel with good rooms and sports facilities, boasting a cinema and bowling alley. Ideal for families.

Cuernavaca Racquet Club
Francisco Villa 100 (731) 3-0300
A romantic and luxurious hotel with superb sports facilities and exotic 23-acre gardens. Popular with the jet-set. There are 250 members of the club, who regard themselves as the social elite and try to keep the atmosphere exclusive.

Hacienda de Cortés
Plan de Ayala 410 (731) 5-8844 21
A beautifully restored 16thC palace originally built for Cortés, but now modernized for those who invade with dollars rather than swords and offering delightful accommodation.

Las Mañanitas
Ricardo Linares 107 (731) 2-4646 15
A breathtakingly beautiful colonial-style inn which usually needs reservations well in advance. See also ***Restaurants***, below.

Las Quintas
Av. las Quintas 107 ☎ (731) 2-8800 *45*
This downtown Spanish count's mansion comes in second-best only to ***Las Mañanitas*** – and it usually has rooms free.

Posada de Xochiquetzal
Leyva 200 ☎ (731) 2-0220 *to* *13*
The town's foreign colony gather here in yet another flower-filled colonial building. A friendly atmosphere prevails behind grim walls.

Hotel nearby

Vistahermosa (*20km/12 miles S*).

Hacienda Vistahermosa
In San José village, N of Lake Tequesquitengo ☎ (731) 2-0300
A rambling old sugar hacienda, once part of the Cortés estates; the arches of the Spanish aqueduct pass through the swimming pool. Couples on the honeymoon package-deal get priority on a room with its own Roman marble bath – and what better way to start a marriage than parachuting, for which the hotel has an arrangement with a nearby airstrip? The Sunday lunch is very popular with Mexican families.

Restaurants

Las Mañanitas
Ricardo Linares 107 ☎ (731) 2-4646
Cuernavaca's best-known restaurant, indeed one of its more popular sights, is housed in this immaculately restored colonial hacienda, full of flowers, fountains, flamingoes, peacocks and monkeys. Advance reservation is vital; Mexico City executives will happily drive down just for lunch. The menu is French-Mexican, with changing exotic specialities. (See also ***Hotels***, above.)

R Other restaurants include **Harry's Bar** (*Gutenberg 3 ☎ (731) 2-7679*), a lively place for tasty snacks, and **Moby Dick's** (*Plan de Ayala 383 ☎ (731) 5-4081*), which has good meat and seafood. Also recommended are the hotel restaurants at ***Casa de Piedra***, ***Cuernavaca Racquet Club***, ***Las Quintas*** and ***Posada de Xochiquetzal*** (see above).

Places nearby

Amecameca, *Cuautla*, *Malinalco*, *Popocetepetl*, *Taxco*, *Tepoztlán* and *Xochicalco*, can all be visited in a day.
Tequesquitengo (*22km/13 miles S by RF 95*). Heading S out of Cuernavaca, the parallel free and toll roads descend quickly to the tropical lowlands. At 19km (11 miles) from town, a turning to the E leads to **Lake Tequesquitengo**, where many rich Mexicans have second homes. The town is on the E of the lake, where boats can be rented for sailing, waterskiing, or diving in the sunken villages under the lake. 6km (3 miles) S of here are the exotic sulphur baths at **Tehuixtla**, a popular weekend resort.

Culiacán

Map 3E5. Capital of Sinaloa. 222km (137 miles) N of Mazatlán on RF 15. Population: 280,000. Served by air, train (on Guadalajara–Nogales line) and bus. Car rental: Avis, Hotel El Presidente ☎ (671) 2-0322, and at airport ☎ (671) 066-801; Budget, Obregón y Ríos ☎ (671) 3-8866.
A convenient stopover on the main W coast highway, although the town itself is of little interest. Its main attraction is perhaps

its fishing: consult the tourist office for details of which local reservoirs allow visitors to fish.

This area is one of the centres of the drug trade, which leads to occasional disturbances in remote parts of the countryside. Do not buy drugs, and do not stop for hitchhikers, and you should not have any trouble.

H **Econhotel Ejecutivo** (*Obregón and Madero* ☎ *(671) 3–9300*) is located downtown; **Los Tres Ríos** (*on RF15 5km/3 miles N* ☎ *(671) 2–3030*) is an ordinary motel.

Dolores Hidalgo

Map 11C5. Guanajuato. 54km (33 miles) NE of Guanajuato; 265km (164 miles) NW of Mexico City. Altitude: 1,990m (6,530ft). Population: 25,000. Served by train (on San Luis Potosí–Querétaro line) and bus **i** *Plaza Grande Hidalgo 18* ☎ *(468) 2–4424.*

One important event guaranteed this small town in the Bajío (see *Planning*) a place in history, without which it would have remained eternally obscure. On Sept 16 1810, the revolutionary priest Father Miguel Hidalgo rang the church bells to summon his flock, and then proclaimed the famous *Grito de Dolores* (*grito* means shout) to launch an uprising against Spanish rule. After a decade of bloodshed (including Hidalgo's own death at Spanish hands) the rebellion was successful. Every year on Sept 16, the *grito* is proclaimed all over Mexico, the President himself coming to Dolores to do this at least once during his reign.

Sights and places of interest

The **Casa de Hidalgo** (*Morelos 1 open standard hours, closed for lunch*), where Hidalgo lived from 1804–10, is now a museum, containing his possessions and assorted bric-à-brac from the War of Independence. The **church** is on the Zocalo, and although the bell that Hidalgo rang was melted down for bullets, it is worth a visit for the Churrigueresque facade and altarpiece. Opposite the church is a fine Baroque government office.

H There are plans to build two large new hotels here, but until then try **Del Caudillo** (*Querétaro 8* ☎ *(468) 2–0198*).

Durango

Map 4E6. Capital of Durango. 598km (371 miles) N of Guadalajara by RF 54 and RF 45. Altitude: 1,890m (6,200ft). Population: 240,000. Served by air, rail (on lines from Mexico City and Monterrey) and bus. Car rental: Hertz, 20 de Noviembre 1010 ☎ *(181) 1–5925* **i** *Hidalgo 408 Sur* ☎ *(181) 1–1107.*

Like many of the colonial cities, Durango began life as a mining town, with the forcible baptism of the local Indians who were then marched off in chain gangs to the mines. The mines are active, and there is so much iron under the hills that compasses are useless in the area. Many visitors have seen Durango's bare Sierra Madre peaks and canyons before without realising it, for they have starred in more Westerns than John Wayne. Ask at the tourist office for details of which film sets around town can be visited during your stay – with luck, guns may be blasting and cameras rolling at one of them. They will also advise on the good hunting, shooting and fishing to be enjoyed in the surrounding hills.

Event On July 8, fiesta to commemorate the town's foundation.

Sights and places of interest

In the centre of town, on the N of the Zocalo, is the **cathedral**, built in a mixture of Baroque and Churrigueresque styles. The tower is supposedly haunted by the ghost of a young girl who died of a broken heart there. The nearby **Palacio de Gobierno** (*Zaragoza and 5 de Febrero*) has some fine 20thC murals; next to it is the town's theatre, the **Teatro Victoria**, also in a colonial building.

The **Escuela de Artesanías**, on the outskirts of town towards Mazatlán, has exhibits of various local craft products, including Durango blown-glass (see ***Shopping***, below).

H **Campo México Courts** (*20 de Noviembre Oriente* ☎ *(181) 1–5560*) is a good motel on the E edge of town; centrally located is the **El Presidente** (*20 de Noviembre 257* ☎ *(181) 1–0480*).

R **El Far West** (*Florida 1106 Poniente* ☎ *(181) 2–3073*) is a steakhouse with appropriate decor; **El Papagayo** (*Progreso 10* ☎ *(181) 1–5061*) offers delicious regional specialities.

Shopping

Durango blown-glass can be bought either at the **Escuela de Artesanías** (*on the Mazatlán road*), or in the shops and market back in the centre. A particular speciality are the ashtrays with a scorpion cast in the glass (the Durango *alacranes* are deadlier with their sting than any others in Mexico). Semi-precious stones are also a good buy.

Places nearby

Thermal springs (*take road NW from Durango towards Tepehuanes*). The road out of town soon climbs up into the mountains, where the Tepehuan Indians live in the eastern foothills. On the way are a large number of thermal springs, reputed to cure almost every known illness; these include **Narcoyán** and **Valparaiso** on the outskirts of town, and, farther on, **Canatlán** (69km/43 miles) and **Tepehuanes** (172km/107 miles).

El Tajín ☆

Map 13C8. Veracruz. 20km (12 miles) S of Poza Rica by unnumbered road; 223km (136 miles) NE of Mexico City on RF 130 to Poza Rica.

Rearing up from dense tropical jungle, El Tajín is one of Mexico's most striking and important Pre-Hispanic temples, yet it is one of the least visited of the major restored sites, being off the main tourist routes and difficult of access without a car.

Those who make the effort will be well rewarded, although the large 150-acre site amounts to only about a tenth of what is still lying dormant beneath the undergrowth. The site was discovered in 1785, and little is known either of its history or of its builders, who were probably ancestors of the local Totonac Indians. It is thought that the city was flourishing during the Classic Period (3rdC AD), and that it had been long abandoned by the time of the Conquest.

Events On Sat and Sun mornings at about 11am–noon, there is often (but not always) a performance of the Huastec flying pole dance in front of the main pyramid.

The ruins

Open 10am–6pm.

Entering from the road, you will be in front of the great **Pyramid of the Niches**, the masterpiece of the art and architecture of the Totonac culture. At the summit of its six-tiered construction stand the remains of a temple. Each tier has an overhanging cornice, under which there are numerous niches adding up to the magic number of 365. Close your eyes and try to imagine all of the niches painted in the original dark blood-red, with the cornices in aquamarine; suddenly the dignified, crumbling structure acquires a fierce and barbaric splendour. The frieze depicts the gods and sacred animals in heaven.

There are two **ball-courts**, one just by the pyramid, the other a few hundred metres to the N, by which is the **Building of the Columns** with its low-reliefs of human sacrifice. Back by the entrance, there is a small **museum**, where carved stone slabs show in fine detail the playing of the sacred ball-game. When further funds are available, the site will be fully explored, but this is unlikely to be until the 21stC, according to the provisional schedule! Until then, the amateur explorer can have a field day wandering around the hundreds of unrestored structures in the jungle.

Ensenada

Map 2B2. Baja California Norte. 117km (73 miles) s of Tijuana on RF 1. Population: 120,000. Served by air and bus
i Primera 768 ☎ (667) 8–3121.

This resort town is growing in popularity, not surprisingly, as it is only an hour's drive from the US border and enjoys a fine setting on the beautiful white-sand bay of Todos Santos. Although it is an active fishing and shipping port, the central area around the waterfront has the feeling of somewhere much smaller. For a good view of the city, stroll out along Av. Segunda to the lookout point on Chapultepec Hill, or take a boat trip out into the bay from the quayside.

Ensenada first became important during the Gold Rush in 1870, and during the Prohibition era became a centre for smuggling bootleg liquor into the USA. When the gamblers and drinkers departed, it turned for its revenue to shipping cotton and to fishing, augmented today by tourism. Good wines are also produced in the area, and your hotel can arrange a visit to the **Bodegas de Santo Tomás** (*Miramar 666 ☎ (667) 8–2509*) to sample some champagne-style wines. The main attraction of Ensenada, however, is the deep-sea fishing: all hotels can arrange boat rental – or simply walk down to the harbour and ask around.

Events In Mar, Mardi Gras Carnival, and bicycle race from Tecate; in May, Newport–Ensenada yacht race; in June, 800km (500 miles) off-road race departs; in Aug, San Diego–Ensenada motorboat race; in Oct, Ensenada small-plane rally; in Nov, 1,600km (1,000 miles) off-road race departs.

H Estero Beach
11km (6 miles) s ☎ (667) 9–1001/8–1380 to 80 AE CB VISA

A complete vacation resort providing water-sports, boat rental and duty-free shops. Popular for a family weekend.

H Royal Inn
Prolongación Calle San Marcos ☎ (667) 6–2203 100 AE CB VISA

A new and luxurious hotel with aspirations to being the area's best. Service is good, and there are thermal spring waters.

H Travelodge
López Mateos and Blancarte 130 ☎ (667) 8–1601/8–3701 40

A pleasant American-owned Mexican-style hotel, home of the ***El Rey Sol*** restaurant.

R **El Rey Sol** ⏏ (*López Mateos 100* ☎ *(667) 8–1733* ▮▮▮▮) is a real treat for superb French and Mexican cuisine, and as such comes as a delightful surprise after the rough and ready frontier atmosphere of the Baja peninsula. A speciality is steak or quail in a brandy sauce.

Places nearby

La Bufadora (*22km/13 miles* W). An energetic ocean geyser which can either be reached by road or viewed from one of the boats which leave from the harbour.

See also *Baja California*, *Mexicali* and *Tijuana*.

Fortín de las Flores ☆

Map 13E9. Veracruz. 135km (84 miles) W of Veracruz on RF 150; 166km (102 miles) E of Puebla on RF 150.
Population: 14,000. Served by rail (branch line from Veracruz) and bus.

The profusion of flowers and tropical plants after which it is named partly smother the colonial buildings of this very pretty small town. By contrast, the skyline falls away from the airy snow-capped peak of Mexico's highest mountain, the **Pico de Orizaba** (5,700m/18,265ft), an extinct volcano.

The **Hotel Ruíz Galindo** (see below) welcomes non-residents to its large gardens, which contain several buildings of an old hacienda and an 18thC church, as well as a large population of wild orchids and humming birds. The same hotel can also arrange for visitors to play golf at a small course nearby; but be sure to take plenty of balls to replace those lost in the dense bougainvillea and gardenias.

H **Ruiz Galindo**
Calle 7 no.210 ☎ *(271) 3–0055/2–2555* ▮▮▮▮ 153
A pleasant mountain resort famous for its gardenia-filled swimming pool (new flowers daily) and large, beautiful garden.

Guadalajara ☆

Map 10C3. Capital of Jalisco. 574km (356 miles) W of Mexico City on RF 15. Altitude: 1,600m (5,250ft).
Population: 2,100,000. Served by air (international airport 19km/12 miles S), train and bus. Car rental: Avis, Niños Héroes 942 ☎ *(36) 12–3451/068–2725, and at airport* ☎ *(36) 35–8190; Hertz, Hotel Genova* ☎ *(36) 13–1994, and Hotel Posada Guadalajara* ☎ *(36) 21–2424* **i** *Lázaro Cárdenas 3298* ☎ *(36) 21–9162, and Juarez 638* ☎ *(36) 14–2702. UK Consul: Lerdo de Tejada 362* ☎ *(36) 15–1406. US Consul: Progreso 175* ☎ *(36) 25–2700. American Express Travel Service: Convisa S.A., 16 de Septiembre no.730* ☎ *(36) 14–8228/14–5919.*

Once the most Spanish city of New Spain, Guadalajara was for many years proudly remote from the rest of Mexico. Now it is changing rapidly, as if to live up to its position as the country's second city. But despite the building boom and industrial growth, it remains free of the pollution and chaos which hangs over the capital. In the centre of town, where four gracious squares surround the cathedral and stately colonial buildings abound, it does not seem so long ago that haughty Spanish nobles strode out from their mansions. Even now, the locals like to be called *Tapatíos*, after the tasselled cloaks that were the height of elegance during colonial times.

The state of Jalisco was originally a part of the province of New Galicia; its conquest was far from easy, and only in 1560, after years of bloody fighting, was Guadalajara sufficiently established to become the state capital. It soon became an important centre of commerce; much of the wealth generated was poured into the building of the city, and the parks and wide tree-lined boulevards constitute a triumph for Spanish town-planning. Even today, modern buildings have to fit into the original master-plan.

Surprisingly, given its Spanish character, Guadalajara joined the 1810 rebellion, and for a short while was even the seat of a revolutionary government. After this brief spell in the limelight, however, it returned to gracious provincial isolation, shaken only slightly by the revolution of a century later.

The more lasting revolution began when the roads and railways eventually arrived and the city began to resume its former economic importance. The large new international airport opened up the area to tourism; many fly here to explore the colonial cities, the mountains, and the coast of western Central Mexico. Indeed, the excellent climate and relaxed atmosphere have attracted some visitors so much that they have decided to retire to Guadalajara and nearby Lake *Chapala*. To cope with the foreign influx, many new hotels and restaurants have opened in recent years, making the city, and the state of Jalisco as a whole, one of Mexico's most attractive travel destinations.

Nowhere more than in Mexico does human life become isolated, external to its surroundings, and cut off tinily from the environment. Even as you come across the plain to a big city like Guadalajara, and see the twin towers of the cathedral peering around in loneliness like two lost birds side by side on a moor, lifting their white heads to look around in the wilderness, your heart gives a clutch, feeling the pathos, the isolated tininess of human effort.

D.H. Lawrence, *Mornings in Mexico*, 1927

Events See **Zapopán** in ***Environs of Guadalajara***, and **San Juan de los Lagos** in ***Places nearby***.

Sights and places of interest

As in the capital, the main sights are scattered in groups around the city, and are best visited in these groups. The central landmark and point of reference is the cathedral. Even by Mexican standards, opening hours here are notably erratic.

The city centre

Cathedral 🏛 †

The cathedral dominates the city in every respect; when you lose your sense of direction, just look for its twin bell towers, strange Byzantine creations on the skyline. They were rebuilt after an earthquake early this century, and just about complete the collection of architectural styles embodied in the cathedral, which ranges from Moorish through classical Greek to Gothic. It was consecrated in 1616 after nearly 50yrs of construction. There are several fine oil paintings in the side chapels: see especially the *Assumption of the Virgin*, attributed to Murillo. A good way to orient yourself to the city is to climb the bell tower, from where there is a magnificent view.

Hospicio Cabañas 🏛

Calle Hospicio, at end of Morelos 🎫 *Open standard hours.*

An enormous 19thC orphanage, all cloisters, courtyards and flowers, which is still in use and where visitors are invited to meet the children. The building was designed by the great Neoclassical architect Manuel Tolsa, but the main attractions are the 1930s **murals** by Clemente Orozco. They fill the chapel, and each panel has a different theme, including political, Biblical and historical pieces, all adding up to a

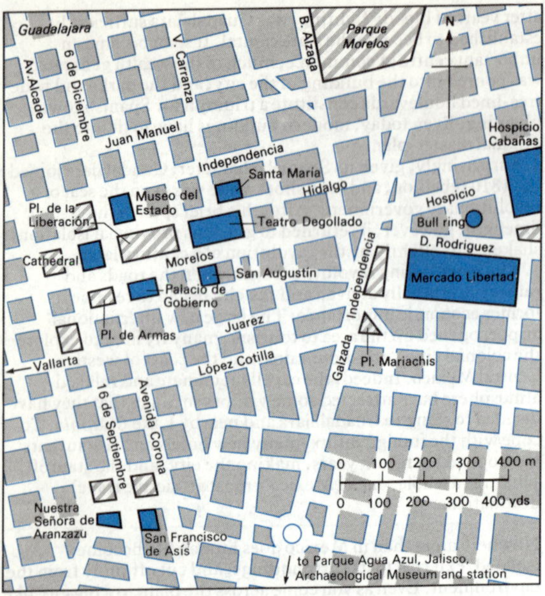

passionately Mexican view of the world. The most famous panel is *The Four Horsemen of the Apocalypse*, a composition of stunning dynamism.

Mercado Libertad

Off Calzada Independencia.

In this enormous marketplace it is the rule to bargain fiercely over the price of any pottery or leatherwork that takes your fancy.

Just S of the market is the **Plaza Mariachis**, blocked with café tables but nonetheless thronging with hundreds of *mariachi* musicians in silver-embroidered costumes cheerfully trying to outplay each other. Just N of the market is the city's **bullring**.

Museo del Estado (*Jalisco State Museum*)

Hidalgo and Liceo Open standard hours.

An amazingly varied range of exhibits fills the maze of rooms, courts and corridors of this 17thC seminary building, opposite the Neoclassical **Rotonda de los Héroes de Jalisco** by the cathedral. Prize pieces include the dried-up arm of a notorious assassin, and the first gramophone to reach Guadalajara, and there is any amount of Pre-Hispanic and colonial relics and art; it is easy to spend a whole day here, poking around, losing oneself and finding wisdom.

In the modern picture galleries, be sure to see the early works of the 1930s muralists, Orozco and Rivera. The colonial section includes a Murillo *Self-Portrait* and *Life of St Francis of Assisi*.

In the same building (*but with a separate entrance at Hidalgo 292*) is the **Museum of Palaeontology**, worth visiting for its fossilized mammoth skeleton, still accompanied by the bones of a hunter and the stone arrowheads he used in a fatal and vain attempt to kill the mammoth.

Palacio de Gobierno

Plaza de Armas.

Behind the impressive Neoclassical facade made of grey volcanic stone, this state house is the home of the huge 1930s **murals** by Clemente Orozco; they show a Stalinist view of the oppression of the Mexican people by foreigners.

Teatro Degollado

Plaza de la Liberación.

An ornate 19thC theatre which is now the cultural nerve-centre of Guadalajara; even if you are not tempted by the various performances, the opulent interior is well worth a look. The theatre is flanked by the colonial churches of **Santa María** and **San Augustín**; both belonged to monasteries which have now disappeared, and are worth a brief visit.

South of the centre

Seven blocks S of the Plaza de Armas, to the right off Corona, is a charming little garden overlooked by the 17thC church of **San Francisco de Asís**, with a fine Baroque facade. Opposite is the church of **Nuestra Señora de Aranzazu**; the exterior is uninspiring, but the high altar is dripping with gold-leaf.

From here it is 12 blocks S to the leafy **Parque Agua Azul**. At its northern tip, on a large roundabout, is the **Museo de Artesanías** (*open standard hours*), where a wide range of folk pottery and weaving is exhibited, most of it for sale at reasonable prices. Ten minutes' walk farther S, by the railway station on 16 de Septiembre, is the small **Museo de Arqueología** (*opening hours irregular*), with some fine human and animal pottery figurines from *Colima*.

West of the centre

Museo Clemente Orozco
Av. Vallarta, near Minerva fountain, 4km (2½ miles) W of centre
Open standard hours.

Housed in his old studio, this museum pays tribute to one of the leading 1930s muralists, who developed the form of the giant polemical mural into one of Mexico's great cultural traditions. On display here are some of the studies Orozco made for his murals, and hundreds of his paintings – but none of the murals themselves. The paintings clearly chart his development from realism in his youth to later symbolism and expressionism.

Environs of Guadalajara

On the outskirts of the city are a spectacular ravine, and two former Indian villages now more or less incorporated into the metropolis.

Barranca de los Oblatos
11km (6½ miles) N along Independencia.

A cable-car makes the dizzying 700m (2,170ft) descent into the ravine, or you can stand at the top and gaze down. It is crowded at weekends.

Tlaquepaque ☆
7km (4½ miles) SE of centre, off Chapala road.

A centre for all manner of traditional Indian crafts, but known above all for its hand-painted pottery. There are numerous shops where you can see weavers, glass-blowers and metal-beaters at work. There is a fiesta on June 29.

Combine this with a look at the spectacular waterfalls at **Juanacatlán**, 20km (12 miles) farther along a turning E off the Chapala road.

Zapopán
8km (5 miles) W of centre, signposted off Vallarta.

The second village has a basilica whose miraculous statue of the Virgin is the focal point of one of Mexico's largest fiestas every October (Oct 4 is the most important day, but it continues to Oct 12). The streets fill with fervent worshippers, *mariachi* bands and dancers, escorting the Virgin on a long procession around the city. At other times, the basilica is barely worth a visit, although it is a good example of 17thC Baroque.

Hotels

Calinda Quality Inn
Juarez 170 ☎ (36) 14-8650
172

Location: Downtown. A chain hotel, well run and economical, and popular with families.

Camino Real
Av. Vallarta 5005 ☎ (36) 21-7217 *224* AE CB Φ ● VISA

Location: 5km (3 miles) W of centre. A colonial-style resort hotel with large airy rooms in low bungalows, a good range of shops and pools.

Fiesta Americana
Av. Vallarta ☎ (36) 90-0536/25-5489 *402* AE CB Φ ● VISA

Location: 4km (2½ miles) W of centre. The most stunning feature of this bold modern building is the 11-storey central lobby between twin towers. Multitude of bars, restaurants and shops, and flamboyantly appointed rooms.

Guadalajara Sheraton
Niños Héroes and 16 de Septiembre ☎ *(36) 14–7272/12–5151* 222

Location: City centre. This downtown high-rise hotel has recently been renovated to keep it in the luxury class; the sumptuous bathrooms seem to have benefited most.

Holiday Inn
López Mateos 2500 ☎ *(36) 21–2400* *068004* to 304

Location: 6km (4 miles) SE, *near Plaza del Sol shopping centre.* A reliable favourite of the worldwide chain.

Plaza del Sol
López Mateos and Manuel Otero ☎ *(36) 21–0515* 194

Location: In a shopping complex near centre. Cheerful modern decor and efficiently helpful management.

El Tapatio
On Chapala road ☎ *(36) 35–6050* 207

Location: 6.5km (4 miles) SE. There are good views of the town from this luxurious multi-level country club resort on a hilltop. There are large rooms, some with fireplaces, pleasant tennis courts attended by a resident professional and plenty of nightlife.

Restaurants

The hotel restaurants at the ***Camino Real, Fiesta Americana, Guadalajara Sheraton*** and ***El Tapatío*** (see above) are among the best in town, all offering an international menu and nightly entertainment. Saturday night at the El Tapatío is always fun, while the Sunday buffet lunch at the Camino Real should not be missed. The restaurants at the ***Holiday Inn*** and ***Plaza del Sol*** are also good.

Le Bistro
Vallarta 1275 ☎ *(36) 25–8239*

Exotic and imaginative cooking in intimate surroundings.

Brazz Campestre
López Mateos 6022 ☎ *(36) 21–1356; also Morelos and Gakana* ☎ *(36) 2–0324, and Plaza del Sol shopping centre* ☎ *(36) 21–3355. All* to

All three branches offer good steaks and meats. Service is impeccable.

Camelot
Libertad 1951 ☎ *(36) 25–1715*

Delicious game dishes are served amid medieval-style decor.

Cazadores
Américas 159 ☎ *(36) 15–8878; also Jalisco 606* ☎ *(36) 35–1983, Niños Héroes 62* ☎ *(36) 14–8235, and Unión 405* ☎ *(36) 15–9710. All*

A family-run chain of restaurants serving delicious Mexican food.

Also at Tlaquepaque, 6km (4 miles) SE, in a beautiful country setting – the best branch of all. Arrive early, as there is no telephone and it is very popular.

La Gran Fonda
Avila Camacho 2012 ☎ *(36) 23–0566*

For the best Mexican food in town try this large, elegant and airy dining room.

Hacienda de la Flor
A. Ortega 764, Zapopán ☎ *(36) 33–3126/24–8419*

Excellent seafood and regional dishes served by candlelight in an old hacienda.

Recco
Libertad 1973 ☎ *(36) 25–0724* to

Good Italian food, not common in Mexico, in an Italian-villa setting. The tourist menu is especially good value.

Suehiro
Av. de la Paz 1801 ☎ *(36) 26–0094*

Traditional hand-and-foot Japanese service accompanies such superb delicacies as raw fish and fried seaweed.

Tekare
16 de Septiembre no. 157 ☎ *(36) 14–9791*

High up in a penthouse with wonderful views. Good Mexican and international food.

Nightlife

Until recently, the conservative local authorities discouraged any sort of after-hours liveliness, and even now most of the action is at the hotels, with the obvious exception of the **Plaza Mariachi** (see ***Mercado Libertad*** in ***Sights***), where you should certainly go once during your stay. Hotels will provide free English-language listings of the shows, fiestas and entertainments being held at the hotels (there is usually something going on most nights), and what is on at the ***Teatro Degollado*** (see ***Sights***), which can range from classical opera to folkloric ballet. (*For cultural information in English ☎ (36) 15–7992*).

The luxury hotels all have bars with entertainment, and discos. The newest and most elegant is at the ***Fiesta Americana***, and disco-lovers should also check out the **Felix** and the ***Holiday Inn***.

Places nearby

Colonial towns to the north The potters' village of **Tonalá** ☆ is 15km (9 miles) from the city. Its finely painted animal figurines can be seen in souvenir shops all over Mexico. They are cheaper here, and you have the fun of seeing them being made and fired. All along this road there are little colonial towns whose churches are worth a quick visit. **San Juan de los Lagos** (250km/155 miles), the most interesting town on the road, is renowned for its religious festivals, spectacular enough to attract pilgrims from all over the state and beyond. The main dates are approximately Jan 20–Feb 6 (especially Feb 2), Aug 1–6 and Nov 21–Dec 12, depending upon days of the week (ask tourist office at Guadalajara). The festivals are accompanied by all the usual bullfights, fireworks and processions. The nearest accommodation is at *Aguascalientes*.

Tequila (*60km/37 miles W of Guadalajara, on RF 15*). A small town which has given to a grateful world the ambrosial and alcoholic bliss of the drink which bears its name. A must for tipplers is a visit to one of the distilleries, where cactus juice is processed into firewater for worldwide consumption. Feast days here are May 3 and Dec 8, when the town's liquor flows freely.

La Magdalena (*78km/49 miles W of Guadalajara, on RF 15*). A pleasant colonial town which has become a centre for trading in semi-precious stones. Magpies will find irresistible the glittering arrays of opal, agate and jade.

Guanajuato ★

Map 11C5. Capital of Guanajuato. 366km (226 miles) NW of Mexico City on RF 57. Altitude: 2,050m (6,725ft). Population: 50,000. Served by train (on Querétaro–Aguascalientes line) and bus ***i*** *in arcades by Parroquia ☎ (473) 2–0244.*

A labyrinth of a city, a maze of narrow streets and small tree-shaded squares, and underneath it all a strange subterranean road winding along the bottom of the steep valley in the town's old main sewer. For years Guanajuato was the richest city in New Spain, producing nearly half the world's silver, and the wealthy mine-owners have left their mark in the mansions and richly endowed churches which hide around every corner. It has also been a seat of learning since the Jesuits opened a university in 1732; it is now housed in a modern building near the Plaza de la Paz, carefully designed to complement the predominant colonial style.

Even when there are no festivals, Guanajuato is a wonderful place to spend a few days, taking in the sights at a leisurely pace, and sitting on the ornate cast-iron benches under the trees drinking coffee and chatting to the students, who are often keen to practise their English.

Leave your car and explore the town on foot, but only after you have driven around the **Carretera Panorámica**, the road which makes almost a full circuit of the city high in the surrounding mountains. The best view is from the statue of *El Pípila*, a local hero from the War of Independence, which can also be reached by 10mins' energetic climbing up a steep lane signposted off Juarez.

Events Every year during spring, costumed students put on a series of weekend performances of Spanish one-act plays (*entremeses*) by writers such as Lope de Vega or Cervantes. The Plaza de San Roque is candlelit for the outdoor performances. Not to be missed even by non-Spanish speakers; tickets in advance from the Teatro Juarez.

In May, the more serious International Cervantes Festival is held. Theatre groups and orchestras come from all over the world to perform in the squares and the two theatres. The festival lasts two weeks, and hotel rooms are reserved months in advance.

Apart from these cultural events, there are several religious fiestas of interest, usually featuring processions, dances and fireworks. Dates include: May 21–31, feast of the Virgin of Guanajuato; Nov 7–14, the colourful *Fiesta de las Illuminaciones*; at Christmas-time, candlelit processions through the streets. For all these, check at the tourist office.

Sights and places of interest

Alhóndiga de Granaditas

Calle 5 de Mayo ▣ *Open standard hours, closed for lunch.*

A massive, grim stone structure with horizontal slit windows, built by the Spanish as a grain warehouse. During the War of Independence, the royalists were besieged here by Hidalgo's revolutionary mob. It seemed that they could manage to hold out indefinitely, when a young miner, nicknamed *El Pípila*, managed to blast open the heavy wooden doors. The defenders were massacred, and Guanajuato thus became the first major city to fall to the insurgents. It was recaptured some months later in 1811, however, and subsequently Hidalgo's head was displayed on a hook high on the Alhóndiga, being removed only in 1821 with the final defeat of Spain. The building now houses a local museum containing all manner of historical memorabilia, Pre-Hispanic remains, and some colourful murals depicting violent episodes in Guanajuato's past.

Mercado Hidalgo 🏛

Av. Juarez. Open daily: best in morning.

Built during the 19thC period known as the *Porfiriato*, this huge and impressive cast-iron and glass market is very like contemporary English Victorian stations and markets. Up on a first-floor gallery is a handicrafts section where energetic bargaining may secure tin-work, leather, weaving or pottery at good prices.

La Parroquía 🏛 †

Plaza de la Paz.

A 17thC church with a magnificent facade in the local pink sandstone. Inside is a highly venerated wooden **statue of the Virgin** sent as a gift by Philip II of Spain in 1557, and known to have been in existence since the 8thC, making her the oldest Christian religious statue in Mexico. She stands on a pedestal of solid silver, and her robes are liberally studded with precious stones.

Teatro Juarez 🏛

Jardín de la Unión.

An extraordinary Neoclassical building finished in 1903. Even if you are not attending a performance, it is worth persuading the doorman to let you look inside at the plush extravaganza of red velvet, brass lamps, ornate carving and intricate cast-iron railings. In the interests of symmetry, the roof-line statues of the *Muses* are supplemented by a tenth member.

Other sights

The church of **San Diego**, next to the ***Teatro Juarez***, has a fine Churrigueresque doorway. Nearby, close to the modern university buildings, is the later church of **La Compañía**, built in 1747–65 by the Jesuits who ran the university. Its great dome dominates the city, and its Baroque facade, with three ornate doorways, is one of the best in Mexico.

For a change from churches, head back past the university down Calle Pocitos to the **Museo Rivera** (*open standard hours*) where the muralist Diego Rivera was born in 1886. It is also a cultural centre; drop by during the day to see if any of the evening events interest you. Just outside the town on the Guadalajara road is the **cemetery** (*Panteón Civil*), where guides enthuse about the collection of mummies.

Sight nearby

Cerro del Cubilete

30km (19 miles) W; take Silao road and turn N at 10km (6 miles).

Well before you get there, the vast 1922 **statue of Christ** comes into view, standing on a bizarre domed structure. A popular picnic spot, it is said to be at the geographical centre of the Republic. The views of the Bajío (see *Planning*) are excellent.

La Valenciana

3km (2 miles) from centre on road for Dolores Hidalgo.

Dominating this small village is one of Mexico's most magnificent Baroque churches, built from 1765–88 by the Count of Valenciana, who owned the nearby silver mines. Steps lead from the village square up to the Churrigueresque facade, of which only one bell tower was completed. Before entering, walk around to the side of the tower to see the statue of *St Joseph* above the door. The church is vaulted in sombre volcanic stone, and contains three ornate altars, covered in gold-leaf, and adorned with religious statues and oil paintings.

On the other side of the road, it is a short walk to the **Valenciana mineshafts**. Some are long abandoned, and others still in use. It is said that silver dust from these mines was mixed into the church mortar.

Hotels

Castillo de Santa Cecilia

1km (½ mile) N on RF 110 (473) 2-0477 to 81

This fantastical medieval castle affords an excellent view of the town and provides all modern comforts. Romantic vaulted restaurant.

Hacienda de Cobos

Padre Hidalgo 3 (473) 2-0350 40

A romantic small inn, housed in converted colonial silver-ore-processing buildings, in the centre of town. Simple, small rooms, and tables in the courtyard for dining.

Hostería del Fraile

Sopeña 3 (473) 2-1179 33

Formerly a coin mint in the 17thC, it is located opposite the ***Teatro Juarez*** (see ***Sights***). Full of character, but parking can be a problem.

Parador San Javier

Plaza San Javier (473) 2-0626 120

A colonial inn located 2km (1¼ miles) N on RF 110. Fireplaces in the older rooms.

El Presidente

Km 2 on Marfil road (473) 2-3980 69

A beautifully converted hacienda surrounded by ornamental gardens. First choice in the town, worth visiting anyway for its superb Spanish chapel, including a 12thC altarpiece.

Real de Minas
Nejayote 17 ☎ (473) 2-1460 to 175
North on RF 110, a large new hotel on the outskirts of town. Motorcycle rental for guests is a useful idea.

San Diego
Jardín de la Unión ☎ (473) 2-1300 to 60
The San Diego is housed in a 17thC convent building in the middle of town. Ask for a room with a balcony, as views are superb.

Restaurants

There are excellent hotel restaurants at the ***Castillo de Santa Cecilia***, ***Hacienda de Cobos***, ***Parador San Javier***, and ***El Presidente*** hotels (see above), which are all open to non-residents.

For a less formal meal, the following establishments are recommended: **La Galevena** (*Sopeña 18* ☎ *(473) 2-0529*), for delicious Mexican food in a beautiful 16thC galleried courtyard; **Pizza Piazza** (*Plaza San Fernando* ☎ *(473) 2-3094*), a popular place for students; **Tasca de los Santos** (*Plaza de la Paz* ☎ *(473) 2-2320*), for Spanish food.

Guaymas

Map 3D4. Sonora. 413km (256 miles) s of Nogales on RF 15. Population: 100,000. Served by air, boat (three ferries per week to and from Santa Rosalia in Baja California), train (on Guadalajara–Nogales line) and bus. Car rental: Hertz, Posada San Carlos, Miguel Alemán 290 ☎ (622) 2-1010.

Along with the nearby tourist development of **San Carlos**, Guaymas is being widely tipped as the Acapulco of the 1990s. The qualifications are certainly all there: it is near the US, and has perfect climate, excellent fishing and natural beauty. On three sides are the desolate and impressive mountains and deserts of Sonora, and on the fourth, palm-shaded beaches face out over the clear waters of the Sea of Cortés. Resort hotels have opened, and others will follow, but the main attraction for the time being is the deep-sea fishing for marlin, sail-fish and others. There is a good secure marina for boat owners, with a multitude of small-time rental-operators – if you rent a boat, check the radio and safety equipment. Hotels can help, and can also arrange hunting and riding up in the hills, or fowl-shooting down by the coast for those less nautically minded.

There are few surviving reminders of Guaymas' disturbed history. During the 19thC it was attacked from all sides. A period of peace has now emerged, and the best place to enjoy it is on Guaymas' premier beach at **Bocochibampo**. The beaches around San Carlos, just to the NW, are less crowded and offer good scuba-diving.

For places of interest nearby, see *Ciudad Obregón*.

Events In May, July and Sept, fishing tournaments. On Mar 18 and June 24, local fiestas.

Hotels

Miramar de Cortés
Playa de Cortés ☎ (622) 2-0135 to 135
Located on the bay, 10mins' taxi ride N from the centre, this is a pleasant and traditional hotel, popular with water-sports enthusiasts.

Posada de San Carlos
12km (7 miles) N ☎ (622) 6-0015 153 AE CB Ⓓ VISA
This hotel, with a good seafood restaurant, is pleasantly relaxing.

Punta del Sol
On San Carlos bay ☎ (622) 6-0235 49 AE CB Ⓓ VISA
A beach hotel with its own trailer park. Popular for family vacations.

Rubi ✿
Serdan and Calle 29 ☎ (622) 2-0169 to 110
A downtown hotel for serious sportsmen: fishing and hunting arranged.

Hermosillo

Map 3C4. Capital of Sonora. 277 (170 miles) S of Nogales on RF 15. Population: 280,000. Served by air, train (on Guadalajara–Nogales line) and bus. Car rental: Avis, Kino and Villareal ☎ (621) 5-1455; Hertz, Abelardo Rodriguez and Guerrero ☎ (621) 9-8500, and at airport ☎ (621) 5-8789 i Calle de los Nogales 13 ☎ (621) 4-7399. US Consul: Blvd. Hidalgo 15 ☎ (621) 3-8922.

The first major town on the road S from Mexicali and Nogales, and well provided with hotels to make it a convenient stopover.

Places of interest nearby

Bahía Kino
104km (65 miles) W by a good road.
A small fishing village which is gaining in importance as a resort, and is now especially popular with the camper crowd. The sea fishing and scuba diving are good, and all equipment can be rented on the spot. Across the alarmingly named Estrecho del Infiernillo (Straits of Hell) is the **Isla del Tiburón** (Shark Island) nature reserve; it is also inhabited by Seri Indians, who now make a living selling woodcarvings to tourists.

Hotels

Internacional
Rosales and Morelia ☎ (621) 3-8960 111 AE CB Ⓓ VISA
A new downtown high-rise hotel with three restaurants.

Vallegrande
Padre Kino and Ramón Corral ☎ (621) 4-4570 142
A pleasant modern motel with colonial-style rooms.

Hotel nearby

Kino Bay (*104km /65 miles W of Hermosillo*).

Posada de Santa Gemma ✿
Morale Cortés and Río de Plata ☎ (621) 2-0026 14
This small motel boasts pleasant bungalow rooms and good service.

Isla Mujeres

Map 9F13. Quintana Roo. 45mins E of Puerto Juarez; 30mins E of Cancún/Punta Sam. Island 8km (5 miles) at longest and 4km (2½ miles) at widest. Population: 10,000. Served by air and frequent ferry services i Aeroméxico building ☎ (988) 20-0044.

Mexico's third Caribbean island paradise (see *Cancún* and *Cozumel*), this is where the friendly, scruffy crowd come to relax after an exhausting second-class bus-tour of the Yucatán. Here, you can spin out those last few dollars for as long as possible before starting the long walk home. There are one or two good hotels for those who enjoy the island's bohemian atmosphere but not its poverty.

The island

'Isla Muj' is a long, low strip of jungle, fringed by coconut groves, white sand, luminous blue waters and coral reefs. The town, little more than a tropical village, is on a spit of land to the N. The whole island can easily be explored on foot – even the airfield is only 15mins' walk from the town. Otherwise, taxis (always arrange the trip back in advance) and rented motorbikes are the best way of getting around.

To see everything in comfort, take one of the daily boat-trips around the island, which also go to the bird sanctuary on nearby **Isla Contoy**. On the way, the boat stops over the skeleton of a sunken galleon, where lurid-looking fish glide in and out of its shattered ribs. Take along snorkel gear and join them. Another stop is at the **Mayan temple**, near the lighthouse on the southern tip of the island.

The best beach near town is the **Playa Cocos**, and about 5km (3 miles) to the S is the **Playa Garrafón**, where the underwater life is worth seeing. On the way back, stop off at the **Mundaca pirate fortress**, which was a centre for the white-slave trade during the 19thC.

Another possible excursion is to the **turtle farm** halfway down the W coast. Large crowds gather to try and ride on the hapless animals – an unpleasant experience for them, and for any watching animal lovers.

Sleeping on the beach is not recommended. It is safer to hire a hammock in one of the enclosures. Despite the name (Island of Women), women on their own on the island are better off staying in hotels (the name derives only from the large number of female statues found here by the Spaniards). Finally, if you have an important travel connection to make on the mainland, it is advisable to take a ferry in good time, for the locals are as happy-go-lucky as anyone else here.

H **Posada del Mar**
Almirante Rueda ☎ (988) 2-0198 IIII 45
This is the best hotel in town. Some rooms are air conditioned.

H **Zazil-ha**
Playa de los Cocos ☎ (988) 2-0155 IIII 100 AE CB DC MC VISA
On the northern tip of the island, this beautiful new resort hotel overlooks the Zazil-ha (Luminous Waters) lagoon. The food and service, however, are not up to luxury standard.

R For an elegantly served seafood meal, go to **María's** at El Garrafón, S of the town. Elsewhere, the prices are lower and the service more relaxed, but the seafood is delicious. To start with try **Ciro's Lobster Pot** (III), in the town.

Ixtapa
See *Zihuatanejo*.

Jalapa (*Xalapa*) ☆

Map 13D9. Capital of Veracruz. 330km (205 miles) E of Mexico City on RF 136 and RF 140; 119km (84 miles) NW of Veracruz on RF 140 and RF 180. Population: 250,000.
Served by train (on Mexico City–Veracruz line) and bus. Car rental: Avis, Hotel María Victoria, Zaragoza 6 ☎ (281) 7-0986 i Primo Verdad 25 ☎ (281) 7-3030.

This capital, like Rome, is built on seven hills, and was put there by rich Spaniards who, finding the steamy climate of Veracruz unhealthy, preferred to conduct their business from the rainy semi-tropical hills of Jalapa. It is a typical colonial city, with fine red-tiled mansions and churches. In recent years Jalapa has become an important cultural centre; it hosts a theatre, an orchestra, a ballet company, an opera company, a large university, and a fine archaeological museum.

For a stroll around the old town, start at the central **Parque Juarez** and walk S; on the E side of the park are the government buildings where some interesting modern murals can be seen. If you are feeling energetic, the highest of the hills, **Macuiltepec**, has good views of the city and, on a clear day, of the Gulf.

Although a pleasant town, Jalapa is not on the main tourist track, and only a limited amount of its cultural life will appeal to the non-Spanish speaker; the tourist office and hotel desks will be glad to offer advice.

Museo Arqueológico *(Archaeological Museum)* ☆
W outskirts of town, on RF 140 to Mexico City *Open standard hours.*

Containing the finest collection of Olmec and Totonac art from the Gulf area, the two rooms of this museum are approached through a park, among the trees of which stand giant Olmec carved stone heads, with typical negroid lips and jaguar-like smiles. Inside, the exhibits are well laid out in two main circular rooms.

The Olmec sculptures show their mastery at all levels of work, from the colossal to the miniature. Especially fine is a green stone statue of a priest or noble, holding the jaguar-child that seems to have been the most important Olmec god.

Although of later date, Totonac art is less advanced. Its most typical products are objects of polished stone incised with intricate designs. The various forms are known as 'yokes', 'palms' and 'votive axes', but their actual function is a mystery.

In two of the smaller adjoining rooms is a collection of costumes and crafts from the native peoples of the Gulf, among them the modern Totonacs.

H **María Victoria** (*Zaragoza 6* ☎ *(281) 7-5600*) has a pleasant central location; **Xalapa** (*Victoria and Bustamante 1* ☎ *(281) 7-1700*) is the best hotel in town.

R **La Parroquía** (*Zaragoza 18* ☎ *(281) 7-4436*) serves Mexican specialities.

Lagunas de Montebello

Map 9I12. Chiapas. 142km (88 miles) SE of San Cristóbal de las Casas, turning E off RF 190 after 102km (63 miles).

There are about a hundred lakes, large and small, in the National Park of Montebello, a remote area of wild forests and mountains near the Guatemalan border. After the park entrance, the road comes first to the group known as the **Lagunas de Colores**, where each lake is a different colour. This is caused by minerals reflected in their waters; on a good day, they range from opalescent violet to emerald green. Parts of the area are now being developed for organized tourism.

At the end of the paved road is the village of **San Rafael**, where guides can be hired for more serious exploration into those depths of this extraordinarily beautiful area which still remain untouched by its increasing popularity.

Chincultic ☆
2km (1¼ miles) N of the road, 5km (3 miles) before the park entrance.

Climb the central acropolis of these Mayan ruins for a superb view of the surrounding forest and of the various pyramids, ball-courts and the deep *cenote* (well) of the old city.

León

Map 11C4. Guanajuato. 228km (141 miles) E of Guadalajara on RF 80 and RF 45. Altitude: 2,052m (6,733ft). Population: 700,000. Served by air, train (on Mexico City–Aguascalientes line) and bus. Car rental: Hertz, Blvd. López Mateos 1774 ☎ (471) 6–6020.

The largest, most industrialized of the Bajío cities. Since it has the only major airport in the region, you may find yourself spending a night here. It is not a major tourist destination in its own right.

Sights and places of interest

There are several agreeable parks near the centre, and on the Zocalo the pleasant church of **Nuestra Señora de la Luz** (1746). Behind the square is the church of **Nuestra Señora de los Angeles**, where there is a collection of religious wood-carvings. E along Madero is the magnificent 18thC church of **Templo Expiatorio**, with some ornate marble carving, plenty of gold-leaf and a fascinating catacomb underneath.

León is the leather capital of Mexico, and all around the centre are shops for footwear and riding gear.

[H] **La Estancia** (*López Mateos 1311* ☎ *(471) 6–3939* ▮▮□ *to* ▮▮▮▮□ ═) offers agreeable motel-style accommodation; another large motel with a pleasant garden is **Real de Minas** (*López Mateos s/n* ☎ *(471) 4–3677* ▮▮□ ═).

Los Mochis

Map 3E5. Sinaloa. 206km (127 miles) NW of Culiacán on RF 15. Population: 136,000. Served by air, train (on Guadalajara–Nogales and Chihuahua–Pacific lines), bus, and ferry to and from La Paz in Baja California ☎ (681) 2–0109.

The main distinctions of this agricultural town are its rich hunting and fishing hinterland and, above all, its position at the head of the spectacular railway line over the Sierra Madre from Chihuahua (see *Chihuahua* for details). The train leaves here every morning, but some are more comfortable than others: try to take the *Auto-Vía*, which runs twice weekly (timetables are subject to change). When making your hotel reservation, ask them to reserve rail tickets at the same time.

The ***Santa Anita*** hotel (see below) can also make reservations at mountain hotels for hunters and anglers, or at their own fishing lodge at **El Fuerte**, 92km (57 miles) to the NE. If you just want a day's deep-sea fishing, rent a boat from the railhead and shrimping port of **Topolobampo**, 16km (10 miles) W on the coast. While out at sea, pass by the **Isla Farallón** to enjoy the noisy spectacle of the sea-lions fighting for space in which to sun themselves.

Places of interest nearby

Guasave
60km (37 miles) SE on RF 15.
Just to the W of the road is this small town, where on Oct 7 the feast of the Rosary is celebrated in pagan style. The highlight is the performance of Mayo Indian dances, including the stag dance and the coyote dance.

Mochicahui
24km (15 miles) NE; turn NE off RF 15 after 16km (10 miles).
Follow the road alongside the railway to this Mayo pueblo, where the fiesta on June 24 involves the 'baptism' of a sacred statue in the river Fuerte, accompanied, of course, by fireworks, processions and dancing. After another 70km (44 miles), the road reaches the colonial mining town of **El Fuerte**, near a large reservoir with good fishing (see ***Santa Anita*** hotel).

Santa Anita
Hidalgo and Gabriel Leyva (681) 2-0046 to 133

This central hotel runs its own bus service to the railway station, and boasts a fine restaurant as well as a private fishing lodge for guests at ***El Fuerte*** (see above). Hunting and sightseeing trips are organized into the Sierra Tarahumara (see *Chihuahua*).

Holiday Inn (*s of town, on International Highway (681) 2-0101*).

Malinalco ★

Map 12E6. State of Mexico. 49km (30 miles) w of Cuernavaca via Ocuilán; 100km (62 miles) s of Mexico City via Cuernavaca, or RF 15 to La Marquesa and turn s.

A small Aztec ceremonial centre carved out of volcanic crags high above the plains to the w of Cuernavaca. Although easy to reach and of great beauty and interest, it is inexplicably off the beaten track for tourists. Leave your car at the end of the track which is signposted from the Zocalo in the village of Malinalco.

Events On Thurs before Good Fri and Pentecost Sun, local fiestas.

The ruins

15mins' walk up a stone stairway

The main group of ruins lies about halfway up a mountain above a village, strategically placed for the Aztec knights who were here to control the local Matlazinca population. Begun in 1501, the buildings had not been finished when the Spaniards arrived 20yrs later – such large structures were a lifetime's work for craftsmen who had no metal tools.

In the main **temple** are sculptures of a jaguar and two eagles around the walls and, in the middle of the floor, another eagle in front of a round hole used for the hearts of sacrificial victims. The other nearby structures were partly hewn from the rock and partly made of stone blocks, most of which the Spaniards hauled back down to build the church and monastery in the village. Cut into the cliffs are the remains of a drainage system.

Sight nearby

Chalma ☆
11km (7 miles) E.

A small village where religious fervour enters into full swing every Sunday. Leave your car on the main road, push down through the crowds of pilgrims and hawkers of garish religious items, and eventually you will reach the church, which contains a miraculous **statue of Christ**. This 'Christ' is probably a Pre-Columbian idol – the god of the caves beneath the church. A spring flows from them, and there are extraordinary Dante-esque scenes as all of the pilgrims try to bathe in the waters, believed to be sacred. At times of special fiestas, there are fireworks and dancing, and it is a lucky person who can even get near the church at such times.

See also *Cuernavaca* and *Toluca*.

Manzanillo

Map 10E2. Colima. 351km (217 miles) sw of Guadalajara on RF 80 and RF 200. Population: 35,000. Served by air (international airport 8km/5 miles N), train (terminus of line from Guadalajara) and bus. Car rental: Avis, at airport (333) 3-0238; Hertz, at airport (333) 3-0418 i Juarez 111 (333) 2-2090.

One of the country's most important commercial ports, with a bustling downtown area behind the cranes, railway lines and wharves. Until a new airport was opened in 1974, this was a minor tourist destination, although always a favourite with the surfing fraternity. All that is now changing, and both in and near Manzanillo, hotels and mini-resorts are springing up.

Manzanillo is on a wide double bay, with a sweeping backdrop of volcanic hills. Here the Spaniards built the galleons that set out to conquer the Philippines, but few buildings from this period remain, although in the narrow streets leading to the Zocalo there are some old, pretty wooden houses. Back around the Zocalo are arts and crafts shops selling (expensive) knick-knacks. More important are the shops selling equipment for fishing expeditions. Hotels or waterfront restaurants will help to arrange boat rental – you have more security if you do it this way; although dealing with the owners direct is cheaper, the boats are less reliable.

The beaches nearer town are quite crowded and occasionally polluted, although you will find there the full range of water-sports. The **Playa Azul** becomes more pleasant as it curves N away from the centre. Beyond the ***Las Hadas*** hotel (see below) is the small **Playa de la Audiencia**, and then the larger **Playa de Santiago** where the surf can be quite rough. Lovers of solitude will need to head farther out, but will not be disappointed. The beaches to the N are renowned for surfing.

Hotels

Club Maeva *Near Las Hadas hotel (see below)* ☎ *(333) 3–0396* 482 AE CB VISA

A self-contained beach resort which will eventually comprise 100 villas set in attractive tropical gardens. There are reciprocal arrangements with ***Las Hadas***, and both are good places to take children.

Club Santiago
Playa Miramar ☎ *(333) 3–0413* 210 AE CB VISA

The Santiago has a mixture of villas, hotel rooms and condominium apartments, but not all the rooms have air conditioning. Despite being much cheaper than ***Las Hadas*** it is still an excellent resort hotel, with facilities for all sports, some lively nightlife, and a superb beach.

Las Hadas
Peninsula de Santiago ☎ *(333) 3–0000/09* 204 AE CB VISA

One of the world's great super-luxury resorts. The fairy-tale Moorish-style village festooned with flowers provides superb sporting facilities, a well-organized social programme and almost miraculous service. Also available are villas within the grounds. A special feature of the water-sports provided is paragliding. The 'Cocktail Cruise' yacht leaves at sundown – the trip is stunningly beautiful.

Playa de Santiago
On Playa Santiago ☎ *(333) 3–0344* to 170 AE CB VISA

This used to be the best in town, and is still a good-value resort hotel, with a nice little beach and its own small island.
(mini)

La Posada
Las Brisas Peninsula ☎ *(333) 2–0805* 23 AE CB VISA

An intimate American-run hotel with striking all-pink decor and a relaxed atmosphere. Occasionally the nearby condominium apartments are available.

H In addition, there are any number of condominium hotels, apartments, suites and bungalows. These are best arranged through a travel agent beforehand. Some recommendations follow: **Arco Iris** (*9km/5 miles N* ☎ *(333) 3–0168*); **Marlyn** (*Playa Santiago* ☎ *(333) 3–0107*); **Playa Sol las Hadas** (*near Las Hadas hotel* ☎ *(333) 3–0308*); **La Siesta** (*Calle del Mar s/n* ☎ *(333) 2–0130*); **Vida del Mar** (*on Juluapán headland* ☎ *(333) 2–1818* AE CB).

Hotels nearby

Bahía Tenacatita (*90km/56 miles* N).

Tenacatita
60

Simple modern decor and restful atmosphere at this secluded beachside establishment. Good sporting facilities, and opportunities for a variety of water-sports.

Barra de Navidad (*56km/34 miles* N).

Cabo Blanco
☎ (321) 7-0182/0046 59

A small Mediterranean-style beach hotel.

Sands
☎ (321) 7-0018 to 42

Sands is for fishermen and those keen on water-sports. Simple accommodation and food.

Chihuatlán, Costa de Careyes (*39km/23 miles* N).

Club Med Playa Blanca
☎ (321) 2-0005. Reservations: Mexico City ☎ (5) 533-4800.

The place for sophisticated and well-organized holiday fun in a beautiful colonial-style resort village. They offer superb sporting facilities and as much wine as you can drink. Non-residents are not allowed in.

Restaurants

At ***Las Hadas*** (see ***Hotels***) there are two super-deluxe restaurants for that last-day-of-vacation feast. The **Terral** is a romantic dream of candles, flowers and gentle music, while the **Lazcapi** tends towards formal elegance. The cuisine in both is international, and reservations are necessary.

Restaurants nearby

The best non-hotel restaurants are on the road N to Santiago. At **El Camión Despierto** (*Centro Commercial del Puerto* ☎ *(333) 2-0505*), in the downtown area near the port, the unexciting ambience is more than compensated for by the marvellous seafood. Farther out of town, **El Dorado** (*13km/8 miles towards Santiago* ☎ *(333) 3-0102*) serves an imaginative menu amid tropical elegance; for an amazing view go to **El Faro** (*La Audiencia, Santiago* ☎ *(333) 3-0216*), which has reasonable international food; **Los Carrizos** (*Independencia 28, Santiago* ☎ *(333) 3-0014*) produces delicious grilled meats; to eat good local food in a relaxed atmosphere, try **Money Pancho's** (*12km/7 miles towards Santiago* ☎ *(333) 3-0452*).

Nightlife

Apart from those in hotels, discos come and go like summer rain. A more permanent fixture is **La Girafa** (*8km/5 miles towards Santiago* ☎ *(333) 3-0020*). Of the hotels, ***Las Hadas*** has by far the best and most expensive nightlife.

Places nearby

Heading down the coast, the road passes the tropical **Laguna Cuyutlán** after 41km (25 miles) and then arrives at a stretch of black-sand beaches. The villages along here never achieved resort status, partly because black sand becomes scorchingly hot, and also because of the vast spring waves which, while almost a tourist attraction in themselves, unfortunately bring with them masses of seaweed which subsequently decays on the beaches. The most agreeable of the villages is **Boca de Pascuales** (60km/37 miles S), where you can sit in a thatched beach hut and eat freshly-caught fish. All have simple (but no better) accommodation, and offer the independent traveller an idyllic seclusion.

See also Colima and Puerto Vallarta.

Matamoros

Map 5E9. Tamaulipas. 323km (200 miles) E of Monterrey on RF 40 and RF 2. Population: 220,000. Served by air (international airport 11km/7 miles NE), train (terminus of line from Monterrey) and bus. Car rental: Avis, Alvaro Obregón 1 ☎ (891) 3-8416, and booth at airport (no telephone) i 'Gateway to Mexico' tourist area ☎ (891) 3-7741. US Consul: Primera 232 ☎ (891) 2-5250.

So turbulent has been the history of this border town that it has a story to tell from almost every regional conflict that has taken place since its foundation in 1765. Raids by pirates, Apaches and Comanches were only the start. It was then occupied by the US Army during the 1846 war, and Maximilian's troops were besieged here at the end of the French intervention. During the American Civil War, it became an arms supply point for the Confederates. Despite all this, it is now a peaceful, prosperous border city which welcomes thousands of visitors every month who come in a vain search for Mexico.

Few stay for long; if you are here overnight, a stroll near the Zocalo should take in the French-built **theatre**, **cathedral** and **fort** – a small local museum is located in the fort (*open standard hours*), but the historical bric-à-brac is of less interest than the building in which it is housed.

Also nearby, on Calle 9, are three markets selling a variety of folk art and crafts from all over Mexico. On the outskirts of town, towards the **International Bridge** and the soaring arches of the **Gateway to Mexico**, is a large new tourist area with recreational facilities and a helpful tourist office.

H **Holiday Inn** (*Obregón 249* ☎ *(891) 2-3600*) is the best in town; **Nieto** (*10a Bravo and Bustamante 140* ☎ *(891) 2-4550*); **Ritz** (*Matamoros and Calle 7* ☎ *(891) 2-1190/94*).

Mazatlán ☆

Map 6F6. Sinaloa. 505km (313 miles) NW of Guadalajara on RF 15. Population: 150,000. Served by air (international airport 13km/8 miles S), train (on Guadalajara–Nogales line), ship (daily ferry to and from La Paz in Baja California ☎ (678) 1-7020/06-6823) and bus. Car rental: Avis, Camarón Sábalo 1000 ☎ (678) 3-6200/06-6801, and at airport ☎ (678) 2-1487; Hertz, Av. del Mar ☎ (678) 1-6303 i Claussen and Zaragoza ☎ (678) 4-0894/1-4966. US Consul: Circunvalación 6 and Venustiano Carranza ☎ (678) 1-2905.

The name of this thriving resort and port means 'Place of Deer', but it should now perhaps be rechristened 'Place of Fish', so numerous are the sportsmen who congregate here all year around to try their luck in the Sea of Cortés. Set on a peninsula, Mazatlán has two waterfronts: to the W, gleaming luxury hotels and long white-sand beaches look out over the Pacific; facing inland, over a natural harbour, are the commercial docks, always busy with luxury cruisers, freighters and trawlers, and a rather scruffy town.

The frivolous elegance of Acapulco or Puerto Vallarta would not appeal to the Mazatlán regulars, who are not jet-setters, but arrive for the most part by car – there are said to be more camper parks here than in all the rest of Mexico. They come to get value for money, a suntan and, if all their dreams come true, a 600lb marlin.

Sights and places of interest

After a hard day's fun, a stroll down the waterfront, the **Olas Altas**, is best punctuated with frequent refreshment stops. If you still feel energetic, it is a short climb up to the lighthouse on the southern tip of the peninsula, from where the views of the city are excellent. On the way, pause at **El Mirador**, where the young bloods of Mazatlán perform a perilous dive off a high rock into shallow water. Behind the Mirador is the **Cerro de la Nevería**, or Icebox Hill. Before the days of refrigerated ships, ice was stored here for shipping shrimps up to the US. The lighthouse is said to be second in height only to that at Gibraltar, and can be seen from as far as 60km (37 miles) out to sea. At sunset, you can see the ships in the distance, reflected in red and gold shimmering waters.

Hotels

There are a large number of condominium apartments for rent which can be arranged through a travel agent, as well as numerous good hotels.

Camino Real
Punta del Sábalo (678) 3-1111/2-3322 172

Mazatlán's most glamorous hotel resort, with very lively nightlife and two excellent restaurants. Linked to the beach by its own funicular railway down the cliffside.

El Cid
Playa Sábalo (678) 2-5199/4078 600

A self-contained holiday town, including six restaurants, three swimming pools, a squash club, sauna and health centre, and social programme.

Don el Guía
Playa Sábalo (678) 2-1688/1777 103

A smaller and very sophisticated beach hotel with a good variety of water-sports on offer.

Holiday Inn
Playa Sábalo (678) 3-2222/2-6222 200

A favourite place for families, as efficient as all hotels in the chain. Paragliding is available for guests.

Oceano Palace
Playa Sábalo (678) 2-0666/3-0777 200

The young jet-setters' disco-hotel. There is a cheerful restaurant, and the bars are open until all hours.

El Pescador
Playa Sábalo (678) 3-4611/2-5500 240

The rooms in this large, modern hotel are spacious, and it is much favoured for family vacations by virtue of being at the centre of things, with a lively disco and bars.

Playa del Rey
Playa Sábalo (678) 1-7520 166

Relaxed atmosphere and friendly service – ask for a room with a view of the ocean.

Puesta del Sol Quality Inn
Playa las Gaviotas (678) 3-5544/2-3366 72

A pleasant, small hotel with the personalized service lacking in some of its sister establishments, although it also lacks some of their facilities.

Playa Mazatlán
Playa las Gaviotas (678) 3-4455 to 365

The special feature here is a giant jacuzzi. The general air is lively, and social life is well organized and varied.

La Siesta
Olas Altas 11 (678) 1-2640 58

Nearer to the centre than any of the other hotels mentioned, La Siesta is the oldest, favoured by a regular clientele. The bar and disco are always entertaining and its **El Shrimp Bucket** restaurant is fun.

Restaurants

At the last count Mazatlán had around one hundred restaurants. Of the hotel restaurants, those at the ***Camino Real***, ***La Siesta*** and ***Oceano Palace*** are the best (see above).

El Camarón
Av. del Mar s/n ☎ (678) 2-6761
Seafood and steaks are served amid bullfighting decor.

Casa Lorna
Gaviotas s/n ☎ (678) 2-3434
AE CB Φ MC VISA
In this beautiful old colonial townhouse, there is a choice between well-prepared international and local cuisine.

Mamucas
Bolivar 73 ☎ (678) 1-3490
The shrimp dishes here are excellence itself, but the decor is rather basic.

Señor Frog
Av. del Mar s/n ☎ (678) 1-4367/2-1925 to
A 'fun' place indeed, specializing in delicious seafood with silly names. Not the restaurant for a quiet evening out.

R Two smaller, family-run establishments serving local dishes are **Doney** (*5 de Mayo and M. Escobedo* ☎ *(678) 1-2651*) and **Plaza de Tony** (*Plaza las Gaviotas* ☎ *(678) 2-0377*).

Nightlife

Now that the serious sportsmen are being joined by more relaxed pleasure-seekers, the nightlife of Mazatlán has become more exciting. Discos abound and are so popular that, in the smart hotels, reservations are sometimes necessary. The ***Camino Real*** has a wild, space-age light-and-sound show, but ***La Siesta*** and ***Oceano Palace*** are considered more trendy. All along the beaches there are smaller establishments which can be short-lived. But for more organized entertainment go to the 'Mexican Fiesta' at the ***Playa Mazatlán***, which happens twice weekly (*ring hotel for details*).

Sports and activities

The seasick and the abandoned families of fishermen need not fear restless inactivity. Hotels can arrange golf, tennis, or riding and hunting trips up into the hills. Game is limited but wild-fowl plentiful, and guns can be rented here.

Up on the wide northern beaches in front of the new hotels, waterskiing and paragliding are available. If business looks slack, try to bargain for a family reduction.

Mérida ☆

Map 9G12. Capital of Yucatán. 206km (127 miles) NE of Campeche on RF 180. Population: 300,000. Served by air (international airport 6km/4 miles SE), train (on line from Mexico City) and bus. Car rental: Avis, Hotel Montejo, Calle 57 no.507 ☎ (992) 3-6191, and at airport ☎ (992) 3-7849; Hertz, Hotel Panamericana, Calle 59 no.455 ☎ (992) 3-9111, and at airport ☎ (992) 1-3828 ℹ Calle 20 no.89 ☎ (992) 7-2652. US Consul: Paseo Montejo 453 ☎ (992) 7-7011.

If you stroll down the Paseo Montejo, Mérida's wide boulevard with its elegant buildings, you could almost be on the Champs Elysées. The local passer-by, on the other hand, might be straight off the Mayan murals at Bonampak. The Yucateco, with flat, almost Asiatic features, looks different from other Mexicans. Nothing is quite like the rest of Mexico here – the food, dress, manner of speech, music, or even the sense of humour. Nowhere else in the country, for instance, do you hear so many men giggling.

Until modern roads and railways linked Mérida with the rest of the Republic in the 1960s, it took almost as long to get to

Mexico City as it did to get to Paris. The wealthy owners of the sisal plantations looked to Europe for their culture, and liked to refer to Mérida as 'The Paris of the West'. The atmosphere is still a blend of Mayan and European influences, and the Yucatecos are proud of their separate identity. Most visitors to Yucatán spend a few nights in Mérida, making excursions out to the ruins. The choice of hotels is greater here than at the sites, especially for those on a budget, and in any case, it is a pleasure to stay in this lively and attractive city and mix with its courteous inhabitants.

Mérida was founded in 1542 by Don Francisco Montejo the younger, on the site of a Mayan city. An army of 60,000 Mayan Indians promptly laid siege to the new city, but were routed by a force of 250 Spaniards (Spanish figures). Because of its remoteness, the upheavals of Mexican history more or less passed Mérida by, but in the late 19thC, Yucatán was racked by its own peculiarly vicious civil war. The Mayan tribes rebelled and savagely butchered most of the whites and *mestizos* on the peninsula. Only Mérida and Campeche were able to hold out. Not until 1901, after 50yrs of fighting, were the last rebels driven down to the remote forests of Quintana Roo by the Mexican army, who then exacted their own appalling vengeance.

Mérida used to be known as 'The White City', for the white *guayaberas* (see ***Shopping***, below), the white buildings, the white sails of the artesian windmills pumping up water, and its general cleanliness. Nowadays, both shirts and houses are any colour, the windmills have disappeared, and the city is no cleaner than anywhere else.

Event There is a lively but movable Carnival Friday.
Early Oct, religious fiesta at the cathedral.

Nothing in a tropical town can fill the place of a church for the most mundane use; a church is the one spot of coolness out of the tropical sun.

Graham Greene, *The Lawless Roads*, 1939

Sights and places of interest

Mérida has streets with numbers, not names, and the point of reference is the Zocalo, **Plaza Mayor**, at the intersection of Calles 60 and 61. The odd-numbered streets run E–W, with higher numbers at the S, and even-numbered streets run N–S with higher numbers at the W.

Cathedral †
Plaza Mayor.

An oddly proportioned 16thC construction of no great intrinsic interest, but notable for the widely venerated *Christ of the Blisters*. This statue was carved in the 16thC from the wood of a tree said to have remained miraculously undamaged despite burning all night. The blisters came from another fire, from which the statue was rescued later on, although it was thought miraculous that the damage was no worse. The miracles are celebrated in early Oct with an orgy of popular devotion.

Museo Arqueológico (*Archaeological Museum*) ★
Paseo Montejo and Calle 43 ▣ *Open 10am–1pm. Closed Mon.*

A more informative introduction to the ruins of the Yucatán than any amount of reading, this excellent museum is housed in an elegant Parisian-style mansion once used by the governors of the state. The emphasis is, of course, on the Mayan culture, but exhibits from the Valleys of Oaxaca and Mexico help to place the Maya in their general context.

Perhaps most striking is a grisly collection of skulls, showing how the Maya purposely distorted the heads of their children to produce a permanent elongation. The results can be seen on the subjects of many ancient works of art.

The museum contains architectural fragments from many sites: ornamental masks, steles, large sculptures of gods, and a finely carved altar from Chichén Itzá. Smaller pieces include musical instruments and beautifully worked jade jewellery. The various masks of the gods, still with traces of paint, are impressive, and there is a rare collection of shell ornaments and copperwork. The collection of highly realistic pottery figurines from the island of Jaina shows how skilfully the Mayan craftsmen could occasionally transcend the almost universal religious symbolism of their culture.

Palacio Montejo
Plaza Mayor Open Mon–Fri 10am–noon, 4–6pm. Closed Sat, Sun.
Until 1980 this building remained in the hands of the Montejo family, for whose ancestors – a father and son who subdued the Yucatán – it was originally built in 1549. It now belongs to a bank, who have restored it to a high standard and opened most of it to the public as one of the city's best pieces of colonial architecture. Of particular interest is the magnificent Plateresque **doorway**, with carvings of Conquistadors trampling Indians underfoot.

Other sights

While in the Zocalo, take a look at the modern murals in the **Palacio de Gobierno**, painted by Pacheco. Following Calle 60 N towards the **Museo Arqueológico** leads you to a pretty little plaza on the right, the **Parque Cepeda Peraza**, facing a large library of the same name and the 17thC Jesuit Church of Jesus. A block farther on is the grand Italianate **Peón Contreras** theatre, built in 1900–8 and, opposite it, the **university**, founded in 1618 but recently modernized. Farther N, a detour down Calle 50 leads to some gates from the old city fortifications.

Hotels

Casa del Balam
Calle 60 no.78 (992) 1–9474 54
An elegant and traditional hotel, with colourful tapestries in the rooms. The pool is in a colonial courtyard, and the atmosphere relaxed and uncrowded.

Cayre
Calle 70 no.543 (992) 3–6024 100
A comfortable hotel near the Zocalo, the Cayre is housed in a splendid old colonial palace.

El Castellano
Calle 57 no.513 (992) 3–0100 to 180
Both a pleasant vacation and commercial hotel: centrally placed, with a good nightclub and shops, and comfortable, modern rooms.

Hacienda Inn
Av. Aviación 709 (992) 1–1680 68
A plush motel, located near the airport, which attracts passing motorists.

Holiday Inn
Calle 60 and Av. Colón (992) 7–8877/8555 to 211
Designed in a Neo-Mayan style, this is a new and luxurious hotel aimed at the tourist. It has a good and popular disco.

Montejo Palace
Paseo de Montejo 483 (992) 1–1641 90
A modern hotel, but built in the colonial style.

Panamericana
Calle 59 no.455 (992) 3–9111/1–7960 103
An older hotel with large, airy rooms. The upper rooms enjoy fine rooftop vistas of the city.

H Other recommended hotels are: **Alfonso García** (*Calle 86 no.587* (992) 1–6496); **Colón** (*Calle 62 no.483* (992) 3–4355 to); **María del Carmen** (*Calle 63 no.550* (992) 3–9133); **Paseo de Montejo** (*Paseo de Montejo 482* (992) 3–9033), which also has a good restaurant.

Restaurants

Alberto's Continental Patio
Calle 64 no.482 ☎ (992) 2-2298
One of Mexico's better restaurants, serving local specialities, Arabic and international dishes.

Los Almendros
Calle 59 no.434 ☎ (992) 1-2851
The best place for excellent regional dishes. Try the *pollo pibil*.

El Faisán y el Venado
Calle 59 no.617 ☎ (992) 1-8352/Calle 86 no.526 ☎ (992) 1-9955
Neo-Mayan atmosphere. Spicy game dishes are the speciality.

Las Palomas
Calle 56 no.481 ☎ (992) 3-1545
International and regional cuisine are offered in this fine old hacienda.

Soberani's
Calle 56 no.468 ☎ (992) 7-7186/Calle 62 no.503 ☎ (992) 1-8363/Calle 56 no.504 ☎ (992) 1-0288/Calle 60 on Calle Nueva ☎ (992) 1-1971
Although the decor is basic, the freshly caught seafood is delicious at this reliable and useful chain of restaurants.

Nightlife

Most of Mérida's nightlife takes place at the main hotels. The best folkloric shows happen every night at the ***Panamericana***, while the wildest disco is at the ***Holiday Inn***. At the **Misión Mérida** there is a lively 'human sacrifice' every day except Sunday. For a quieter time, head for the bar at ***El Castellano*** or the ***Casa del Balam***.

Some other places are: **Barba Azul** (*Paseo de Montejo Norte ☎ (992) 2-7834*), a lively disco; **Carrillon** (*Campestre 271*), with an international flavour; **Tulipanes** (*Calle 43*), offering a Mayan sacrifice routine and other entertainments.

For information in English on cultural events ☎ (992) 3-0123.

Shopping

Most visitors to Mérida cannot resist one of the hammocks for which it is famous. You can even buy a 'familial' size one (200 strings), but it takes years of practice for a family to sleep in one. The cheapest place to buy them is at the market on Calles 56 and 65. Hat stalls are also abundant – the best hats can be rolled up and passed through a ring; these are the true Panama hats which, curiously, have always been manufactured in Yucatán for export to Panama. Another good buy are the pleated *guayabera* shirts that have caught on all over Mexico as elegant semi-formal wear. Originally they were always white, but they can now be any colour.

Places nearby

Dzibilchaltún ☆ (*25km/15 miles NE: turn E off Progreso road after 15km/9 miles*). A Mayan ceremonial centre which was still in use when the Spaniards arrived, and a particular pleasure to visit, although of less importance than the great ruins. It was a large city, but only a small part near the central *cenote* (well) has been restored. Human remains and jewellery have been found at the bottom of the *cenote* (and swimming is allowed).

Valladolid (*160km/100 miles E on RF 180*). For lunch on the way to the coast, Valladolid is a good place to stop. While there, the 16thC monastery of St Bernard is worth a quick look.

From Valladolid, the RF 295 leads N to the Gulf Coast at **Río Lagartos** (103km/64 miles), where there are beautiful and deserted beaches. At **Tizimín**, 51km (32 miles) along this road, there is an important fiesta of the Tres Reyes (Three Kings) on Jan 1–6, which attracts pilgrims from the whole peninsula.

R At Valladolid, **Cenote Zaci** (*Calle 36 ☎ (985) 6-2107*), near a *cenote* (well), serves regional specialities including venison.

Mexicali

Map 2A2. Baja California Norte. 189km (118 miles) E of Tijuana on RF 2. Population: 400,000. Served by air (international airport 10km/6 miles SW), rail (end of line from Mexico City and Guadalajara) and bus. Car rental: Avis, Juarez 1010 ☎ (656) 83518, and at airport ☎ (656) 8-3060; Hertz, Juarez 2151 ☎ (656) 8-2244.

A popular border crossing-point at the head of the Pacific Highway. It is a prosperous agricultural town, with an 'Amexican' atmosphere. Only souvenir shops and the occasional bullfight contribute the Mexican element . . . so press on for the real Mexico.

Places nearby

To get to the main highway down *Baja California*, either head back via *Tijuana* or make a wide loop to *Ensenada*. A small road leads S to the fishing village of **San Felipe** (149km/93 miles), where boats can be rented for deep-sea fishing. Accommodation is primitive. The roads beyond here cannot be recommended for cars.

Mexico City ★

*Maps **14–16**. Distrito Federal (D.F.). 1,820km (1,138 miles) SE of US border at Ciudad Juarez. Altitude: 2,240m (7,350ft). Population: 14 million. International airport: E of the city in ZP9, served by frequent buses to downtown area. Railway station: Estación Buena Vista, Insurgentes Norte ☎ (5) 547-1084/6593. Bus stations: Terminal del Norte, Av. de los Cien Metros, ZP14 ☎ (5) 587-1552, for the N and US border; Terminal Oriente, Ignacio Zaragoza 200, ZP9 ☎ (5) 542-1582, for the E, Oaxaca and Yucatán; Terminal del Poniente, Rio Tacubaya, ZP18 ☎ (5) 567-7131, for the W Pacific coast; Terminal del Sur, Taxqueña 1320, ZP21 ☎ (5) 532-0280, for the S Pacific coast; central bus reservations at Central de Autobuses, Londres 161, Plaza del Angel, ZP6 ☎ (5) 533-2047. Car rental: Avis, Dr. Velasco 138, ZP7 ☎ (5) 578-1177 Ⓣ 1773073, and at airport ☎ (5) 762-3688; Budget, Reforma 60, ZP6 ☎ (5) 566-7923, and at airport ☎ (5) 762-0900; Hertz, Versalles 6, ZP6 ☎ (5) 566-0099 Ⓣ 1774316, and at airport ☎ (5) 762-8977; car rental booths also at all luxury hotels* ***i*** *Juarez 92, ZP1 ☎ (5) 250-0123, for information and emergencies; also Mariano Escobedo 726, ZP5 ☎ (5) 533-0540. American Express Travel Service: Hamburgo 75, Zona Rosa, ZP6 ☎ (5) 533-0380/511-0309.*

A sprawling, fascinating monster of a city, and without doubt one of the great world capitals, Mexico City seethes with cultural and artistic life, and is the intellectual focus of all Hispanic America. It has a unique anarchic vitality, the result of the bloody forced marriage in fire and steel of the Spanish and Pre-Columbian civilizations, but now transcending both. The kaleidoscopic and turbulent past has left its mark everywhere, on the buildings, the political institutions, and most important, on the people themselves. As well as tourists, many distinguished refugees from more oppressive regimes of right and left have found here a tolerant haven; their contributions are Mexico's gain.

The colonial heart of the city is the **Zocalo**, the great main square, with the **Palacio Nacional** and the **Catedral Metropolitana**. Here and in the surrounding area it is only necessary to raise the eyes above the commercial bustle at street level to glimpse the gracious capital of the viceroys of New Spain. The centre of the Aztec capital of Tenochtitlán was also here, built on artificial islands in the lake which then filled the Valley of Mexico. When Cortés and his men first marched over the mountains and caught sight of the silver-glinting pyramids, they were entranced by its beauty. Nonetheless, they tore it down stone by stone, using the temples as quarries for their own churches and palaces. Behind the cathedral, some colonial buildings have recently been demolished and archaeologists have reconstructed the base of the Aztec Great Temple, the **Templo Mayor**. Cortés would have turned in his grave, but this bold homage to the past is proof of Mexicans' belief in the mixed origins of their race and culture.

Mexico City's main avenue, the grandiose and tree-lined **Paseo de la Reforma**, passes a few blocks from the colonial area. It was laid out in the 19thC as a new Champs-Elysées, although at the time it passed mostly through countryside. Since then, the explosive growth of the city has justified the planners – it takes an hour to drive out of the city in either direction to reach the open fields. To the N, Reforma leads to the holiest shrine in the country, the **Basilica de Nuestra Señora de Guadalupe**, shrine of the Virgin, patron saint of all the country. To the W, it first passes the **Zona Rosa** (Pink Zone), the smartest commercial area, near where the best shops, restaurants and hotels are concentrated. Then it comes to the city's green lung, **Bosque de Chapultepec** (Chapultepec Park), where every visitor should spend a day at the stunning **Museo Nacional de Antropología** seeing the best of Pre-Columbian art amid the finest of modern Mexican architecture.

Despite all this, nobody can deny that Mexico City has alarming problems to face. Every day the grim slums spread farther across the old dried-up lake bed, and up onto the slopes of the encircling volcanoes; the shanty town of Netzahualcoyotl, E of the centre, is already in theory the country's second largest city, with millions of inhabitants. Every day industry and vehicles pour thousands of tons of polluting chemicals into the thin mountain air, while the labyrinthine expressways become more congested. The snow-covered peaks of *Popocatepetl* and Ixtaccihuatl can hardly ever be seen, yet not so long ago they were a familiar and well-loved part of the city skyline. At present rates of growth the population will rise to 25 million by the year 2000, making it the largest city in the world. If that happens, the traffic jams will last all night as well as all day, and the city will literally be choking to death. No doubt something will be done, maybe too little and too late, but just enough to keep life tolerable for inhabitants and visitors. Even so, it is hard not to feel optimistic about a city that has so much energy and life.

The result of these urban problems is that affluent Mexicans prefer to live well away from the centre. Many have built luxurious villas on the wooded hills to the W, out past **Chapultepec Park** on Reforma. Others prefer the old houses of the charming colonial villages to the S of the city. Places such as **San Angel** and **Coyoacán** have retained their character, despite having been surrounded by the city.

Despite the minor irritations and hazards of life in the 'Distrito Federal', a visit to Mexico is incomplete without spending at least a few days in the capital. In so many ways it epitomizes the whole country – in everyday conversation, it is often referred to simply as *Mexico*, while the country is called

La república. Quite apart from the multitude of sights, the city's hotels, restaurants, nightclubs and shops rank among the best in the world. Within easy reach of the city lies a galaxy of archaeological sites and colonial monuments; even on a day-trip it is possible to combine these with a long forest walk around mountain lakes, and a visit to a bustling native market.

If the history of a city can be expressed in its buildings, then the **Plaza de las Tres Culturas** (Square of the Three Cultures) sums it up for Mexico. In the middle of a large housing development to the N of the centre stand the restored remains of the Aztec centre of Tlatelolco. By their side are a fine colonial church and a soaring modern skyscraper. In the middle of the plaza is a plaque inscribed 'On the 13th of August 1521, defended by the heroic Cuauhtemoc, Tlatelolco fell under the power of Hernán Cortés. It was neither a triumph nor a defeat, but the painful birth of the mixed race that is the Mexico of today.' By one of history's cruel and symbolic ironies, Tlatelolco was also the scene of a massacre of students by police and army units during protests before the 1968 Olympic Games. Hundreds died and were buried in unknown graves in yet another episode of this 'painful birth'.

Events In Sept, Independence Day. Vast crowds gather on the evening of Sept 15 for the President's traditional *grito* (shout) at 11pm, followed by fireworks and much throwing of flour and eggs (which can get rough); there is a 5hr military parade the following morning; good views of both from the Hotel Majestic's terrace restaurant.

On Dec 12, Día de Guadalupe. Millions of pilgrims gather at the Basilica of Guadalupe for the feast of Mexico's patron saint; very colourful but also very crowded.

See also ***Calendar of events*** in *Planning*.

Sights and places of interest

Mexico City's sights are concentrated in quite distinct areas which are most conveniently explored separately. The sights and places of interest are therefore grouped together in these areas and arranged in alphabetical order. The following list identifies and explains the main area headings, and includes the sights described under each.

West of the centre
Sights in and around Chapultepec Park
Castillo de Chapultepec
Museo de Arte Moderno
Museo Nacional de Antropología

The centre
Sights in and around the Zocalo, followed by three suggested excursions in the city centre
Alameda Central
Catedral Metropolitana
Monte Nacional de Piedad
Museo Nacional de Arte
Palacio de Bellas Artes
Palacio Nacional
Templo Mayor
North and east of the Zocalo (excursion)
South of the Zocalo (excursion)
West towards the Alameda Central (excursion)

North of the centre
Basilica de Nuestra Señora de Guadalupe
Plaza de las Tres Culturas
Pyramid of Tenayuca

South of the centre
Sights, followed by two suggested excursions
Convento de Churubusco
Copilco
Cuicuilco
Museo Rivera
Poliforum Cultural Siqueiros
University City
Xochimilco
East of the Monumento Obregón (excursion)
West of the Monumento Obregón (excursion)

Walks near the city
Ajusco
Desierto de los Leones
Lagunas de Zempoala

West of the centre

From the heart of Mexico City, the **Paseo de la Reforma** sweeps W to the huge **Bosque de Chapultepec** (Chapultepec Park) (*map 14D2*), and its numerous sights.

The main part of the park is on the other side of Reforma from the **Museo Nacional de Antropología**. It is the largest park in the city, with several museums, an amusement park, zoo, boating lake and luxury restaurant. The best day to visit is Sunday – especially if you like seeing a lot of people enjoying themselves. The **Museum of Technology** and **Museum of Natural History** (*both*) may be worth a visit for those with children. It is inadvisable to enter the park on foot after dark.

Castillo de Chapultepec (*Chapultepec Castle*) ☆
Map 14D2. Chapultepec Park. Castle, museum and gallery open Tues–Sat 9am–5.30pm, Sun 10am–1.30pm; closed Mon.

This imposing 18thC building up on the hill overlooking Chapultepec Park houses the **Museum of National History** () containing a collection of memorabilia and bric-à-brac from the Conquest up to the 1910 Revolution. There are also vivid 1930s frescoes by the great Marxist muralists, Siqueiros, Orozco and O'Gorman, showing their polemical interpretation of Mexican history. The Emperor Maximilian, during his short and ill-starred reign, had rooms here, which can be visited. His richly decorated Imperial Coach is on display, providing a striking contrast to the simple coach used by his rival, Benito Juarez, as the actual seat of the provisional government during Juarez' evasion of Maximilian's troops. Beneath the castle, these and other important episodes in Mexico's history are depicted in the three-dimensional son-et-lumière **Gallery of History** ☆ ().

Museo de Arte Moderno (*Museum of Modern Art*) ☆
Map 14D3. Chapultepec Park. Open 10am–5pm. Closed Mon.

An interesting modern building at the end of the park by the impressive marble **monument to the Niños Héroes** (Boy Heroes). In 1847, these six cadets leaped to their deaths from Chapultepec Castle after fighting against the invading Americans. The museum has a good permanent collection of Mexican art, and there are frequent visiting exhibitions of work by major foreign artists.

Museo Nacional de Antropología (*National Museum of Anthropology*) ★
Map 14D2. Reforma, opposite Chapultepec Park. Open Tues–Sat 9am–7pm, Sun 10am–6pm. Closed Mon.

This unique museum, itself a stunning example of modern architecture, contains an unrivalled collection of Pre-Hispanic treasures, and the displays are so imaginative and effortlessly informative that even a confirmed museum-hater must be enthralled. Even the **mural decorations** by Rufino Tamayo, not actually part of the exhibitions, demand considerable attention. So many cultures and civilizations are represented, including those of the indigenous peoples of modern Mexico, that it is impossible to do them all justice in a single visit; try to come several times during your stay, seeing just one room at a time.

The museum's entrance off Reforma is guarded by a giant statue found near the capital, thought to be of the rain god, Tlaloc; on the day that it was moved here, Mexico City was drenched by unseasonal rain. The galleries are on two floors around the courtyard; the ground floor houses the Pre-Hispanic collections, with one room given over to each main cultural group; upstairs are the modern native items. In each case, it makes sense to concentrate on areas of the country which you plan to visit.

On the left of the foyer is the bookstall, which has an excellent selection of maps, cards, and books on archaeology. Over on the right are the temporary exhibition rooms, where the latest finds from various excavations are displayed. To reach the permanent galleries, head into the central court under the amazing **umbrella fountain**.

Start on the right with the three small galleries containing an introduction to anthropology and to the development of Mesoamerican civilization; these rooms can be omitted from a hurried visit. The next three rooms are given over to the three main periods of civilization in the Valley of Mexico: the Pre-Classic, the Classic (Teotihuacán), and the Post-Classic (Toltec and Aztec).

In the **Pre-Classic Room**, see especially the pottery figurines from Tlatilco, and the 'Acrobat's Vase' from near the same site; the life and imagination in these simple pieces remain fresh after hundreds of years. In the **Teotihuacán Room**, the inlaid funerary masks are the main attraction. The **Toltec Room** is smaller and less interesting, but the adjacent **Aztec Room** is not to be missed, especially after the recent finds at the ***Templo Mayor***. The centrepiece is the **Aztec calendar**, a 25-tonne circular basalt stone, which bears engravings symbolizing the Aztec system for measuring time, a vital part of their cosmology and religion.

The Aztec room is at the end of the courtyard. Back down the other side are the rooms dealing with civilizations from other parts of Mexico. First come the civilizations of the Valley of Oaxaca: the Classic Zapotecs, and the Post-Classic Mixtecs. The latter were famous for their especially fine pottery and jewellery. The next room goes back in time to the Olmecs of the Gulf coast, the first important culture of Mesoamerica, whose sculpture was highly accomplished at all scales, from giant monolithic heads down to beautifully carved miniature jade figurines. Next door is the room of the Mayan people, the most advanced civilization of Mesoamerica.

Outside the room, in the garden, are reproductions of the famous mural paintings from the remote jungle site of *Bonampak*. Finally comes a room of artifacts from the N and W of Mexico; both areas were remote from the more advanced cultures but, in the W especially, a high artistic level was reached. See in particular the delightful little pottery figurines, illustrating every aspect of everyday life.

The first-floor galleries are devoted to the modern descendants of the Pre-Hispanic master-craftsmen. In much of the country the traditional costumes and customs are disappearing fast, so this may be the best chance to see life as it existed for the Mexican Indian for countless centuries, up until only a few years ago.

Free guided tours of the museum are available in Spanish, but a small fee is charged for other languages. The large catalogue serves not only as a guide, but as an excellent reference book for all the civilizations of Mesoamerica.

Museo Rufino Tamayo (*Rufino Tamayo Museum*)
Map 14D3. Reforma, opposite Museo de Arte Moderno Open 10am–7pm.
An interesting modern building, but the permanent art collection is disappointing. Excellent temporary exhibitions are staged from time to time, however; they are advertized in the press and on large boards which can be seen from Reforma.

The centre

At the centre of every town of New Spain, the main church and government buildings were built around a wide parade ground. In the middle was a pedestal (*zocalo* in Spanish) waiting to receive a statue of the Spanish monarch. When the statues failed to arrive on time, the word *zocalo* became universal slang in Mexican Spanish for the whole square.

Known formally as Plaza de la Constitución, Mexico City's **Zocalo** (*map 16C7*) is the largest and most grandiose in the country, and on a world scale is second in size only to Red Square in Moscow. It was built over the great Aztec marketplace of Tenochtitlán, whose stones were used to construct the **cathedral** and the original **Palacio Nacional**.

Concentrated around the Zocalo is a wealth of sights, highlights of which are individually described in alphabetical order. These are followed by three suggested excursions radiating from the Zocalo, which incorporate numerous other places of interest.

Alameda Central (*Alameda Park*)
Map 16C6
This pleasantly shaded park was laid out in the 16thC as a suitable venue for the burning of heretics. Starting at the western end, the former

monastery of San Diego, now the **Pinacoteca Virreinal museum** (▣ *open 10am–7pm, closed Mon*), houses a collection of colonial paintings, and the chapel contains a 1959 mural by Cantu depicting monastic life.

From here, walk down the W side of the park and over the wide shopping street of Juarez to the **Hotel del Prado**. In the foyer is the huge mural by Rivera, *A Sunday Afternoon Dream in the Alameda* ☆ showing important characters in Mexico's history strolling around the park. Also on Juarez and facing the middle of the Alameda is a **museum of popular arts** (▣ *open during shopping hours*), housed in the old church of Corpus Christi; many of the crafts exhibited are for sale. Cross the park for the two adjacent 17thC churches of **Santa Veracruz** and **San Juan de Díos**.

Catedral Metropolitana (*Cathedral*) 🏛 † ☆
Map 16C7. N side of the Zocalo.

The largest church in Mexico, the cathedral was originally meant to have been built in Lima, Peru, but the plans got mixed up and, once the mistake had been discovered, it was decided to leave things as they were. The cathedral then took two-and-a-half centuries (1573–1813) to complete, encompassing a wide variety of architectural styles. The facade has both Neoclassical and Baroque elements, while altars inside are in the heavily ornamented Churrigueresque style. Unfortunately many of them were destroyed in a disastrous fire in 1967.

The adjacent 18thC church, the **Sagrario**, was built to house sacred vestments and treasures from the archbishopric, and possesses one of the finest Churrigueresque facades in the country.

Monte Nacional de Piedad (*National Pawnshop*)
Map 16C7. On the NW corner of the Zocalo ▣ Open Mon–Fri 10am–2pm, 5–7pm; Sat 10am–2pm. Closed Sun.

This 18thC building functions as a giant pawnshop. Walk in and stroll around the amazing variety of objects left by the needy to secure loans. These are mostly jewellery, antiques and furniture – larger items such as cars and washing machines are now handled elsewhere. Prices of unredeemed objects are not especially low, but you may find something you like at one of the occasional sales, which are advertised in the press.

Museo Nacional de Arte (*National Museum of Art*) ★
Map 16C6. Calle de Tacuba 8, near the Alameda Park ▣ Open 10am–5.30pm. Closed Mon.

The building which houses this new museum, opened in 1982, was until then merely the Ministry of Telegraphs, yet it is so grandiose that it might have been a presidential palace. The collections range from Pre-Columbian to the present, with examples of the very best from each epoch. It is fascinating to see the broad sweep of Mexican cultural history under one roof, and it is worthwhile coming here more than once.

Start on the second floor, where the first room is devoted to the history of the building itself. In the other rooms, the works are divided by period and also, more imaginatively, by theme and technique.

The **Pre-Hispanic rooms** (2 and 3) are disappointingly small, but there are some well-chosen pieces, such as the exquisitely carved Mayan altar, and a large Aztec carving of a snail from the ruins of the ***Templo Mayor***. **Colonial art** is well represented (Rms. 4–7), mostly by religious works which originally hung in churches. On the same floor, a 19thC room contains landscapes by foreign artists travelling in Mexico, all straining to capture the country's wild splendour and great open skies.

With the exception of engravings, all 20thC art is on the first floor. A room is given over to popular or folk art, and its influence on modern Mexican art is easily seen by comparing the works in other rooms.

Palacio de Bellas Artes (*Palace of the Fine Arts*) 🏛 ☆
Map 16C6. At E end of the Alameda Park ▣ Open Mon–Sat 10am–5.30pm, Sun 10am–1.30pm.

A grandiose Italianate palace, containing an opulent theatre, recital room, and collections of paintings and murals. The building, completed in weighty Italian marble in 1934, has sunk an average of 9cm (3½ ins) every year into the soft soil. It is the home of the **Ballet Folklórico** (see *Mexico City/Nightlife*), which every visitor to Mexico should try to see at least once. Those who cannot go to a performance should at least see the remarkable **Tiffany glass curtain** in the proscenium arch.

Palacio Nacional (*National Palace*) 🏛 ☆
Map 16C7. On the Zocalo ▣ Open irregularly 10am–1pm. Closed Mon.

Frequently rebuilt through the centuries, the Palacio Nacional has been used by all Mexico's rulers from Cortés onwards. The central courtyard, passing under the **Bell of Liberty** (see *Dolores Hidalgo*), is open to visitors. On Independence Day (Sept 15), the President rings the bell at 11pm to signal the start of celebrations. Around the grand stair and galleries of the courtyard are **murals** by Diego Rivera illustrating various scenes from Mexican history. In the left hand courtyard is a small **museum** (*open Mon–Sat 10am–8pm, Sun 10am–1pm*) dedicated to the memory of Benito Juarez.

Templo Mayor ☆

Map 16C7. Calle de Guatemala, behind the cathedral Open standard hours.

After the Conquistadors destroyed the Aztec city of Tenochtitlán and built over the ruins using the same stones, it was thought that Tenochtitlán had disappeared forever. Descriptions by Spanish chroniclers, and their inaccurate sketches, enabled archaeologists to make theoretical reconstructions. It was known that the main temple enclosure was nearly 0.5km (⅓ mile) square, and contained around a hundred buildings, including temples on pyramid bases, altars of skulls (*tzompantli*), ball-courts for the sacred game, houses for pilgrims, and the palaces of nobles. The city was on a largely man-made island in a lake, and was linked to the mainland by wide causeways.

The main temple was surmised to be under the cathedral. It was therefore a great discovery when, in 1977, workmen of the electricity company uncovered the base of the temple while excavating. The surrounding buildings were compulsorily purchased and demolished, and the work of reconstruction then started in earnest, ending in 1982. The base of the pyramid was about 80 by 100m (90 by 110yds); it had steep stepped sides, with two parallel staircases up the W front, leading to a terrace at a height of 30m (90ft). Set back from the stairs were two tall temples, one dedicated to the god of fertility and rain, Tlaloc, the other to the Aztec tribal god of war and the sun, Huitzilopochtli. This dualism was fundamental to the Aztec system of beliefs.

The quantity and quality of the archaeological finds during the excavations far surpassed anything previous, and included statues, weapons, everyday objects, and jewellery from all over Mesoamerica. Their significance is still being assessed, but is certain to lead to a major reappraisal of the importance of the Aztecs in the development of Pre-Hispanic art. Some of the best pieces have joined the permanent displays at the ***Museo Nacional de Antropología***; others are shown at a small museum near the site.

North and east of the Zocalo

Map 16C7.

This and the following two areas of the centre are each most conveniently explored on foot. Leaving the Zocalo with the cathedral on your right, walk N up Brasil three blocks to the charming little Plaza Santo Domingo. Colonial mansions line the S and E sides, on the W side stands a gallery occupied by professional letter-writers, while to the N is the Baroque church of **Santo Domingo**.

Go back a block, turn left into Donceles, and on the left is the church of **La Enseñanza**, notable for its exuberantly ornamented Churrigueresque high altar. One block farther down Donceles, on the left, is the former Jesuit college of **San Ildefonso** † which now contains a school. In the courtyards (*open 9am–2pm, closed Sat, Sun*) are **murals** by Rivera, Orozco and Siqueiros.

Continue E down Donceles (here called Justo Sierra), then turn left into Loreto, thereby reaching the nearby Plaza Loreto. Inside the elegant Neoclassical church of **Santa Loreto**, be sure to see the religious oil paintings ☆ by the Zapotec Indian painter Miguel Cabrera (*died* 1768). The other church on the plaza, **Santa Teresa**, is also worth a quick visit.

Walking back down Loreto, turn left after three blocks into Emiliano Zapata to visit the gracious church of **La Santísima Trinidad**, the bell tower of which is fashioned to resemble a pope's crown. Then head W for the Zocalo, down Zapata which becomes the pedestrian precinct Moneda. On the left after two blocks is the **Museo de San Carlos** (*open 10am–6pm, closed Mon*), known also as the Academy of the Three Noble Arts. This contains works by colonial artists, and some lesser known paintings by European masters such as Bosch, Rubens and Murillo.

Finally, by the Zocalo, in the same block as the Palacio Nacional, on the left, is the great carved wooden door of the **Museo Nacional de las Culturas** (*open 9am–6pm, closed Fri*). The collections themselves are of no great interest, being mostly reproductions. However, the old mansion in which they are housed, with its arcaded court, fountain and flowers, is an agreeable place to sit and recover after the walk.

South of the Zocalo

Map 16C6&7.

Leave the Zocalo with the Palacio Nacional immediately to the left, and head S down Pino Suarez, past the Supreme Court of Justice on your left. On the left, at the end of the third block from the Zocalo, is the old 18thC mansion of the Counts of Santiago, now the **Museo de la Ciudad de Mexico**, or Museum of the City of Mexico (*open 10am–5.30pm, closed Mon*). Here can be seen assorted historical memorabilia and an interesting model of the city centre of Tenochtitlán. On the corner of the building are some re-used stones bearing Aztec carvings.

A block farther down the street, on the right, is the church of **Jesús de Nazareth**, burial place of Hernán Cortés, whose vault displays an alarming mural by Orozco painted in 1944, illustrating the Book of Revelations. Five minutes' walk away is the **Metro station of Pino Suarez**, where Aztec ruins were found during construction; these have been preserved, and are worth a look.

To continue the walk, turn right, walk three blocks W, then turn right again up Isabel la Catolica. Four blocks away is the **Biblioteca Nacional**, the national library (*open 9am–1.30pm, closed Sun*), housed in the huge old Baroque church of San Agustín. Two blocks farther N is the busy shopping street of 16 de Septiembre. Turn right to return to the Zocalo.

West towards the Alameda Central

Map 16C6.

Leave the Zocalo on Madero, with the Merchants Arcade on the left. At the beginning of the third block on the right is the 18thC Jesuit church of **La Profesa**, with an especially fine Baroque doorway. Another two-and-a-half blocks on the left is the magnificent **Palacio Iturbide** (Iturbide Palace) where the hapless would-be Emperor of Mexico, Agustin Iturbide, lived in 1821–22. It is now used by the Banco de Mexico; visitors are allowed into the courtyard during office hours, and paintings are sometimes on show.

Next, on the right, is the unmistakable 16thC **Casa de los Azulejos** or House of Tiles ☆ (*open during shopping hours*). The facade of this pretty colonial residence is entirely covered in blue and white Puebla tiles. The great courtyard, roofed in amber-coloured glass, is used as a restaurant by ***Sanborn's***; be sure to stop here for at least a coffee (see *Mexico City/Restaurants*). Opposite is the equally unmistakable **Torre Latino Americana** (*open 10am–11pm,*); from the observation deck on the 44th floor there are good views of the city or, more likely, of the photochemical smog. This is the tallest building in any earthquake zone; but rest assured that it has survived some mighty shakes.

Next to the tower, also on Madero, is the church of **San Francisco**. It once belonged to a monastery, the central Franciscan headquarters for all New Spain, which was demolished during the anti-clerical period in the 19thC. The church was gutted at the same time, although the especially fine Churrigueresque doorway remains. From here, the Alameda Park is only a block away.

North of the centre

The following principal sights to the N of the city are all within easy reach of the centre and can therefore be conveniently visited as a group.

Basilica de Nuestra Señora de Guadalupe (*Shrine of the Virgin of Guadalupe*) ☆

At end of Calzada de Guadalupe.

Reforma Norte continues N of the ***Plaza de las Tres Culturas*** (see below), changing its name to become Calzada de Guadalupe and ending in front of this huge modern basilica.

The Virgin of Guadalupe has been Mexico's patron saint since 1531, when the Virgin appeared to a humble peasant, informing him of her wish to have her shrine built on this spot. The local bishop was sceptical, but the Virgin appeared again, telling the peasant to return to pick the roses that he would find miraculously growing there. This he did, wrapping them in his cloak to show the bishop. When he arrived, the cloak was found to bear an image of the Virgin, and a church was built to house it.

The Virgin rapidly gained popularity, partly because of her Indian features and partly because her church was built on the site of the temple of a Pre-Columbian goddess. She was the symbol of the 1810 revolutionaries, and millions of reproductions of the miraculous image are to be found in cars, homes, factories and churches. Every year on December 12 vast crowds of pilgrims gather to venerate the Virgin with fervent religious devotions punctuated by magnificent firework displays.

Next door is the **old basilica**, a large colonial church of no great merit, and behind it the **Capilla del Pocito**, marking the place where a well materialized miraculously during an apparition of the Virgin. The **Capilla de las Rosas**, where the roses were gathered, can also be visited. In the **Capilla del Tepeyac**, on the hill, are murals depicting all the miraculous episodes previously mentioned.

Plaza de las Tres Culturas *(Square of the Three Cultures)* ☆
Map 16A6. Reforma Norte. 3km (2 miles) N *of the city centre.*
The symbolic importance of the place where the Aztecs met their final defeat is described in the introduction to *Mexico City*. Both the **Aztec ruins** and **colonial church** are interesting.

Pyramid of Tenayuca 🏛 ☆
4km (2½ miles) E *of Calzada Vallejo* 🎫 🚗 *Open 10am–6pm. Closed Mon. Calzada Vallejo forks left from Insurgentes Norte at the Monumento de la Raza; the ruins are then signposted to the right.*
These are smaller than the ruins of *Teotihuacán* but much closer to the centre of the city, and can be combined with a visit to the ***Basilica de Guadalupe***. The main pyramid contains no less than five earlier pyramids, and was itself built over once, although this seventh layer has disappeared. The first pyramid, dating from about the 13thC, was built by the predecessors of the Aztecs. Of particular interest is the row of serpents' heads along the base of the pyramid – there were originally about 750, but over the years some have disappeared.

South of the centre

Where Insurgentes Sur passes through the wealthy suburb of San Angel, the **Monumento Obregón** provides a useful reference point for visiting the many interesting and varied sights in this outer part of the metropolis. The highlights are described in alphabetical order. These are followed by two suggested excursions starting from the monument; both are within walking distance and include numerous other sights.

Convento de Churubusco
Between División del Norte and Calzada Tlalpán on Churubusco 🎫 *Open 9am–1pm, 3–5pm. Closed Mon.*
An old Franciscan monastery in well-kept grounds. A battle took place here in 1847 between Mexican and US troops and, as a result, it has been turned into a museum dedicated to the history of foreign military interventions in Mexico. Most foreigners will find something here to be embarrassed about.

Copilco ☆
🎫 🚗 *Open 10am–6pm. Closed Mon. Take Insurgentes Sur 1km (½ mile)* S *of the Monumento Obregón, turn left (*S*) into Av. Copilco, then left again following signposts to the site.*
Under the thick layer of lava that covers most of this archaeological site, various tombs – some of them 3,500yrs old – have been discovered. The tunnels used for the excavation now form a **museum** where pottery, obsidian tools and skeletons from the graves are displayed. The great heat and pressure from the volcanic eruption has twisted and deformed the bones.

Cuicuilco ☆
To the left of Insurgentes Sur, just after the Periférico. Site and museum both 🎫 *and open 9am–6pm, closed Mon* 🚗
The archaeological site of Cuicuilco, a circular pyramid of great antiquity, lay covered by lava for thousands of years until excavations,

using high explosives, began in 1922. On the site is a small **museum** containing artifacts from Cuicuilco and from contemporary sites all over central Mexico.

Museo Diego Rivera ★

Calle del Museo *Open 10am–6pm. Closed Sun, Mon and Dec 15–Jan 5.*

A massive and sombre building, designed by the famous muralist Diego Rivera to house his magnificent Pre-Hispanic collection. In the entrance hall, a stone plaque bears Rivera's dedication of the museum: 'I return to the people the artistic heritage which I was able to redeem from their ancestors.'

The ground floor houses collections of pieces from the three main civilizations of the Valley of Mexico: Teotihuacán, Toltec and Aztec. Especially fine are the lifesize Teotihuacán **funerary stone masks**. Some of the rooms are devoted to Pre-Hispanic gods common to all three cultures, emphasizing the importance of the ancient religious symbolisms for Rivera's art.

The first floor is dominated by the great central room which Rivera intended to use as a studio, although he died before the building was completed. It contains charcoal studies for murals, unfinished paintings, and Pre-Hispanic pieces from the cultures of western Mexico, which also fill the other rooms on the first floor. It is in this area that Rivera's collection surpasses all others, even that in the Museo Nacional de

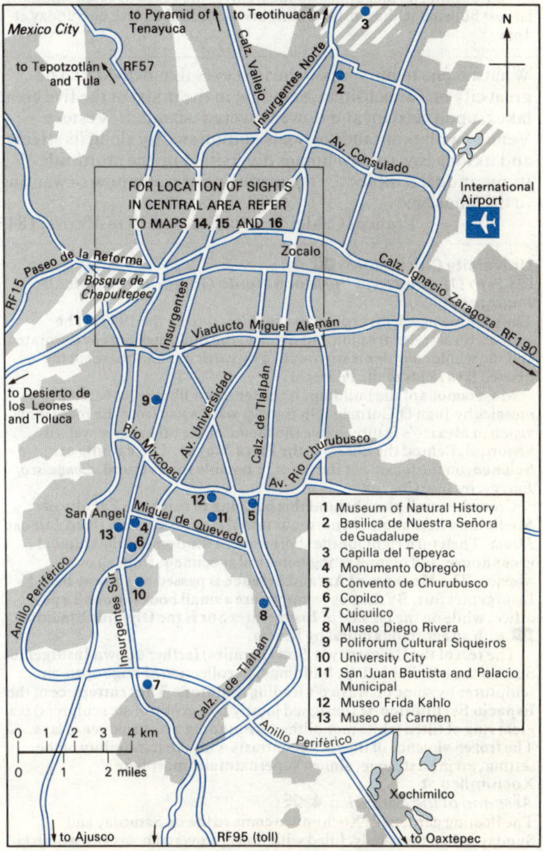

Antropología. The most important exhibit in the main room is the **ball-game** from the state of Nayarit, a model of players, spectators and the actual court of the sacred ball-game; its vivid realism is rare in Mesoamerican art. See also the charming little potbellied dogs from Colima. Known as *escuintles*, they were highly valued as a delicacy by all Pre-Hispanic peoples.

On the smaller top floor are further Aztec pieces, and some Totonac work from the E coast. Although their region was removed from the mainstream of civilization, the Rivera collection shows that the Totonacs were artistically accomplished. The most remarkable piece is a **head of a coyote**, with a collar and enormous ears. Among the other pieces are several small 'smiling faces'; it is rare to see such joyous expressions in Mesoamerican art, which tended to take an austere and dramatic view of the world.

On the Sunday nearest to Dec 8, Rivera's birthday is celebrated with Indian dancing all day on the patio of the museum.

Poliforum Cultural Siqueiros ☆
Insurgentes Sur 700. 3km (2 miles) S of centre
A large, strange, modern building, providing space for a great variety of cultural performances. It also has a good selection of folk art on display, mostly for sale. The walls are covered in passionately Marxist murals by David Siqueiros, paid for by the wealthy capitalist who financed the centre.

1km (½ mile) farther S, also on the right, is the **Plaza Mexico**, the largest bullring in the world. Bullfights usually take place on Sunday at 4pm.

What a scene to burst upon the first eyes that beheld it: The great city of Tenochtitlán, standing in the midst of the five great lakes, upon verdant and flower covered islands, a Western Venice, with thousands of boats gliding swiftly along its streets, and its long rows of low homes diversified by the multitude of its pyramidal temples . . . the profusion of water now so wanting to the landscape . . . .

Frances Calderón de la Barca, *Life in Mexico*, 1843

University City *(UNAM)* ☆
2km (1¼ miles) S of the Monumento Obregón, turn left off Insurgentes Sur.
The exciting new University City was built during the 1950s. The architectural styles are bold and diverse, the buildings heavily decorated, and the whole complex is surrounded by gardens and squares in the twisted lava fields of the Pedregal.

Most famous of the buildings is the ten-floor **library**, covered in mosaics by Juan O'Gorman. On the east wall (away from the road) is his vision of Mexico's future, while the theme of the other three walls is historical. Behind the library is the **Plaza Mayor**. The **Faculty of Science**, on the far side of the plaza, is notable for its mural, *Conquest of Energy*, by José Chavez.

Cross the small plaza behind this building to reach the **Faculty of Medicine** where another enormous mural is appropriately titled *Life and Death*. Then turn right for the short walk to the dome of the **tropical greenhouse**, full of interesting botanical specimens from all over Mexico. The **Museum of Art and Science** is passed on the way back to Insurgentes Sur. By the bus terminus are a small bookstore and a post office, while on the far side of Insurgentes Sur is the **Olympic Stadium** with an enormous mural by Rivera.

The rest of the University is 2km (1¼ miles) farther S down Insurgentes Sur, on the left. Behind the buildings is a collection of huge open-air sculptures by some of Mexico's leading sculptors. The centrepiece of the **Espacio Escultórico** ☆ (designed jointly by a group of six sculptors) is a great ring of tilted white monoliths surrounding a tortured sea of lava. The frozen violence of the rocks contrasts with the tranquillity of the setting, giving a strange, almost supernatural atmosphere.

Xochimilco ☆
At SE end of the Periférico
The floating gardens of Xochimilco come to life on Saturday and Sunday, when the canals, filled with flower-covered boats and *mariachi*

bands, become the scene of an agreeably languid water-borne carnival. Just as the gardens of Babylon were not hanging, however, these gardens are not actually floating, but are little artificial islands. The Aztec word for them was *chinampas*, and all of Tenochtitlán's fruit and vegetables were grown on these islands. Even today, Xochimilco provides a proportion of Mexico City's needs in this respect.

Boats, each with a gondolier, can be rented (*in daylight hours*) on a fixed hourly rate. Take a picnic and some cold drinks, and go off to explore some of the quieter backwaters.

Recently there has been much concern over the falling water level in the canals and the infestation of water hyacinths which threatens to take over, and it is feared that the days of the canals may be numbered.

East of the Monumento Obregón

A taxi is recommended for the foot-weary.

Starting at the monument, turn right down Insurgentes Sur then right again down Miguel de Quevedo, and at the roundabout turn left into Universidad. On the right is an interesting modern **church** designed by Mexico's well-known modern architect, Felix Candela. Opposite, over Francisco Sosa, is an 18thC Baroque **chapel**.

It is about 25mins' walk along Francisco Sosa to the central plaza of **Coyoacán**, a pleasant, narrow street of low colonial houses now providing homes for affluent Mexicans. Like San Angel to the W of the Monumento Obregón, Coyoacán was once an independent village which, although swallowed up by the city, has lost little of its charm in the process. On the plaza, see the early colonial church of **San Juan Bautista** and the **Palacio Municipal**, said to have been built for Cortés. On Sat and Sun there is a lively market here with bookstalls.

From the plaza, head N up Centenario for six blocks, then turn right into Londres. At no.127 is the **Museo Frida Kahlo** ☆ (*open 10am–6pm, closed Mon*), studio of the artist who for many years was married to Diego Rivera. It contains a large number of Kahlo's works and some of Rivera's, as well as a large collection of Pre-Columbian, colonial and folk art. Of particular charm are the little pictures commemorating lucky escapes from disaster.

West of the Monumento Obregón

Cross over Insurgentes Sur from the monument and walk W up Av. de la Paz. On the left, just before the traffic artery of Revolución, is a 17thC Carmelite convent, now the **Museo de Carmen** (*open 10am–6pm, closed Mon*). The courtyard is full of trees and flowers, with a tiled fountain at its centre. Rather more gruesome are the mummified bodies on display in the crypt. In the church, see the colonial oil paintings, especially the *Marriage of the Virgin* by Cristóbal de Villalpando.

Cross over Revolución, keeping the flower market on your right, and carry on E up Av. de la Paz. This leads to the charming and fashionable area of **San Angel**, once a colonial village outside the city. Several fine houses are passed on the way to the **Plaza San Jacinto**, where each Saturday there is a lively arts and crafts market (see ***Bazaar Sábado*** under ***Markets*** in *Mexico City/Shopping*). At no.15 is the luxuriously furnished mansion known as the **Casa del Risco** or 'House of Broken Porcelain' (). In the courtyard stands a fountain whose decoration gives the house its name.

From here, head down Alvaro Rivera, then turn right up Santísima to Altavista, where to the left will be seen the restored 18thC **hacienda of San Angel**. It is now a luxury restaurant, but even those on a budget should have a drink in the beautiful courtyard.

To return to the Monumento Obregón, head back E down Altavista and take the left fork into Desierto de los Leones. Crossing over Revolución, it is worth stopping at the interesting small **gallery of modern art** at no.1608 () where the works of Picasso and Kandinsky rub shoulders with homegrown masters. A short distance E from here is Insurgentes Sur, where a right turn takes you back to the monument.

Walks near the city

Perhaps surprisingly, within an hour's drive of the capital there are quiet mountains and forests where the air is fresh and clear. They are deserted during the week.

See also *Popocatepetl* and Nevado de Toluca (under ***Places nearby*** in *Toluca*).

Ajusco ☆
Take the road sw towards the village of Ajusco (a continuation of Paseo del Pedregal beyond the Periférico Sur), and park at the Albergue Alpinista hostel, about 12km (8 miles) from the Periférico.
One of the tallest of the volcanoes near the city, easily climbed in a morning. It is a stiff climb of 1½ hrs to the summit; avoid the cliffs over to the left. During the rainy season, the climb is best undertaken early so as to be back before the afternoon downpours. The views and solitude make all the effort most worthwhile.

Desierto de los Leones
Leave the city w along Reforma; follow signposts for Toluca and after 22km (14 miles) take the mountain road left, signposted to Parque Nacional Desierto de los Leones. Alternatively, leave the city s along Altavista, which becomes Av. Desierto de los Leones after crossing the Periférico.
The car park is by a beautiful half-ruined **monastery** ☆ (▣ *open standard hours*) surrounded by tranquil pine forests. There are no maps of the area, but it is hard to get lost if you stick to the forest paths. The name ('Desert of the Lions') refers to the pumas which used to haunt the area. 5km (3 miles) farther w along the Toluca road, another left turning leads s to the area known as **La Marquesa**. All along this road are picnic spots with paths snaking off into the forests on the foothills of the Ajusco mountain range.

Lagunas de Zempoala
Take the old free road s towards Cuernavaca; just past Tres Cumbres, 51km (32 miles), turn right heading w.
A region of mountain lakes surrounded by forests is reached after 11km (8 miles). There are numerous paths, rather popular at weekends but empty at other times. Horses may sometimes be hired, and there is pleasant riding among the verdant alpine scenery.

Where to stay

There are hundreds of hotels in Mexico City ranging from the great international luxury palaces to rock-bottom boarding houses, where rooms can be rented by the hour. Although tourists never have to sleep on the street, those with prior reservations are more likely to obtain rooms at the right price and location. Demand for rooms is unpredictable, but if you arrive without having reserved a room, as a general rule it is wisest to take whatever accommodation is available for the first night, then hunt around the next day for something more appropriate.

Hotels in Mexico are relatively less expensive than those in the USA and Europe, although the higher the category, the smaller the differential; the same applies to standards of hygiene and service. At the time of writing, the price advantage enjoyed by Mexican hotels was rapidly being eroded by repeated increases in the official scale of tariffs, another result of the economic crisis. As the situation changes so rapidly, it is impossible to give here any precise guidance on prices, and it is best to check before departure. Prices in Mexico City are 50 to 100 percent higher than in the rest of the country. Visitors planning a longer stay and aiming at comfort without financial ruin may prefer to reserve accommodation in one of the numerous service-suite hotels, often furnished to the highest international standards, of which a good example, **Suites Amberes**, is included in the following selection of hotels.

There are two main hotel areas, both convenient for sightseeing and shopping. Most of the cheaper establishments are to be found in the streets surrounding the Zocalo, and hotels in this area have a ZP1 postcode. Most of the luxury hotels are on Reforma near the Zona Rosa, the triangular shopping district off Reforma by the Angel of Independence, and along towards the centre. The postcode here is ZP6.

Alameda
Map 16C6. Juarez 50, ZP1 (5) 518-0620 1772416 350 AE CB VISA
Location: Facing Alameda Park. International-style comfort with an unmistakably Mexican atmosphere. The upper-floor rooms have magnificent views of downtown Mexico, and the lobby café is good for a quick snack while sightseeing. In the evening, the rooftop restaurant offers dining and dancing, with the lights of the city far below.

Aristos
Map 15C4. Paseo de la Reforma 276, ZP6 (5) 533-0560 1771067 360 AE CB VISA
Location: In Zona Rosa. Visiting diplomats and executives favour this 15-storey hotel. The rooms are well furnished, and facilities include a sauna, gymnasium, travel agency and a unisex beauty parlour.

Calinda Geneve
Map 15D4. Londres 130, ZP6 (5) 525-1500 450
Location: In Zona Rosa. A friendly central hotel, with a remarkable cocktail bar containing more plants than a greenhouse, and a pleasant lobby furnished with colonial carved chairs and tables. The rooms are adequate if a trifle cramped; the clientele is almost exclusively foreign. Service has improved steadily ever since it joined the Quality Inn chain.

Camino Real
Map 14D3. Mariano Escobedo 700, ZP5 (5) 545-6960 1773001 720 AE CB VISA
Location: Near Chapultepec Park. People have been known to come to Mexico just for the experience of staying at this super-luxurious neo-Aztec city-within-a-city. From dancing at the wildest disco to dining at the smartest restaurant, from playing energetic rooftop tennis to lounging languidly by one of the pools, residents and Mexican high society are entertained and pampered around the clock. Rooms are large and cheerfully decorated, while service is rapid if impersonal. The only complaint: it is easy to get lost in the corridors of this architectural masterpiece.

Century
Map 15D4. Liverpool 152, ZP6 (5) 584-7111 to 143 AE CB VISA
Location: In Zona Rosa. Expensive modern elegance – rooms even have Roman-style marble baths. Weeping Hungarian violins add a romantic touch at the **Régine** restaurant, and the African safari bar is fun if incongruous. The large penthouse suites are superb.

De Cortés
Map 16C6. Hidalgo 85, ZP3 (5) 585-0322 27 AE CB VISA
Location: Near Alameda Park. A delightful small hotel, in a colonial building designated a national monument. Rooms are cool and airy, surrounding a tree-shaded courtyard restaurant with a fountain at the centre. Popular with an arty crowd, and often reserved long ahead. The *mariachi* fiesta every Sat is usually fun, making an early night out of the question.

Del Paseo
Map 15C4. Paseo de la Reforma 208, ZP6 (5) 525-7600 107 AE CB VISA
Location: Near Zona Rosa. Agreeable small hotel atmosphere, but no lack of facilities – shops, travel agent, rooftop restaurant, and even a massage parlour. A small orchestra plays nightly in the restaurant. Rooms and service would be passable for a much more expensive establishment.

Del Prado
Map 16C6. Juarez 70, ZP1 (5) 518-0040 to 507 AE CB VISA
Location: On Alameda Park. Although often reserved for conventions, there are usually last-minute cancellations. In the lobby, a magnificent Diego Rivera **mural** ☆ shows the nearby Alameda Park in 1900, with a multitude of historical characters strolling around (*explanations at 1 and 5pm daily*). Simple rooms and adequate service, but excellent facilities.

Fiesta Palace
Map 15C5. Paseo de la Reforma 80, ZP4 (5) 566-7777
628

Location: Between Zona Rosa and centre. Luxurious and well-organized for the international tourist, with a large selection of bars, restaurants and entertainment, including the lively **Stelaris** rooftop nightclub. Not much Mexican atmosphere, but even if the sun doesn't shine, you can get a good Mexican suntan in the solarium.

Galeria Plaza
Map 15D4. Hamburgo 195 (Varsovia), ZP6 (5) 286-5444/250-6540
1771808 360

Location: In Zona Rosa. Part of the prestigious Camino Real chain, conveniently placed for shopping and dining out in the elegant Zona Rosa. Faultless rooms, service, and facilities, but it is hard to know whether you are in Mexico or anywhere else in the world. Advantages include cable-TV from the USA, the popular 24hr **Plaza** restaurant, and a secure underground car park.

Gran Hotel de la Ciudad de Mexico
Map 16C7. 16 de Septiembre no.82, ZP1 (5) 510-4040
125

Location: On the Zocalo. Ideally located for central sightseeing, this is an older, more traditional luxury establishment, but with up-to-date service and large rooms. The magnificent lobby is worth a visit in its own right, with a beautiful stained-glass Tiffany dome, chandeliers, mirrors, and 19thC cage-lifts gliding smoothly up and down. The best value in town at the time of writing.

Holiday Inn
Blvd. Puerto Aereo 502, ZP9 (5) 762-4088 334

Location: Near airport. Reserve well in advance through your nearest Holiday Inn, for this is the only good accommodation near the airport. It is not really convenient for visiting Mexico City, so there is little point in spending more than one night here. The building is an agreeable, low, neo-colonial structure, and the hotel has its own shops, travel agency, and helpful English-speaking staff.

Hyatt Continental
Map 15C4. Paseo de la Reforma 166, ZP6 (5) 518-0700 to
359

Location: Between Zona Rosa and centre, at intersection with Insurgentes. Since Hilton sold this hotel to the Hyatt chain, the rooms have been modernized and the facilities generally improved. Spectacular views from the upper floors, and from the **Belvedere** nightclub on the 15th floor. Service is a little lackadaisical, but the rooms are fine.

Krystal
Map 15D4. Liverpool 155, ZP6
(5) 533-3500 1772349
335

Location: In middle of Zona Rosa. Once a Holiday Inn but now under new management, the high-rise Krystal's quality of service and level of appointments remain excellent, while the restaurants and nightlife have if anything become livelier.

María Isabel Sheraton
Map 15D4. Paseo de la Reforma 325, ZP5 (5) 546-9880/525-9060 850

Location: Across from Zona Rosa, overlooking the Angel of Independence. Those feeling perhaps just a little jaded after sampling the excellent restaurants and nightclubs can get back into form with a session in the Turkish bath or the gymnasium. There is even a movie theatre showing English films. The new rooms on the upper floors are the best furnished, and have terrific views. The daily buffet lunch is recommended for hungry shoppers from the Zona Rosa.

Plaza Florencia
Map 15D4. Florencia 61, ZP6
(5) 533-6540 1776354
140

Location: In Zona Rosa. A new, ultra-modern hotel in a smart shopping street. Rooms are well furnished, cheerfully decorated, and soundproofed against traffic noise; the higher floors have a view of the Angel monument. Some larger family suites are available. A good place for a restful stay yet right at the centre of city life.

El Presidente Chapultepec
Map 14C2. Campos Elíseos 218, ZP5 (5) 250–7700
900
Location: Overlooking Chapultepec Park. A modern super-luxury hotel, only just behind the Camino Real in the race to be the capital's best. The grandiose five-storey lobby is a hollow pyramid of balconies, with daily music at the lively lobby bar. There are any number of smart shops, and no less than six restaurants to choose from (see ***Restaurants***), including a branch of **Maxim's** from Paris. The rooms are large, and from the upper floors the volcanoes can be seen early every morning.

El Presidente Zona Rosa
Map 15D4. Hamburgo 135, ZP6 (5) 525–0000/528–5100
136
Location: In Zona Rosa. Although not any longer the really 'smart' place to stay in Mexico City, this remains an elegant, well-run and comfortable hotel, ideally located amid the bright lights. A small hotel with all of the advantages of belonging to the Presidente chain.

Reforma
Map 15C5. Paseo de la Reforma (Paris), ZP4 (5) 546–9680
269
Location: Between Zona Rosa and centre. The Reforma was to the 1930s what the ***Camino Real*** is to the present day, and it still manages to resist the challenge of the newcomers. Recommended for its traditional decor, good service, and central location.

Suites Amberes
Map 15D4. Amberes 64, ZP6 (5) 533–1306 to
28
Location: In Zona Rosa. Some family units are available in this first-class modern apartment hotel. Each spacious room has a small kitchen and balcony, and modern colonial furniture. Recommended for a longer stay.

Other hotels

The pleasant, modern **Brazilia** (*map 15A5, Av. de los 100 Metros, ZP14* *(5) 587–8577*) is the only hotel near the Terminal del Norte bus station; get away from international food and ambience at the **María Cristina** (*map 15C4, Lerma 31, ZP5* *(5) 546–9880*), a slightly run-down colonial inn with a fine garden, near the Zona Rosa; among the high-rise glass towers along Reforma, the small colonial **Montejo** (*map 15C4, Reforma 240, ZP6* *(5) 511–9840*) combines traditional decor with modern comfort, although rooms are rather small; new and ultra-modern, the **Plaza Florencia** (*map 15D4, Florencia 61, ZP6* *(5) 524–4000* *1776354* *to*), in the Zona Rosa, has comfortably furnished and soundproofed rooms and some large family suites; the centrally located **Royal** (*map 15D4, Amberes 78, ZP6* *(5) 525–4850*), opened in 1982, welcomes families.

Other recommended hotels, each with its own restaurant: **Ambassador** (*map 15C5, Humboldt 38, ZP1, near Alameda Park* *(5) 518–0110* *to*); **Bristol** (*map 15C4, Plaza Necaxa 17, ZP5, across Reforma from Zona Rosa* *(5) 533–6060*); **De Carlo** (*map 15C5, Plaza Republicana 35, ZP1, by the monument to the Revolution* *(5) 535–4946*); **Del Angel** (*map 15C4, Lerma 154, ZP5, by the Angel of Independence* *(5) 533–1032*); **El Diplomático** (*Insurgentes Sur 1105, ZP18* *(5) 563–6066* *to*); **Majestic** (*map 16C7, Madero 73, ZP1, in city centre* *(5) 521–8600*); **Polanco** (*map 14D3, Edgar Allan Poe 8, ZP5, w of centre* *(5) 520–6040*); **El Romano Diana** (*map 15C4, Lerma 237, ZP5, near British and American Embassies* *(5) 525–7765*); **Suites Havre** (*map 15D4, Havre 74, ZP6, in Zona Rosa* *(5) 533–5670* *to* *apartments*); **Versalles** (*map 15C5, General Prim 59, ZP6, in Zona Rosa* *(5) 546–9300* *to*).

Where to eat

Mexicans love eating out, and nowhere is this more true than in Mexico City. Every imaginable national cuisine is represented, as is the enormous regional diversity of Mexican cooking. The cost of a good meal can vary enormously, but prices are lower than in the USA or Europe, while the standard of cooking and service is at least comparable. Visitors new to the city can thus afford to avoid the cheaper restaurants, and those who venture no farther than hotel dining rooms and fast-food bars are therefore missing an important part of the Mexican experience.

For that one really unforgettable evening out, there are two rivals for the first choice, the **San Angel Inn** and the **Hacienda de los Morales**. The colonial atmosphere, sophisticated cooking and excellent wines available in both place them firmly among the ranks of the world's greatest restaurants.

Every neighbourhood has its small family restaurants, but the smarter establishments favoured by executives and tourists are concentrated mostly in the fashionable Zona Rosa. The southern district of San Angel and the areas around the Zocalo also have a good selection. Telephone reservations are advisable on the day before for luxury restaurants, and on the same day for others.

The following selection of restaurants concentrates mostly on places offering Mexican food and ambience, and some of the better hotel restaurants are also represented.

Ambassadeurs
Map 16A7. Reforma 12, ZP1
(5) 535–6435/546–1663
AE CB Φ VISA
Considered one of the finest French restaurants in the world, certainly the best of its kind in Mexico City. This is a favoured haunt of the very rich, and has received international awards for its classical French menu.

Anderson's
Map 14D3. Reforma 400, ZP6
(5) 525–1006/511–5187
AE CB Φ VISA
The menu may be written to amuse, the decor off-beat, the waiters relaxed and casual – but the food in this lively, crowded restaurant is usually reliable. There is a sister branch in the southern suburb of San Angel (*Calzada Desierto 67, ZP20 (5) 548–1265*) serving the same international menu; steaks are especially good. There is always music to add to the clamour.

Arroyo
Insurgentes Sur 4003, Tlalpán, ZP22 (5) 573–7745
South of University City, and great for *al fresco* barbecue lunches at weekends. It is justifiably popular with families, who can include it in a visit to Xochimilco or any of the other sights s of the city centre. The food is reliable if unadventurous.

La Calesa de Londres
Map 15D4, Londres 102, ZP6
(5) 533–6625
AE CB Φ VISA
Located in the former US Embassy in the Zona Rosa; serves enormous Chihuahua steaks.

La Cava
Insurgentes Sur 2465, ZP20
(5) 548–8275
AE CB Φ VISA
Good for lunch or dinner while visiting the s of the city, with elegant but restrained decor, a piano bar and an attractive interior garden. Regional dishes from all over Mexico, but the specialities are Spanish.

Cicero's
Map 15D4. Londres 197, ZP6
(5) 525–6130
AE CB Φ VISA
Very fashionable, this is a beautifully furnished old mansion in the Zona Rosa; it is crammed with antiques and serves seafood specialities.

Circulo del Sureste
Map 15C5. Lucerna 12, ZP6
(5) 535–2704
To sample the aromatic spicy food of the Yucatán peninsula, very different from typical Mexican food, try this simple and unpretentious restaurant. a must if you don't intend to travel to the Yucatán itself.

Del Lago
Map 14D2. Chapultepec Park, ZP18 (5) 515–9350/546–1663
A flamboyant modern glass and shell-concrete fantasy on the lakeside, providing international cuisine in a formally elegant atmosphere.

Delmonico's
Map 15D4. Londres 87, ZP6 (5) 528–7530/514–7003
The menu is international and the service superb in this elegant restaurant, favoured by executives, in the Zona Rosa.

Fonda del Recuerdo
Map 14C3. Bahía de las Palmas 39-A, ZP17 (5) 545–7260
Seafood is the speciality here, and the cooking is typical of that found in the state of Veracruz. There is always a party atmosphere.

Fonda del Refugio
Map 15D4. Liverpool 166, ZP6 (5) 528–5823/525–8128
The traditional Mexican food is supplemented by specialities from the individual regions of the country. One of the capital's better cellars. It is necessary to make a reservation the day before.

Hacienda de los Morales
Vázquez de Mella 525, Polanco, ZP10 (5) 540–3125/3225
This beautifully restored 16thC hacienda provides impeccable international cuisine and also gourmet Mexican specialities. It is patronized by executives and politicians, therefore dress is formal. A favourite for riotous high-society parties.

Hostería de Santo Domingo
Map 16C7. Domínguez 72, ZP1 (5) 510–1434
Still going strong after 100yrs of preparing good traditional Mexican food. Especially lively at lunch.

Loma Linda
Reforma 1105, ZP10 (5) 520–0024
Situated in the fashionable Lomas residential area, w of centre. Recommended for its large Argentinian-style steaks and relaxed atmosphere.

La Marinera
Map 15D4. Liverpool 183, ZP6 (5) 511–3568
This pleasant, clean and unpretentious Zona Rosa restaurant produces the best seafood in Mexico City at modest prices.

Mesón del Caballo Bayo
Conscripto 360, ZP10 (5) 589–3000
Mexican specialities are served in this old colonial hacienda. Its proximity to the race-track attracts a lively, horsey crowd. For the popular Sunday lunch reserve your table on Friday.

Mesón del Perro Andaluz
Map 15D4. Copenhague 20, ZP6 (5) 533–5306
For pavement-café atmosphere sample the well-prepared Spanish food in this establishment in the Zona Rosa.

Les Moustaches
Map 15C4. Rio Sena 88, ZP5 (5) 533–3390
Although served in an elegant setting in an old mansion, the French-style food is over-rated.

Muralto
Map 16C6. Floor 41, Latin American Tower, Juarez, ZP1 (5) 521–7751
Come here for amazing views (smog permitting) of the city. The international/French food is not special but is acceptable.

Normandie
Map 15D4. Niza 5, ZP6 (5) 521–7124/553–0906
For a taste of France, this restaurant is highly recommended for its delicious cuisine and refined atmosphere.

El Paseo
Map 15D4. Reforma 146, ZP6 (5) 546–5124
An informal, crowded, fun place to go, similar to a New York supper-club.

Prendes
Map 16C6. Av. 16 de Septiembre, ZP1 (5) 521–8600/585–4199
A popular venue for lunch, equally famous for its seafood dishes and for its murals.

Rivoli
Map 15D4. Hamburgo 123, ZP6
(5) 525–6862
Located in the Zona Rosa and considered to be the best of those restaurants offering international and French cuisine. The menu and surroundings provide an air of sophistication. Perhaps not now the temple of French cuisine that it once was.

San Angel Inn
Palmas 50, San Angel, ZP20
(5) 548–6746
Delicious, gourmet Mexican food in an 18thC colonial building with furnishings from the same period. Combine a visit here with an excursion to the S of the city. Smooth, professional service and an elegant atmosphere ensure that a visit here is more than a chance to sample the native cuisine.

Sanborn's Casa de Azulejos
Map 16C6. Madero 4, ZP1 (5) 512–1331
The most interesting feature of this restaurant is the magnificent colonial courtyard, covered with amber glass, and its **Orozco murals**, but the food is ordinary, mainly hamburgers and snacks.

Suntory
Torres Adalid 14, ZP12 (5) 536–7754/6884
This elegant restaurant offers an extensive range of delicious Japanese food combined with very efficient service.

Tampico Mirador
Hotel de Mexico, Insurgentes Sur (Filadelphia), ZP18 (5) 687–1000
A revolving restaurant at the top of the long-unfinished Hotel de Mexico. There are wonderful views of the Valley of Mexico and the volcanoes, but a fairly uninspiring seafood menu. Be sure to choose a clear day.

Other restaurants

Also worth noting are the following hotel restaurants. Names given in brackets refer to the respective hotels, whose addresses and telephone numbers can be found in *Mexico City/Hotels*, and all accept

Fouquets (*Camino Real* (5) 545–6960) serves both international and French cuisine; for truly authentic French flavour, however, **Maxim's** (*El Presidente Chapultepec* (5) 250–7700) tries with some success to live up to its Parisian namesake; within the same hotel is the **Arrecife** (*El Presidente Chapultepec* (5) 250–7700), noted for its excellent seafood; the **Grill del Prado** (*Del Prado* (5) 518–0040) is another seafood specialist, but the steaks are also recommended; for those seeking entertainment with their dinner, the **Veranda** (*María Isabel Sheraton* (5) 525–9060) is the answer, and it also offers a daily buffet lunch; for colonial atmosphere, try the restaurant in the **De Cortés** (*De Cortés* (5) 585–0322).

Nightlife

Two essential experiences are the **Ballet Folklórico** and a visit to the **Plaza Garibaldi**.

Some performances of the ballet take place at the ***Palacio de Bellas Artes*** (see *Mexico City/Sights*), but most are now downtown outside the Alameda Park, on Wed, Fri and Sun, in the Auditorio Nacional. Pick up tickets beforehand at the Bellas Artes, or ask your hotel to arrange tickets and transport. The 2hr performance features dances from all over the country, with superb costumes and choreography, and the interior of the Bellas Artes itself is well worth a visit.

The Plaza Garibaldi (*on Eje Lázaro Cárdenas, about five blocks N of the Bellas Artes*) is the home of Mexico's renowned *mariachi* musicians. Plan to arrive after dinner, on Fri and especially Sat night, then drift around the square listening to all the competing bands. Later, head for one of the café/bars around the square to sip tequila and be entertained by the bar's own band. Best of these is **Tlaquepaque**, which is untroubled by the drunken brawls that occasionally erupt in less salubrious establishments. The area is well patrolled by police, but it is wise to avoid carrying large amounts of money.

Another recommended spectacle is the son-et-lumière show at the pyramids of *Teotihuacán*. Hotels will either arrange a tour to these or will put you in touch with an agency.

Times and places of concerts, ballets and Spanish-language plays are given in the *Mexico City Daily News* and in the weekly *Tiempo Libre* (Free Time) magazine.

Bars and discos

For non-stop nightlife, it has to be admitted that Mexico City is neither the equal of Acapulco nor New York, yet there is plenty to beguile and amuse the visitor into the small hours. Offices close around 7pm and business moves to the bars; luxury hotel bars are a favourite meeting place, the most glamorous being those at the ***Camino Real*** and the ***El Presidente Chapultepec***, both offering music every night. The ***Del Prado*** hotel, with its famous Rivera mural, is also popular, and is known for a rather more Mexican atmosphere. For a quieter, more discreet ambience, try the **Bar Inglés** at the ***El Presidente Zona Rosa***, all black leather and gleaming chrome.

For details of the various entertainments and spectacles laid on by the luxury hotels, check in the free information sheet available at all hotel desks. The ***María Isabel Sheraton*** and the ***El Presidente Chapultepec*** usually have a big foreign name performing at one of their clubs or restaurants. The Saturday night fiesta at the ***De Cortés*** hotel is always fun, with guitar music and Mexican fare.

The hotel discotheques rank among the best. The **CeroCero** at the ***Camino Real*** and the **Club 84** at the ***El Presidente Chapultepec*** both offer loud rock music and more flashing lights than a funfair. Most of the other good discos are private clubs; ask Mexican friends to take you to the amazing **Circo Mágico** ('El Magic') or to the smaller **Bandasha** – non-members are not admitted on their own.

Three other non-hotel establishments worth a visit after dinner are listed below.

Bar el Opera
Map 16C6. 5 de Mayo 31, ZP1, near the Palacio de Bellas Artes
A lunch and drinking spot downtown. Ornate mirrors and mahogany panelling. Light Mexican snacks, and heavy Mexican drinking.

Catacumbas
Map 16C6. Dolores 16B, ZP1 ☎ (5) 518–4027
An old tourist favourite, with its subdued B-horror-movie feeling and plenty of spooky surprises.

Gitanerías
Map 15D4. Oaxaca 15, ZP6, near Zona Rosa
Flamenco floor-show and good Spanish food. Open until late.

Shopping

Anything from other parts of the country and, indeed, almost anything from other parts of the world can be bought in Mexico City. Those with their wits about them can avoid expensive worthless rubbish and enjoy a bargainer's paradise, even in the most surprising places; the trick is to look doubtful and see what happens. It is important, however to examine all goods thoroughly before purchase – for example, check hinges when looking at silver, and examine the stitching in leatherwork.

The best place to start is the central Zona Rosa, between Chapultepec Park, Reforma and Insurgentes, where among the vast number of restaurants, cafés, nightclubs and hotels are found hundreds of small shops selling silver, jewellery, leather, clothes, paintings and antiques. Similar shops are also located in the downtown area along Reforma and Insurgentes, and around the Zocalo and Alameda Park. Luxury hotels also have their own boutiques which, although expensive, are useful for those in a hurry.

Department stores and shopping centres provide a helpful starting point for newcomers, while the capital's markets and craft centres should be on every visitor's list of places to visit. A selection of these follows.

Department stores and shopping centres

Centro Comercial Perisur
Insurgentes Sur and Periférico, ZP20 AE CB VISA
Three large department stores, plus many boutiques and shops. Closed Mon. The **Centro Comercial Ciudad Satelite**, w of the centre on the road to Querétaro, is similar.

El Palacio de Hierro
Map 16C7. Av. 20 de Noviembre, ZP1 AE CB VISA
A large downtown department store, good for international fashions. There is another branch at Durango and Salamanca, ZP7 (*map 15D4*).

Polanco shopping centre
Map 14C2. Horacio, ZP5 AE CB VISA
Three large stores in one block: **El Puerto de Liverpool, Paris Londres** and **Woolworth's**, all behind the ***El Presidente Chapultepec*** hotel.

Sanborn's
There are about 20 branches in strategic locations, all good for silver souvenirs and aimed at foreign visitors (*all take* AE CB VISA). The most notable one is in the **House of Tiles** (*map 16C6, Madero 4, ZP6*).

Markets and craft centres

Bazar Sábado
Plaza San Jacinto, San Angel, ZP20.
Jewellery, painting, and folk art. Open on Sat only.

Bodegas Oaxaca
Tlalpán 2191, ZP21 ☎ *(5) 689–0212.*
A large selection of weaving and crafts; combine with an excursion to the s of the city.

Centro de Artesanías Buenavista
Map 15B5. Aldama 187, ZP3.
An arts and crafts warehouse near the railway station.

Centro de Artesanías Carreta
Insurgentes 2105, San Angel, ZP20.
In the basement under Sanborn's; native art from all over Mexico is straightforwardly displayed.

Ciudadela
Map 15C5. Av. Balderas, six blocks s of the Alameda Park.
Hundreds of little stalls in a purpose-built development, with glass-blowers, metalworkers and weavers at work. Good for silver.

FONART
Patriotismo 691, ZP19. Near Plaza Mexico bullring.
Map 16C6. Juarez 70, 89 and 92, ZP1. Near Alameda.
Avenida de la Paz 37, San Angel, ZP20.
Map 15D4. Londres 136, ZP6. In the Zona Rosa.
Good value and choice are to be found at these government-run stores, which buy direct from the native artisans. Crafts from the whole country at good prices.

Indios Verdes
1km (½ mile) to the N of the Basilica de Guadalupe.
A large open-air tourist market, which makes a good place to stop on the way to Teotihuacán.

Lagunilla

Two blocks E of the Cuitlahuac monument on Reforma Norte (*map 15B7*), this is a large covered market, open daily. Only worth visiting on Sun, when the streets to the N (especially Comonfort) fill with the stalls of what is known as the 'thieves' market'. Crafts, antiques, and general bric-à-brac are sold for prices that vary according to the apparent wealth of the purchaser. Three blocks E of here is the **Tepito market** (*map 15B7*), where much of what is on sale is smuggled or stolen. It used to be easy to buy such things as illegal guns, drugs and brass-knuckles here, but recently controls have become tighter. Hold on to your money.

Palacio de Artesanías

Map 16C6. Hidalgo 45, ZP1.

Near the Alameda; craftsmen at work, with a good selection of their products for sale.

San Juan Market

Map 16C6. Aranda and Ayuntamiento, ZP1, four blocks S of the Alameda.

A large modern building, with stalls on three floors.

Places nearby

An early priority should be an excursion to the NE of the city to the great pyramids at *Teotihuacán*, usually combined with a trip to the monastery at Acolmán. North of the city, the ruins of *Tula* and the superb church at *Tepotzotlán* can be visited at the same time as the large monastery at Actopán (see *Pachuca*). Restful weekend retreats from the city include *Cuernavaca*, *Pachuca*, *San Juan del Río* and *Valle de Bravo*. Numerous other excursions from Mexico City are suggested in *Planning*.

Mitla ★

Map 8H10. Oaxaca. 42km (26 miles) SE of Oaxaca on RF 190. Served by bus.

The intricate geometric stonework of the palaces at Mitla is unique among Mexico's major ruins, and a visit to the site is essential for anybody interested in the country's past. Just who was responsible for this masterpiece, though, has long been a point of considerable academic controversy. When the Spaniards arrived, it was inhabited by Zapotecs, but the architecture is more typical of the greater artistic sophistication of the Mixtecs, who are known to have arrived in the area around the 10thC when the Zapotec civilization was in decline.

It is possible that Mitla was built during the 13thC by Zapotecs heavily influenced by the Mixtec culture. Unlike many of Mexico's ruins, it was not overgrown by jungle, nor was it used as a stone quarry by the Spaniards, who merely contented themselves with building a church in one of the less important courtyards, at the end of the track through the site.

The ruins

Open 8am–6pm.

The most important group of ruins is known as the **Columns Group**, just to the S of the Church Group, and consists of two diagonally adjacent courts surrounded by chambers. On the N side of the largest court, a stair leads up to a triple doorway through which the long and narrow **Hall of Columns** is entered. A passage from here leads to a small court, where the walls are decorated in the typical Mitla style with thousands of small interlocking pieces of stone used to create complex patterns. The number of precisely carved stones is well in excess of 100,000 – like Rome, Mitla was not built in a day. In the smaller court of the group, there is a cruciform tomb decorated in the same way; the contents were lost to grave-robbers who got there before the archaeologists. In another tomb to the N of this court there is a large column which supported the roof of an adjacent tomb. Local superstition has it that if you embrace this column you will know the day of your death.

There are three other groups of buildings: the **Adobe** and **Arroyo** Groups, over a small *barranca* to the W, and the **South** group. These smaller and less well-preserved buildings are of no great interest.

The many market stalls near the entrance to the ruins sell native embroidery at low prices.

Monte Albán ★

Map 7H9. Oaxaca. 12km (7 miles) W of Oaxaca. Altitude: 2,113m (6,500ft). Served by bus.

Around the time of the fall of Rome in 410, this breathtaking ceremonial centre of the Zapotec people was a large and flourishing city. The mountain which it crowns was terraced right down to the plain with houses and temples. It was about 1,000yrs ago that decline set in, as the Zapotecs came under pressure from the Mixtecs, invading from the N. By the 15thC they had been driven out of the city, by now in use only as a burial centre for Mixtec kings. Dating from this period are the hundreds of tombs dotted around the site, some of which yielded rich treasures which can be seen in the Museo de Oaxaca in *Oaxaca*. By the time the Spaniards arrived, the Mixtecs themselves were more or less under Aztec domination, and Monte Albán was falling into ruin. Today it is still a place of inspiring natural and man-made grandeur, and should be the first destination for any visitor to Oaxaca.

The ruins

Open 9am–6pm.

The restored part of the city is a large group of buildings around the great esplanade on the artificially flattened hilltop. If at first you feel impressed by the restrained dignity of the architecture, remember that the Zapotecs painted it in as many colours as Joseph's coat. The site is entered from the N, passing on the left a court for the sacred ball-game. Before you are three large structures aligned N to S down the centre of the esplanade; behind these is a smaller, older building which is out of alignment – parts of this date from nearly 2,000yrs ago and were built by the unknown predecessors of the Zapotecs.

The S edge of the esplanade is bordered by a large raised platform with the remains of a temple in the centre. Standing here, and facing back up the esplanade, the building on the right is known as **El Palacio**. The second building on the left is the remarkable **Monumento de los Danzantes**, the sides of which are decorated with reliefs of dancers who have notably negroid features, suggesting that the Zapotecs may have been descended from the Olmecs of the Gulf. On a few of the stones are glyphs indicating the age of the carvings.

There are other structures to the S of the main groups. Around here you are likely to meet youths trying to sell artifacts 'from the tombs'. If they are fake (and 99.9% are) they are of no value; if not, it is breaking the law to buy one.

Monterrey

Map 5E8. Capital of Nuevo León. 228km (141 miles) S of Nuevo Laredo on RF 85. Population: 1,400,000. Served by air (international airport 22km/14 miles NW), train (on line from Mexico City) and bus. Car rental: Avis, Padre Mier 647 ☎ (83) 44–7230, and at airport ☎ (83) 38–2590; Hertz, Hotel Ambassador, Hidalgo & Galeana ☎ (83) 38–2795, and at airport ☎ (83) 44–7031 i Hidalgo and Zaragoza ☎ (83) 42–3488, and Emilio Carranza 730 ☎ (83) 44–0172. US Consul: Constitución 411 ☎ (83) 43–0650.

As befits one of Mexico's great industrial cities, Monterrey is rapidly catching up with the capital in terms of pollution, congestion and over-population. Like Mexico City, it is ringed by mountains which trap and concentrate the smog, much of it produced from a giant steelmill near the city centre which has been 'due for closure' for years but which continues to make money and, therefore, continues to make smoke. Despite all this, Monterrey has enough compensations to reward the unhurried for a day or two, including some spectacular areas of natural beauty nearby.

For information in English on cultural events in Monterrey ☎(83) 43–5060.

Events On May 20 for one week, agricultural fiesta. Bullfights, horse races, dancing and fireworks.

On Dec 12, local centre of pilgrimage for fiesta of the Virgin of Guadalupe.

Sights and places of interest

Around the main square, **Plaza Zaragoza**, there are some elegant, flower-filled cobbled streets, and on the square itself the **cathedral**, a bold new **Palacio Municipal**, and the old one it replaced, now more of a cultural centre where occasional concerts are held on the patio. Just s are the twin avenues, Constitución and Independencia, that flank the dry bed of the river Catarina. Plaza Zaragoza is the night-time focus of the city, and in the six blocks up to Plaza 5 de Mayo to the N are concentrated the hotels, restaurants and shops. Up on Plaza 5 de Mayo is the **Palacio de Gobierno**, the state seat of government, and in its small museum room (*usually open during office hours*) are the actual guns used for the execution of Emperor Maximilian in 1867.

Padre Mier leads w past Enrique de la Mora's beautiful modern church of **La Purísima** to Chepe Vara hill, overlooking the town, and the **Palacio del Obispo** (Bishop's Palace). Because of its dominant position, it was a centre of action during the Mexican-American War of 1846, the French intervention and the Revolution, and now contains a small **museum** (*open standard hours*) telling the story of this turbulent period.

After all this culture, leave the children at the excellent **Planetarium** (*on Gómez Marín and Coatzacoalcos open 10am–6pm*) and head N for the huge **Cuauhtemoc brewery** on the outskirts of town (*open Mon–Fri 9am–3pm, closed Sat, Sun*), where the visit ends with free beer.

Sights nearby

Cola de Caballo

40km (25 miles) sw; turn w off RF 85 after 35km (22 miles).

The impressive waterfalls, cascading over jagged rocks, are a popular weekend picnic spot, and horses are available for hire to ride in the hills around. The name means 'Horse-tail' falls.

Grutas García and the Huasteca Canyon

w on RF 54 to Saltillo.

The dizzyingly deep **Huasteca Canyon** is a favourite outing from town, 3km (2 miles) s of the main road after 16km (10 miles). After 25km (15 miles) on the main road, turn N and drive a further 21km (13 miles) to the **Grutas García**, the best of all the sights around Monterrey. Access to the caves is by cable-car, and the visit includes an underground lake and forests of stalactites and stalagmites; it is safe and well lit.

Mesa Chipinque

18km (11 miles) w; leave city by Colonia del Valle.

Monterrey's favourite weekend resort is at the end of a steep, winding road on a mountain plateau with fine views over the city. Hire horses at the Motel Chipinque for rides through the quiet pine forests.

Hotels

Ambassador

Hidalgo and Galeana ☎ (83) 42–2040 300 AE CB DC MC VISA

A large, comfortable downtown commercial hotel popular with executives. Pleasant garden.

Gran Ancira
Hidalgo and Escobedo (83) 43-2060/1870 300
For turn-of-the-century atmosphere and elegance, this is the hotel you should choose. Large, well-furnished rooms.

Holiday Inn
Universidad 101 (83) 52-3390 190
This luxurious colonial-style hotel is located 13km (8 miles) N of the centre and has good sports facilities.

Ramada Inn
Almazán s/n (83) 52-2270 138
This resort is based on the country club idea and is on the W outskirts.

Hotels nearby

(*On RF 40, 18km/11 miles SW of Monterrey*).

Motel Chipinque
(83) 78-1257 60
A pleasant mountain resort, but rather crowded at weekends. Fireplaces in some rooms.

(*On RF 85, 40km/25 miles S of Monterrey*).

Hacienda Cola de Caballo
(83) 43-7730 to 75
For good sports facilities and great views, this country motel fits the bill.

Restaurants

Henry VIII
Hidalgo 2726 Poniente (83) 48-5671
A mock-Tudor hostelry with food to match. Incongruous and amusing.

Residence
Degollado and Matamoros (83) 42-7730
Located near the Bishop's Palace (see ***Sights***), this elegant 19thC mansion provides an international menu.

Santa Rosa
Plaza Hidalgo (83) 42-7111 to
Regional specialities are served in the flower-filled garden of an 18thC mansion. Candlelit tables create a soft ambience.

El Tío
Hidalgo and Mexico (83) 46-0291
The place for dedicated carnivores, with appropriate bullfighting decor.

Places nearby

Monclova (*194km/120 miles NW on RF 53*). The first major city on the road S from *Piedras Negras*, and capital of Texas in the 19thC when that state was part of Mexico. The hotel will arrange a visit to the steelworks on the edge of town. It is surprisingly interesting – you will see scenes straight from Dante's *Inferno*.

H **Gil Cantú** (*Carranza 410* (863) 3-1333 to).

Morelia ☆

Map 11D5. Michoacán. 311km (193 miles) w of Mexico City on RF 15; 363km (223 miles) SE of Guadalajara on RF 15. Served by air, train (on Mexico City–Guadalajara line) and bus. Altitude: 2,080m (6,400ft). Population: 300,000. Car rental: Budget, Héroes de Nocupetaro 46 ☎ (451) 2-5019/2-1276/2-6351; Hertz, Madero 348 ☎ (451) 2-8303 i Santos Degollado 357 ☎ (451) 2-4898.

In colonial times, Morelia was known as Valladolid, because it reminded the Conquistadors of that Spanish city, and in fact it has retained a much more historic atmosphere than its former namesake. Travellers come here less than to the colonial cities to the N, and there is a calmer, less touristic atmosphere. In charm and interest it is certainly the equal of its better-known rivals, and with the forthcoming opening of the new airport seems certain to attract more visitors.

In 1828, it took the present name in honour of its most famous son, José María Morelos, a revolutionary priest who led the struggle for independence against the Spanish and was eventually executed in 1813. The man who signed his death warrant was another son of Morelos, although you will see no statues to Agustín Iturbide. He was an opportunistic professional soldier who fought on several sides during the War of Independence. In 1822 he was crowned Emperor of the Catholic Kingdom of Anahuac. Like Morelos, though, his luck ran out, and in 1824 he too found himself blindfolded and up against a wall.

For a good orienting view, take a walk in the hills up towards Santa María, S of town. The spires, domes and treetops of this charming city are spread out in the valley below.

Sights and places of interest

Bosque Cuauhtemoc
Twelve blocks E of the Zocalo.
Through this large, pleasant park runs an impressive 18thC aqueduct, close to a small and unremarkable **Museo de Arte Contemporáneo** (▣ *open standard hours*). In the centre of the park is a fine orchid garden which catches the tropical colonial atmosphere of the whole town, and to the E is the **Sanctuary of the Virgin of Guadalupe**, dazzlingly over-decorated.

Casa de Morelos
Iturbide and Morelos ▣ Open standard hours, closed for lunch.
A 1758 house, bought by Morelos in 1801 and now a museum to his memory. There are various documents and personal possessions, and even the blindfold which he was wearing when executed. In the courtyard are two antique carriages: Morelos used one of them to carry the Last Sacraments to the sick and dying.

Colegio de las Rosas Teresitas 🏛 †
20 de Noviembre.
The oldest music college in the Americas, and still in use as a choir school by the famous *Niños Cantores de Morelia*. The church of **Santa Rosa**, part of the college, has a Baroque facade and a beautiful altarpiece. To attend a rehearsal or performance of the choir, ask at the college.

Colegio de San Nicolas 🏛
Madero ▣ Open standard hours.
This college was founded in 1540 by the first Bishop of Michoacán, Vasco de Quiroga, and moved to this location in 1580. The court of the main building is arcaded in the Baroque style, and the walls are decorated with murals.

Zocalo
Colonnaded on three sides, the Zocalo is a good place to sit out at a café, drinking in coffee and atmosphere and listening perhaps to one of the evening concerts often held on the central bandstand. On the E side is the Plateresque **cathedral**, built in the 17thC, with the two bell towers added

in the 18thC. Notable are the low reliefs on the doorways and the religious oil paintings inside, and the largest organ in the Americas.

Opposite the cathedral is a large colonial mansion, once the seminary for all Michoacán, and now the **Palacio de Gobierno** (*usually open during office hours*). On the main staircase are some fine murals showing historical scenes from the Conquest to the 1917 Revolution. On the SW corner of the Zocalo is the **Museo de Michoacán** (*open standard hours*), housed in a small 18thC palace, with collections of Pre-Columbian and colonial art, especially of the local Tarascan culture. On the second floor is a large mural of *The Four Horsemen of the Apocalypse* by Cantu.

Other sights

If there is time, visit also the 16thC church of **San Agustín** (*Corregidora and Hidalgo*) and see beside the church the house where Morelos was born. To the E, five blocks behind the cathedral, is the 16thC church of **San Francisco**, with a massive bell tower and a tiled dome. A final church to visit is the 18thC monastery church of **El Carmen**, four blocks N of the Zocalo on Benito Juarez, which has a very pretty cloister.

Hotels

Albergue de la Calzada
Fray Antonio de San Miguel 173 (451) 2-7518 24
Originally the town house of an aristocrat. Reserve ahead, as it has a regular clientele.

Villa Montaña
Patzimba s/n (451) 2-2588/4-0231 to 65 AE CB VISA
Located 5km (3 miles) S of the centre, the Montaña is one of Mexico's very special hotels. It comprises beautifully furnished private villas which surround a rambling colonial hacienda. There are five things not found here – no children, no air conditioning, no disco, no telephones and no television. The food is disappointingly dull.

Virrey de Mendoza
Portal de Matamoros 16 (451) 2-0633 52 AE CB VISA
Traditional comfort and a good restaurant are the main features of this 18thC mansion on the Zocalo.

H Less interesting but also good are: **Alameda** (*Madero and Prieto* (451) 2-2023); **Villa Capri** (*Madero Poniente 2069* (451) 2-7293).

R The best food is to be found in the hotel restaurants (see ***Hotels***).

Shopping

The state of Michoacán is well known for its arts and crafts, largely due to the efforts of the first Bishop of Michoacán, Vasco de Quiroga, who encouraged suitable crafts for his Indian flock. In Morelia you will find pottery, wood-carving, copper, and lacquerware. A good place to start is at the **government store** (*Madero 492*), although there is more bustle and bargaining at the **Mercado Independencia** (*Lázaro Cárdenas*).

Places nearby

Cuitzeo (*35km/22 miles N on Salamanca road*). A small fishing village on Lake Cuitzeo, whose Zocalo is also the forecourt of a 16thC monastery. The two churches and the monastery cloister are fine examples of 16th–17thC colonial architecture.
San José Purua (*137km/85 miles E to the S of RF 15*). The inhabitants of this small spa town never tire of telling visitors that they live in Mexico's Shangri-La: the claim has some apparent justification, for it is a pretty place, set in a small canyon and surrounded by luxuriant vegetation. It is a good

place to spend a night, and wallow awhile in the health-giving geothermal waters.
Yuriria (*66km/40 miles* N*; turn* E *off Salamanca road after 62km/37 miles*). A large fortified lakeside Augustinian monastery which has recently been declared a national monument. After visiting the monastery, relax by the lake, or rent a boat and go fishing. Beyond here, the road passes through some magnificent volcanic country.

Nuevo Laredo

Map 5D8. Tamaulipas. 223km (137 miles) N *of Monterrey on RF 85. Served by air (international airport 10km/6 miles* SW*), train (line to Monterrey) and bus. Population: 275,000. US Consul: Allende and Nayarit ☎ (871) 4–0512.*
An ordinary border town, with reasonable hotels and a variety of souvenir shops. If you are lucky, you may catch a bullfight.

[H] Nuevo Laredo is well provided with hotels and motels, and the following are recommended: **Hacienda Motor Hotel** (*Reforma 5530 ☎ (871) 2–6666/4–4666*), a resort hotel to the S of the town; **Reforma** (*Guerrero 882 ☎ (871) 2–6250*), the best downtown hotel.

Oaxaca

Map 7H9. Capital of Oaxaca. 541km (335 miles) SE *of Mexico City on RF 150 and RF 190. Altitude: 1,694m (5,070ft). Population: 150,000. Served by air, train (terminus of line from Mexico City) and bus. Car rental: Avis, Alameda de León 1 ☎ (951) 6–5030, and at airport ☎ (951) 018–857 i García Vigil and Independencia ☎ (951) 6–3810.*
If you want to see all of Mexico in a week, come to Oaxaca, a beautiful colonial city, surrounded by great archaeological sites such as *Mitla* and *Monte Albán*, Indian villages, old monasteries and magnificent scenery; it is also only a half-day's drive or a short flight down to the unspoiled beaches of the Pacific. The state which it commands is poor in minerals, and just as it escaped the ravages of the Spanish mine-owners, it now looks set to avoid the ravages of Pemex (Petróleos Mexicanos), who have laid waste to so much of the neighbouring states of Campeche, Tabasco, and Chiapas.

Unknown civilizations flourished in the Valley of Oaxaca as much as 3,000yrs ago, making it one of the oldest continuously inhabited areas in the country. When the Spaniards arrived, the two great cultures of the Valley, the Zapotec and Mixtec, were exhausted by their struggles, and had both fallen under the sway of the Aztecs. Cortés himself fell in love with the area and intended to retire to his large estates there. Although he died too soon, his descendants retained the title of 'Marquis of Oaxaca' until the Revolution of 1917.

The famous sons of Oaxaca include two presidents of Mexico. The first was Benito Juarez, hero of the bitter war against the French. The second was the rather less popular dictator, Don Porfirio Díaz, who ruled Mexico with an iron hand for the 35yrs before the 1910 Revolution. Recently, his achievements in creating the infrastructure for Mexican industrial development have been re-assessed, but during the *Porfiriato*, as today, the rich got richer and the poor stayed poor. Nowhere is this truer than in the state of Oaxaca.

A note of caution: Oaxaca is one of the centres of the Mexican drug trade, and this is the cause of violence and corruption at all levels of society; you would therefore do well to steer clear of trouble.

Events Many of the native dances of the state of Oaxaca are performed regularly in town at special nights in the major hotels – inquire for details at your hotel, or at the tourist office, who will also be able to help if you wish to go to a village fiesta nearby. There is almost bound to be a fiesta during your stay. A selection of important dates in Oaxaca follows.

At Easter, festivities in all villages. Processions, dances and fireworks.

On last two Mondays of July, Lunes del Guelaguetza. Major dance festival on summit of Cerro de Fortín and at various hotels.

On Dec 16, feast of the Virgin of La Soledad. Start of the elaborate Christmas celebrations at church of La Soledad.

Sights and places of interest

Cathedral and Zocalo

Days in Oaxaca all seem to start and end under the trees of the Zocalo. Before dawn, the Indians walk in from their villages, and sit talking until the market starts; long after midnight, the last tourist staggers back to his hotel. Nearly all around the clock, it hums with social, musical and commercial activity – although creative inactivity over a glass of beer or a coffee is the rule.

On the N side of the Zocalo is the **cathedral**, started in 1544 and finished some two centuries later. The facade is Baroque, with an old wooden-cogged clock presented to the city by the king of Spain. Standing opposite is the splendid 19thC Neoclassical **Palacio de Gobierno**.

Museo Rufino Tamayo ☆

Morelos 503 Open 10am–6pm. Closed Mon, Tues.

In an old, carefully restored colonial mansion is a fine collection of Pre-Hispanic pottery and sculpture, originally the personal collection of the artist Rufino Tamayo, who presented it to his home state. There are exhibits from all over the country, arranged geographically and chronologically. Perhaps the most delightful item is the model of a ball-court for the sacred game, with figurines for the participants and spectators.

Santo Domingo and Museo de Oaxaca ✝

5 de Mayo Open standard hours, closed for lunch.

A massive 16thC monastery church with an ornately carved facade between two high bell towers. The interior is an opulent profusion of white and gold, typical of the amazing energy with which Mexico seized on the Baroque style and made of it something quite unique. During the anti-clerical upheavals of the 1860s, the church was turned into a stable and suffered severe damage. All except the side chapels have now been fully restored.

In the old monastery behind the church is the state museum of Oaxaca, laid out in a series of galleries around the cloister. Pride of place goes to the rich treasures of gold and jade from the tombs at *Monte Albán*. There is also a large collection of ceremonial masks and costumes from the different tribes of the valley; some of the Indian women in town for the market still wear the traditional costumes, and with a bit of study here, you will be able to identify their home village.

La Soledad ✝

Independencia.

A Baroque church, built in 1682, housing the statue of the Virgin who is Oaxaca's patron saint. She stands in a gilded shrine, and wears a magnificent robe of jewel-studded black velvet. She was found in the pack of an unaccounted-for stray mule which had died. This event was construed as miraculous and a church was built to commemorate it. The statue then proved to have supernatural healing powers, and ever since has been the object of fervent piety from a devout populace.

Villages nearby

At **Cuilapán** ☆ (12km/8 miles SW) the Dominicans decided to build their largest monastery in New Spain. The ruins are indeed vast, and although the project was never completed, they are well worth a visit. The church, now roofless, has a simple Renaissance facade flanked by round towers, and next to it is another smaller church that would have been for the use of the monks only. **Zaachila** (6km/4 miles farther) is on the site of the last capital of the Zapotec kingdom. There is one small restored structure and many burial mounds. Two of the tombs in the main court have been excavated, and their contents are in the Museo Nacional de Antropología in *Mexico City*.

San Bartolo and **Santa Rosa Coyotepec** ☆ (12km/8 miles s by the Puerto Angel road) are two potters' villages famous for their black terra-cotta crockery and figures. The workshops welcome visitors, who can watch pots and plates being made without the benefit of a wheel. On Aug 23–24, San Bartolo celebrates its patron saint's day with some unusual dancing, involving performers with wooden masks and wigs of cactus fibre.

Hotels

Hotel Victoria [symbol]
Pan-American Highway km 545 ☎ *(951) 6–2633* [symbol] *to* [symbol] [symbol] *151* [symbol] AE CB [symbol] [symbol] VISA

The Victoria has a prominent position overlooking the city, with a good restaurant and gardens.
[symbols]

Marqués del Valle [symbol]
Portal de Claveria 1 ☎ *(951) 6–3198* [symbol] [symbol] *84* [symbol]

Due to its location in the plaza, parking can be difficult. A traditional establishment with smallish rooms.
[symbol]

Misión de los Angeles
Porfirio Díaz 102 ☎ *(951) 5–1000* [symbol] [symbol] *60* [symbol] AE CB [symbol] [symbol] VISA

A well-run, quiet hotel about 15mins' walk from the Zocalo. Local tours arranged.
[symbols]

El Presidente [symbol]
5 de Mayo no.300 ☎ *(951) 6–0611* [symbol] [symbol] *91* [symbol] AE CB [symbol] [symbol] VISA

The most interesting hotel: a beautifully restored 16thC monastery decorated in colonial style with native weavings. Pleasant cocktail bar open to non-residents.
[symbol]

Restaurants

R **La Flor de Oaxaca**
López 311 ☎ *(951) 6–5522* [symbol]

Regional cuisine is served amid simple decor.

R **El Tule** [symbol]
Portal de Flores 3 ☎ *(951) 6–2917* [symbol]

Located on the plaza, this restaurant provides Oaxacan specialities – try something with the *mole oaxaqueño* sauce.

R The ***Misión de los Angeles***, ***El Presidente*** and ***Hotel Victoria*** hotels all have good restaurants. **El Patio** [symbol] (*Hidalgo 819* ☎ *(951) 6–1885* [symbol] *to* [symbol]) is decorated in the colonial style, and specialities include regional meat dishes.

Shopping

The villages around Oaxaca each have their own craft speciality, and every day, but especially on Saturdays, the villagers pour into the **Mercado Juarez**, s of the Zocalo. This is the place to buy weaving, embroidery, pottery, hammocks, baskets and so on. Alternatively, visit the tourist office, who can tell you at which of the villages nearby there will be a special market and fiesta.

A speciality of the jewellery shops near the Zocalo are reproductions of the Monte Albán tomb finds.

Places nearby

Besides the great archaeological sites of *Mitla* and *Monte Albán*, both less than an hour from the city, the state of Oaxaca offers a generous variety of possible excursions.

The road to Mexico City via Cuautla

Take RF 190 NW.

The village of **Atzompa** (6km/4 miles S at 3km/2 miles) is known for the green-glaze pots and fine figurines of its many potters. At **San Pablo Etla** (10km/6 miles) there is a Plateresque church and a 16thC Dominican monastery, whose sister establishment is at **Huitzo**, 22km (13 miles) farther on. On Apr 1, there is a large market and some lively celebrations at Etla. Of particular interest are the church and monastery at **Yanhuitlán** ☆ (119km/74 miles). The monastery has a fine collection of painted wooden effigies of saints, and in the church is a caissoned ceiling, in the upper gallery, which is a good example of a difficult technique. Under the rib-vaulted nave of the church stands an ornate altarpiece.

Take the road S to Costa Chica after 130km (81 miles) and after 13km (8 miles) you will reach the 16thC monastery church of **Teposcolula**, with an interesting open chapel. It suffered some earthquake damage, but most of the fine decorative stonework is intact. In the village of **Coixtlahuaca** (10km/6 miles N at 135km/84 miles), the Aztec language of Nahuatl is still spoken, rather than the local Mixtec, as it was an Aztec trading post after it declined from the Mixtec period. The Spaniards used the stones from the temples to construct the large monastery and church; the latter has a large rose window, uncommon in Mexico. A possible overnight stop is at **Huajuapán**, after 195km (122 miles).

The road to Mitla

Take RF 190 SE.

Readers of books of records will know that the enormous cypress tree at **Santa María del Tule** (10km/6 miles) has the greatest circumference of any tree in the world. The girth and the height are nearly equal – 41m (135ft) each way – and the age is approximately that of the number of the year. There is dancing in front of the church on Aug 15.

Teotitlán del Valle (20km/12 miles) is a Zapotec village of weavers, famous for its *sarapes*. In Holy Week, the colourful Feather Dance is performed in front of the church. The site of **Dainzu** (just S of road at 21km/13 miles) is best seen on the way back from *Mitla* – if you still have the energy. The most important structure is a pyramid faced with carved stone slabs, most of which show players of the sacred ball-game.

The fortified hill which dominates the archaeological zone of **Yagul** (N of road at 34km/22 miles) has a magnificent view of the whole Oaxaca Valley. It was occupied throughout the life of Monte Albán, but the main buildings date from the later period. A large ball-court has been fully restored, and is flanked by two courts. Overlooking the area is the **Palacio**, with a series of chambers around small terraces.

Orizaba

Map 13E8. Veracruz. 132km (82 miles) E of Puebla on RF 150 and RF 190. Population: 140,000. Served by train (lines to Mexico City and Veracruz) and bus.

Not only does Orizaba lie at the foot of Mexico's tallest mountain, but it also possesses the country's largest brewery, the **Cervecería Montezuma**, on the W of town. Turn up during working hours, or get your hotel to ring and arrange a guided tour – it is both interesting and refreshing. The 5,700m (18,851ft) **Pico de Orizaba** is more demanding to explore. There is always a cone of snow on the summit of the extinct volcano, and to climb it an experienced guide is needed. Only those in perfect condition can hope to reach the top without experiencing oxygen starvation. You might care to make a petition for success at the colonial church on the Zocalo.

[H] **Aries** (*Oriente 6 no.265* ☎ *(272) 5–3699* ▮▯ ⇉) has an astrological theme; **Trueba** (*Oriente 6 and Sur 11* ☎ *(272) 5–2144* ▮▯ ⇉ ≈) is a downtown commercial establishment.

Pachuca

Map 12D7. Capital of Hidalgo. 91km (56 miles) NE of Mexico City on RF 85 and RF 45. Altitude: 2,430m (8,747ft). Population: 115,000. Served by train (line from Mexico City) and bus. Car rental: Budget, Glorieta Revolución 18 ☎ (771) 3–3215 i Victoria 202 ☎ (771) 2–5960.

An unremarkable and little-visited old mining town which is nonetheless surrounded by places of interest, including two of the finest colonial monasteries in Mexico, and the ruins of *Tula*. The old part of town around the Zocalo retains some of its colonial flavour, but Pachuca is only worth a longer stay if you have already been to Mexico several times, and wish to explore some of the lesser-known places nearby. Otherwise, if you are passing through, just take your pick of the nearby sights that interest you and set off into the beautiful hill country around the town. The best hotel for a stopover is at San Miguel Regla (see ***Places nearby***, below).

H **El Dorado** (*Guerrero 721 ☎ (771) 2–0082* to) is a modern hotel; **Grenfell** (*Plaza Independencia 116 ☎ (771) 2–0207*) was originally a 19thC stagecoach stop.

Hotel nearby

Huasca (*25km/15 miles NE of Pachuca*).

Hacienda San Miguel Regla

No telephone 53

A colonial hacienda located near fascinating old silver mines and ore-extraction water-works. This used to be a luxury weekend spot, and although the service and food are no longer in that class, it is still the best in the area.

R **General de Pachuca** (*Rojo Gómez ☎ (771) 2–7439*) serves regional specialities.

Places nearby

Actopán ☆

Take RF 85 N.

At the town of **Actopán** (36km/23 miles), there is a large and beautifully restored complex of ecclesiastical buildings which now serves as a **museum of colonial art** (*open 10am–6pm*); there are also exhibits of native Otomi arts and crafts. Beside the dignified Plateresque church is a large open chapel, with murals showing graphically the sufferings of the damned. The hall of the monastery has contrasting murals showing the tranquil benefits of the monastic life.

48km (30 miles) farther is the smaller sister-establishment at **Ixmiquilpán**. Every Monday, there is a colourful Otomi market in the village, and on Aug 14 the local fiesta is celebrated with a procession over a carpet of flowers.

The road to Tampico

Take RF 105 NE.

The road winds up into the wooded hills of the state of Hidalgo. After 10km (6 miles) the attractive 18thC mining village of **Mineral del Monte** is reached. The Cornish miners who came out to work the mines here have left their mark on the local cuisine in the shape of pasties: meat and vegetable pies identical to the originals in all respects, except for the addition of chili.

A turning E after 21km (12 miles) leads to **San Miguel Regla** (12km/8 miles). Even if not planning to stay at the hotel here, it is worth a detour to see the disused silver-refining works. On the main road beyond here there are interesting 16thC monasteries at **Atotonilco** (40km/25 miles), **Molango** (137km/86 miles) and **Huejutla** (204km/126 miles). The cliffs and mountains along this road are spectacular, with amazingly twisted rock formations.

Palenque ★

Map 8H11. Chiapas. 150km (93 miles) SE of Villahermosa on RF 186. Population: 4,000. Served by air (air taxi from San Cristóbal de las Casas, Tuxtla and Villahermosa), train (on Coatzacoalcos–Mérida line) and bus.

Of all Mexico's Mayan cities, it is usually Palenque that enchants and fascinates visitors the most. The buildings are on low hills surrounded by the exuberant tropical jungle that concealed them for nearly a millenium. Although they are smaller than the great monuments of Yucatán, the delicate proportions and intricately modelled stucco decoration are unrivalled. Some observers have found here similarities to the temples of Cambodia, and the burial chamber at the heart of the **Temple of the Inscriptions** is paralleled only in the Middle East. This all adds to the mystery of the Maya.

Palenque was inhabited long before the Christian era, rose to become a powerful independent city, and was abandoned as the Dark Ages waned in Europe. Restoration work began in 1940, but much remains to be done on the myriad green-covered mounds that spread out far into the jungle.

. . . if you like wild nature, the setting of Palenque is a finer one – on a great circular plateau half-way up the mountainside, with the jungle falling precipitously below into the plain and rising straight up behind . . . temples or palaces open up, emerging obscurely from the jungle . . . they have looked out for a minute, old wrinkled faces, and will soon withdraw.

Graham Greene, *The Lawless Roads*, 1939

The ruins

Open 8am–6pm.

The Palace

Entering the site, directly in front is a striking four-storey tower, rising over a group of buildings known as The Palace. The tower may have been used for astronomical observation, but it is unique in Mexico and its purpose is not known. In the small temples around the courts of the Palace are many examples of the finely detailed stucco reliefs for which Palenque is famous, and leading down to the E court is a beautifully ornamented stairway. After leaving the Palace, walk around the exterior retaining walls, which are decorated with large carved panels of gods.

Temple of the Inscriptions

Near the Palace is a steep pyramid crowned by the Temple of the Inscriptions, where there are a large number of carved hieroglyphs relating to the Mayan calendar. The most remarkable thing about this pyramid is the existence of a burial chamber at its centre, discovered only in 1952. It is reached down a narrow tunnel, and now contains a single 5-tonne sarcophagus, richly carved. When found, it contained the remains of a priest or king, and the skeletons of some hapless servants sent with him to the underworld. Together with the funerary offerings, they are now all at rest in the Museo Nacional de Antropología in *Mexico City*. This discovery upset the conventional wisdom that the pyramids of Mesoamerica were never used as burial places.

Other buildings

On the other side of the stream running through the site there are several smaller buildings, widely spaced out. From the great pyramid, you arrive first at the **Temple of the Sun**; to its N is a building known as **Edifice XIV**, with a fine low-relief of a prince accepting offerings from a humbly genuflecting woman. Behind are the carved **Temples of the Cross** and, to the S, of the **Foliated Cross**.

500m (550yds) S down the course of the stream stands the **Temple of the Jaguar**, on a low hill. Unfortunately, only parts of the reliefs remain here, so unless you feel energetic, miss it, and head N up the stream to the temples and ball-court of the **North Group**. Near them is a small **museum**, containing stucco masks and sculptures from the ruins.

Hotels

Accommodation in Palenque has long been an object of complaint by travellers, but the new Hotel Misión (opening 1983/4) should set a new standard.

La Cañada
Cañada 18 ☎ (934) 5–0102 20
Located on the outskirts of town, this is a good place for archaeological enthusiasts. Accommodation is in thatched bungalows.

Motel de las Ruinas
Near the ruins ☎ (934) 5–0109 30
A new, efficient and clean motel.

Palenque
5 de Mayo no. 15 ☎ (934) 5–0103 40
This is the best place to stay in the village. Some of the rooms have air conditioning.

R **The best restaurant is to be found in the hotel *La Cañada* (see above).**

Places nearby

A reasonable all-weather road leads over the mountains to *San Cristóbal de las Casas*, via the little known but fascinating ruins of Toniná. After about 20km (12 miles), a turning to the W leads to the local beauty spot of Agua Azul, where you can swim beneath the cascades.

See also *Bonampak*.

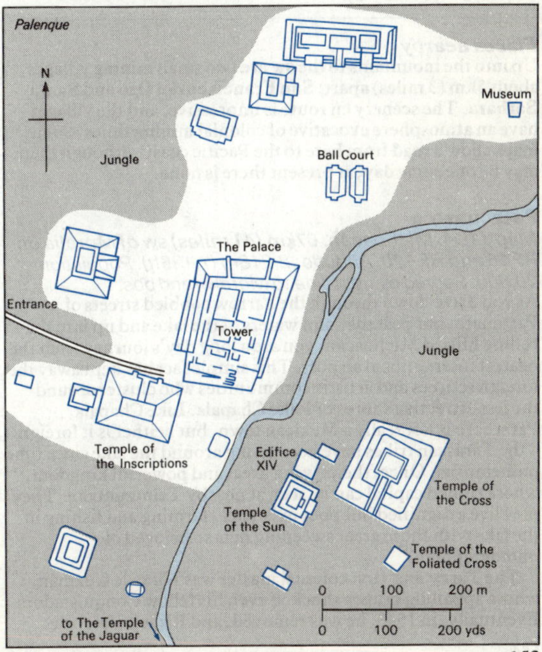

Parral (*Hidalgo del Parral*)

Map 4D6. Chihuahua. 300km (186 miles) s of Chihuahua on RF 45. Altitude: 1,660m (6,450ft). Population: 80,000. Served by train (branch line from Jiménez on Torreón–Chihuahua line) and bus.

A small colonial mining town in the dry and dusty mountains of the Sierra Madre that makes a fascinating diversion and is only an hour's drive from the main N to S highway.

Event On May 3, Festival of the Cross.

Sights and places of interest

On the Zocalo is the colonial **Palacio Municipal**, with its own pleasant gardens, and the **parish church**, completed in 1710, with a fine Churrigueresque altar.

Two blocks away, towards the river, is the **Palacio Pedro Alvarado**. The building is only irregularly open, but is worth visiting for its ornate interior, all marble and onyx, with crystal chandeliers. It was built by a humble silver miner, who struck so lucky that at one point he offered to pay Mexico's national debt.

Another miner who struck lucky was an Indian who financed the building of the 17thC church of **La Virgen del Rayo** (Our Lady of the Thunderbolt), on the other side of the river. Parral was at that time the capital of the colonial state of New Biscay, and the governor had the Indian tortured to reveal the location of his gold mine. However, he died silent. Today, the church, colourfully decorated with Indian motifs, is still used with pride by local Indians.

Parral's most famous son was the notorious revolutionary, Pancho Villa. His house is now a grocery store, and the place of his sudden and violent death in 1923 is marked by a plaque, in Calle Barreda.

[H] Although there are no luxury hotels here, two reasonable choices are **Camino Real** (*Prolongación Av. Independencia* ☎ *(152) 2-2050* ▮□ ⇌ ≋), a motel s of town, and the central **Turista** (*Plazuela Independencia* ☎ *(152) 2-4784* ▮□ ⇌).

Places nearby

Up into the mountains to the SW are two small mining villages, about 5km (3 miles) apart: **San Francisco del Oro** and **Santa Barbara**. The scenery en route is impressive, and the villages have an atmosphere evocative of colonial mining times. Some maps show a road from here to the Pacific coast; although there may be one some day, at present there is none.

Patzcuaro ☆

Map 11D4. Michoacán. 67km (41 miles) sw of Morelia on RF 15 and RF 120. Altitude: 2,218m (7,135ft). Population: 28,000. Served by train (line to Morelia) and bus.

As you drive down through the narrow cobbled streets of Patzcuaro, out past the calm waters of the lake and up into the rolling hills of Michoacán, you are a long day's journey from the nearest international airport. This simple fact has kept away the foreign retirees and artistic communities who cluster around the less attractive shores of Lake Chapala. Like Chapala, Patzcuaro is not really a Mexican town, but neither is it foreign – the Tarascan tribes have been living around the lake since time immemorial. Once, theirs was a great and powerful kingdom, whose ruined capital can be seen at nearby **Tzintzuntzán**. They now live a dignified but poor existence, farming and fishing in the lake with those great sweeping nets so beloved of photographers.

The Tarascans' first colonial master was Nino de Guzmán, whose appalling crimes shocked even his fellow Conquistadors. Eventually, in 1540, he was removed, and Bishop Vasco de

Quiroga was sent to bring life back to the devastated area. One of his methods was to teach the Indians of each village a different craft. To this day his name is venerated by Tarascans, and the area remains rich in handicrafts. On Fridays there is a big market, and this is the day to buy weaving, copperware or any other of 'Tata Vasco's' many legacies.

Events The tourist office will advise on details, but some special dates for religious celebrations are Good Friday and Oct 8, both celebrated with processions and dances. During Holy Week in Tzintzuntzán, locals re-enact the Passion with alarming realism. At Quiroga on first Sunday in July, candlelit procession in honour of the Precious Blood of Christ.

In early Aug, copper fair at Villa Escalante (see ***Sights***, below).

On Nov 1, Day of the Dead on island of Janitzio (see ***The lake and islands***, below). One of Mexico's best fiestas.

Sights and places of interest

The centre

The colonial buildings around the **Zocalo** could well take half a day to visit before you even start on the lake. Begin on the Zocalo itself with the **Casa del Gigante** (House of the Giant), named for the large painted statue of a soldier, up on the first floor. Leave the square on Portugal, right of the Casa del Gigante, and turn left for the **Museo de Arte Popular** (Museum of Folk Arts), which is housed in the 16thC Colegio de San Nicolás (*closed Mon*). Exhibits demonstrate the range of the crafts devised by Don Vasco for his Tarascan flock, including some fine ceremonial masks. Just a block to the N is the large unfinished **Basilica de Nuestra Señora** (of the Virgin). The Virgin in question is a statue, made from a special worm-proof vegetable on a frame of cane, which is the object of frenzied devotion at fiesta times.

From the W door of the basilica, the narrow Calle del Conejo leads straight ahead to the **Plaza de San Agustín**, where the 16thC church has been converted into a library. On the walls are murals by Juan O'Gorman, one of the 1930s Marxist muralists, showing the history of Michoacán, with plenty of evil-looking Spaniards grinding the faces of the Tarascan poor. Finally, before going down to the lake, visit the **Casa de los Once Patios**, a thriving little crafts centre in the old residence on Colimilla, SE of the Zocalo, which also houses the tourist office.

The lake and islands

It is about 25mins on a small ferry to the largest of the seven islands, **Janitzio**, mostly occupied by a pretty little fishing village dominated by the tiled dome of the church and a rather dreadful monument. On the night of The Day of the Dead, on Nov 1, the villagers stay up till dawn in the graveyard, chanting by candlelight; all the while boats come and go with offerings for the dead, with the candles on the prows glinting over the dark waters of the lake. It is an eerie and moving scene, well worth travelling a long way to see.

If there is time to spare, engage a boatman at the jetty and explore the lake and islands at leisure. At sunset, the elegant geometric shapes of butterfly nets reflect in the shimmering water – photographers should stock up on film.

For a good view of town and lake, head W out of the Zocalo along Ponce de León, past the old Customs House and the pottery market in front of San Francisco church. It is about 5km (3 miles) to the summit of an extinct volcano called **El Estribo**. By the time you return, a supper of grilled whitefish from the lake will be more than welcome.

Sights nearby

Tzintzuntzán ruins ☆

17km (10 miles) N by Morelia and lakeside roads.

Near the village of Tzintzuntzán are the ruins of the old Tarascan capital, on the side of a hill looking out over the lake. Although only partly restored, the grandeur of the five main temples around the great terrace is proof of the high level of civilization that had been reached by the time of the Conquest. Indeed, the Aztecs, with whom the Tarascans had occasional skirmishes, regarded them as artistically superior. Near the site is a large 16thC monastery, built using stones from the pyramids. In the forecourt are some of the only olive trees grown in New Spain; their planting was generally forbidden to protect the farmers of Spain.

From here the road around the lake leads to the village of **Quiroga**, 9km (5 miles) farther on. It is known for its intricately decorated wooden boxes and furniture, one of Vasco's industries still flourishing after four centuries. Another of these can be seen at **Santa Clara del Cobre** (now **Villa Escalante**), 15km (9 miles) s of Patzcuaro. Copper-working is the speciality here, and the sound of metal-beating echoes right through the village. The copper fair in early August is an impressive sight, with great regiments of pots and kettles shining in the sun.

All around the lake and in the hills are hundreds of villages worth exploring for their churches, crafts and timeless charm. Two of the most interesting and unspoiled are **Erongaricuaro** (w of the lake) and **Ario de Rosales** (25km/15 miles s of Santa Clara).

H **Posada de Don Vasco**
Calzada de las Américas 450 ☎ (454) 2-0227 66 AE CB DC MC VISA

A colonial-style country hotel between the town and lake, which puts on Tarascan dancing in the evenings.

H Also recommended: **Mesón del Gallo** (*Doctor Coss 20* ☎ *(454) 2-1474*), a small, pleasant, downtown hotel, and **San Carlos** (*Av. Caltzonzir, on the lakeside* ☎ *(454) 2-1274/1359*).

R Visit **Hostería de San Felipe** (*Calzada de las Americas s/n* ☎ *(454) 2-1298*) for local specialities and atmosphere.

Piedras Negras

Map 5C8. Coahuila. 442km (274 miles) N of Monterrey on RF 57 and RF 53. Population: 60,000. Served by air, train (line to Monterrey) and bus.

An important border crossing-point from the US with little to interest the tourist.

H **Autel Río** (*Padre de las Casas 121 Norte* ☎*(878) 2-0180*); **California** (*Emilio Carranza 1006* ☎ *(878) 2-2453*), a motel.

Popocatepetl

Map 12E7. State of Mexico. 89km (55 miles) SE of Mexico City by RF 190 and RF 115. Altitude: 5,450m (17,881ft).

The 'Smoking Mountain' dominates the skylines of *Mexico City*, *Puebla* and *Cuernavaca*, with its tapering mass of rocks and snow often showing above a layer of clouds. The last major eruption was in 1802, so it is fairly safe to climb 'Popo'; a path leads all the way to the summit from the mountain hostel at Tlamacas, not far from the Paso de Cortés where Cortés first caught sight of the Aztec capital laid out in the valley below him. If intending to go all the way, it is advisable to spend the night here and set out at dawn. The climbing gets slower and slower as the oxygen in the air diminishes (anyone who faints should immediately be escorted back to the hostel). Do not start the climb unless the weather looks good (ask advice locally), and take warm clothing and some supplies. When the crater is reached, spare a thought for the heroes whom Cortés caused to be lowered down there, while it was still active, to scrape out sulphur for gunpowder.

On the other side of the pass is the 'Sleeping Lady', **Ixtaccihuatl**, a more difficult peak to climb, only to be undertaken by experienced, fully equipped mountaineers.

Poza Rica

Map 13C8. Veracruz. 265km (164 miles) NE of Mexico City on RF 85, RF 45 and RF 130. Population: 230,000. Served by air and bus.

An industrial town of little interest for the tourist. It may however be a convenient place to spend the night before visiting the archaeological site of *El Tajín*.

Papantla

30km (19 miles) SE on RF 180.

A small agricultural centre in the middle of Totonac Indian country. It is famous for the **'Danza de los Voladores'**, which takes place every year on Corpus Christi, and on some Sundays throughout the year. Four costumed dancers, ropes around their waist, climb up a 30m (100ft) pole, then launch themselves into space, spiralling down to the ground in dizzying loops. This is a Pre-Hispanic pagan rite of unknown significance; the missionaries, who regarded it only as a dangerous game, failed to stamp it out.

30km (19 miles) farther E is the tranquil beach of **Tecolutla**, near a Totonac township known for its hats of woven palm-fibre.

See also *El Tajín*.

H **Poza Rica** (*10 Oriente and Kehoe* ☎ *(782) 2–0112*); **Robert Prince** (*6 Norte and 10 Oriente* ☎ *(782) 2–5455*).

Hotels nearby

Papantla (*20km/12 miles SE of Poza Rica*).

Totonocapán (*Olivo and 20 de Noviembre* ☎ *(784) 2–1218*).

Tecolutla (*60km/37 miles SE of Poza Rica*).

Tecolutla (*Matamoros s/n* ☎ *(784) 5–0901*).

Tuxpán (*60km/37 miles NE of Poza Rica*).

Reforma (*Juarez 25* ☎ *(784) 4–0210*).

Puebla ☆

Map 12E7. Capital of Puebla. 132km (82 miles) SE of Mexico City on RF 150 and RF 190. Altitude: 2,160m (7,086ft). Population: 600,000. Served by train (line from Mexico City) and bus. Car rental: Budget, Juarez 1703 ☎ (22) 41–2650; Hertz, 4 Poniente no.2910 ☎ (22) 48–4345 i 5 Oriente no.3 ☎ (22) 46–0928.

A city of colonial mansions and churches, with walls, facades and domes covered in brightly coloured *faïence* tiles. The original colonists came from an area of Spain famous for its intricately patterned ceramics; unlike most Spaniards, they came to stay and not to amass a fortune for retirement to Spain, so they tried to make Puebla as much like their home as possible. The Spanish atmosphere is all the stronger because, unlike most cities of New Spain, Puebla was not built over the ruins of pyramids. Nearby *Cholula* would have been the obvious site, but it seems that the blood-encrusted temples and piles of skulls proved too much for the early settlers.

It is said that the first Bishop of Tlaxcala dreamed of Puebla's beautiful fertile valley under the shadow of snow-covered volcanoes, and ordered the city to be founded there in 1531. Puebla remained strongly royalist during the War of Independence, although it established more patriotic credentials during the war with the French. General Ignacio Zaragoza, leading a citizen army, inflicted a heavy defeat here on the French army in 1862. Although they were not finally defeated for another five years, the day of the battle, May 5, has become a national holiday, celebrating the rejection of all foreign interventions.

The *poblanos* have always been proud of their separate character, and as well as in their architecture, this is reflected in their cooking and in the women's costumes. The famous *mole* sauce, of spices, chili and chocolate, was first prepared by the nuns of Santa Rosa as a special saint's day treat for their bishop. Another speciality is *chiles en nogada*, also first prepared as a saint's day treat, this time for General Iturbide. His admirers decided to fête him with a patriotic dish of green chili, white sauce and red topping, representing the Mexican flag; it is now served all over the country during Independence celebrations in September.

Alas, the traditional costume is harder to find than the traditional food, and you are unlikely to see a *poblana* in full rig, although some smart Mexican ladies do wear it as formal dress. Known as *china poblana* after a Chinese girl who originally designed it, it is also red, white and green, covered with rich embroidery and sequins.

Industry and the ravages of the internal combustion engine have not passed Puebla by, but it makes an excellent day-trip from Mexico City. The city centre itself repays any amount of exploration, and the countryside around is one of the most fascinating areas in Mexico.

Event On May 5, fiesta to commemorate Battle of Puebla.

Sights and places of interest

Most of Puebla's colonial monuments are within a few minutes' walk of the pleasantly shaded **Zocalo**. The streets are numbered in a semi-logical but confusing way, the streets to the N or E of the Zocalo even-numbered, and the others odd-numbered. Moreover, each street bears the name of the direction in which it points from the Zocalo. Once you have mastered it, however, it is impossible to get lost.

Biblioteca Palafoxiana

7 Oriente, behind cathedral. Open 9.30am–1pm.

An old tiled palace containing thousands of books in dark, carved shelves. There is a 15thC *Nuremburg Chronicle*, and a 16thC Bible printed in Greek, Latin, Aramaic and Hebrew. Sitting quietly at one of the tables, you can hardly avoid absorbing some of the ancient wisdom.

Casa del Alfeñique (*Puebla Regional Museum*)

4 Oriente. Open standard hours.

The excellent local museum is housed in a typical tiled residence whose name means 'Barley Sugar House'. There is a fine collection of Puebla ceramics and costumes, and up on the first floor some paintings of the Battle of Puebla.

Cathedral †

The huge Renaissance cathedral is the largest in the country outside Mexico City, and dominates the Zocalo from the S. Although begun in the mid-16thC, it was not completed until 1649, and so the great west **doors** are wonders of the Baroque. Also notable on the exterior are the statues of Spanish kings, on the N doorway. Inside, the Neoclassical high altar is made from the onyx for which Puebla is famous; the intricately carved doors and choir stalls are inlaid with onyx and mother-of-pearl. One of several ornate side chapels, the **Capilla Real**, houses 17thC paintings by Martínez Montañes.

La Compañía †

4 Norte.

Inside the fine Churrigueresque facade and the typical blue-and-white-tiled cupola is the resting place, according to legend, of the original *china poblana*. If she did exist, she may have been a Mogul princess captured by pirates in the Philippines and sold into slavery.

Guadalupe and Loreto forts and Museo del Estado *(State Museum)*
3km (2 miles) NE of centre. Open standard hours.
The two 19thC forts which look over the city centre mark the site of the Battle of Puebla in 1862; inside the Loreto fort there is a small military museum commemorating the occasion. The fine modern building between the forts is the Puebla State Museum, with archaeological remains and native artifacts from the state. The centrepiece is a **jade statuette** of Olmec origin.

Santo Domingo ✝
4 Poniente.
This 17thC Baroque church contains one of the most breathtakingly opulent chapels in all Mexico, the **Capilla del Rosario**. The central statue of the Virgin is festooned with more jewels than Cleopatra, and on every surface, walls, ceiling and altar, is a confusion of lavishly gilded cherubs and intricate carvings.

Santa Monica Convent
5 de Mayo (1 Norte). Open 10am–4pm.
When the Mexican state expropriated all church property in 1857, the nuns here literally went underground, into the honeycomb of secret passages, hidden doors and hollow walls. They lived there, with local cooperation, until their discovery by the authorities in 1934. The building was turned into a museum and now houses a large collection of religious sculpture and painting.

Santa Rosa Convent
3 Norte and 14 Poniente. Open 10am–6pm.
The historical kitchen where *mole* was invented has been fully restored, and there is even a small restaurant where it may be sampled.

Other sights

Worth a quick visit is the small colonial **Museo Bello** (*3 Sur open 10am–5pm, closed Sun*), containing Puebla furniture and glassware. As you make your way across the Zocalo, do not be surprised to see a bus with zebra stripes – it is picking up passengers for the **Safari Park**, 21km (13 miles) s of town towards the Valsequillo dam (*open 10am–6pm*). Private cars are also admitted to the park (but not soft-tops), which is an amusing trip for those who really wanted Africa.

Sights nearby

Huejotzingo
26km (16 miles) NW on road to San Martín Texmelucan.
A good detour on the road to Mexico City. Passing Cholula on your left, you come to the town of Huejotzingo, built around one of the best 16thC monasteries in Mexico and known also for its refusal to submit to the Aztecs in Pre-Hispanic times, for its (lapsed) tradition of banditry, the Lent Carnival, and the Saturday market. Start your visit to the monastery with the finely carved stone cross in the atrium; all around the atrium are the open chapels used by pilgrims and unbaptized converts. From here, enter the grim-looking church, with its great Gothic vault soaring over the Plateresque high altar. In the monastery itself, see the murals, in the cloister, of the *Immaculate Conception*.

15km (9 miles) farther is the town of **Texmelucan**, where the highway can be re-joined. Here too there is a monastery, and at the Tuesday-morning market can be found the geometrically-patterned *sarapes* (ponchos) for which the area is known.

Puebla churches to the south
Follow road for Izúcar de Matamoros.
Two of the most perfect Puebla-style churches are on this road at **Tlaxcalancingo** (8km/5 miles) and **Acatepec** ☆ (10km/6 miles). San Francisco ✝ at Acatepec has a fine intricately tiled and ornamented facade and a heavily carved and gilded Baroque wooden altarpiece. The Cholula road out of Acatepec leads to the village of **Tonantzintla** ☆ (2km/1¼ miles), where the Churrigueresque church is a good example of the way in which this lavish style was so enthusiastically developed by native craftsmen.

After 34km (22 miles) on the main road is the pleasant small town of **Atlixco**, with a leafy Zocalo surrounded by tiled Puebla buildings. Visit the parish church and the Hospital de San Juan, built around a galleried court. Up on the hill overlooking the town is an austere fortified monastery with a commanding view of the valley.

Hotels

Lastra
Calzada de los Fuertes 2633 ☎ *(22) 42–4630* 52
A taxi ride from the centre, this hotel is set in semi-tropical gardens, and has an excellent restaurant, popular for Sunday lunch.

Mesón del Angel
Hermanos Serdán 807 ☎ *(22) 48–2100* 185
Puebla's best-known hotel is located in a southern suburb. A popular weekend spot with colonial decor.

Posada San Pedro
2 Oriente 202 ☎ *(22) 46–5077* 80
A good new downtown hotel 5mins from the Zocalo.

Restaurants

There are a large number of smart commercial international restaurants, catering for Puebla's business community.

La Bola Roja
17 Sur no.1305 ☎ *(22) 43–7051*
Simple decor, but good Mexican and regional cuisine.

Charlie's China Poblana
Juarez 1918 ☎ *(22) 46–3184*
A cheerful place to go for Mexican and international dishes.

Fonda Santa Clara
3 Poniente no.307 ☎ *(22) 42–2659* to
For the best *mole poblano* in town, come here; they grind their own spices and take hours to prepare it.

Hostería del Virrey
11 Sur no.1306 ☎ *(22) 43–8439*
The Virrey provides an interesting combination of an art gallery and a Mexican restaurant.

Puerto Escondido

Map 7I9. Oaxaca. 242km (149 miles) s of Oaxaca on RF 200. Population: 20,000. Served by air and bus. Car rental: Avis, Rancho El Pescador ☎ (958) 2–0391.

A supposedly 'undiscovered' fishing village, whose beautiful beaches and relaxed atmosphere are in fact being discovered by quite a crowd. Luxury hotels are in the offing, but the emphasis for the time being is definitely on the beachlife rather than the nightlife.

H **Paraíso Escondido** (*Unión 10* ☎ *(958) 2–0444*); **Rancho el Pescador** (*coast road s/n, km 1* ☎ *(958) 2–0391*), a small fishing and beach resort; **Viva Puerto Escondido** (*Juarez 1* ☎ *(958) 2–0133* to), a modern hotel.

Place nearby

Puerto Angel (*68km/43 miles* E *on RF 200*). Another idyllic, small fishing village with some fine tropical beaches, but no facilities for jet-set vacationers.

H **Angel del Mar** (*Playa del Panteón, no telephone*)

Puerto Vallarta

Map 6G6. Jalisco. 395km (240 miles) W of Guadalajara on RF 15 and RF 200. Population: 80,000. Served by air (international airport 11km/7 miles N), ferry (twice weekly to and from Cabo San Lucas in Baja California ☎ (322) 2-0476/06-527) and bus. Car rental: Avis, at airport ☎ (322) 2-1412; Budget, Olas Altas 428 ☎ (322) 2-1980, and at airport ☎ (322) 2-0188; Hertz, Hotel La Perla, 1.5km (1 mile) N on RF 200 ☎ (322) 2-0054, and at airport ☎ (322) 2-0473 i Independencia 8 ☎ (322) 2-0242, and Malecón s/n ☎ (322) 2-0242. American Express Travel Service: c/o Millers Travel Service, Paseo de las Garzas ☎ (322) 2-1197/2-1297/2-1397.

The badly kept secret of Puerto Vallarta's delights finally leaked out in the early 1970s, and in no time a picture-book fishing village blossomed into one of the country's top five resorts. It all began during the local filming of *Night of the Iguana*, when (off-screen) Richard Burton and Elizabeth Taylor titillated the world's voyeurs with an extravagant pre-marital dalliance. With such a start, an international airport was bound to follow. The town, with its narrow streets and low red-tiled houses, has kept most of its charm, all the same.

Most of the old houses are on the N bank of the river Cuale, which flows into the Bahía de Banderas under the 'Gringo Gulch' cliffs, named for the wealthy foreign community who followed in the footsteps of the superstars to settle in luxury eyries above the town and bay. The older hotels and restaurants are mostly in the commercial district to the N, although some of the cheaper establishments are in the blocks to the S of the Cuale Bridge. The luxury hotels are on the beaches on both sides of town, and thus do not set the tone of the place.

The atmosphere at 'P.V.' (as it is known) is less hectic than at Acapulco, although far from inhibited or unsophisticated. It now seems unlikely that there will be further massive investment here, for financial attention is now focused instead on the new super-resorts. Life at P.V. should therefore carry on at its own pace, no longer an undiscovered hideaway but by no means an out-and-out tourist-exploitation machine.

Hotels

Calinda Puerto Vallarta
Playa las Glorias ☎ (322) 2-2224 IIII 404 AE CB Φ MC VISA
One of the Quality Inn chain, this hotel was only opened in 1982. Next door is its slightly cheaper sister hotel, **Plaza las Glorias**.

Camino Real
Playa las Estacas ☎ (322) 2-0002 IIII 250 AE CB Φ MC VISA
A beach resort for those who enjoy the high life with lively and well-organized social arrangements. The only snag is that there is a seven-day minimum stay in high season.

Fiesta Americana
Playa los Tules ☎ (322) 2-2010 IIII 282 AE CB Φ MC VISA
A spectacular modern pyramid on the beautiful Los Tules beach. Also nearby are a cluster of more secluded Mediterranean-type villas, under the same management (*for details* ☎ *(322) 2-0570*).

Garza Blanca
Playa Palo María ☎ (322) 2-1023 IIII 46 AE CB Φ MC VISA
This isolated and intimate hideaway comprises the main hotel on the beach and several small villas up on the cliffs above.

Holiday Inn
3.5km (2¼ miles) N of Puerto Vallarta ☎ (322) 2-1700 IIII 230 AE CB Φ VISA
The Holiday Inn provides dependable fun for all the family, including paragliding for the more adventurous. Set on a quiet beach away from the town.

Lagunita
Playa Yelapa (reservations from 31 de Mayo no.62) II 13

Accessible only by boat from Puerto Vallarta, this group of thatched cabins is set on what is a truly secluded South Sea Paradise island. There are beautiful white-sand beaches, palm trees, and no telephones. Accommodation is fairly simple, however, and it is only for those who want complete isolation.

Posada Vallarta
Playa Vallarta ☎ (322) 2-1459 IIII 550 AE CB Φ VISA
The Posada has the most character of all the deluxe hotels, with its rambling complex of courts, gardens, pools and villas.

Quinta María Cortez
Playa Conchas Chinas ☎ (322) 2-1317 IIII 8 AE CB Φ VISA
A beautiful little colonial inn suitable for affluent sophisticates.

Sheraton Buganvilias
Playa las Estacas ☎ (322) 2-2050 IIII 328 AE CB Φ VISA
The penthouse suites here are the ultimate in luxury and the other rooms not far behind. All facilities.

Restaurants

The luxury hotels all have excellent and expensive restaurants, of which the ***Fiesta Americana*** and ***Posada Vallarta*** win the most acclaim. The **Playa de Oro** is a good place for lunch.

Carlos O'Brian's Bar and Grill and Pawnshop
Malecón 286 ☎ (322) 2-1444 IIII AE CB Φ VISA
A lively and popular place, with a joke-filled menu and easy-going waiters serving good food.

Casablanca
Díaz Ordaz 570 ☎ (322) 2-1723 III *to* IIII AE CB Φ VISA
An interestingly decorated *papier-mâché* zoo specializing in game and seafood dishes.

La Cebolla Roja
Díaz Ordaz 822 ☎ (322) 2-1087 III AE CB Φ VISA
Vegetarian and salad specialities.

Chez Elena
Hotel los Cuatro Vientos, Matamoros 173 ☎ (322) 2-0161 IIII AE CB Φ VISA
Located in the hills above the town, this is a restaurant not to be missed for its delicious and adventurous food.

Daiquiri Dicks
Olas Altas 246 ☎ (322) 2-0566 III *to* IIII AE CB Φ VISA
Imaginative decor and food are the features of this American-owned establishment.

La Fonda del Sol
Morelos 54 ☎ (322) 2-0743 IIII AE CB Φ VISA *Closed lunch.*
International and Mexican cuisine served amid soft music and dim lights.

La Iguana
Lazaro Cardenas 169 ☎ (322) 2-0105 III
Oriental and Mexican dishes, and frequent and lively fiestas.

Ostión Feliz
Libertad 177 ☎ (322) 2-2508 II
Distinctly downbeat decor, but excellent and varied seafood.

El Set
Km 3 on the road to Mismaloya ☎ (322) 2-0302 IIII AE CB Φ VISA
This cliff-top luxury restaurant is a favourite with celebrities for cocktails at sunset.

Restaurant nearby

(*20km/12 miles S*).

Chico's Paradise
III *Closed eve.*
A 'tropical fantasy' restaurant in luxuriant jungle near some waterfalls, serving simple food.

Nightlife

Inquire at your hotel for details of beach parties, shows and Mexican fiestas at other hotels. Some of the best discos and nightclubs are at the main hotels. The ***Holiday Inn*** has the wildest electronic equipment while the ***Camino Real*** boasts the loudest rock-and-roll music. There are also piano bars with entertainment and dancing at the ***Fiesta Americana***, and at the **Playa de Oro** and **Siesta** hotels.

The main discos include: **Capriccio** (*Olas Altas and Dulpito* ☎ *(322) 2–1593* ✿ ▥ ◉), for elegant decor and high decibels; **Cuckoo's Nest** (*Díaz Ordaz 570* ▥ ▣ ◉), a small and friendly place; **Los Lobos** (*Madero 17* ☎ *(322) 2–0154* ▥ ▣ ♫ 👣), for *mariachis* and local entertainment; **The City Dump** (*Ignacio Vallarta 278* ☎ *(322) 2–0719* ▥ ▣ ◉), open until very late and popular with the trendy young crowd: outrageous elegance is the style.

Sports and activities

As might be expected from a luxury resort, every imaginable water-sport is available, including even the exhilarating and perilous paragliding. It is also possible to arrange riding and hunting in the hills behind the town. As always, hotels are the best source of advice. For golfers, there is a new club, for which hotels can arrange temporary membership.

The beaches The main beach is the **Playa del Sol**, to the S of the river. It was formerly known as Playa de los Muertos (Dead Men's Beach), after some unseemly episode during the 17thC involving pirates. The name was thought unduly morbid for P.V.'s new fame, however, and was changed quite recently. As for the other beaches, the farther you go out of town, the more square metres of sand you get per person and the fewer services and activities are available. One of the best is at **Mismaloya**, 11km (7 miles) to the S, where *Night of the Iguana* was actually shot. It is best reached by boat from the *malecón* (waterfront).

For latterday Robinson Crusoes, the boat carries on to the small island and village of **Yelapa**. Here you can either laze around in the sun, eating fresh grilled fish, or explore the island, which has an impressive waterfall far into the uncharted (but small) interior.

Querétaro

*Map 11C5. Capital of Querétaro. 220km (136 miles) NW of Mexico City on RF 57 and RF 45. Altitude: 1,970m (6,463ft). Population: 240,000. Served by air, train (on Mexico City–San Luis Potosí line) and bus. Car rental: Hertz, Colón 2 no.7 ☎ (463) 2–3591 **i** Sierra Gorda 30 ☎ (463) 2–4898.*

Although set in an unattractive and dusty industrial hinterland that threatens to spread far into the Bajío, Querétaro is still one of the most attractive colonial cities. It is also being used to house some of the capital's overflowing multitudes, however, and is paying a high price for growth and progress. The historic centre has been turned into a pedestrian zone, and some of the revenues from industry have been used to restore older buildings.

Querétaro has been at the centre of events in Mexican history ever since the conspiracy to overthrow the Spanish was hatched here in the years leading up to the Proclamation of Independence on September 16 1810. The plotters were warned of their impending arrest by the sympathetic wife of the local provost, and fled to nearby *Dolores Hidalgo* to start the struggle. By the time independence was achieved in 1821, they were nearly all dead, although the *Corregidora*, as she was known, lived on to a ripe old age.

Later, in 1848, it was in Querétaro that the treaty handing over Texas and New Mexico to the USA was signed. Also here, the would-be Emperor Maximilian was executed in 1867, while in 1917, after the Revolution, the new Constitution was drawn up in the town. Finally, for the time being, in 1927, Mexico's dominant political party was founded here; they have ruled ever since, now as the Party of Institutional Revolution (PRI).

Sights and places of interest

The centre

The main square, with its pretty little **Jardín Obregón**, is about four blocks N of the large **Alameda Park**. In its centre is an ornate cast-iron bandstand where concerts are given on Sunday evenings. Just S of here along Juarez is the **Plaza de la Constitución**, ringed by stone posts each bearing the name of a state of Mexico, and commemorating the writing of the 1917 Constitution. The square is dominated by the church of **San Francisco**, and in the large adjacent monastery is the **Museo Regional** (*open standard hours*). It contains bizarre historical memorabilia, such as the actual keyhole through which the *Corregidora* whispered her warning to the plotters, and also collections of colonial paintings and other assorted relics.

Leave the square along 5 de Mayo; on the arcaded Plaza Independencia can be seen the actual **Casa de la Corregidora**, now the **Palacio Municipal**. Unless some function is taking place, you can view the room in which the *Corregidor* imprisoned his wife to prevent her warning the plotters of their danger.

Convento de la Cruz (*Monastery of the Cross*)
Independencia, six blocks E of centre.

This fine monastery is named after the miraculous cross which appeared in the sky during an early encounter between the Spaniards and the local Indians in 1531. A chapel and a stone cross were immediately erected, but the monastery was not completed until the late 17thC. Around the Baroque cloister are rooms containing rare antique books, testifying to the monastery's position as a great centre of learning.

There is a lively religious festival at the monastery on September 14.

Plaza de Santa Clara

A short distance W of the Plaza de la Constitución along Madero, and once the forecourt of a rich convent, Plaza de Santa Clara is now a small garden. The church of **Santa Clara** has an almost austere facade, but inside is a riot of Churrigueresque gold archangels and cherubs. In the centre of the square is the beautiful Neoclassical **Fountain of Neptune**, designed in 1797 by the Bajío's own architect, Eduardo Tresguerras.

For two blocks around the plaza, there is a heavy concentration of churches, monasteries, and mansions. Stroll around and visit a few: of particular interest is the **Palacio Federal**, housed in an old Augustinian monastery a block to the S. The mansion **Casa de los Perros**, behind the Palacio, is decorated with some delightfully ugly gargoyles.

Other sights

The spot where the Emperor Maximilian was executed, atop the **Cerro de las Campanas**, 1.5km (1 mile) W of centre, is marked by a statue of his victor, President Benito Juarez, glaring down on the small chapel to Maximilian's victory. Along Ejercito Republicano, on the E edge of the town, is the impressive **aqueduct**, finished in 1735, still in use.

H **Casa Blanca** (*Constituyentes 69 (463) 2-1134*) is a good motel for one night; **Holiday Inn** (*Constitución 13 Sur (463) 4-1202 to*) is a modern hotel on the outskirts of town; **Real de Minas** (*Constituyentes 124 Poniente (463) 4-0444*) is the best hotel in town, with a good restaurant.

Hotel nearby

(4km/2½ miles N on San Luis Potosí road).

Jurica

Km 217 on RF 57 (463) 2-1081/1084 187

A beautiful country club hotel in an old colonial hacienda.

R **Fonda San Antonio** (*Corregidor 44 Norte (463) 2-0299*) serves Mexican cuisine.

Shopping

History apart, Querétaro is also famous for its semi-precious stones. Items of onyx, amethyst and opal are widely sold: chess sets, ashtrays, imitation Pre-Columbiana, and so on. Basket-work is another good buy.

Reynosa

Map 5D9. Tamaulipas. 225km (139 miles) E of Monterrey on RF 40. Population: 280,000. Served by air, train (on Monterrey–Matamoros line) and bus.

A pleasant enough border town, but with little of note except reasonable accommodation and the usual seedy nightlife.

Sight nearby

Presa del Azúcar

80km (50 miles) NW by RF 2.

Literally 'Sugar Dam': sweet to anglers, as the lake teems with black bass and other species.

[H] **Conchita** (*Hidalgo 1510 Poniente* ☎ *(892) 2–1977* ▮▯ *to* ▮▮▯ ≡ ≈); **Virrey** (*Hidalgo and Balboa* ☎ *(892) 3–1050* ▮▮▮ ≡ ≈), a modern motel.

Saltillo

Map 5E8. Capital of Coahuila. 85km (53 miles) SW of Monterrey on RF 40. Population: 300,000. Served by air, train (on Piedras Negras–Mexico City line) and bus. Car rental: Avis, Victoria 718 ☎ *(841) 2–4046* **i** *Felipe Pescador 651* ☎ *(841) 2–6373.*

Most people just pass through Saltillo, although the city fathers would like them to stay longer and enjoy the dry, sunny climate, and the excellent sporting facilities. There is a good tourist office, which does its best to lure you into spending time and dollars here, and which has the latest details of activities and facilities. The sights of the city are of no great distinction, although the 18thC **cathedral** on the Zocalo is a fine example of the Churrigueresque style.

Events On Aug 6, important festival. Celebrating the arrival in town of a donkey, which delivered a statue of Christ and then disappeared miraculously.

On Oct 4, wine fair.

[H] Saltillo is well provided with good motels, but the following are especially recommended: **Camino Real** (*5km/3 miles S on RF 57* ☎ *(841) 4–1515* ▮▮▮ ≡ ≈) is a pleasure to stay at; **El Morillo** (*Prolongación Obregón Sur* ☎ *(841) 2–6300* ▮▮▯ ≡ ≈) is a weekend ranch 3km (2 miles) W of town.

Shopping

Saltillo is famous for its brightly coloured *sarapes* (ponchos); the shops around the Zocalo will arrange for you to visit a weaving workshop. Other local products include silver, leather, and grotesque masks hammered out of sheet-tin.

San Blas

Map 6F6. Nayarit. 302km (187 miles) NW of Guadalajara on RF 15. Population: 5,000. Served by bus.

When Cancún and Ixtapa were computer-selected to become Mexico's space-age resorts, lovers of San Blas could breathe again. It is a sleepy place, surrounded by the palm-shaded ruins of great colonial mansions. Up on a hill overlooking the town are the remains of a **fortress**, built as a defence against the depredations of ruthless English buccaneers; San Blas was the home port for galleons arriving from the Far East with precious cargoes, and thus came under frequent attack. Nowadays the only ships using the port are deep-sea fishing launches, the occasional yacht, and motor boats off on daily trips around the jungle lagoons and estuaries. Your hotel, or the marina, can arrange fishing trips, and boats for the jungle leave from the waterfront beneath the fort.

In the absence of any serious nightlife, the beaches are the main attraction: for the authentic shipwrecked experience, head for the **Playa de Matanchén**, 4km (2½ miles) down the coast. One word of caution: do take plenty of insect repellent.

H None of the following hotels have air conditioning, so insist on a fan: **Casa Morales** ☎ (*Cuauhtemoc s/n* ☎ *(321) 5–0023* ▮▢ ≡ ≈) is located on the edge of a lagoon, and is a useful motel for fishermen; **Casino Colón Moderno** ✿ (*Bahía de Matancher* ▮▮▢ ≡) is just out of town, on an isolated bay; **Suites San Blas** (*Aticama and Palmas* ☎ *(321) 5–0047* ▮▮▢ ≡ ≈) is a modern hotel. Two other possibilities are the **Flamingo** ▮▢ and **Bucanero** ▮▢ both on Juarez and both in romantically crumbling 19thC mansions.

R **Torino** (*Juarez 56* ▮▢) is good for seafood and international cuisine.

San Cristóbal de las Casas ★

Map 8H11. Chiapas. 85km (53 miles) E of Tuxtla Gutiérrez on RF 190. Altitude: 2,050m (6,726ft). Population: 40,000. Served by air and bus. Car rental: Budget, Adelina Flores 2 ☎ (967) 8–1817.

An attractive colonial city high in the mountains of the Sierra Madre Sur; or, more specifically, an island of Spanish-speaking culture in a great and diverse sea of Indian tribes, each with its own language, costumes and culture. In town, there are other tribes – the anthropologists and missionaries – and a few hapless *gringos* in the town jail for drug offences. The tourist tribe is not heavily in evidence, a further attraction for the independent traveller who has made the effort to get here.

The houses are low and stuccoed, with a few larger colonial mansions around the Zocalo; the town is dominated by two strategically placed churches up on the hills on the outskirts. But the architecture is only second of San Cristóbal's attractions: pride of place must go to the local population. Every day of the week except Sunday is market day, and the Indians flock into town on foot, on donkeys and in buses. The market is one of the most animated and colourful in Mexico – noisy, too, for the different tribes cannot understand each other and tend to yell in broken Spanish. Sadly, not many of the men now wear the traditional costumes; to see them in full splendour, you will have to go out to the villages on market day (usually Sunday), or for one of the frequent fiestas.

The town was founded in 1528 after savage battles between the Chamula Indians and a Spanish army led by the soldier and chronicler Bernal Díaz, famous for his eye-witness account of the Conquest. The town's patron saint was promptly designated as St Christopher, but it was soon more widely known as *Villaviciosa* (Wicked City) because of the appalling exploitation of the Indians by Spanish landowners. This was at its height when Bishop Bartolomé de las Casas arrived in 1544 and promptly began to fight for their rights, much to the displeasure of his compatriots. He wrote a long report on the situation, which finally had some effect in 1565, when the King of Spain decreed that improvements should take place. As a result, de las Casas is to this day the (uncanonized) patron saint of the Indians.

Events All the usual religious feasts are celebrated, but are even more memorable here. Particular to San Cristóbal is the day of the patron saint, on July 25. Festivities start as early as July 18, and culminate in a candlelit procession and vigil on the night of July 24. The day of the Virgin, Dec 12, is celebrated with horseback processions, *marimba* music, and dancing. The Indians from all around flock into town, and the market is even fuller than usual.

See also ***Places nearby***, below.

Sights and places of interest

The town

The 16thC Plateresque **cathedral** on the Zocalo is outwardly unremarkable but contains some fine Baroque altars and an ornately carved and gilded pulpit. On the opposite side of the Zocalo is a fine unnamed mansion of similar age, with a statue of a mermaid on the facade. Leave the Zocalo on 20 de Noviembre and walk six blocks N to the church of **Santo Domingo**, where rose-coloured statues of the Apostles guard the Baroque facade. Inside, kneeling before the gilded altars, will be Indians making their devotions, prostrating themselves with loud protestations, making small offerings, and lighting a multitude of candles.

Na-Bolom Centro de Estudios Científicos (*Na-Bolom Centre*) ☆
Vicente Guerrero 33, on outskirts of town along Real de Guadalupe.

A remarkable establishment: museum, library, photographic archive and home-from-home for archaeologists, anthropologists and Lacandon Indians. It is housed in a colonial seminary, with the buildings grouped around an elegant plant-filled courtyard. Exhibits include Lacandon artifacts and artworks. Visits are in the afternoon only: your guide will be able to answer any questions about the Chiapas area or about your stay there. The centre was founded by the Danish explorer Frans Blom and his wife Gertrude, who settled here in the 1920s and devoted their lives to the study and help of the people of Chiapas under pressure from the evangelizing 20thC. The Lacandon Indians, in particular, they literally saved from extinction.

If the house is not full of academics, it may be possible to stay here, and to dine at the high table with the other guests and residents (better than any hotel).

[H] **Molino de la Alborada** ✿ (*Periférico Sur s/n* ☎ *(967) 8–0935* [III] [≡]) is an American-run, relaxed motel; **Na-Bolom Centre** (*Vicente Guerrero 33* ☎ *(967) 8–1686* [IIII]) is an exclusive establishment (see ***Sights***, above); **Parador Ciudad Real** (*Diagonal Centenario 32* ☎ *(967) 8–1886* [III] [≡]) is a comfortable new downtown inn; **Posado Diego de Mazariegos** (*María A. Flores 2* ☎ *(967) 8–1313* [III] *to* [IIII] [≡]), an elegant downtown hotel, has fireplaces in the rooms.

[R] **La Parroquía** (*Guadalupe Victoria 3* ☎ *(967) 8–1354* [II]) serves delicious regional cuisine.

Shopping

San Cristóbal is the best place in Mexico to buy native weaving and other handmade goods; most of the shops are down the **Calle Real de Guadalupe**, off the Zocalo. Do not however wear in town any Indian costumes you may have bought, for this is resented. Among the best buys are intricately knotted string bags, straw hats, leatherware, and embroidered blouses.

Places nearby

Comitán (*88km/55 miles SE on RF 190*). The last town before Lagunas de Montebello and the Guatemalan frontier is bisected by a dusty expanse on each side of the Pan-American Highway, but has a pleasant hill-town climate. The small **museum** ([ticket] *open standard hours, closed for lunch*) has ruins from nearby Chincultic, including a fine stele.

[H] The **Internacional** (*B. Dominguez 22* ☎ *(963) 2–0110* [□]) and **Los Lagos** (*3km/2 miles S of centre* ☎ *(963) 2–0657* [□]) are full during Feb because of prolonged religious celebrations.

Indian villages nearby There are a large number of fascinating Indian villages within a short distance of San Cristóbal; the ***Na-Bolom Centre*** will advise on special markets or fiestas during your stay. Two of the nearest and most important villages are described below.

San Juan Chamula, 5km (3 miles) N, is a large Tzotzil village of thatched adobe homes clustered around a 16thC Dominican church that is now the centre for their semi-pagan Catholic religion. The village administers itself with a minimum of interference from the federal authorities, and is one of the few places where traditional costumes are widely worn by men and women. The women wear *huipils* (embroidered blouses) and a heavy dark blue skirt with thin embroidered bands. The men wear rough white cotton shirts and trousers covered by a black woollen tunic; ribbons on the hat indicates a village official. Market day is Sunday; be warned that photography is discouraged by the smashing of cameras. Some of the main fiestas are: Easter Carnival (fascinating dances), May 3 (Day of the Cross), June 24 (patron saint's day), and Dec 31 – Jan 4 (civil ceremonies).

Zinacantán, 5km (3 miles) W of San Juan Chamula, is another Tzotzil village, run along the same lines as San Juan. The costumes here are the finest in Chiapas: the embroidery on the women's *huipils* is intricate and superb, the men wear pale pink tunics and very short trousers, and they all wear flat straw hats, the men trailing brightly coloured ribbons from the rim. If they are blowing free, this means that the wearer is a bachelor, for only married men can tie them. Fiestas worth attending are on Jan 20 (San Sebastián) and Aug 10 (San Lorenzo).

See also *Lagunas de Montebello*.

San Juan del Río

Map 12D6. Querétaro. 168km (105 miles) NW of Mexico City on RF 57 and RF 45; 52km (32 miles) SE of Querétaro on RF 57. Population: 25,000. Served by train (on Mexico City–Querétaro line) and bus.

Until the new toll road to Querétaro was opened, the country's main N to S road passed through the centre of this colonial town. It became as a result an important centre for handicrafts, but was noisy, dusty and crowded. Now it is returning to a more tranquil existence, but remains the best place in the country to buy semi-precious stones. Around the Zocalo and on the main street are innumerable shops selling opals, amethyst, aquamarine and other stones from all over Latin America. It is known also for the local basket-work, cheese and wine – cheap wine can be bought by the case at the **Cavas de San Juan**, about 1km (½ mile) out of town towards Tequisquiapán.

Sights nearby

The five churches of the Sierra Gorda

From San Juan, a road leads NE through the land of the Otomi Indians and up into the wild mountains of the Sierra Gorda towards *Ciudad Valles*. The Otomi village of **Tequisquiapán** is 20km (12 miles) from San Juan; it has become a fashionable weekend resort and has lost much of its charm.

The Sierra Gorda was inhabited by wild and rebellious Jonace Indians, never conquered by the Aztecs, who submitted to the Spanish only in the 18thC. The missionaries who took on the dangerous task of evangelizing the area built five churches, known as 'The Five Churches of the Sierra Gorda', all within a day's walk of each other. The two finest are on the main road at **Jalpán** (181km/112 miles) and at **Landa** (201km/124 miles), both notable for their profusely decorated Baroque facades. The other three are at **Tancoyol** (23km/14 miles to the W at 144km/90 miles), **Conca** (50km/31 miles to the W at Jalpán) and **Tilaco** (23km/14 miles to the E at 213km/131 miles). The side roads are rough, and there is no good accommodation until *Ciudad Valles*.

Hacienda Mansión Galindo
8km (5 miles) N of San Juan on RF 57, turn left (s) towards Amealco for 5km (3 miles) (467) 2–0050 177

A former luxury weekend resort in a beautifully restored old hacienda. There are good sporting facilities but service has fallen from luxury standards.

La Mansíon
8km (5 miles) N of San Juan on RF 57 (467) 2–0120 108

Similar to the ***Mansión Galindo*** and under the same ownership, but less grand. More of a motel, but with equally fine old buildings.

Hotel nearby
Tequisquiapán (*20km/12 miles NE of San Juan del Río*).

Balneario el Relox
Morelos 8 (467) 3–0006 to 101

A weekend resort and also a thermal spa in lovely hill country; go during the week to avoid the crowds.

San Luis Potosí

Map 11B5. Capital of San Luis Potosí. 202km (125 miles) N of Querétaro on RF 57; 535km (332 miles) S of Monterrey on RF 57. Altitude: 1,965m (6,447ft). Population: 360,000. Served by air, train (on Mexico City–Monterrey line) and bus i Jardín Hidalgo 20 (481) 2–3143.

The small Franciscan settlement of San Luis gained the name 'Potosí' after the discovery of rich gold and silver mines nearby in the early 17thC; it means 'of great wealth' in the South American tongue of Quechua. The town then grew rapidly, and although it is now an important industrial centre, it retains much of its charm from those days. For a while, San Luis was the provisional capital of Mexico, after President Benito Juarez, evading the French armies, set up his government here in 1863. Later it became the capital of all northeastern Mexico, and has always had strong links with Texas – to this day, Texans come here to consult the land registry in cases of dispute. If you are driving N to S, San Luis is a natural place to break your journey for a night or two.

Sights and places of interest

On the E side of the Zocalo is the 17thC **cathedral**, which provides examples of most available architectural styles from Gothic to Byzantine via Baroque. It faces the **Palacio de Gobierno**, where during office hours you can visit a Hall of Mirrors and a patriotically inspiring gallery of Mexican heroes. Two blocks to the E of here, on Calle de Villerías, is an 18thC Baroque jewel, the **Templo del Carmen** whose Neoclassical high altar was designed by the famous Bajío architect, Eduardo Tresguerras.

Make sure that you also see the **regional museum** (*on Galeana 450, SW of the Zocalo open 10am–1pm, closed Mon*) an interesting collection of Huastec antiquities and local crafts housed in an old Franciscan monastery. The adjacent **Aranzazu Chapel** boasts a fine Churrigueresque facade and religious oil paintings. The church of **San Francisco**, looking over the Jardín Guerrero, is on the far side of the chapel.

Sights nearby

Real de Catorce ☆

191km (107 miles) N; turn W off RF 57 at Matehuala.

A short detour from the old mining town of Matehuala, a convenient stopover, lies this even better-preserved mining outpost, named after the fourteen (*catorce*) bandits who made their headquarters here. It is also known for the hallucinogenic cacti growing in the hills all around, the goal of the long pilgrimages made by the Huichol Indians of Nayarit who collect them for their religious rites. There are fiestas on Jan 6 and June 13 at Matehuala and on Oct 3 at Real de Catorce.

[H] **Cactus** ✿ (*Glorieta and Juarez ☎ (481) 2–1871* ▮▮□ *to* ▮▮▮▮ ≡ ≈) is an excellent motel; **Panorama** (*Av. Carranza 315 ☎ (481) 2–1777* ▮▮□ ≡ ≈) provides the best choice downtown.

San Miguel de Allende

Map 11C5. Guanajuato. 60km (37 miles) NW of Querétaro on RF 57. Altitude: 1,970m (6,463ft). Population: 37,000. Served by train (on Mexico City–San Luis Potosí line) and bus **i** *Palacio Municipal ☎ (465) 2–1747.*

Not only is San Miguel one of the finest colonial cities of the Bajío, but within that category it also has a unique atmosphere, resulting from the presence of a large number of foreign residents. Unlike other Mexican towns, it offers dog-training classes, Scrabble competitions, a large branch of the American Legion, and a host of other unlikely activities. In the bars or the Zocalo, you are bound to run into one of the artists, writers or retirees who have chosen to make their home in the land of cheap tequila and servants. You may even be convinced to stay and start writing that novel.

It all began in 1938, when a Mr Sterling Dickinson founded an art school. Success came after World War II, as returning GIs found that their education grants went further S of the border; the school now offers courses in almost any art medium imaginable. The town was declared a national monument in 1926 and, despite some uncontrolled development on the outskirts, the centre is in an excellent state of preservation, thanks largely to the efforts of the foreign community.

The best way to discover the town is a leisurely ramble through the narrow streets – punctuated by frequent stops at the abundant cafés, bars, restaurants, art galleries and craft shops – past enchanting little street-corner fountains, churches great and small, the ornately carved facades of colonial mansions, and a hundred-and-one flower-filled courtyards glimpsed through open doorways. End up sitting under the trees at the Plaza Allende – the central meeting place for everyone.

The 'Allende' in the name is in honour of the local hero of the War of Independence, Don Ignacio Allende. He was a Mexican-born Spaniard, who along with his fellow conspirators resented being treated as a second-class citizen by native Spaniards. His career began in the royalist army, but he deserted to become the leader of the peasant army that stormed the towns of *Dolores Hidalgo* and *Guanajuato*. After a defeat at Chihuahua in 1811, Allende was executed. He rapidly became a popular martyr, and his memory inspired further revolts until final success was achieved in 1821.

Some useful addresses in San Miguel are: **Academia Hispano Americana** (*Insurgentes 21 ☎ (465) 2–0349*), the language school; **Centro Cultural Ignacio Ramirez** (*Calle Canal ☎ (465) 2–0289*), the gallery, museum and art school; **Centro**

Internacional (*H. Macias 101* ☎ *(465) 2–0435*), the school of writing; **Instituto Allende** (*San Antonio 20* ☎ *(465) 2–0190*); and the **public library** (*Insurgentes 25*), for both Spanish and English books.

Events Towards end of Sept, Day of St Michael the Archangel. One of Mexico's most riotous, colourful fiestas, celebrated on a Friday. Festivities last all weekend; hotels are full of fun-seekers from Mexico City, so reserve well ahead.

Sights and places of interest

Instituto Allende
Calzada Ancha de San Antonio 20 ☎ *(465) 2–0190. Open 10am–1pm, 4–7pm. Closed Sun.*
An old hacienda building, on the outskirts of town towards Celaya, which is the powerhouse of San Miguel's cultural revolution. Even if you have no wish to enrol as a student, it is well worth a visit to find out about cultural events in town during your stay. While out in this area, take the opportunity of a stroll in the **Juarez Park** and up to the **Cerro de los Chorros** (Hill of the Springs), for an excellent view of the city.

Plaza Allende
On the S side of this central square stands the **Parroquia**, a bizarre and towering late 19thC Gothic construction, which serves as a good landmark during exploration of the town. It is said to have been designed by an illiterate stone-mason, inspired by picture postcards of European churches. Although inside it is ordinary, there is an alleged piece of the True Cross to add interest. On the left of the church is an arcade housing a café and the tourist office. To the right, just S of the square, is the house where Ignacio Allende was born, with a plaque over the door reading *Hic natus, ubique notus* (Born here, famous everywhere).

Also on the square, on the NW corner, is the most opulent of San Miguel's mansions, the **Casa del Mayorazgo de Canal**, built during the 18thC by the mining dynasty of Canal. One block away to the W, down Calle Canal, is the old convent housing the **Bellas Artes Cultural Institute**. The great twelve-sided dome of the church is said to have been designed by the same mason as the Parroquia; the postcard this time was doubtless of the Duomo in Florence.

Plaza de San Francisco
A group of churches embellish this open square a block from the Zocalo down the Calle de San Francisco. In the middle of the square is a statue of *Allende* on horseback. The facade of San Francisco itself, built in the late 18thC, is in the ornate Churrigueresque style, but the tower and interior are more coolly Neoclassical.

The largest of the churches is the **Oratorio de San Felipe Neri**, which houses several large **murals** showing the life of San Felipe, attributed to Miguel Cabrera (*died* 1768), an Indian painter whose work far outclassed that of his Spanish mentors.

Leave the square by Insurgentes, passing a number of churches, each worth a visit, until after five blocks you reach the church of **San Juan de Díos**, facing a large courtyard with a bronze head of *Miguel Hidalgo*.

Sights nearby

Atotonilco
16km (10 miles) N just W of RF 51.
The 18thC monastery is a religious shrine which attracts pilgrims from all over Mexico. The decoration of the chapels is typical of Mexican popular religious art, and it was here that Allende took the religious banner of the Virgin which served as his battle colours.

See also *Dolores Hidalgo* and *Guanajuato*.

Hotels

There is a fair selection of interesting hotels at good prices.

Hacienda Taboada
8km (5 miles) towards Dolores Hidalgo ☎ *(465) 2–0888*
72 AE CB VISA
A pleasant resort hotel with its own mineral waters and a volcanically heated pool. The Sunday lunch is a San Miguel social event.

Parador San Miguel
Instituto Allende gardens (465) 2-0392 57
Homesick Americans will find plenty of company at this friendly small hotel set in attractive gardens.

Posada la Ermita
Calle Real 64 (465) 2-0777 25
Once the home of Mexico's biggest film star, Cantín Flas, and now a luxurious colonial-style inn.

Posada de San Francisco
Plaza Allende (465) 2-0072 50
Hard to believe that this ancient-looking hotel is only 35yrs old. Fireplaces in the larger rooms and a busy cocktail bar.

Rancho el Atascadero
1km (½ mile) towards Querétaro (465) 2-0206 51
Expert riding instruction is provided at this colonial hacienda, and other sports are well catered for. Pleasant rooms.

Sierra Nevada
Hospicio 35 (465) 2-0415 10
A beautiful little colonial inn, with a good restaurant.

Villa Jacaranda
Aldama 53 (465) 2-0811 12
This hotel was originally the town house of a Spanish nobleman. The original 19thC furniture is still there adding a touch of style.

Restaurants

Hotel dining rooms are all open to non-residents, although it is wise to make a reservation. The best are at the ***Posada la Ermita*** and ***Sierra Nevada***. For Sunday lunch head out to the ***Hacienda Taboada***.

La Bodega del Marqués (*Correo 34 (465) 2-1481*) is a romantic old wine-cellar serving Americanized Mexican cuisine; **El Carousel** (*Canal 15 (465) 2-0076*) is cheap and cheerful, with a good disco; **La Fragua** (*Cuna de Allende 3 (465) 2-0109*) has a lovely old courtyard, and serves Mexican food accompanied by lively entertainment until the early hours; **El Patio** (*Correo 10 (465) 2-0017*), for international cuisine with Mexican entertainment.

Nightlife

There are plenty of discos, bars, restaurants with entertainment, and more earthy dives. A few examples are: **Laberintos** (*near the Instituto*), for the young crowd; **La Princesa** (*Recreo 5 (465) 2-1403*), a dangerous bar; **Los Topos** (*Hidalgo 46 (465) 2-0489*), a nightclub with superior entertainment; **The Ring** (*Hidalgo 15*), which has a loud disco.

Tampico

Map 13B8. Tamaulipas. 604km (373 miles) NE of Mexico City on RF 105 and RF 70. Population: 280,000. Served by air, train (on lines from San Luis Potosí and Monterrey) and bus. Car rental: Avis, Carranza 508 (121) 3-2356; Budget, Hidalgo 4308 (121) 3-4264 i Palacio Municipal (121) US Consul: Hidalgo 2000 (121) 3-2217.

A busy industrial port surrounded by rather grim, flat marshes. Although founded in 1533, occasional floods and hurricanes have ensured that no early colonial buildings survive. Nonetheless it is not an unpleasant place to stop for the night.

The central **Plaza de Armas**, the focus of the town, comes to life in the evening, when there are often bandstand concerts. You may be surprised by the swastika pattern on the floor of the strange 1930s **cathedral** but, architecturally, the cathedral is quite outclassed by the bandstand which can be best described as a psychedelic Moorish wedding cake of cast-iron.

Culture-seekers should not miss the **Museo de la Huasteca** (*open 10am–1pm, closed Mon*) in the satellite town of Ciudad Madero (1km/½ mile W), where you can learn about the past and present of the local Huastec people. They inhabit a large area, from *Veracruz* to *San Luis Potosí*, and live now as an agricultural people who also produce a wide variety of handicrafts.

H Camino Real
Hidalgo 2000 (121) 3-1101 100

Nothing special, but luxury for this area, with a good restaurant.

H Posada de Tampico
Prolongación Hidalgo km 2 (RF 80) (121) 3-3050 130

This is a good second choice to the ***Camino Real***.

H Inglaterra (*Salvador Díaz Mirón 116 (121) 2-5678*) is the best central hotel.

R Try **Del Mar** (*Aduana Sur 309 (121) 2-5035*) for fresh seafood.

Sports and activities

The wildlife in the area around Tampico has suffered under the onslaught of industrial pollution, although some hunting is possible in the coastal lagoons. Deep-sea fishing is a better bet, and is best arranged through your hotel. The beaches near town are sometimes polluted, but there is a beautiful unspoiled island off the coast, which can be reached by boat from the harbour (*no organized service*).

Tapachula

Map 8I11. Chiapas. 256km (157 miles) SE of Tuxtla Gutierrez on RF 190. Population: 90,000. Served by air, train (on line to Mexico City) and bus.

A steamy tropical city on the coastal plain near the Guatemalan border, at the foot of a towering extinct volcano, Tacaná (4,064m/13,300ft). It is a good overnight stop on the way to Central America.

Sights nearby

Izapa
15km (9 miles) E on RF 200.

The last ruin before the border should not be missed by addicts. The chief attractions are the relief sculptures on the stele, showing the sacred ball-game, the execution of prisoners and other cheerful scenes of everyday Mayan life.

Puerto Madero
27km (17 miles) SW.

Tapachula's beach, where sun-lovers can waterski, and lunch on freshly caught grilled fish at a palm-thatched beach restaurant.

H Loma Real (*Coastal Highway km 244 (962) 6-1440 to*), a luxury motel; **San Francisco** (*Central Sur 94 (962) 6-1454*).

Taxco ★

*Map **12E6**. Guerrero. 185km (115 miles) sw of Mexico City on RF 95. Altitude: 1,662m (5,453ft). Population: 40,000. Served by air taxi and bus* ℹ *on RF 95 at N end of town* ☎ *(732) 2–0579.*

Even those preferring to stay off the main tourist circuit would make a mistake in staying away from Taxco. It is a colonial mining town of irresistible charm, with narrow cobbled streets winding up, down, and around the hills, and domes and spires of churches rising above terra-cotta roofs. The town should be explored on foot; just walking around the streets is such a pleasure that it should keep one busy for a morning or so, and will provide such arresting moments as a flower-filled court glimpsed through an intricate cast-iron gate, or perhaps just a languid cat gazing down from a picturesque balcony.

You may end your walk rather poorer than when you started – for this is a city of silver. There are in the region of a hundred silver shops, glittering and beckoning the visitor. The standard of design is very high and amazingly varied, including ancient, modern and Neo-Aztec jewellery, dinner services, and indeed anything else that can be made of silver. Prices are fairly uniform, although a little preparatory comparison is wise.

It was Cortés himself who ordered the initial explorations for silver in the locality, and these met with some success, although Taxco's prosperity really dates from the 18thC, when the French nobleman José de la Borda struck the fabulously rich San Ignacio vein. After his death in 1778, the town's fortunes waned, not to be revived again until an American, William Spratling, came to Taxco in 1929, just after the opening of a new road. He was a writer and university lecturer, but gave all this up to throw himself into the business of designing, producing and marketing silver jewellery. There are now over 2,000 people working in the silver industry, and many more in the tourist business. William Spratling, who died in 1967, is already more or less a patron saint of Taxco, and his home is now a museum of silverware.

Events At Easter, processions throughout Holy Week. The most exciting time of year in Taxco, culminating in a gruesome re-enactment of the Passion, on Good Friday.

On Jan 18, Feb 24, Mar 8 and May 3, other important religious festivals. Check at the tourist office for exact dates.

At end of Nov, silver festival. Jewellers submit their latest designs to a prize-giving committee.

Sights and places of interest

For a good view of the town, leave the Zocalo on Calle Guadalupe and climb the narrow lane up to the church of the **Virgin of Guadalupe**. The energetic can continue for another 2km (1¼ miles) up a mountain path to the summit of the **Cerro de Atachi**, from where the entire Valley of Taxco and the surrounding villages can be surveyed.

The principal sites are in and around the Zocalo.

Casa Figueroa
Open 10am–1pm.
Now an art gallery and museum, the house is named after the Mexican artist who restored it in the 1940s to serve as his own studio and home. It was originally built in the 18thC by a local magistrate, using the forced labour of Indians unable to pay their debts.

Museo Guillermo Spratling *(Spratling Museum)*
Behind Santa Prisca *Open 10am–1pm, 4–7pm.*
The museum now occupying the old home of William Spratling contains

a history and description of the local silver industry as well as prize pieces of work. Also on display is Spratling's collection of Pre-Columbiana.

Santa Prisca

The great Baroque facade of Santa Prisca dominates the laurel trees of the charming little Zocalo, and is thought by many to be the finest church in Mexico. It was built in the 1750s by Count de la Borda as a special thanksgiving for his good fortune. Over the doorway, exquisitely carved in the local pink stone, is a relief of *St John the Baptist and the Infant Christ*. Inside, the altars are a profusion of carved and gilded decoration. Over the doorway to the **Chapel of the Indians** hangs an oil painting of *The Martyrdom of St Prisca in Rome*, painted by Miguel Cabrera (*died* 1768), a Zapotec Indian who became a great (Christian) religious painter. There are more of his works in the sacristy.

Other sights

The home of Taxco's original silver king, José de la Borda, is now occupied by a silver shop which bears his name in Munoz.

On the other side of the Zocalo, in Plaza San Juan, is the **Casa Grande**, (*open 10am–1pm, closed Sat, Sun*), the house of the mayors of Taxco, with various exhibits commemorating the revolutionary José Morelos' short stay here in 1815. Dedicated sightseers should also see the **Casa Humboldt** (*N of Zocalo, on J.R. Alarcón*), named after the famous explorer who stayed here for one night in 1803. The facade is adorned in the Mudejar style, with complex interlocking geometric designs; it is usually possible to walk into the lovely little courtyard.

Five minutes' walk from here, past the Palacio Municipal, is the large old monastery of **San Bernardino**, rebuilt after a fire in 1805. About 1km ($\frac{1}{2}$ mile) from here, up Morelos and along the Cuernavaca road, is the interesting old **Hacienda del Chorillo**, near the ruins of a silver-ore-refining works. A taxi may be the best way to get here, but, beyond, a cable car runs up to the ***Monte Taxco*** hotel (see below). It is worth going up for a drink and the view, even if you are not a guest there.

Sights nearby

Cacahuamilpa ★

49km (30 miles) N; W off Cuernavaca road after 39km (24 miles).

The vast network of caves at Cacahuamilpa (*open 11am–3pm*) are well lit and safe. The tour passes through forests of stalagmites into chambers the size of concert halls, and past historical graffiti by such distinguished folk as Maximilian's empress, Carlota (for those not of royal blood, graffiti are now forbidden). Tours are at irregular intervals, depending on the number of people waiting.

See also *Cuernavaca*.

Hotels

Los Arcos

Juan Ruiz de Alarcón 12 ☎ (732) 2-1836 25

Formerly a monastery in the 17thC, the cloister is always filled with flowers. Its location is central.

Los Castillo

Juan Ruiz de Alarcón ☎ (732) 2-3471 22

This pleasant small inn is housed in a 17thC mansion; the owners are a well-known family of silversmiths.

Hacienda del Solar

Taxco Viejo ☎ (732) 2-0323 17 AE CB VISA

Set in vast grounds, this beautiful resort hotel boasts the best restaurant in Taxco. Children are not allowed here.

Monte Taxco

Fracc. Lomas de Taxco, to the N off RF 95 ☎ (732) 2-1300 156 AE CB VISA

Until recently this was a Holiday Inn. It is located upon the hills overlooking town, and has a cable-car link to the **Hacienda del Chorillo** (see ***Sights***), but, sadly, it lacks atmosphere.

Posada de la Misión
Cerro de la Misión 32 (732) 2–0063 100
Colonial-style rooms, O'Gorman **murals** and a good restaurant are the main features of this establishment.

Rancho Taxco Victoria
Carlos J. Nibbi 12 (732) 2–0004 to 140
Large and well run; not far from centre.

Apart from the hotel restaurants, which rank among the best in Mexico, there are several cheap, cheerful and clean places around the Zocalo. To start with, try **Los Balcones** (*Los Gallos 5 (732) 2–0680*) for Mexican specialities. Of the hotel restaurants, the best is at the ***Hacienda del Solar***, serving gourmet Italian food.

Nightlife

Apart from the hotels, the only place for nightlife is **Cantarranas** (*RF 95*), a taxi ride from town. Riotous goings-on in this old hacienda – a good time to arrive is between 9 and 10pm.

Tehuacán

Map ***13****F8. Puebla. 283km (177 miles)* SE *of Mexico City on RF 150. Population: 65,000. Served by air, train (on Mexico City–Oaxaca line) and bus.*

'Tehuacán' is a household word in Mexico, meaning any kind of sparkling mineral water, and reasonably so, as the town is by far the largest producer in the country. It is also a fairly pleasant resort for liverish and infirm Mexicans, who come to take the mildly radioactive waters. Travellers often stop for a night on the way from Mexico City to *Oaxaca*.

The health-giving waters can be sampled free of charge at a fake Aladdin's cave by the Peñafiel bottling plant. Other worthwhile sights in town include the church of **El Carmen** (*Reforma Norte*) with its dazzling *faïence* dome, and the **Museo del Valle de Tehuacán** (*Calle 1 Norte*). Exhibits prove that this valley was where the cultivation of maize began 7,000yrs ago, a vital stage in the development of Mesoamerican civilizations from hunter-gatherers to settled villages.

Events On night of Nov 1, Day of the Dead. Fascinating and macabre ceremony at San Gabriel Chilac (20km/12 miles SE; turn W off RF 131 after 10km/6 miles).

Hacienda Spa Peñafiel (*Carretera Estación Peñafiel (238) 2–0190*), a slightly dilapidated resort hotel with its own thermal waters; **Mexico** (*Reforma and Independencia (238) 2–2319*), another hotel with its own mineral water spring.

La Oaxaqueña (*5 Oriente 406 (238) 2–3189*) serves specialities from the state of Oaxaca such as chicken in the aromatic *mole* sauce.

Tehuantepec

Map ***8****I10. Oaxaca. 250km (155 miles)* SE *of Oaxaca on RF 190. Population: 20,000. Served by air, train (on Mexico City–Guatemala line) and bus.*

Considering the reputation and geographical importance of this town (it gives its name to the isthmus of tropical lowlands dividing North and Central America), it is a disappointing place, dusty and squalid, with indifferent hotels. With the influx of oil wealth to the area have come plans to revitalize the isthmus rail link between here and the Gulf, which would be a rival to the Panama Canal; so Tehuantepec may yet achieve world prominence.

Until then, its main claim to fame is one that causes much concern to men all over Mexico – by popular repute, it is a town run by women, where men take the orders. The women are tall and renowned for their beauty. Unlike the men, who wear appropriately drab clothing, many of them frequently wear the magnificent traditional costume of rich gold embroidery on red cloth. On fiesta days, their splendour is such that they rival European royalty, with heavy necklaces of gold coins and an extraordinary head-dress resembling a baby's dress.

Events From around June 21 for a week, fiesta. A colourful, lively occasion; photography is tempting but risky – the Tehuanas are said to treat roughly anyone suspected of ogling.

Other fiesta dates are Jan 22, June 24, June 30, Aug 15 and Oct 1; the dull town is enlivened by its colourful fiestas.

Place of interest nearby

Juchitán
26km (16 miles) E on RF 200.
Run along similar matriarchal lines to Tehuantepec, this is a better place to buy the local costumes. It has important fiestas on Aug 13 and Sept 3, when the women of the town perform graceful dances.

[H] **Calli** (*RF 190 6km/4 miles S* ☎ *(971) 5–0085* ▮▮▮▮ ⚌ ≈) is the best place to stay; **Tehuantepec** (*RF 185 20km/12 miles N* ☎ *(971) 5–0003* ▮▮▮□ ⚌ ≈) is suitable for a one-night stay.

Teotihuacán ★

Map 12D7. State of Mexico. 49km (30 miles) NE of Mexico City on RF 85 and RF 45. Served by bus.

For centuries, the great pyramids of Teotihuacán have dominated the surrounding plains, and are dwarfed only by the encircling mountains. Grouped along a monumental avenue, as long, wide and straight as an airport runway, they are the best known and most imposing of Mexico's Pre-Hispanic ruins.

When the Aztecs came upon the vast ruined city, already abandoned for centuries, they could not believe that it had been built by mere mortals – the name in their language means 'City of the Gods'. It is still hard for us to believe that it was the work of a civilization which did not even know the wheel. The original name of the city is not known, and little is known of the people who built it, between the 2nd–7thC AD, only to abandon it for mysterious reasons. The evidence of the buildings tells us that they were highly advanced in the fields of geometry, architecture, astronomy and the arts. We can also surmise that they were not a militaristic race, partly from the subject matter of their murals, partly because the buildings are laid out to comply with astronomical rather than defensive necessities.

All over the site are images of the gentle god Quetzalcoatl – The Plumed Serpent – whose legend bears startling resemblances to the story of Christ. It is thought by some scholars that he may have been a real man, maybe even a European, who somehow travelled to Mexico. When Cortés arrived, he was mistaken for the long-predicted second coming of Quetzalcoatl, an illusion of some considerable use to him in the Conquest.

Events From Oct–May, regular performances of son-et-lumière show, with historical narrative. English show at 7pm; hotels arrange tickets and transport. Six shows per week only; the night off varies, so check first.

The ruins

but *on Sun* *Open 9am–5pm.*

The main entrance is through a group of modern buildings, including shops, a cafeteria and a well laid-out little museum. You should expect to spend at least half a day at the ruins, and may find your visit enhanced by engaging an official guide from the museum.

Avenue of the Dead (*Calle de los Muertos*)

Running the entire length of the site is this broad avenue, stretching away through the unexcavated areas to the S and N to the ***Pyramid of the Moon***, nearly 2km ($1\frac{1}{4}$ miles) from the museum. Opposite the museum is a large construction, about $\frac{1}{2}$km (550yds) square, wrongly known as the **Citadel** (Ciudadela). In the large central court is the **Temple of Quetzalcoatl**, where there are some remarkable stuccoed statues and reliefs of plumed serpents and other deities. On the way N to the great pyramids, the road passes the **'Superimposed Buildings'** (Edificios Superpuestos), and the **'Viking Group'**. In the former there are remains of frescoes and, in the latter, a courtyard covered in two layers of loose, shiny mica. Its use is unknown, and it is difficult even to dream up a convincing one. You will have to get a guardian to uncover the mica.

Pyramid of the Moon

The Avenue of the Dead ends at the courtyard in front of the Pyramid of the Moon (only a little smaller than the ***Pyramid of the Sun***) which is now being restored and explored internally for chambers or caves. Around the court are several temples of interest. See especially the ornate **Temple of the Plumed Butterfly** (Quetzalmariposa), W of the pyramid.

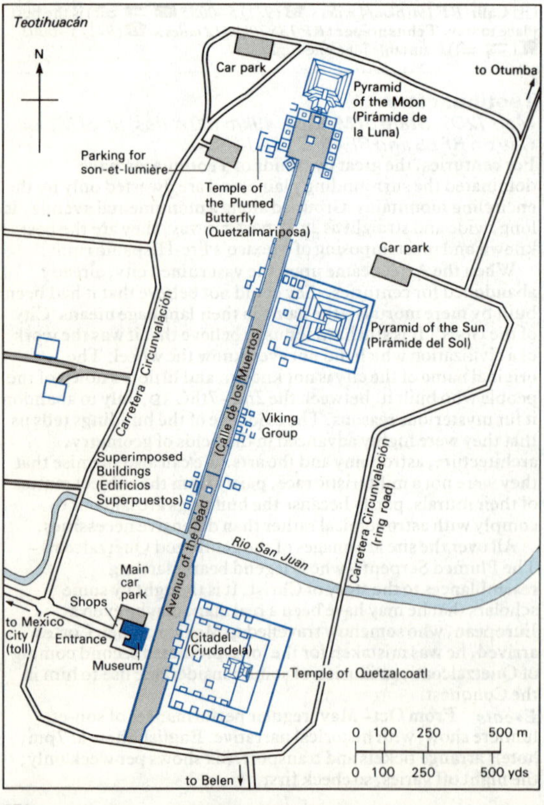

Pyramid of the Sun
Dominating the countryside in every direction, the great pyramid compares in size to the Pyramid of Cheops in Egypt, although, because of the stepped construction, the actual mass is smaller. Five levels can be seen, but it is now known that it was wrongly restored in 1910, and should have only four. The view from the top is excellent, taking in the entire site and the plains and mountains around. Deep under your feet, at the heart of the pyramid, are some chambers and a natural cave, joined by tunnels (*not open*). Its exact symbolic significance probably will never be known, although its careful astronomical orientation has been worked out. It was probably central to the religion of the inhabitants, being maybe even the mythical place of creation, for deep chambers are often prominent in contemporary religious paintings.

Sights nearby

Acolmán 🏛 ✝ ☆
8km (5 miles) SW 🎫 ✗ *Closed Fri.*
A large, fortress-like Spanish monastery, with a serenely beautiful **church** (1560) with a fine 17thC Churrigueresque altarpiece. The carved **cross** in front of the Plateresque facade carries native motifs.

Tepexpán
7km (4½ miles) SW, just E of Mexico City road.
A small museum (🎫 *open standard hours*) contains remains of mammoths which roamed the Valley of Mexico some 10,000yrs ago.

Tepic

Map 6F6. Capital of Nayarit. 226km (140 miles) NW of Guadalajara on RF 15. Population: 145,000. Served by air, train (on Guadalajara–Nogales line) and bus **i** *Mexico 253-a Sur* ☎ *(321) 2–1552.*

Tepic was founded in 1542 on the fertile slopes of the extinct volcano Sanguangüey, but its position on the edge of the mountain territory of the marauding Huichol and Cora Indians prevented the town from prospering until after the 1910 Revolution, when a railway arrived. On the central square is the 18thC **cathedral**, in the Neo-Gothic style, and nearby the church of **Santa Cruz**, built in 1744 around the site of a miraculous growth of grass in the shape of a cross in the middle of bare ground, which can still be seen. The more Christianized of the Huichols come here to venerate the cross.

Those who admire the Huichol beads and costumes can purchase them from shops and vendors around the Zocalo, but they should not be worn in the area out of respect for the Indians. Examples of Huichol weaving and artifacts can be seen at the **Museo Regional de Antropología e Historía** (*on Zapata and Mexico*), together with local archaeological finds.

Expeditions to the wild Huichol mountains will need an official permit (*issued from the Palacio de Gobierno*), the fiestas and villages being of more interest to the anthropologist than to the tourist: the Huichols have never really been conquered.

Sight nearby

Ahuacatlán
75km (47 miles) SE on RF 15.
The small 16thC monastery here is a good place to stop off briefly and enjoy the shade of the cloister. A short distance beyond the town, an extraordinary desolate moonscape of black sands and twisted rocks is encountered, left by the 1885 eruption of nearby Monte Ceboruco.

[H] **Fray Junípero Serra** (*Lerdo 23 Poniente* ☎ *(321) 2–2051/2525* ▮▮□ ⇌) has a central location; **La Loma** (*Paseo de la Loma 301* ☎ *(321) 2–2922* ▮▮▮▮ ⇌ AE CB Ⓓ ⊙ VISA ≈) is a motel.

[R] **Betos** (*Insurgentes 282 Poniente* ☎ *(321) 2–6061* ▮▮□) serves seafood; **Cazadores Nayar** (*Insurgentes 280 Poniente* ☎ *(321) 3–1109* ▮▮□) for meat.

Place nearby

Mexicaltitlán (*97km/60 miles NW; turn W off RF 15 after 57km/34 miles*). As you drive N, there are several roads leading down to tropical beaches and little fishing villages. The best known of these is at *San Blas* (turning at 40km/25 miles). At 57km (34 miles) a turn W leads through Santiago Escuintla down to the amazing village of Mexicaltitlán, built on a circular island with radiating streets. Some academics believe that the Aztecs originated here, but there is little evidence one way or the other. Every June 29, there is a canoe race around the island followed by cheerful celebrations to mark the feast of St Peter and St Paul.

Tepotzotlán ☆

Map 12D6. State of Mexico. 45km (28 miles) N of Mexico City on RF 57. Altitude: 1,660m (5,446ft). Population: 23,000. Served by bus.

A small colonial town, containing one of the three finest churches in Mexico and a large museum of colonial art. It makes a good detour on the way to *Querétaro* from Mexico City, or can be combined with the ruins at *Tula* to make a day's excursion from the capital.

Events On June 29, local fiesta.

Around Christmas time, traditional plays (*pastorellas*), performed in the cloister.

Sights and places of interest

The church and Museo Nacional de Arte Virrenial (*Viceroy's Museum*) 🏛

On the Zocalo 🎫 *for museum. Museum open 10am–6pm; closed Mon, Tues.*

The profusely Churrigueresque facade of the church, completed in 1762, represents one of the peaks of this architectural style in Mexico. Five years after its completion the Jesuit seminary, of which the church was part, was closed down, and it became the parish church. Inside, amid cascades of gold-leaf, is a superb painting of the *Virgin of Guadalupe* in the N transept; the artist was Miguel Cabrera. A small door leads from the nave through a chapel to a remarkable eight-sided chamber, so heavily ornamented that you will get a stiff neck before you have finished counting the cherubs on the ceiling.

The **Viceroy's Museum**, occupying the old seminary buildings, is reached through some cloisters on the right just inside the church. It boasts an extensive collection of holy relics and religious paintings, rather haphazardly distributed on several floors. Highlights are the bone relics of St Peter and St Paul in their silver cases, and the room full of pictures composed of nothing but inlays of different-coloured precious woods.

Tepoztlán

Map 12E7. Morelos. 84km (52 miles) S of Mexico City on RF 95 and RF 115; 27km (17 miles) E of Cuernavaca on RF 115. Population: 10,000. Served by bus.

Some years ago, Tepoztlán was a remote village surrounded by majestic volcanic crags, its narrow streets dominated by a massive 16thC monastery. The only inhabitants were Nahuatl-speaking Indians, and a large number of anthropologists studying their customs and frequent fiestas. New roads and weekend homes have broken this isolation, and it is now both easy and worthwhile to come here for the day from Mexico City or Cuernavaca.

The great **monastery** on the Zocalo not only looks like a fortress, but was used as one by Emiliano Zapata during the 1910 Revolution. It is now in use as a local museum, containing a collection of Pre-Hispanic objects found at the temples high in the hills above town. The most interesting of these is at the top of the **Cerro del Tepozteco** ☆ about an hour's energetic climb up a well-marked path from the edge of town. The summit is reached up a steep gully and an alarming iron ladder. The pyramid here was dedicated to Tepoztecatl, a god of drunkenness, who is represented symbolically by four hundred rabbits – the Aztec equivalent of pink elephants. When the Spaniards arrived, they righteously hurled the idol over the cliffs, but legend has it that he landed unharmed, which only encouraged his followers.

On the night of Sept 7 Tepoztecatl is still venerated, with dances and scenes of universal drunkenness, both in town and up at the temple. The carnival, in the first week of Lent, features colourful dances. Holy Week here is also a lively occasion, with dancing and a large market. At the weekly Sunday market, local handicrafts are sold, and you can gaze at the bright costumes and beads of foreign hippies who live here.

H **Hotel Tepoztlán** (*Industrias 6* ☎ *(738) 5–0522* ▮▮◻ *to* ▮▮▮▮ ≡ ≈) is a pleasant, modern building.

R **Hosteria del Convento** (*Plaza Hidalgo 32; reservations* ☎ *Mexico City: (5) 876–0243* ▮▮◻) has irregular opening hours, good food and lively music.

Texcoco

Map 12E7. State of Mexico. 41km (26 miles) E of Mexico City on RF 190, RF 150 and RF 136. Altitude: 2,280m (7,480ft). Population: 30,000. Served by bus.

Now a small, dusty town on the banks of a dry lake-bed, but before the Conquest a great and beautiful city, with pyramids and temples towering over the lake. There is little to see in the town itself, but nearby are enough places of interest to make a good day's excursion from Mexico City.

Sights nearby

Chapingo and Huexotla

N on Tlalpán road.

The **agricultural school** at **Chapingo** (3km/2 miles) is worth a visit to see the striking murals by Diego Rivera (*open 9am–1pm, 3–5pm, closed Sun*), showing scenes of the Mexican Revolution. At **Huexotla** (4km/2½ miles W at 8km/5 miles), Pre-Hispanic fortifications surround a small Franciscan monastery, flanked by a Churrigueresque church. The stone carvings are clearly by native craftsmen – just look at the faces of the saints.

Chiconcuac and Papalotla

N on Tepexpan road.

Most people come to the small village of **Chiconcuac** not for the fine Baroque church, but to shop for woollen clothing; it is a centre for the production of thick knitted jackets, and they are cheaper here than anywhere. The nearby village of **Papalotla** (10km/6 miles by small unnumbered road) has a church in front of an especially fine arcaded atrium, with Baroque decoration, and, inside, some fine carved wooden altar pieces from the 18thC.

Molino de Flores and Tepetlaotzoc

E on Calpulalpan road.

In the pleasant gardens around the old disused hacienda of **Molino de Flores** (8km/5 miles) stand a ruined mill and several Baroque chapels. Nearby are the remains of Aztec gardens, with irrigation channels carved into the rocks. There are more Pre-Hispanic remains at **Tepetlaotzoc** (6km/4 miles S at 12km/7 miles), where the wide stairway leading up to the monastery was once part of a pyramid. The buildings, although now very old, are well preserved.

Tijuana

Map 2A2. Baja California Norte. 763km (474 miles) NW of Hermosillo on RF 2 and RF 15. Population: 900,000. Served by air (international airport 16km/10 miles SE), train (terminus of line from Mexico City) and bus. Car rental: Avis, Agua Caliente 1 ☎ (66) 86–4004/056–6865, and at airport ☎ (66) 3–2310; Hertz, El Conquistador hotel, Agua Caliente Sur 700 ☎ (66) 6–4902 i Guanajuato 1020 ☎ (66) 85–0476. US Consul: Tapachula 96 ☎ (66) 86–1001/86–3003.

For countless Americans, 'TJ' is all they have ever seen of Mexico. With its slums, beggars, and seedy sex-joints, it is hardly the greatest advertisement. All the same, it is visited by nearly twice its own population each month. The attractions are many: cheap false teeth and auto repairs, bullfights, *jai-alai* (see below), and simple curiosity to see another country. Sex is no longer a big draw, the permissive society over the border being bad news for the porn barons of TJ. The notorious Zona Norte however is still in action and could be a nostalgic stroll if you were last here as a lonely young serviceman during World War II, but vice here just isn't what it was. Until the 1920s, TJ was no more than a dusty frontier village. The meteoric urban and industrial growth began with Prohibition in the USA, when suddenly every humble liquor-vendor became rich beyond the wildest dreams of avarice.

For those here just for the day, formalities are minimal. The problems are encountered on the way back, on those days when the US Customs are meticulously searching vehicles for drugs and contraband. Time may be saved by leaving your car in the USA and taking taxis in TJ. A good way to pass time while waiting for a backlog of cars to pass through Customs is at the **Palacio de Jai-Alai** (*on Revolución*); here the amazingly fast hand-ball game of *jai-alai* is played daily (*except Thurs*) in the evening, and the betting is fast and furious. Bullfights are usually on Sundays, but the tourist office will advise. The largest bullring is the **Plaza Monumental**, by the port.

See also *Ensenada* and *Mexicali*.

[H] The **Baja Inn** (*Agua Caliente s/n* ☎ *(66) 6–5000* ▮▮▮) is an adequate large, modern hotel; **El Conquistador** (*Agua Caliente Sur 700* ☎ *(66) 6–4801/4902* ▮▮▮) offers colonial-style accommodation in a pleasant southern suburb; nearer the town centre is **Palacio Azteca** (*16 de Septiembre no.213* ☎ *(66) 6–5301* ▮▮□).

Shopping

Not only does Tijuana have a large selection of Mexican handicrafts and souvenirs, but it is also a duty-free zone. There are bargains to be had, but be sure of the prices at home before buying. In the shopping district around and along Constitución, anything from Taxco silver to Japanese cameras can be bought.

Tlaxcala

Map 12E7. Capital of Tlaxcala. 115km (72 miles) E of Mexico City on RF 150, RF 190 and RF 119. Population: 20,000. Altitude: 2,250m (7,382ft). Served by train (on Mexico City–Puebla line) and bus i Diego M. Camargo 32-2 ☎ (246) 2–2369, and Constitución 21 ☎ (246) 2–0027.

The capital city of Mexico's smallest state is an attractive but little visited place which, together with the places of interest nearby, makes a fascinating excursion.

Historically, Tlaxcala has the unique distinction of remaining unconquered by the Aztecs, despite frequent attempts to bring it under their control. When Cortés arrived, he fought several savage battles with the Tlaxcalans before they surrendered and joined him to attack the Aztecs. One of the reasons for the subsequent Aztec defeat was simple demoralization: the knowledge that the Spaniards had succeeded where for so many years they had failed. Throughout the colonial period, Tlaxcala enjoyed special privileges; it was, therefore, on the wrong side during the War of Independence, and as a result has been starved of federal funds ever since.

Events On Oct 12 and Dec 30, fiestas.

Sights and places of interest

Start your visit in the **Zocalo**, where there are two 16thC palaces now housing the local government; the modern murals on the main stair of the **Palacio de Gobierno** are both vibrantly colourful and historically informative. From here, it is 5mins' walk across the square and up a wide cobbled stairway to the **monastery of San Francisco** ☆ The roof of the church was rebuilt during the 17thC in Mudejar timberwork.

On the outskirts of town, 2km (1¼ miles) SE of the centre, is the pueblo of **Ocotlán** ☆ where red pottery figures of animals are for sale. The 18thC church, with two bell towers decorated in typical Puebla tilework, should certainly be visited. Another 2km (1¼ miles) farther S is the weaving village of **Santa Ana Chiautempán**; fiesta on July 26.

Sight nearby

Cacaxtla ★

26km (16 miles) SE on unnumbered road Open standard hours.

These are the remains of a large city which flourished some 2,000yrs ago, and was abandoned around the 9thC. There are several low temple bases, a few of which have been restored, but the main interest here lies in the remarkable **murals**, probably the best preserved and finest Pre-Columbian paintings in the country, excelling those of *Bonampak*. They are painted on stucco in eight colours, some showing vivid and gory scenes of war, and are of especial interest to archaeologists because of the Mayan faces of the warriors, who appear to be locked in combat with more negroid adversaries. Some of the dateglyphs show resemblances to those of the Olmec culture; one can only speculate why.

H **Campo Real** (*Revolución 6* ☎ *(246) 2-1947*).

Toluca

Map 12E6. State of Mexico. 65km (41 miles) W of Mexico City on RF 15. Altitude: 2,680m (8,793ft). Population: 200,000. Served by train (on Mexico City–Guadalajara line) and bus. Car rental: Hertz, Paseo Tollocán 721 Oriente ☎ (721) 4-6510.

A large industrial city, with all the accompanying disadvantages you might expect, and few buildings of merit to compensate. It is, however, within reach of many beautiful and interesting places; although they can easily be reached within a day from Mexico City, some travellers prefer to stay at one of Toluca's excellent hotels and save time on the road.

Toluca's Friday market is a lively and colourful place to buy Mexican crafts; weaving and pottery are good value, and also on offer are leather, wood-carving and basket-work. To see examples of the entire range of local crafts, go to the **Casa de las Artesanías**, a government-run museum and shop (*Paseo Tollocán, near the market*).

Sights nearby

Calixtlahuaca ☆

11km (7 miles) NW; turn W off San Juan del Río road after 8km (5 miles).

A large and interesting archaeological zone, with remains of a Matlazinca town and of its Aztec garrison's ceremonial centre. The most important building on the site is the circular **Temple of Quetzalcoatl**, constructed on four levels, with a wide stair on the E side. A short walk to the SE is the **Temple of Tlaloc**, built in pink and grey volcanic stone. The small adjacent structure is the **Altar of Skulls**, used for human sacrifice. From the hill to the S can be surveyed the other important structures.

Nevado de Toluca ☆

43km (27 miles) SW; turn S off Ciudad Altamirano road after 18km (11 miles).

The rough mountain track from the main road finishes only about 1km (½ mile) from the summit of the extinct volcano of **Xinantecatl**. Struggle on up the wall of the crater, with the two smooth lakes beneath you. Just as your lungs are bursting in the thin mountain air, you will suddenly find yourself on the roof of the world, with the Valley of Mexico and all its teeming millions spread out at your feet.

Hotels

Few tourists stay here, and downtown hotels are geared towards executives. Try the following: **Del Rey** (*Paseo Tollocán ☎ (721) 4–9888* ▮▮□ *to* ▮▮▮▮ ⇌ ≈), a good motel, 2.5km (1½ miles) from the centre towards Mexico City; **Plaza Morelos** ✤ (*Aquiles Serdán 115 ☎ (721) 5–9200* ▮▮□ ⇌), which has a good restaurant.

Hotel nearby

(*8km/5 miles NE of Toluca*).

Castel Plaza las Fuentes

Carr. Mexico–Toluca km 57 ☎ (721) 6–4666 ▮▮▮▮ *150* ⇌ AE CB ⊕ ⊙ VISA

If driving down from Toluca, this is a good place for a rest before pressing on into Mexico City. A plush country-club-style hotel.

≈ ⚲ Y ●

Places nearby

Teotenango and Taxco road (*S on Taxco road*). After 6km (4 miles), turn E on a road for **Metepec** (a further 2km/1¼ miles), a small town whose brightly coloured ornamental ceramics can be seen in shops all over the country. A speciality is the 'Tree of Life', but there are also animals going into the Ark, and many other themes.

Near the village of **Tenango** (on W of road at 26km/15 miles) are the **Teotenango remains**, once a large Matlazinca city crowning some craggy uplands. The entrance to the site is at the foot of the hill, where there is also a small and well-laid-out museum (▣ *open 9am–6pm*). The best exhibit is a large wooden drum from the nearby ruins of **Calixtlahuaca**, the only one of its kind in existence. Either drive or walk up to the ruins, which are imposingly grouped around a wide, grassy esplanade. Archaeologists are still at work, and will be for years yet.

The road continues to **Tenancingo** (54km/33 miles), a good place to buy the intricately woven *rebozos* (shawls). From here a poor road branches off E for *Malinalco*.

The waters at the thermal spa of **Ixtapán de la Sal** (85km/53 miles) are so mineral-rich that they are almost solid.

Torreón

Map 4E7. Coahuila. 375km (233 miles) W of Monterrey on RF 40. Population: 300,000. Served by air, train (on Mexico City–Ciudad Juarez line, and link line to Monterrey) and bus. Car rental: Avis, Independencia 999 ☎ (171) 3–9850, and booth at airport (no telephone); Budget, Independencia 295 ☎ (171) 6–1805; Hertz, Morelos 60 ☎ (171) 2–0991.

Mexico's youngest city, founded in 1875, and so therefore having few colonial buildings. Together with the linked cities of

Gomez Palacio and **Ciudad Lerdo**, it is an important part of the country's industrial base and, if you are passing through, not a disagreeable place to spend the night.

H **Palacio Real** (*Morelos 1280 Poniente* ☎ *(171) 6–0000* ▮▮▮▮ ≡ ≈); **Paraíso del Desierto** (*Independencia and Jiménez* ☎ *(171) 6–1122* ▮▮▮▮ ≡ ≈), a plush motel.

R **Apolo Palacio** (*Valdez Carrillo 258 Sur* ☎ *(171) 2–0436* ▮▮□ *to* ▮▮▮▮) serves Mexican and international cuisine; **Buffalo Steak House** (*Independencia 725 Oriente* ☎ *(171) 3–4521* ▮▮□).

Tula ★

Map 12D6. Hidalgo. 98km (61 miles) N of Mexico City on RF 57.

One of the more interesting archaeological sites, although you should expect neither the grandeur of *Teotihuacán* nor the beautiful surroundings of *Malinalco*. It was founded in the 10thC, probably by one of the tribes sweeping down from the N to sack Teotihuacán. Two centuries later, they had changed their barbaric ways and Tula had become the highly advanced and civilized capital of the Toltec domain. But then, in its turn, Tula also came under attack from nomadic and warlike tribes and was destroyed by fire. The people dispersed all over Mesoamerica, many migrating to the Yucatán, where they were an important influence on the development of Mayan culture.

One of the legendary rulers of Tula was the gentle god-king Quetzalcoatl, known for his dislike of human sacrifice and violence. It now seems likely that his legend pre-dates the Toltecs, who simply adopted it from the Teotihuacán culture; during the time of his supposed reign, the Toltecs were engaged upon the military conquest of the Yucatán, and are known to have introduced human sacrifice to that area. One possibility is that there was a Toltec ruler of that name who was confused with the mythical figure. In any case, his second coming was awaited by later cultures, including the Aztecs, and when Cortés arrived the emperor Montezuma made the fatal mistake of taking him for the gentle god.

The ruins 🏛

Pyramid of the Morning Star (*Templo de Tlahuizcalpantecuhtli*)

At the centre of the site is the Pyramid of the Morning Star, bearing four giant statues of warriors (*atlantes*) who gaze out impassively over the valley. They are probably representations of Quetzalcoatl, for one of the versions of the legend has him rising into the sky like a burning bird to become the Morning Star. Around the pyramid are various subsidiary structures of which the walls and pillars remain; they contain richly carved reliefs, some bearing traces of the bright colours in which they were painted. On the walls of the pyramid itself are remains of a frieze showing eagles and jaguars bearing human hearts. To the N, on a flanking wall, there are intricate geometric patterns and a relief.

The last building of this central group is the **Burnt Palace** (Palacio Quemado), on the W side. Two reclining statues stand in the main court, similar to others found all over Mesoamerica; these *chac-mools*, which were used to receive hearts from human sacrifice, show the extent of Toltec influence on other cultures.

Other ruins

The other buildings at Tula have not been substantially restored, although there are plans for the **Templo Mayor**, which faces the main terrace. There are also two ball-courts for the playing of a sacred game. Myth has it that the captain of the winning team was sacrificed, although it is hard to understand why this should have been an incentive to win. By the entrance to the site is a small **museum** (▪ *open 9am–6pm*), with a collection of pottery and sculptures from the site and some fine stone reliefs taken there for protection. A quick look around here should make it clear that the individuals outside selling 'genuine' relics are up to no good.

Tulum ★

Map 9G13. Quintana Roo. 224km (138 miles) E of Mérida on RF 180 and unnumbered road; 131km (81 miles) S of Puerto Juarez on RF 307.

Perhaps the most beautiful of the Yucatán's ruins, this is a small city walled on three sides and on the fourth looking out over the clear blue waters of the Caribbean. Architecturally it is less important than the great cities of the peninsula, but when you sit in the sun, idly watching the giant basking lizards and listening to the surf and the rustle of the palm trees, such academic matters will be far from your mind. Tulum was one of the few cities still inhabited when the Spaniards arrived, and was seen and described by explorers as early as 1518.

The ruins

Open 8am–6pm.

At the centre of the city's coastline, over some cliffs, stands the **Castillo** (Castle); it is in fact a temple with a pyramidal base and a wide ceremonial stair leading to an upper sanctuary. To the N of the courtyard behind the Castillo is the small **Temple of the Descending God**, where a stucco relief shows just that. A short distance W of here, the **Temple of the Frescoes** has one of the rare surviving examples of Mayan painting, showing divinities, serpents and sacred offerings, all in blue-green on a black wall. Outside, on the main facade, the Descending God appears again on a stucco relief; he is to be found at several places in Tulum.

H Villa Arqueológica

2 Poniente no.501 ☎ (22) 47–1966. Reservations: Mexico City ☎ (5) 583–4800 40

Location: In centre of the Cobá site (see below). A beautiful Club Mediterranée inn surrounded by ruins and tropical jungle. For those who prefer archaeology to sunbathing, there is a good library for serious study of the Maya. The management is young and friendly.

Place nearby

Cobá ☆ (*39km/25 miles NW by unnumbered road leading to RF 180*). The paved road leads to the archaeological zone of Cobá, which was one of the main centres of Mayan civilization from the 7thC right up until the Conquest. Excavations are at an early stage, but eventually Cobá will become one of the wonders of the world. The main group of buildings stands in the jungle between two opaque green lakes, and is dominated by the **Castillo**, taller even than the Castillo at *Chichén Itzá*. All around, there are somewhere in the region of 7,000 ruined structures, and satellite pictures have also revealed a network of wide avenues of crushed limestone running through the jungle to link Cobá with other cities; one of these runs nearly 100km (62 miles) to Chichén Itzá. The pictures also reveal the existence of an extensive network of irrigation canals.

Tuxtla Gutierrez

Map 8H11. Capital of Chiapas. 294km (182 miles) S of Villahermosa on RF 190 and RF 195. Population: 118,000. Served by air and bus. Car rental: Hertz, 14 de Septiembre 1418 ☎ (961) 2–4375 i Central Poniente 1454 ☎ (961) 2–0732/2–7773. US Consul: Laureles 26 ☎ (961) 2–3013.

Not one of the country's most magnificent tourist towns, but a pleasant place to spend a night after the steamy heat of the isthmus or the rigours of travelling in Chiapas. The tourist office is helpful and well informed.

Tuxtla's main attraction is the **zoo** (*open 9am–6pm*), where you can see animals native to the forests and mountains of Chiapas. You are unlikely to see many of them elsewhere during your stay: most are elusive and shy, although monkeys and parrots can be spotted near the ruins in the jungle. The **Museo del Estado** or Chiapas State Museum (*Av. Central, towards Tehuantepec open 8.30am–2pm, closed Sun*) contains Olmec sculptures from the N of the state and various Mayan artifacts from nearby sites.

Sights nearby

Chiapa de Corzo
14km (9 miles) E on RF 190.
At the centre of this small town's Zocalo is a bizarre 16thC **fountain**, built in the Moorish style to resemble the crown of the kings of Spain. Near the Zocalo is a small **museum** of regional handicrafts and Mayan artifacts from the oldest known sites. Enterprising local boatmen offer roller-coaster rides ✩ on the river Chiapas from the town down to the canyons, an hour or two away.

El Sumidero Canyon
23km (14 miles) N.
The **gorge** cut by the river Chiapas near the village of El Sumidero is one of the most spectacular natural sights in Mexico. It is hard not to believe you are flying when you look down the full dizzying mile to the churning white waters below. Legend has it that a whole tribe of Indians cast themselves to their death here rather than submit to the Conquistadors.

Ocozocoautla
36km (23 miles) W on RF 190.
A *pueblo* of the tall and graceful Zoque Indians, an agricultural people who have more or less adopted the Catholic faith, with a few pagan improvisations. At fiestas, they wear beautiful embroidered tunics to perform the traditional dances; if you buy one, do not wear it until you have left the area, out of respect.

Simojovel de Allende
78km (49 miles) NE; turn N onto RF 195 after 34km (22 miles) on RF 190.
Since Pre-Columbian times this fascinating hillside village has been a source of amber. In the village can be bought small pieces of jewellery, cigarette holders and so on. Rarer, and more expensive, are the pieces containing fossilized insects.

[H] Here are some good places to spoil yourself after a hard journey, although prices are high for the area: **Bonampak** (*Belisario Domínguez 180 ☎ (961) 2-0201*) is a clean, comfortable and modern hotel with its own sauna; **Castel Flamboyant** (*Belisario Domínguez km 1,081 ☎ (961) 2-9259*) is a new resort hotel; **Real de Tuxtla** (*Pan-American Highway km 1,088 ☎ (961) 2-5958*) is the best and most luxurious hotel in the state.

[R] **La Selva** (*Belisario Domínguez km 1,360 ☎ (961) 2-6251*), although not the grandest restaurant, is good for regional specialities.

Uruapán

Map 11E4. Michoacán. 186km (115 miles) SW of Morelia on RF 15 and RF 37. Population: 117,000. Served by bus.

A quiet and pretty town in the semi-tropical hills of Michoacán, whose name in the language of the local Tarascan Indians means 'Place of Flowers', a title still justified by the impressively luxuriant parks. At the centre is a large market square occupying four blocks of the town's grid plan; every Sunday it fills with Tarascans selling the crafts of their villages. On the main square is a fine Plateresque doorway which leads to some old ecclesiastical buildings now in use as a **museum of Tarascan crafts** (*open 9am–1pm, 3–5pm*), showing especially the lacquerware for which Uruapán is famous.

Events On July 22 and Oct 4, local fiestas.

Sights nearby

Paracho

36km (23 miles) N on RF 37.

A small village which attracts musicians because of the hand-made violins and guitars produced in its many workshops. Fiesta on Aug 8.

Parangaricutiro

20km (12 miles) NW; engage guides with ponies at Angahuán, W of RF 37 after 11km (7 miles).

From Angahuán, where there is a fine 16thC church, guides will take you to the deserted village of Parangaricutiro, which was half buried by lava from an eruption of the volcano Paricutín. The volcano started as a smoking hole in the middle of a cornfield in 1943, and blasted its way up to 700m (2,310ft) above the land before ceasing activity as suddenly in 1951. The thick covering of volcanic ash, which made life a choking misery during the eruption, has repaid local farmers by markedly improving the fertility of their land.

H **Mansión de Cupatitzio**

In the National Park, W of town ☎ *(452) 3–2100* 56 AE CB Φ MC VISA

Located amid beautiful countryside, this is a good place to go for the weekend. Country-club-style accommodation and fine restaurant.

H **Paraíso Uruapán** (*Km 2 on Patzcuaro road* ☎ *(452) 2–1640*) is an excellent motel; **Tarasco** (*Independencia 2* ☎ *(452) 2–1680*) is a modern downtown hotel; also **Victoria** (*Cupatitzio 11* ☎ *(452) 2–1500*).

R **Papillón** (*Madrid 12* ☎ *(452) 3–4380*) is reasonable for steaks.

Uxmal ★

Map 9G12. Yucatán. 78km (49 miles) S of Mérida on RF 261 and RF 180. Served by bus.

When Uxmal was built, it was surrounded by luxuriant tropical jungle, but the fires that devastated the Yucatán in the 16thC have left no more than thorny scrub. This does not detract from the glory or allure of some of the finest remaining Mayan buildings and one of the world's great archaeological sites, rivalling Ephesus, Luxor and Macchu Pichu in beauty and splendour. Along with *Chichén Itzá*, Uxmal is the central part of any visit to the Yucatán. The very name embodies its past – in the Mayan tongue, the word means 'thrice built', and indeed the Mayans returned after abandoning the city at least that number of times, having been forced to leave because Uxmal, unlike the other cities, relied entirely on rainwater, having no *cenote* (well), and ran dry when the rains failed.

The earliest buildings date from the Classic period of the 6thC. In the 10thC, the city was occupied by an invading Toltec tribe and became a part of the Mayapan League of cities. It was deserted for the last time in the 14thC as the League broke up.

Many of the buildings are unrestored, and archaeologists will be working here for many years to come. To have the latest discoveries pointed out, it is necessary to engage an official guide. The tour lasts up to 4hrs, but most people like to stroll around on their own afterwards.

Events Daily at 9pm, son-et-lumière in English. Not performed one day every week, which varies.

The ruins 🏛

Open 6am–5pm.

The Magician's Pyramid (*Pirámide del Adivino*)

As you enter the site, this steep, elliptically-based pyramid is immediately opposite. It is said to have been built in a single night by a magician, an unlikely story since it shows evidence of various architectural styles from the 6th–10thC. The stairs to the apex are hard to climb, and much harder to descend.

The Nunnery (*Cuadrángulo de las Monjas*)

Just behind the pyramid is the entrance to 'The Nunnery', which consists of four buildings around a large, nearly square court. The monumental entrance to the S building is especially fine, while the most important building of the group is on the N side, raised on a terrace, and with a heavily ornamented frieze; note especially the masks of the rain god Chac, of vital importance in a city which depended entirely on rainfall for its water. Far from being a nunnery as the Spaniards supposed, there is evidence that these buildings were used to house young women passing a final debauched year before being sacrificed to Chac.

The Palace of the Governor

Due S of the Nunnery is this magnificent long building, thought by many authorities to be the finest achievement of Mayan architecture. It was probably the administrative centre of the city, so, for once, the Spaniards guessed more or less right. The contrast between the elegant simplicity of its proportions and the geometric complexity of the frieze provides an entirely satisfying artistic tension.

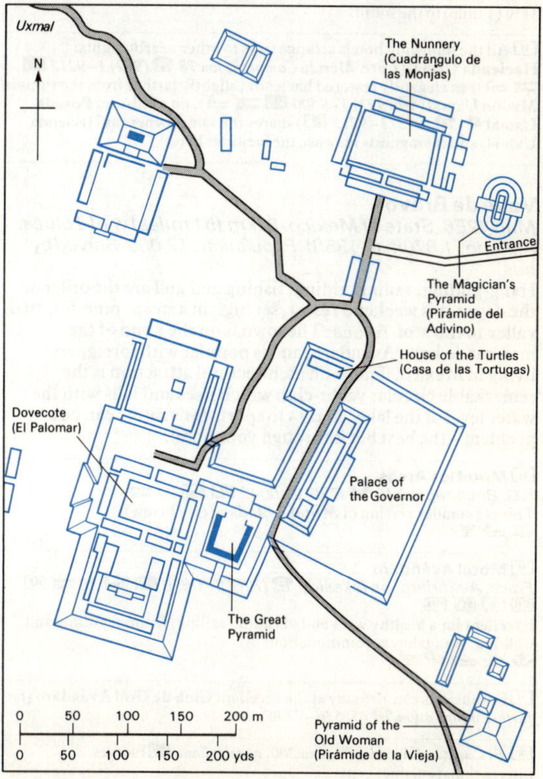

The Great Pyramid

In the same group of buildings, on the SW corner of the Palace, is the Great Pyramid, from the summit of which there is a good view of the city. Over to the W can be seen the **'Dovecote'** (El Palomar), incorrectly named by the Spaniards. Looking N, the small **House of the Turtles** (Casa de las Tortugas) is near the Palace – walk over here to see the turtles carved in relief over a simple frieze. In the opposite direction is the oldest building on the site, the small **Pyramid of the Old Woman** (Pirámide de la Vieja).

Sights nearby

The countryside around Uxmal is one great archaeological zone. There are three sites of importance to the E and SE which can be quite easily visited by road. The hotels at Uxmal can arrange tours and guides.

Kabah is 22km (14 miles) S on RF 261. Just to the E of the road stands the amazing **Temple of the Masks** (also known as 'Codz Pop'). The facade is decorated with hundreds of masks of the rain god Chac, from the cornice to the base. Other buildings are less restored, but there are plans to renovate the main pyramid and the large arch which was the ceremonial entrance to the limestone causeway leading to Uxmal.

Labna is reached 41km (26 miles) E by turning E off RF 261 at Sayil and taking the road for Xul. The most important structure in this jungle-covered site is the massive **Arch of Labna**, which once linked two courts. Nearby is a high pyramid with a roof-comb and, over to the N, a complex of courts and chambers known collectively as **El Palacio**.

The jungle is still master of most of **Sayil**, 27km (16 miles) S on RF 261, but the large three-storey **Palacio** has been partly restored. Another temple, known as **El Mirador**, with a tall open stonework roof-comb, is ½km (⅓ mile) to the south.

[H] All the following hotels arrange trips to other nearby sights: **Hacienda Uxmal** (*Carr. Mérida Campeche km 78* ☎ *(992) 1–9212* ▮▮▮▮ ≡ ≈), an elegantly restored hacienda; slightly farther from the ruins is **Misión Uxmal** (☎ *(992) 3–9500* ▮▮▮▮ ≡ ≈), on a hill-top; **Posada Uxmal** ✿ (☎ *(992) 1–9212* ▮▮▯) shares the same owners as Hacienda Uxmal, and their guests may use the facilities here.

Valle de Bravo

Map 12E6. State of Mexico. 82km (51 miles) W of Toluca. Altitude: 1,870m (6,135ft). Population: 12,000. Served by bus.

Hang-gliding, sailing, riding, fishing and golf are the order of the day at this weekend resort, set high in a steep, pine-forested valley to the W of *Toluca*. The town is on the E end of the man-made Lake Avándaro, and is popular with foreigners living in Mexico. The main architectural attraction is the remarkable circular yacht-club which rises and falls with the water level of the lake. Access to sports for visitors can be a problem – the best bet is through your hotel.

[H] **Motel los Arcos**
F.G. Bocanegra 310 ☎ *(726) 2–0042* ▮▮▯ 24 ≡
This is a smaller version of ***Motel Avándaro*** (see below).

[H] **Motel Avándaro**
Fracc. Avándaro, on lakeside ☎ *(726) 2–0626* ▮▮▮▮ 36 ≡ AE CB ◉ ⊕ VISA
Excellent for a healthy weekend of riding, sailing, fishing, golfing and walking. Bungalow accommodation.

[H] Enthusiasts can also stay at the excellent **Club de Golf Avándaro** (*for further information* ☎ *(5) 536–7736*).

[R] **El Capitán** (*Arcadio Pagaza 200, no telephone* ▮▮▮▮) serves international cuisine.

Veracruz

Map 13E9. Capital of Veracruz. 431km (268 miles) E of Mexico City on RF 190 and RF 150. Population: 375,000. Served by air (international airport 12km/7 miles NW), train (on line to Mexico City) and bus. Car rental: Avis, Hotel Veracruz, Plaza de Armas ☎ (293) 2–2516, and booth at international airport (no telephone) ℹ Palacio Municipal ☎ (293) 2–2151. US Consul: 5 de Mayo 1082 ☎ (293) 4–5809.

The people of Mexico's oldest and busiest port are renowned for the warmth of their welcome, and yet, although visitors fit happily into the bustling life of the city, it does not revolve around them and they can enjoy the welcome relief of being out of the focus of economic attention. Unlike any other city in Mexico, there is a strong Afro-Caribbean influence on the people and culture of Veracruz, and this can be seen every day in the faces in the streets. But it is at carnival time that Veracruz becomes a Caribbean city. Fireworks light up the sky from dusk to dawn, while dancers, musicians and costumed revellers throng the streets. The lilt of the calypso and the African rhythms of the local dances fill the air, and everyone has a wonderful time.

The Spanish influence is more apparent in the buildings and especially in the area around the Zocalo, where the street life is even more active than in other Mexican towns. At numerous small pavement cafés, *Veracruzanos* sit out talking, drinking and eating delicious seafood snacks. On most evenings in the square there are bandstand concerts, and the ritual evening stroll, the *paseo*, keeps the streets busy and the atmosphere relaxed.

It was near Veracruz, on Good Friday 1519, that the Conquistadors first landed, and founded the city a short distance from the modern town. For a long time it was the only port allowed to trade with the Old World, and therefore offered rich pickings for the buccaneers who infested the sea; the town was sacked and plundered on several occasions between the 16th–18thC. Nor did the eventual disappearance of the pirates end the troubles of Veracruz. Long after Mexico had achieved independence, Spanish troops on the island fortress of San Juan de Ulúa kept the city under sporadic shell fire. There was then a French invasion in 1838, followed by an American occupation in 1847 and a further French invasion in 1862, this time with English and American help. Finally, in 1914, there was yet another American occupation, preceded by a bombardment.

None of this will be held against you, however, so long as your foreign intervention is restricted to such peaceable activities as eating seafood, strolling around the lively docks, and buying hammocks and cigars from the vendors in the Zocalo.

Event There is a large and exciting Easter carnival.

Sights and places of interest

The centre

The Zocalo, the **Plaza de Armas**, said to be the oldest in Mexico, is arcaded on two sides and overlooked by a small and well-worn **cathedral**. Six blocks NE is the waterfront (*malecón*); while there to take a boat to the islands, take a look at the **Biblioteca Juarez**, a library housed in an old bell tower overlooking the port, and the nearby monastic buildings now in use as a hotel.

On the way S from the Zocalo, the small regional **museum** (🎫 *open standard hours*) in the Baluarte Santiago building on 16 de Septiembre contains some of the offerings found on Isla de Sacrificios. Six blocks S of

Plaza de Armas is the pleasant **Parque Zamora**, by the trolley-bus terminal, and E of the park is the church of **Santo Cristo del Buen Viaje** (Christ of the Safe Voyage), where Spanish sailors would pray for deliverance from English pirates on the way back to Spain.

Isla de Sacrificios

A boat from the main quay takes you to this small island, a short distance into the Gulf. The Spaniards discovered a shrine here where numerous human sacrifices had evidently been performed (some of the offerings found can be seen at the small museum in town). There is not much to see here, but the view of the town from the sea is excellent.

San Juan de Ulúa

This massive, dismal fortress on a small island opposite the port was originally built to defend Veracruz, although its principal use was as a dungeon for dissidents or criminals, who were immersed in sea water every high tide. It was started in 1528 and eventually finished in 1771, at a cost of some 40 million gold pesos to the treasury of Charles V.

Sight nearby

Zempoala ☆

34km (21 miles) NW on RF 180. Open 9am–6pm.

The ruins of the large Totonac city which was the first in Mesoamerica to be visited by Cortés. At the centre of the main group is the **Great Temple**, atop a 13-tier pyramid, and nearby a 4-tier **Great Pyramid**, finished just in time for the Spaniards to ransack. The **Templo de las Caritas** ('the small faces') is decorated with rows of grinning skulls.

Hotels

Calinda Quality Inn

Boca del Río Playa (293) 4-5100 128

A new chain hotel 10mins' taxi ride from the centre of town.

Emporio

Malecón and Xicotencatl (293) 2-0020 20

Fishing trips can be arranged from this traditional waterfront hotel.

Hostal de Cortés

Avila Camacho and las Casas s/n (293) 2-0065 108

It is advisable to avoid conventions at this excellent hotel.

Mocambo

Playa Mocambo (293) 7-1500 90

A vacation resort hotel, good for all kinds of water-sports, with a reasonable beach.

Playa Paraíso

Mocambo Highway km 3.5 (293) 7-8399 32

A luxurious beach hotel, although the beach is not special.

Prendes

Independencia 1064 (293) 2-0153 to 34

This traditional downtown establishment has the best seafood restaurant in Veracruz.

Pardino (*Boca del Río, no telephone*) and **El Pescador** (*Zaragoza 335 (293) 2-5252*) are both seafood restaurants. The best seafood restaurant in town, however, is the one at the ***Prendes*** hotel (see above).

The Beaches

The nearest beaches to the town centre are N out along Independencia at **Villa del Mar** and **Hornos**. Six blocks N of the Villa del Mar beach is an aquarium (☎ *open 10am–6pm*), with a large collection of marine life from the Gulf. A little farther from the centre, at **Boca del Río** (10km/6 miles S along the coast road), there are more deserted beaches. Some development is now taking place here, and also at **Mocambo**, a village between Boca del Río and Veracruz. To get even farther away from it all, take the road beyond Boca del Rio as far as the jungle lagoon of **Mandinga**, 20km (12 miles) to the S.

Places nearby

The Gulf road (*SE on RF 180*). The first stop along the steamy Gulf of Mexico road is at the fishing port of **Alvarado** (72km/45 miles); try to be here at a meal time, since the unpretentious Port Authority canteen on the waterfront offers top quality seafood at low prices. The men of Alvarado have a reputation for brawling and foul language, however, so before getting into a fight, press on to **Tlacotalpán** (16km/10 miles S at 89km/55 miles), a small, pretty town of thatched cottages, where you can buy local handicrafts and take a boat trip up the river.

The next stop is at **Santiago Tuxtla** (144km/90 miles), where there is an interesting archaeological museum by the Zocalo. Only 20km (12 miles) beyond here is **Lake Catemaco**, a tranquil lagoon where many *veracruzanos* have weekend houses. At the village of Catemaco, there is a lively fiesta on July 16 in honour of the Virgin, and a few decent hotels.

Villahermosa

Map 8H11. Capital of Tabasco. 245km (151 miles) E of Coatzacoalcos on RF 180. Population: 130,000. Served by air and bus. Car rental: Avis, at airport ☎ (931) 2-9214; Hertz, Hotel Maya Tabasco, Grijalva, 907 ☎ (931) 2-1111 ***i*** *Lerdo 101 ☎ (931) 2-3171.*

The name Villahermosa means 'beautiful town', but sadly any charm it may have had has been swept away by oil wealth. It is a hot, crowded, congested and polluted city, but most travellers in this part of Mexico end up spending a night here (it is well worth staying in an expensive hotel here). However, the two museums are excellent, and you should stop to see the **Parque La Venta** even if you are just passing.

Sights and places of interest

Museo Tabasco ☆

Calle Vicente Guerrero ☎ Open standard hours.

A well-laid-out museum, containing Mayan and Olmec artifacts from all over the state of Tabasco. It provides an easy, enjoyable way to familiarize yourself with the art of these vanished cultures before going on to visit the major sites.

The first two rooms contain mostly Olmec work, with small sculptures of warriors, monkeys and semi-human jaguars. On a larger scale, there is a fine colossal **head of a warrior** with a jaguar-like smile or snarl. In the following smaller rooms are less important collections from Central and Western Mexico; up a staircase in a small room are copies of Pre-Hispanic *códices* (painted scrolls). The Mayan collections are in the last few rooms. Do not miss the reproductions of the **murals** from the remote jungle site of *Bonampak*. The **pottery figurines** from the island of Jaina show a realism which is rare in Mayan art, whose emphasis is more usually on religious symbolism and stylization.

Parque la Venta ★

On road to Coatzacoalcos, 1.5km (1 mile) from centre ☎ Open 8.30am–5pm. Closed Mon.

An open-air museum which is a painstaking re-creation of a part of the ruins found at La Venta, in the swamps of western Tabasco. La Venta was a major centre of the mysterious Olmec people, who were the first urban civilization of Mesoamerica. There is now little to see at La Venta itself, since most of the finer pieces have been transferred to the park.

The highlights are four of the giant **monolithic heads**, which are a typical product of Olmec sculpture. They weigh up to 20 tonnes apiece, and facially they are a mixture of negroid and jaguar-like, for the Olmecs were a negroid people who worshipped a jaguar god. Other pieces include the famous *Madonna and Child*, probably a goddess holding a jaguar-featured baby. There are also some low-relief steles (stone tablets), showing gods, animals and richly caparisoned nobles. As part of the effort to ensure the realism of the park, there is a small zoo containing animals which roam the swamps around La Venta; quite often they escape from their cages and are pursued by staff and visitors. The Olmecs may also have kept a similar zoo; a construction of thin stone cylinders in the park was almost certainly a cage for captured jaguars.

H **Cencali** (*Juarez and Laguna de las Ilusiones* ☎ *(931) 2–6000*) is near the airport; near the bus station, try the new **Maya Tabasco** (*Grijalva 907* ☎ *(931) 2–1111* to), which has a good restaurant; **Olmeca** (*Reforma 304* ☎ *(931) 2–0022*) is located downtown and has helpful staff; **Villahermosa Viva** (*Paseo Tabasco 1201* ☎ *(931) 2–5555*) is near to the *Cencali* hotel and offers similar facilities.

R **Club de Pesca** (*2 de Febrero no.812* ☎ *(931) 2–2197*) serves seafood; **D'Alrio** (*Hotel Manzur, Madero 422* ☎ *(931) 2–2499*), whose specialities include turtle and shrimps, served to the strains of organ music.

Places nearby

Comalcalco ☆ (*96km/60 miles NW; turn N off RF 180 at Cardenas, 58km/36 miles W*). A recently restored Mayan site of great beauty, of which few people have even heard. Near the large pyramid is a burial chamber decorated with stucco reliefs of Mayan princes and gods. The **Building of the Masks** (Edificio de los Mascarones), also in the main group, is heavily decorated with stucco masks. 19km (11 miles) beyond here is the coastal village of **Paraíso**, which does indeed have a heavenly beach.

Tenosique (*219km/135 miles SE; head SE on RF 186 and turn S after 134km/84 miles*). A small trading outpost on the banks of the river Usumacinta, which flows through the Lacandon rain-forest. From here, the enterprising can venture into the jungle in canoes or on mules to see remote Mayan ruins. It would be unwise, however, to set out without a local guide.

Xochicalco ☆

Map 12E6. State of Mexico. 36km (22 miles) SW of Cuernavaca. Served by bus.

Like so many of the great ruined ceremonial centres of Mexico, little is known of the history of Xochicalco. Archaeologically, it does provide important clues to the history of the whole region; artifacts and inscriptions link it not only with *Teotihuacán* and *Tula*, but with the Mayan and Zapotec cultures far to the E. It was abandoned in the 10thC, perhaps because of plague, invasions or famine, and the inhabitants literally disappeared from history. The ruins are in a commanding position on the artificially flattened summit of one of the foothills of Mount Ajusco.

The ruins

Open 10am–6pm.

The entrance to the site is from the S, into the **Plaza Inferior**, where a tall stele carved with calendrical symbols stands between two pyramids. When the site was abandoned, the stele was overturned and painted red – the colour of death throughout Mesoamerica. From here a wide avenue leads past a ball-court for the sacred game, to some unrestored buildings on an artificial mound.

To the N of the Plaza Inferior is the site's finest monument, the **Pyramid of the Plumed Serpents** (Pirámide de las Serpientes Emplumadas). It is built on two levels, and around the walls of the lower stage are reliefs of numerous plumed serpents twisting around the seated figures of priests. Over to the N and down the hill is the entrance to a network of chambers and tunnels beneath the site, some of which have been opened. In one of the chambers, an opening to the roof is oriented to admit direct sunlight only on the days of full equinox. It is possible, with the help of a flashlight, to make out the remains of murals.

Yaxchilán

See *Bonampak (and Yaxchilán).*

Zacatecas

Map 10A3. Capital of Zacatecas. 318km (196 miles) N of Guadalajara on RF 54. Altitude: 2,440m (8,005ft). Population: 100,000. Served by air, train (on Mexico City–Chihuahua line) and bus ℹ *Adolfo L. Mateos 923* ☎ *(492) 2–6750.*

One of the old mining towns of Central Mexico, with some fine colonial architecture. The skyline is dominated by the ragged rocks of the Cerro de La Bufa, from which the chapel of **La Virgen del Patrocinio** commands a bird's-eye view of town. The pink-stone mansions and churches are eloquent testimony to the wealth that silver once brought to the town, but the rather run-down and sprawling outskirts, of more modern origin, suggest that the good times have passed. The town was founded in 1546, and silver mining began 2yrs later, reaching a peak in the next century. In the 1910 Revolution, Zacatecas was the scene of the dictator Huerta's final defeat by Pancho Villa.

Events Between Aug 27–31, fiesta. Mock battle on Cerro de la Bufa between dancers dressed as Franks and Saracens.

On night of Dec 31, lively celebrations for the New Year.

Nearby, there are worthwhile fiestas on Jan 20 at Saín Alto (116km/72 miles NW on RF 49), on Jan 22–24 at Jerez de García Salinas (31km/20 miles S on RF 54), and on Oct 28 at Villanueva (55km/36 miles S on RF 54).

Sights and places of interest

For a good orienting view of the city, the chapel of **La Virgen del Patrocinio** can be reached either by car (the turning is signposted off the Durango road), or by the scenic cable-car.

Cathedral 🏛 ✝ ☆
Plaza de Hidalgo.

On the S side of the main square, this cathedral is probably the finest example of the amazing flowering of the Churrigueresque style in 18thC Mexico. Every part of the facade is profusely ornamented, with the extravagant fantasies of the rich mine owners frozen in stone. Work was started in 1612, but the building was not completed until 1760, and the dome is a later 19thC addition.

Santo Domingo 🏛 ✝
Callejón de Veyna.

Just W of the Zocalo, past the Palacio de Gobierno, the facade of this Jesuit church has a restraint and elegance which offers a sharp contrast to the excesses of the cathedral. The main door is at the top of a wide, curved stair, and inside is a fine Churrigueresque altarpiece.

The part of town to the W of here is known as **Old Zacatecas** (Vieja Zacatecas), with pretty little squares with their 18thC palaces.

Sight nearby

La Quemada (*Chicomoztoc*) 🏛
40km (25 miles) S on RF 54 🎫 *Open 9am–6pm.*

Nobody knows who erected these important buildings on a natural terrace high above the plain; one theory is that the Aztecs lived here during their migration to the Valley of Mexico from their unknown home. Halfway up the wide causeway is the group known as **The Cathedral**, because of a line of large columns, and at the summit are the sturdy bulwarks and a **votive pyramid**.

H **Aristos** (*Loma de la Soledad s/n* ☎ *(492) 2-1788*) is an excellent hotel; **Calinda Quality Inn** (*López Mateos and Callejón del Barro* ☎ *(492) 2-3311*) is a modern, central hotel; located by the scenic cable-car station is **Del Bosque** (*Periférico and Díaz Ordaz* ☎ *(492) 2-0745*), a motel with bungalows.

R **El Caballo Loco** (*Pan-American Highway 101* ☎ *(492) 2-6343*) serves western-cut steaks.

Zihuatanejo (and Ixtapa) ☆

Map 6H7. Guerrero. 241km (150 miles) NW of Acapulco on RF 200. Population: 11,000. Served by air (international airport 24km/15 miles N) and bus. Car rental: Avis, Juan Alvarez 7 ☎ (743) 4-2275, and at airport ☎ (743) 4-2248; Hertz, Hotel Posada Caracol, La Madera ☎ (743) 4-2035, and at airport ☎ (743) 4-2590 **i** *Paseo del Pescador ☎ (743) 4-2207.*

Some years ago, Zihuatanejo was a small, isolated fishing port, exporting bananas and attracting a few intrepid seekers after unspoiled beaches. The computer of Mexico's Tourist Ministry changed all that when, in the early 1970s, it selected the deserted beaches of Ixtapa, just up the coast, as the site for an entirely new luxury resort.

Ixtapa has a futuristic image, with gleaming high-rise pleasure machines sitting like a row of interstellar cruisers along the beach. Unlike *Cancún*, founded at the same time, it has not rocketed immediately to commercial global status and, despite offering the very latest in jet-set glamour and luxury, is altogether a more relaxed place. Of the two, Zihuatanejo is more popular with budget-conscious travellers who prefer atmosphere to comfort. The particular advantage of a vacation at either of these two resorts is that a quick escape to a completely different style of entertainment is always possible.

Isla Ixtapa

A small island about 15km (9 miles) off the coast from Zihua, with an irregular boat service from Zihua and Ixtapa. There is a regular boat service to near the Club Med on the mainland opposite, the last boat leaving at about 5pm. There are three beaches on the island, each with several small restaurants serving fresh seafood. The woods of the interior are a wildlife reserve, with semi-tame deer and noisily squawking parrots of all colours. A good place to spend an idle day.

Hotels

Ixtapa

For the following hotels in Ixtapa, it can be much cheaper to arrange a package through a travel agent.

Aristos

Paseo Ixtapa ☎ (743) 4-2265 (016206 226 AE CB DC MC VISA

This was the first luxury hotel to be built here, and it still ranks as one of the top four. A lively social programme is organized for guests. It has all facilities, and is one of the smaller of the concrete monsters.

Camino Real

Playa Vistahermosa ☎ (743) 4-3300 016203 450 AE CB DC MC VISA

Every facility is offered here, with three restaurants, four bars, vast swimming pools and its own beach. The rooms are superb and there are six special suites, each with its own swimming pool.

Club Med
Playa Quieta (743) 4-3440
375

Attractive villas clustered on a secluded beachfront form this exclusive club with its highly organized social life.

Holiday Inn
Blvd. Ixtapa (743) 4-2396
to 240

One of the best of the Holiday Inn chain, with a most attractive flower-filled lobby. The watersports provided include paragliding.

Krystal
Paseo de Ixtapa (743) 4-2618 016201 to
260

This high-rise tower is a newcomer to the scene and provides an organized social programme.

El Presidente
Paseo Ixtapa (743) 4-2013 016205 300

An attractively designed, low building with an extraordinary multi-level swimming pool. There is plenty of entertainment for children, and a good seafood restaurant.

Riviera del Sol
Paseo de Ixtapa (743) 4-2406 320

The twin towers of this hotel rise out of its pleasant garden. Diving instruction is given.

Sheraton
Blvd. Ixtapa (743) 4-2819
358

The Sheraton is the newest luxury hotel, with striking twin towers.

Viva Ixtapa
Av. del Palmar (743) 4-2341
to 110

A friendly atmosphere is a feature of this, the smallest luxury hotel in Ixtapa.

Zihuatanejo

Posada Caracol
Playa Madera (743) 4-2036
to 60

Stay in the new air conditioned wing of this friendly establishment: near the beach.

Villa del Sol
Playa la Ropa (743) 4-2239/3239 17

This is a small, family-run inn, with a South Sea Island decor.

Restaurants

Hotels in Ixtapa all have excellent restaurants, with an emphasis on international seafood and some Mexican dishes. There are all sorts of arrangements for hotel-hopping diners, some of which include a restaurant in Zihuatanejo.

Coconuts
Agustín Ramirez 1 (743) 4-2518
Closed lunch.
An elegant restaurant serving international food. Friendly foreign management, and occasional special fiestas.

Kontiki
Playa la Ropa. No telephone
A lively place on the beach which always attracts sun-lovers with its enormous pizzas, sweet-and-sour and cheesecake. Open all hours.

La Mesa del Capitán
Bravo 18 (743) 4-2027
Fresh seafood and steaks are served here amid a cheerful atmosphere. Best food in Zihua.

La Tortuga y la Rana
Alvarez s/n (743) 4-2323
Romantic atmosphere and an imaginative seafood menu are the two main ingredients of this restaurant.

Nightlife

There is always something going on at one of the hotels, and each one will provide a free entertainment schedule. The two fashionable discos in Zihuatanejo are at the ***Posada Caracol*** hotel and ***Kontiki*** restaurant. For a *dîner-dansant* try the **Adam and Eve** club (*near Kontiki restaurant* ☎ *(743) 4–2135* ▮▮▮).

Shopping

The only places to shop in Ixtapa are at boutiques in the luxury hotels, or at the brand-new **La Puerta shopping centre** where there is better choice but high prices and no bargaining. It is much more fun therefore to shop in Zihua, at the little shops along the **Paseo del Pescador** waterfront and around the **Zocalo**. Prices are low, the selection good, and haggling is expected. The town market, on Paseo del Cocotal, has a small craft section.

Sports and activities

The beaches

The beaches near Zihua are separated by rocky promontories, and are best reached by taxi from the town centre, or by boat from the quayside. There is no regular service to the more remote beaches, so make sure that the taxi driver or boatman has clear instructions when to pick you up. The four main beaches are described below.

Las Gatas

Perhaps the best of all is this isolated beach, out at the end of the bay N from Zihua. It has an excellent pedigree, once being the exclusive preserve of the Tarascan rulers in Pre-Columbian times. The name of Las Gatas (The Cats) is thought to have been given by the Conquistadors; they chose it because of a high wall built around the beach to protect sunbathing monarchs from the fierce jungle wildcats. The wall is no more, but, luckily, the cats have also disappeared. According to some, the cats in question were actually cat-sharks, and the wall was built under water. In any case, there are no sharks either, and scuba and snorkel equipment can be rented on the beach.

Playa Madera

A small and secluded beach, to the S of Playa Principal (see below). Good for children, as no motorboats come in close to the shore.

Playa Principal

The main town beach under the shops and cafés of the waterfront. Becomes crowded at weekends.

Playa La Ropa

The more agreeable of the beaches near Zihua: long, wide and uncrowded. Absolutely the best for water-sports, with windsurfing, waterskiing and paragliding. The name of 'La Ropa' (The Clothes) comes from a time when a ship carrying a cargo of shirts was wrecked and the contents washed up on the beach. Overlooking the beach is an amazing, vast Greek temple surrounded by marble statues and manicured lawns. This is the holiday home of a former chief of police who became fabulously rich in an inexplicable way!

Other sports

Most water-sports are on offer on the main beaches, so inquire at your hotel if you need to rent any equipment. Deep-sea fishing can also be arranged through the hotels or by bargaining with the characters down at the quay in Zihua. Golf and tennis are available to all at the well-designed **Palma Real Golf Club**, behind the Ixtapa hotel zone, on payment of a small fee.

Places nearby

Acapulco, 3–4hrs' drive S along the coast (241km/150 miles), is worth a day-trip if you have never been there. Rent a car and start early so as to enjoy the unspoiled coast at leisure.

In the other direction is the vast new steel complex at **Lázaro Cárdenas** (98km/61 miles), where visitors who are interested will be given a tour and will not be disappointed. The small beach resort 22km (13 miles) farther up the coast, **Playa Azul**, is now a firm favourite with the steelworkers, but its often-referred-to charm is a thing of the past.

Biographies

This list represents just some of the key figures in Mexican history. See also ***Art and architecture*** in *Culture, history and background*.

Alemán, Miguel *(1900–1983)*
President from 1946–52, a period of spectacular economic growth. Despite major public works, his regime's suppression of workers' movements and the spread of corruption alienated popular support.

Allende, Ignacio *(1769–1811)*
One of the heroes of Mexican nationalists, he left the Spanish royal army to join the rebellion of 1810. As general of Hidalgo's army he achieved important victories, but was eventually captured and executed near Chihuahua.

Cabrera, Miguel *(1695–1768)*
The best-known painter of the colonial era was born an Indian peasant. His religious works are in churches all over Mexico.

Cárdenas, Lázaro *(1895–1970)*
Perhaps the only post-1917 president to effect both economic success and the reformist principles of the Revolution. During his presidency (1934–40) he initiated the first agrarian reforms and the nationalization of the foreign oil companies.

Carranza, Venustiano *(1859–1920)*
A shrewd and moderate politician who emerged from the internal fighting following the 1910 Revolution to become President in 1914. War between the former revolutionary comrades continued, and he was assassinated in 1920. He is still regarded as one of the fathers of modern Mexico.

Cortés, Hernán *(1485–1547)*
The leader of the small band of Spanish adventurers who landed in Mexico in 1519. By a combination of luck, guile, skill, ruthlessness and great courage, they subjected the powerful native civilizations to the Spanish crown within three years. Cortés died in Spain, but his remains were brought to Mexico in accordance with his last wishes.

De las Casas, Bartolomé *(1474–1566)*
A leading Spanish churchman, who by simple Christian example achieved the peaceful conquest of many Indian tribes. In 1544 he became Bishop of Chiapas, where he was shocked by the brutal Spanish treatment of Indians. Returning to Spain, he became their champion at court, eventually persuading the king to make decrees giving them certain civil rights.

De la Madrid, Miguel *(1934–)*
A brilliant administrator, who became President of Mexico in 1982. He gained a doctorate in public administration from Harvard in 1965; was sub-director of finance at PEMEX from 1970–72; became Secretary of Public Finance in 1975 and, in 1979, Secretary of Planning and the Budget. Following his election, he instituted a programme of austerity to deal with Mexico's massive foreign debt.

De Quiroga, Vasco *(1470–1565)*
The first bishop of Michoacán, he saw the suffering of the Indians as analogous to those of Christ, and made great efforts to defend them from exploitation. In each village of his see, he encouraged the development of a different craft, many of which are still thriving.

Díaz, Porfirio *(1830–1915)*
A popular general under Juarez, he took power in 1877 after a succession of short-lived military and democratic governments.

He was to rule, with one brief break, until the 1910 Revolution, and brought wealth and stability to Mexico, giving it an industrial infrastructure. But because of his neglect of social reform, his achievements have been underrated.

Hidalgo, Father Miguel *(1753–1811)*
A philanthropic and learned parish priest, who became the leader of the 1810 rebellion against Spanish rule when he gave the famous *grito* (call to arms) at Dolores Hidalgo. Captured and executed in 1811, he is regarded as the 'Father of Independence'.

Iturbide, Agustín *(1783–1824)*
An ambitious and opportunistic soldier, who led royalist armies against the 1810 revolutionaries. In 1821, he proposed the Plan of Iguala for Mexican Independence, and signed the Treaty of Córdoba by which Spain recognized the new nation. He then declared himself Emperor of New Spain, and was executed by General Santa Anna.

Juarez, Benito *(1806–1872)*
The first Indian president, often known as 'Mexico's Abraham Lincoln'. His greatest achievement was the overthrow of the interventionist French regime of 1861–67. Despite good intentions, the troubled state of the country prevented him from carrying out his proposed social and land reforms.

Madero, Franciso *(1873–1913)*
A mild idealist, who led the 1910 Revolution against the iron rule of Porfirio Díaz. After becoming President, he proved incapable of controlling the country, and was murdered by his former colleague, General Huerta.

Maximilian of Hapsburg *(1832–1867)*
A cousin of Napoleon III, Emperor of France. After the French intervention of 1861, he was made Emperor of Mexico, but when the French troops were withdrawn to meet the Prussian threat, he was defeated and executed by Benito Juarez.

Morelos y Pavón, José María *(1765–1815)*
A revolutionary priest who joined Hidalgo's uprising of 1810. He led an insurgent army in the south of the country, and became a martyr of Independence when captured and shot.

Nezahualcoyotl *(1402–1472)*
The enlightened and humane poet-king of the Pre-Hispanic kingdom of Texcoco. He was a legal and social reformer, but is best remembered for his poems which stress the beauty of life and the inevitability of death.

Paz, Octavio *(1914–)*
Mexico's foremost man of letters and poet laureate; his works have been widely translated and have won major international awards. His best-known work is a penetrating prose study of the Mexican mind entitled *The Labyrinth of Solitude.*

Villa, Pancho *(1878–1923)*
A sadistic bandit who rose to fame as leader of a 1910 revolutionary army in the north of Mexico. After victory was achieved he attempted to seize power, and continued his career of looting and terrorism until bribed into submission. He was eventually assassinated to prevent further revolts.

Zapata, Emiliano *(1879–1919)*
The most famous and flamboyant of all the 1910 revolutionaries, he led a victorious army in the south. The violence of his followers and his radical idealism were troublesome to his colleagues, and he was assassinated by them. His name, which is revered among the impoverished peasantry of the south, is still a symbol of popular protest.

Mexico for children

Mexicans are renowned for their indulgent love of children, and junior tourists can expect to be a centre of attention, pampered, patted and given sweets (although unwrapped sweets should be tactfully confiscated). Even so, an arduous sightseeing vacation in Mexico is not advisable for those with young children. The minor discomforts of heat, insect bites, unfamiliar food and mild stomach upsets can combine to cause prolonged misery, and it is hard to find trustworthy and reliable baby-sitters. Remember also that high altitudes and pollution, such as in Mexico City, can precipitate serious breathing problems in asthmatic children. The relative comfort of car travel can make things easier, but keeping children amused on long journeys is an art in itself.

The best vacation in Mexico for small children is at a first-class hotel at one of the major resorts. Many hotels organize special entertainment programmes involving parties, donkey rides, competitions, and so on. There is often no charge for children staying in their parents' bedroom. A good idea for looking after children while parents are off water-skiing or snorkelling is to team up and take turns with another family in the same position. Luxury hotels all have TV in the rooms, showing various programmes suitable for children including old American cartoons and serials, either dubbed or sub-titled in Spanish. A growing number of the super-deluxe establishments now also have cable-TV direct from USA. Of the resorts, crowded *Acapulco*, with its emphasis on sophisticated nightlife, is probably the least suitable for a family.

Vacations inland are only recommended for older children whose tastes to some extent coincide with those of adults. Clambering over great ruined cities and trying to imagine their colourful past can be a memorable adventure for children with stamina. The ruins of the Yucatán have the advantage of being near to beaches and resorts. Colonial monuments and churches are much less fun, while visits to Indian towns and markets are likely to appeal to only a small minority of children.

In *Mexico City*, there are sufficient attractions to keep children amused for several days. The zoo in Chapultepec Park is a good starting place; the animals are clean and well-kept, and include one of the few giant pandas born in captivity. Junior big-game fanciers will also insist on a day-trip to the big safari park at Totimehuacán (see *Puebla*), about two hours' drive from Mexico City. Large carnivores and other beasts roam around large enclosures through which cars can drive. Further excitement is to be found back in Chapultepec Park, where the funfair has the largest and probably the most frightening roller coaster in the world (inexplicably known as the *montaña rusa* – 'Russian mountain'). The Museums of Technology and Natural Science are worth visiting by small boys of any age. A day at Xochimilco, drifting around the canals in a flower-festooned barge to the strains of *mariachi* music, is another possibility.

For the evenings, the city has many movie theatres showing a good selection of English-language films sub-titled in Spanish. Releases are later than in the USA, and so going to see an old favourite is a painless way to pick up some Spanish. Details are given in the *Mexico City Daily News*. Most children will also enjoy the spectacle of the son-et-lumière at the pyramids of *Teotihuacán*, near Mexico City.

Sports and activities

For those with stamina and a sense of adventure, the possibilities are vast; arrangements are usually best made through a hotel.

Camping

There are plenty of organized campsites and trailer parks with reasonable facilities at all major resorts. Back-packing expeditions into areas of wilderness have not, however, caught on in Mexico, and it is certainly not advisable for foreigners to camp on their own in populated parts of the countryside, as they make a tempting target for small-time bandits.

Camping is legal on all beaches, on common land and in national parks. At all campsites, drinking water should be boiled and/or purified.

The best specialist guidebook is *The Rand McNally Campground and Trailer Park Guide*, which has a long section on Mexico. The American Automobile Association issues a list of campsites near main roads to its members, which may be available through affiliated motoring organizations.

Flying

As the number of private planes in the USA increases, more and more people fly to Mexico for their vacation. Regulations are complicated but not impossible to follow, and for the latest details it is necessary to inquire well in advance at the nearest Mexican consulate.

Golf

Golf is rapidly growing in popularity in Mexico, which is both good and bad news for enthusiastic visitors. Although new and excellent courses are opening all over the country, those at the inland cities are all private and will admit guests only if accompanied by a club member. Only a few have reciprocal facilities with clubs in the USA – inquire before leaving and take your membership card. In Mexico City, green fees are high.

At coastal resorts and inland weekend spots there is no such problem, since most courses are hotel-owned; non-guests are invariably allowed to play, although at crowded times guests will be given preference. There is no difficulty about club rental, but serious players will wish to have their own.

The country's best public courses are the Pierre Marqués at *Acapulco*, the Palma Real at *Ixtapa*, the El Palmar at *Manzanillo* and the Avándaro at *Valle de Bravo*.

Hunting

Although the hunting in some parts of Mexico is good, the red tape involved in obtaining all the necessary permits is fearsome, especially for those planning to bring guns into the country.

The regulations and seasons for different species change from year to year, so a first step in planning a hunting vacation is to write to **Dirección General de la Fauna Silvestre** (*Nezahualcoyotl 109, ZP1, Mexico City*), requesting the latest details (in English). A permit will be required if the game in question is on a special list, so it is advisable to start the procedure about 3–4 months before departure.

For the actual hunting licence, it is necessary to contact the nearest Mexican consulate. Much complication can be avoided if you are prepared to rent guns in Mexico, and go after whatever game happens to be in season with a registered guide (available through hotels or tourist offices).

The wild fowl in Mexico includes duck, geese, wild turkey,

quail, pigeon, pheasant and partridge; game includes bear, wild boar, wild cat, wolf, deer, coyote and rabbit. Of the beach resorts, *Acapulco*, *Mazatlán*, *Manzanillo* and *Zihuatanejo* also have good facilities for hunting. Other places on the west coast are *Guaymas*, Bahía Kino (*Hermosillo*), *Culiacán* and *Los Mochis*. In the Yucatán peninsula, *Mérida* and *Campeche* are not far from rich game areas.

Foreigners who illegally import guns face a stiff jail sentence.

Mountaineering

In recent years, Mexicans have suddenly begun to take an interest in mountain climbing. The volcanoes near Mexico City make an interesting climb, the easiest being *Popocatepetl*. More dangerous and challenging is the 5,714m (18,748ft) Pico de Orizaba (see *Orizaba*), Mexico's highest peak.

In the absence of good maps, expeditions without guides are foolhardy. Organizations through which to contact registered guides are: **Club de Exploraciones de Mexico** (*J.A. Mateos 146, ZP8, Mexico City* ☎ *(5) 578–5730*); **Asociación Alpina de Mexico** (*A.C. Las Huertas 93-c, ZP5, Mexico City* ☎ *(5) 547–3285*); **Socorro Alpino de Mexico** (*Lázaro Cárdenas 80–83, ZP1, Mexico City*).

Guides will have some equipment, but the more you can bring, the better.

Photography

The scenery, the buildings, the people: Mexico is a paradise and a challenge for photographers. It is wise, because of the inferior quality of Mexican-made film, to bring enough for all needs from home (beware X-ray machines at airports). Lighting conditions are harsh, and the use of fast film (ASA 200/400) and filters will ensure better results. Simple automatic-exposure cameras will produce poor results when there are strong lighting contrasts.

Ordinary still photography and 8mm filming are legal for tourists. A permit is required for 16mm movie equipment and above – inquire at any Mexican consulate before leaving.

In some museums, it is necessary to buy a separate ticket to photograph the exhibits. The only other restrictions are on photographing military installations. In native areas, cameras are widely regarded as infernal machines of witchcraft, so it is unwise to take pictures of people without their prior and specific consent.

Riding

Horses for hire and expert tuition for riders at all levels of skill are widely available outside the big inland cities. As always, it is best to make the arrangements through hotels.

Longer expeditions are possible in various places. Two of the best are into the spectacular Copper Canyon from El Divisadero (see *Chihuahua*) and through the jungle and Indian villages from Molino de la Alborada (see *San Cristóbal de las Casas*).

Near Mexico City, good weekend resort hotels which offer riding include Hacienda San Miguel Regla near *Pachuca*; the Hotel Jurica near *Querétaro*; and the Rancho El Atascadero near *San Miguel Allende*.

For further information on stables and specialist riding vacations, write to **Federación Ecuestre Mexicana** (*Cda. Ahumada 31, ZP10, Mexico City*).

Tennis

Tennis is now a popular sport in Mexico, and there are courts all over the country. Tourists are well served by hotels.

For a list of clubs open to non-members, write to the

Federación Mexicana de Tenis (*Durango 225–301, ZP7, Mexico City*).

Spectator sports
Baseball, football (soccer), American football and horse-racing are all popular – hotel desks or tourist offices have details.

Less familiar are the *charreadas*, the Mexican rodeo meetings, and *jai-alai*, an extremely fast ball-game resembling squash, often accompanied by lively betting.

It is harder to decide whether bullfighting is sport or spectacle, for a good fight is an exciting performance combining balletic elegance with traditional ritual. In large cities, hotels organize tours including transport to and from the ring.

Water-sports
Fishing For most species, licences can be obtained cheaply by application in person to any harbour master, wild-life warden, or at the local Secretaría de Comercio; some hotels will handle this. For detailed information on regulations and on dates of tournaments, write well in advance to **Dirección General de Pesca** (*Alvaro Obregón 269, ZP7, Mexico City*), enclosing a large self-addressed envelope. They will also send information on special fishing vacations (all in English).

Excellent deep-sea fishing is available at all the major resorts and ports; hotels will arrange rental of boats and equipment, although better bargains (and sometimes less reliable boats) are sometimes to be found by asking around the docks and at waterfront bars. It is always worth checking safety equipment before signing a charter agreement.

If fishing is your sole purpose, the narrow Sea of Cortés (Gulf of California), which acts as a kind of fish trap, has the richest waters. Places to stay where there are numerous hotels with their own fishing fleets include *Mazatlán* and *Guaymas* on the mainland, and Cabo San Lucas on the *Baja California* peninsula. *Ensenada* on the Pacific coast of Baja is another port which has more or less grown up around deep-sea fishing. The most commonly found large fish include tarpon, sailfish, marlin, shark, tuna, swordfish and bonitos.

Inland fishing, in lakes, reservoirs and rivers, is also possible; equipment rental cannot be relied upon, so it is best to bring your own tackle. In Central Mexico, anglers try their luck on the lakes at *Patzcuaro*, *Chapala* and *Valle de Bravo*. In the N and NW, there are numerous large irrigation projects – see *Ciudad Victoria*, *Los Mochis*, *Culiacan* and *Ciudad Obregón*.
Sailing Small yachts are widely available for charter at coastal resorts and by large inland lakes. For details of regattas and sailing meetings, write to the **Federación Mexicana de Vela** (*Balderas 36–13, ZP1, Mexico City* ☎ *(5) 510–1974*).
Surfing It is down the Pacific coast that the best surfing waters in Mexico are to be found – conditions along the Gulf and Caribbean coasts are not nearly as good. Surfing enjoys no great popularity among Mexicans, and there are almost no rental facilities or shops.

Surfing is prohibited on most crowded beaches, so many serious surfers camp in deserted places away from the main resorts. Sharks are of course a hazard, so be sure to inquire locally about their favourite feeding grounds. Areas with the best reputation for surfing beaches are: S of *Acapulco*; N of *Ensenada*; S of *Manzanillo*; N of *Mazatlán*; and around Puerto Angel (see *Puerto Escondido*).

Excursion to Central America

At the time of writing, the political situation in Central America was prohibitive to leisure travel, but it is an area where things change fast, and conditions may well improve in a short time; make inquiries from a reliable source, such as the Centro Na-Bolom in *San Cristóbal de las Casas*. Places referred to below will be found on Map 9.

Guatemala is a beautiful country, dominated by great volcanoes. The population, largely Mayan Indians like those who live in Chiapas, has been less affected than the Mexicans by the 20thC; travel in Guatemala is likely to appeal to those who knew Mexico 20yrs ago, and who can tolerate a few minor hardships.

From *San Cristóbal de las Casas*, it is a hard day's drive to Guatemala City on the Pan-American Highway (601km/378 miles), and the first town after the border, Huehuetenango, is a good place to spend the night. This is the starting point for exciting expeditions W up into the grandiose Cuchumatanes mountains, and to Mame Indian villages such as Todos Santos. An easier trip is to the well-restored Post-Classic site of Zaculeu ★ just on the N edge of 'Huehue' itself.

Another 60km (37 miles) towards Guatemala City, a turning S leads to the charming little towns around Lake Atitlán, overshadowed by smoking volcanic peaks; the best-known village is Panajachel. North of the Pan-American Highway at this point is the native village of Chichicastenango, famous for its colourful markets and religious celebrations. From here it is an easy 2hrs' drive to the capital, a pleasant enough city with little to detain the traveller beyond the archaeological site of Kaminaljuyu, with Pre-Classic and Classic buildings. A short drive of 40km (25 miles) W lies the strange city of Antigua Guatemala ☆ which was the colonial capital until it was abandoned in the 18thC after a terrible earthquake. Today it has an air of romantic disarray, with great masses of fallen Baroque masonry lying in the old cloisters and courts.

From Guatemala City it is possible to fly up to the ruins of Tikal, Mesoamerica's largest excavated city, on a memorable if exhausting day excursion. Those with time to spare and a car could return to Mexico via Tikal, Belize (formerly British Honduras) and cross the border at *Chetumal* on the Yucatán peninsula.

The road leaves the capital heading NE for Puerto Barrios. The first possible overnight stop is at Zacapa (138km/84 miles); it is from here that the trip to Copán in Honduras can be made, some 100km (62 miles) E on poor roads. The extensive Mayan ruins of Copan ★ are well preserved, especially some fine carving and sculpture.

Back on the main road, try to see the ruins of Quirigua ★ 50km (31 miles) beyond Zacapa, just S of the road to Amates; it is notable for very tall and finely carved steles dating from around the 8thC.

The long haul on jungle tracks towards Tikal leaves the road heading N from Morales, 50km (31 miles) past Amates. It takes at least a day to reach the attractive frontier town of Flores, and Tikal ★ where huge Mayan pyramids tower out of the rain forest is 2hrs farther. The adventurous can reach other ruins in the jungle, such as Uaxactún, a day's walk N of Tikal. From Tikal to Chetumal is likely to involve an overnight stop at Belmopán or Belize City.

A guide to Mexican Spanish

This glossary covers the basic language needs of the traveller: for pronunciation, essential vocabulary and simple conversation, finding accommodation, visiting the bank, shopping, using public transport or a car, and for eating out.

There is considerable regional variation in pronunciation; in areas where indigenous languages are spoken, the local Spanish is almost incomprehensible, even to other Mexicans.

Pronunciation

Spanish is a phonetic language in which the spelling matches the pronunciation. Letters whose pronunciation is not obvious are the r, which is trilled as in Scots; g before e or i and j, which are pronounced like the ch in loch; h, which is always silent; v, which is pronounced like b; and ll, pronounced as y. The letter z and c before e or i are not lisped as they are in Spain.

Stress is on the penultimate syllable in words ending in a vowel, n or s; otherwise the stress is on the last syllable. Exceptions are indicated by a stress mark, e.g. inglés.

Vowels

a	as the a in father; e.g. hamaca
e	as the e in let; e.g. peso
i	as the i in police; e.g. litro
o	as the o in pot; e.g. pollo
u	as the oo in food; e.g. mucho
	before another vowel, as the w in well; e.g. cuando
y	as the Spanish i; e.g. yo

Consonants/letter groups

b	soft, with the lips slightly apart; e.g. sábado
c	hard, as in cat; e.g. catorce
	before e or i sibilant, as the c in race; e.g. doce
g	hard, as in get; e.g. gracias
	before e or i guttural, as the ch in loch; e.g. gente
h	never sounded; e.g. hotel
j	guttural, as the ch in loch; e.g. abajo
ñ	as the ny in canyon; e.g. mañana
r	trilled; e.g. ahora
v	like the Spanish b; e.g. vino
x	like the x in box; e.g. próximo
	after e, as an s; e.g. exportación
	between vowels in proper names, as the h in house; e.g. Mexico, Oaxaca
z	as the s in sack; e.g. diez
cc	as the ks in sacks; e.g. dirección
ch	as the ch in church; e.g. derecho
ll	as the y in yacht; e.g. lleno
qu	as the c in cat; e.g. queso
rr	strongly trilled; e.g. cerrado

Gender

Gender has been indicated where appropriate. Adjectives are given in the masculine form, with the alternative ending used when it accompanies a feminine noun.

Reference words

Monday	lunes	Friday	viernes
Tuesday	martes	Saturday	sábado
Wednesday	miércoles	Sunday	domingo
Thursday	jueves		

January	enero	April	abril
February	febrero	May	mayo
March	marzo	June	junio

July julio	October octubre
August agosto	November noviembre
September septiembre	December diciembre

1	uno	13	trece	32	treinta y dos
2	dos	14	catorce	40	cuarenta
3	tres	15	quince	50	cincuenta
4	cuatro	16	dieciséis	60	sesenta
5	cinco	17	diecisiete	70	setenta
6	seis	18	dieciocho	80	ochenta
7	siete	19	diecinueve	90	noventa
8	ocho	20	veinte	100	cien
9	nueve	21	veintiuno	200	doscientos
10	diez	22	veintidós	500	quinientos
11	once	30	treinta	1,000	mil
12	doce	31	treinta y uno		

First primer(o), -a	Third tercero, -a
Second segundo, -a	Fourth cuarto, -a

Quarter past . . . . y cuarto	Quarter to . . . . menos cuarto
Half past . . . . y media	Quarter to six las seis menos cuarto

Mr señor	Ladies señoras, damas, mujeres
Mrs señora	Gents caballeros, señores, hombres
Miss señorita	

Red rojo, -a	Blue azul
Yellow amarillo, -a	Black negro, -a
Green verde	White blanco, -a

Basic communication

Yes sí
No no
Please por favor
Thank you gracias
I'm very sorry lo siento mucho/perdón
Excuse me perdóneme/con permiso/disculpe
Not at all/you're welcome de nada
Hello hola, bueno (on telephone)
Good morning buenos días
Good afternoon buenas tardes
Good night buenas noches
Goodbye adiós
Morning mañana (f)
Afternoon tarde (f)
Evening tarde (f)
Night noche (f)
Yesterday ayer
Today hoy
Tomorrow mañana
Next week la semana próxima
Last week la semana pasada
. . . days ago hace . . . días
Month mes (m)
Year año (m)
Here aquí
There allí
Big gran(de)
Small pequeño, -a
Hot caliente
Cold frío, -a
Good buen(o), -a
Bad mal(o), -a
Beautiful bonito, -a/hermoso, -a
With con

And y
But pero
Open abierto, -a
Closed cerrado, -a
Entrance entrada (f)
Exit salida (f)
Free (unoccupied or of charge) libre
Left izquierda
Right derecha
Straight on derecho
Near cerca (de)
Far lejos (de)
Above encima
Below abajo
Front delante (de)
Behind detrás (de)
Early temprano, -a
Late tarde
Pleased to meet you. Encantado(a) de conocerle.
How are you? ¿Cómo está usted?/ ¿Qué tal? (informal)
Very well, thank you. Muy bien, gracias.
Do you speak English? ¿Habla usted inglés?
I don't understand. No lo entiendo.
What did you say? ¿Como dice?/ ¿Mande? (colloquial)
Please explain. ¿Puede usted explicarme, por favor?
Please speak more slowly. Mas despacio, por favor.

My name is . . . . Me llamo . . . .
I am English/American. Soy inglés, -esa/americano, -a.
Where is/are . . . . ? ¿Dónde está/están . . . . ?
Is there a . . . . ? ¿Hay un/una . . . . ?
What? ¿Qué?
When? ¿Cuándo?
How much? ¿Cuánto?
That's too much. Eso es demasiado.
Expensive Caro, -a
Cheap Barato, -a
I would like . . . . Quisiera . . . ./querría . . . .
Do you have . . . . ? ¿Tiene usted . . . . ?
Where is the toilet? ¿Dónde está el baño?
Where is the telephone? ¿Dónde está el teléfono?
That's fine/OK. Está bien.
I don't know. No sé.
What time is it? ¿Qué hora es?
I feel ill. Me siento mal.

Accommodation

Making a reservation by letter

Dear Sir/Madam,
Muy estimado/-a señor/señora,

I would like to reserve one double room (with bathroom),
Quisiera reservar un cuarto doble (con cuarto de baño),

one twin-bedded room and one single room
un cuarto con dos camas y un cuarto sencillo

(with bath/shower) for 7 nights from 12 August.
(con baño/regadera) por 7 noches desde el 12 de agosto.

I would like bed and breakfast/half board/full board
Quisiera desayuno/media pensión/pensión completa

and would prefer rooms with a sea view.
y preferería cuartos con vista al mar.

Please send me details of your terms with the confirmation.
Por favor envíeme sus condiciones y precios con la confirmación.

Yours faithfully,
Le saluda atentamente

Arriving at the hotel

I have a reservation. My name is . . . .
Tengo una reserva. Me llamo . . . .

A quiet room with bath/shower . . . .
Un cuarto tranquilo con baño/regadera . . . .

. . . overlooking the sea/park/street/back.
. . . con vista al mar/al parque/a la calle/atrás.

Does the price include breakfast/service/tax?
¿El precio incluye desayuno/servicio/impuestos?

This room is too large/small/cold/hot/noisy.
Este cuarto es demasiado grande/pequeño/frío/caliente/ruidoso.

That's too expensive. Have you anything cheaper?
Eso es demasiado caro. ¿Tiene usted algo más barato?

Where can I park my car?
¿Dónde puedo estacionar?

Is it safe to leave the car on the street?
¿Se puede dejar el coche en la calle?

Have you got a room?
¿Tiene usted un cuarto?

Floor/storey piso (m)/planta (f)
Dining room/restaurant comedor/restaurante (m)
Lounge salón (m)
Manager gerente (m)
What time is breakfast/dinner? ¿A qué hora se sirve el desayuno/la cena?
Is there a laundry service? ¿Hay servicio de lavado?
What time does the hotel close? ¿A qué hora cierra el hotel?
Will I need a key? ¿Me hará falta una llave?
Is there a night porter? ¿Hay un portero de noche?
I'll be leaving tomorrow morning. Me marcharé mañana por la mañana.
Please give me a call at . . . . ¿Puede usted despertarme a . . . por favor?
Come in. Adelante/pase usted.

Shopping

Where is the nearest . . . . ? ¿Dónde está . . . más cercano, -a?
Where's there a good . . . . ? ¿Dónde hay un buen/una buena . . . . ?
Can you help me/show me some . . . . ? ¿Puede usted atenderme . . . . ?
I'm just looking. Sólo estoy mirando.
Do you accept credit cards/travellers cheques? ¿Acepta usted tarjetas de crédito/cheques de viajero?
Can you deliver to . . . . ? ¿Puede usted enviar a . . . . ?
I'll take it. Me lo llevo.
I'll leave it. Lo dejo.
Can I have it tax-free for export? ¿Puedo comprarlo libre de impuestos para exportación?
This is faulty. Can I have a replacement/refund? Este tiene una falta. ¿Puede cambiármelo/devolverme el dinero?
I don't want to spend more than . . . . No quiero gastar más de . . . .
I'll give you . . . for it. Le daré . . . .
Can I have a stamp for . . . . ? Quiero un timbre para . . . .

Shops

Antique shop tienda de antigüedades (f)
Art gallery galería de arte (f)
Baker panadería (f)
Bank banco (m)
Beauty salon salón de belleza (m)
Bookshop librería (f)
Butcher carnicería (f)
Cake shop pastelería (f)
Chemist/pharmacy farmacia (f)
Clothes shop tienda de ropa (f)
Dairy lechería (f)
Department store grandes almacenes (m)
Fishmonger pescadería (f)
Florist florería (f)
Greengrocer tienda de verduras y frutas (f)
Grocer abarote (m)
Haberdasher mercería (f)
Hairdresser barbería (men), la peluquería (women) (f)
Jeweller joyería (f)
Market mercado (m)
Newsstand quiosco de periódicos (m)
Optician óptico (m)
Photographic shop tienda de fotografía (f)
Post office oficina de correos (f)
Shoe shop zapatería (f)
Souvenir shop tienda de recuerdos (f)
Supermarket supermercado (m)
Tailor sastrería (f)
Tobacconist tabaquería (f)
Tourist office oficina de turismo (f)
Toy shop juguetería (f)
Travel agent agencia de viajes (f)

At the bank

I would like to change some pounds/dollars/travellers cheques.
Quisiera cambiar unas libras esterlinas/unos dólares/unos cheques de viajero.
What is the exchange rate?
¿A cuánto está el tipo de cambio?
Can I obtain cash with this credit card?
¿Puedo sacar dinero con esta tarjeta de crédito?
Do you need to see my passport?
¿Quiere usted ver mi pasaporte?

Some useful goods

Antiseptic cream crema antiséptica (f)
Aspirin aspirina (f)
Bandages vendas (f)
Cotton wool algodón (m)
Diarrhoea/upset stomach pills píldoras para diarrea/el estómago trastornado (f)
Indigestion tablets tabletas para indigestión (f)
Insect repellant repelente para insectos (m)
Laxative laxante (m)
Razor blades hojas de afeitar (f)
Sanitary towels compresas (f)
Shampoo champú (m)
Shaving cream crema de afeitar (f)
Soap jabón (m)
Sticking plaster esparadrapo (m)
String cuerda (f)
Sunburn cream crema para quemaduras del sol (f)
Sunglasses gafas de sol (f)
Suntan cream/oil crema (f)/aceite (m) bronceador, -a
Tampons tampones (m)
Tissues pañuelos de papel (m)
Toothbrush cepillo de dientes (m)
Toothpaste pasta de dientes (f)
Travel sickness pills píldoras para mareo (f)

Bra sostén (m)
Coat abrigo (m)
Dress vestido (m)
Jacket chaqueta (f)
Pullover pull (m)
Shirt camisa (f)
Shoes zapatos (m)
Skirt falda (f)
Socks calcetines (m)
Stockings/tights medias (f)
Swimsuit traje de baño (m)
Trousers pantalones (m)
Underpants for women bragas (f), for men calzoncillos (m)

Film película (f)
Letter carta (f)
Money order giro postal (m)
Postcard tarjeta (f)
Stamp timbre (m)
Telegram telegrama (m)

Motoring

Service station estación de PEMEX (f)/gasolinera (f)
Fill it up. Lleno, por favor.
Give me . . . pesos worth. Deme . . . pesos por favor.
I would like . . . litres of petrol. Quiero . . . litros de gasolina.
Can you check the . . . . ? ¿Puede usted mirar el/la . . . . ?
There is something wrong with the . . . . Hay algo que no va bien en el/la . . . .
Battery batería (f)
Brakes frenos (m)
Engine motor (m)
Exhaust tubo de escape (m)
Lights luces (f)
Oil aceite (m)
Radiator radiator (m)
Tyres llantas (f)
Water agua (f)
Windscreen parabrisas (m)
My car won't start. Mi coche no arranca.
My car has broken down/had a puncture. Tengo un coche averiado/una llanta pinchada.
The engine is overheating. El motor se calienta.
How long will it take to repair? ¿Cuánto tardará en repararlo?

Car rental

Where can I rent a car? ¿Dónde puedo alquilar un coche?
Is full/comprehensive insurance included? ¿Está incluido un seguro a todo riesgo?
Is it insured for another driver? ¿Es asegurado para un otro conductor?
Unlimited mileage kilometraje ilimitado
Deposit un depósito
By what time must I return it? ¿Para qué hora tengo que devolverlo?
Can I return it to another depot? ¿Puedo devolverlo a una otra agencia?
Is the petrol tank full? ¿Está lleno el tanque de gasolina?

Road signs

¡Alto! Stop
Calle bloqueada Road blocked
Calle sin salida No exit
Calzada deteriorada Bad road surface
Ceda el paso Give way
Centro ciudad Town centre
Cuidado/con precaución Caution
Cuota Toll
Deslizamientos Slippery surface
Despacio Slow
Desviación Detour
Estacionamiento permitido Parking permitted
Obras Road works
Otras direcciones Other directions
Paso a nivel Level crossing
Peligro Danger
Prohibido estacionar No parking
Salida de emergencia Emergency exit
Senso único One way
Todas direcciones All directions

Other methods of transport

Aircraft avión (m)
Airport aeropuerto (m)
Bus autobús, camión (m)
Bus stop parada de autobús (f)
Coach camión (m)
Ferry/boat transbordador, embarcadero (m), panga (m)
Ferry port puerto (m)
Railway station estación (f)
Train tren (m)
Ticket billete (m)
Ticket office taquilla (f)
Single de ida
Return de ida y vuelta
Half fare medio billete
First/second primera/segunda clase
Sleeper/couchette coche cama, carro dormitorio (m)
When is the next . . . for . . . . ? ¿A qué hora sale el próximo . . . para . . . . ?
What time does it arrive? ¿A qué hora llega?

What time does the last . . . for . . . leave? ¿A qué hora sale el último . . . para . . . . ?
Which platform/gate/quay? ¿Qué andén/puerta/muelle?
Is this the . . . for . . . . ? ¿Es éste el . . . para . . . . ?
Is it direct? Where does it stop? ¿Es directo? ¿Dónde se para?
Do I need to change anywhere? ¿Tengo que hacer transbordo?
Please tell me where to get off. ¿Me diría usted cuándo tengo que bajar?
Take me to . . . . Lléveme a . . . .
Is there a buffet car? ¿Hay un coche-comedor?

Food and drink

Have you a table for . . . . ? ¿Tiene usted una mesa para . . . . ?
I want to reserve a table for . . . at . . . . Quisiera reservar una mesa para . . . personas a las . . . .
A quiet table. Una mesa tranquila
A table near the window. Una mesa cerca de la ventana.
Could we have another table? ¿Nos puede dar otra mesa?
The menu, please. ¿Puedo ver la carta?
I'll have . . . . Tomaré . . . .
Can I see the wine list? ¿Puedo ver la lista de vinos?
I would like . . . . Quisiera . . . .
What do you recommend? ¿Qué recomienda usted?
I did not order this. No he pedido esto.
Lunch/dinner comida/cena (f)
Bring me another. Otro/a, por favor.
The bill please. La cuenta, por favor.
Is service included? ¿Está incluído el servicio?

Restaurant restaurante (m)
Hot caliente
Cold frío, -a
Glass vaso (m)/copa (f)
Bottle botella (f)
Half-bottle media botella (f)
Beer/lager cerveza (f)
Orangeade/lemonade naranjada/limonada (f)
Water agua (f)
Iced . . . . fría/ . . . con hielo
Mineral water agua mineral (f)
Fizzy/still gaseoso/sin carbonato
Flask/carafe jarra (f)
Red wine vino tinto (m)
White wine vino blanco (m)
Cheers! ¡Salud!
Sweet dulce (m)
Salt sal (f)
Pepper pimienta (f)

Mustard mostaza (f)
Oil aceite (m)
Vinegar vinagre (m)
Bread pan (m)
Butter mantequilla (f)
Cheese queso (m)
Egg huevo (m)
Milk leche (f)
Coffee café (m)
white con crema
(without) sugar (sin) azúcar
Ice cream helado (m)
Chocolate chocolate (m)
Honey miel (m)
Sugar azúcar (m)
Tea té negro (m)
Steak filete (m)
well done bien hecho
medium regular
(very) rare (muy) poco hecho

Menu decoder

Cover charge cubierto
Bread pan
Appetizers entremeses
Soups sopas
Pasta pastas
Fish pescados
Seafood mariscos
Vegetables verduras

Minced meat carne picada
Salads ensaladas
Cheeses quesos
Fruit frutas
Sweets postres
White/red/rosé wines vinos blanco/tinto/rosado
Beers cervezas

Aceite (de oliva) (olive) oil
Aceitunas olives
(en) Adobo, adobado marinated, pickled
Aguacate avocado
Agua fresca fresh fruit drink
Ahumado, -a smoked
Ajo (-illo) garlic
Alas wings
Albaricoques apricots

Albóndigas spiced meat balls
Alcachofa artichoke
Alcaparras capers
Almejas clams
Almendras almonds
(en) Almíbar (in) syrup
Anchoas anchovies
Anguilla eel
Apio celery
Arenque herring

Arrachera tripe
Arroz rice
Asado grilled/broiled
Atole corn-meal gruel
Atún tuna
Aves poultry
Bacalao dried salt cod
Barbacoa Mexican barbecued meat
Berenjena aubergine, eggplant
Berros watercress
Besugo sea-bream
Biftec (beef)steak
Birria mutton stew
Bocadillos sandwiches
Bolillo roll
Bonito bonito (striped tuna)
(en) Brochetas skewered
Buey beef, ox
Cabeza head
Cabrito kid
Cacerola casserole
Calabaza squash, pumpkin
Calamares (en su tinta) squid (in their own ink)
Caldo broth or soup-stew of meat and vegetables
Camarones shrimps
Camotes sweet potatoes
Cangrejo crab
Caracoles snails
Carne meat
Carnero mutton
Carnitas cubes of roast meat
(de la) Casa of the restaurant
Caza game
Cazador hunter's style
Cebolla onion
Cecina salty dried meat
Cerdo pork
Cerezas cherries
Cerveza beer
Ceviche fish marinated in lime juice
Chabacano apricot
Chalupas small *tortilla* snack
Chamorro knuckle
Champiñones mushrooms
Chicharrón pork crackling
Chicharros peas
Chilaquiles *tortilla* strips in sauce
Chile chili, red pepper
Chipirones squid
Chipotle a type of spicy pepper
Chongos sticky milk pudding
Chorizo spiced pork sausage
Chuleta chop, usually veal
Cilantro coriander
Ciruela plum/prune
Cochinillo sucking pig
Cochinita sucking pig meat
Cocido, -a cooked, boiled
Codorniz quail
Col cabbage
Cola tail
Coliflor cauliflower
Conejo rabbit
Corazón heart
Cordero lamb
Costilla rib
Crepa pancake
Criadillas bull's testicles ('prairie oysters')
Crudo, -a raw
Dorada gilthead bream
Dulces sweets, desserts
Durazno peach
Duro hard(-boiled)
Ejote string bean
Elote corn, maize
Empanado, -a fried in breadcrumbs
Enchilada filled *tortilla* roll in sauce
Ensalada salad
Entremeses hors d'oeuvres
(en) Escabeche, escabechado pickled, marinated
Espárragos asparagus
Espinacas spinach
Estofado stew(ed)
Filete fillet, usually steak
Flameado flambé
Flan caramel pudding
Flor de calabaza squash (pumpkin) flowers
Frambuesas raspberries
Fresas, fresones strawberries
Fresco, -a fresh, cold
Frijoles beans
Frío, -a cold
Frito, -a fried
Fritura fried dish; fritter
Fruta fruit
Galletas biscuits
Gallina fowl
Gallo cockerel
Ganzo goose
Garbanzos chickpeas
Gazpacho chilled vegetable soup
Gorditas *tortilla* snack
Granada pomegranate
Gratinado, -a browned, with cheese or breadcrumbs
Guacamole avocado purée
Guajolote turkey
Guanabana apple-like tropical fruit
Guayaba guava
Habas broad beans
Hamburguesa hamburger
Helado ice cream
Hervido, -a boiled, poached
Higadillos chicken livers
Hígado liver
Higos figs
Hoja leaf
Hongos mushrooms
(al) Horno baked
Huachinango red snapper
Huevos eggs
cocidos boiled
al plato fried or baked
a la mexicana scrambled with chile
rancheros in red sauce on a *tortilla*
revueltos scrambled

Huitlacoche corn fungus
Jabalí wild boar
Jaiba crab
Jamón ham
Jerez sherry
Jicame sweet parsnip
Jitomate tomato
(en su) Jugo (in its own) juice
Langosta lobster
Langostino crayfish
Lechazo young lamb
Lechón sucking pig
Lechuga lettuce
Lengua tongue
Lenguado sole
Lentejas lentils
Liebre hare
Limón lime
Lombarda red cabbage
Lomo, Lomita loin (prime cut)
Longaniza spicy sausage
Macedonia fruit salad
Machacas dried donkey meat
Mamey sweet tropical fruit
Mango mango
Manitas de puerco pork trotters
Mantequilla butter
Manzana apple
Mariscos seafood
Melón melon
Membrillo quince, quince jelly
Menudo tripe stew
Merengue meringue
Merluza cod
Mojarra perch
Mole spicy chocolate sauce
Moluscos mussels
Naranja orange
Nieve water ice
(en) Nogada walnut sauce
Nopal(-ito) cactus fruit
Nueces nuts, walnuts
Ostiones oysters
Paella saffron rice dish with meat, fish or seafood
País (del) Mexican
Paloma dove/pigeon
Pan dulce sweet rolls
Papas potatoes
Papaya papaya (paw-paw)
(a la) Parrilla grilled, broiled
Parrillada (de mariscos, de pescados) grilled or broiled seafoods or fish
Pasas raisins
Pastel pâté; pie, pastry; cake
Pato duck
Pavo turkey
Pechuga breast (usually chicken)
Pepinillos gherkins
Pepinos cucumber
Pera pear
Perdiz partridge
Pescadilla whiting; small hake
Pescado fish
Pez espada swordfish
Picante hot (spicy)
Pichón pigeon
Pibil spicy roast
Pierna leg
Pimientos sweet peppers
Piña pineapple
Pipián spicy stew
Plátano banana
Plátano macho plantain
Pollo chicken
Pozole meat and hominy soup
Pulpitos tiny octopuses
Pulpo octopus
Pulque cactus beer
Quesadilla *tortilla* snack
Queso cheese
Rábanos radishes
Refresco soft drink
Refritos re-fried beans
Relleno stuffed
Repollo cabbage
Res beef
Riñones kidneys
Róbalo sea-perch, sea-bass
(a la) Romana deep-fried
Salado, -a salted
Salchicha sausage
Salchichón salami
Salsa sauce
  borracha Pulque sauce
  mexicana chile sauce
  veracruzana a spicy red sauce
Sandia watermelon
Sangrita drink of tomato juice, chile, and orange
Sardinas sardines
Sesos brains
Sincronizadas ham, cheese, and *tortilla* snack
Sopa soup
  de Mariscos seafood soup
  de Arroz spicy boiled rice (not soup)
Surtido assortment
Taco a *tortilla* snack
Tamale meat-filled roll of maize dough, steamed
Tarta savoury tart or pie
Tarteleta small sweet tart
Tehuacán soda water
Ternera veal
Tiburón shark
Tocino bacon
Toronja grapefruit
Torta sandwich
Tortilla maize pancake
Tortillas de trigo wheat pancake
Tortuga turtle
Tostado, -a (adj) toasted
Tostada (noun) a *tortilla* snack
Tronco slice
Trucha trout
Trufas truffles
Tuña cactus fruit
Uvas grapes
(al) Vapor steamed
Venado venison
Verduras vegetables
Vino blanco/tinto/rosado white/red/rosé wine
Zanahorias carrots
Zapote sweet tropical fruit

Index and gazetteer

Numerals in ordinary type indicate a mention; numerals in bold type indicate a main entry; and those in italics denote an illustration. Under towns and cities, only general categories (i.e. events, hotels, nightlife) are listed. Individual sights and places of interest are indexed separately under their own names and in general categories such as Archaeological sites and Museums. Map references refer to maps at the end of the book.

MEXICO

LEGEND

Area Maps

0 100 200 Km

- Divided Highway
- Main Through Route
- Other Main Road
- Secondary Road
- Minor Road
- 40 Mexican Road No.
- 10 U.S. Road No.
- Railway
- Ferry
- Airport
- Airfield
- International Boundary
- Ancient Site, Ruin
- Monastery, Church
- Good Beach
- .3703 Heights in Metres
- 10 Adjoining Page No.

City Maps

- Major Place of Interest
- Other Important Building
- Built-up Area
- Cemetery
- Named Church, Church
- Hospital
- Information Office
- Post Office
- One Way Street
- Subway Station

2
SAN DIEGO
TIJUANA
Calexico
MEXICALI
Gila Bend
Rosarito
L. Salada
SIERRA DE JUAREZ
Ensenada
GRAN DESIERTO
Lukeville
Sonoyta
R. Sonoita
Lazaro Cardenas
Golfo de Santa Clara
SIERRA S. PEDRO MARTIR
3078
San Felipe
Observatorio San Pedro
Puerto Peñasco
SIERRA S. ISABEL
San Quintín
El Desemboque
Rosario de Arriba
Golfo de Baja California
Santa Catarina
Isla Angel de la Guarda
Isla del Tiburón
Bahía de los Angeles
San Borja
Santa Gertrudis
Isla Cedros
Guerrero Negro
SIERRA VIZCAINO
DESIERTO DE VIZCAINO
•1996
San Ignacio
Laguna S. Ignacio
OCEANO PACIFICO
Villa Constitución
Bahía Magdalena
A B C D E F
1 2 3

PHOENIX
U. S. A.
4 5
5 6
3
A
B
TUCSON
La Cruces
EL PASO
Palomas
CIUDAD JUAREZ
Nogales
Nogales
Douglas
Agua Prieta
Cananea
Imuris
Santa Ana
SIERRA DE LA MADERA
Janos
CASAS GRANDES
Nuevo Casas Grandes
Nacozari de García
3200
Moctezuma
Divisaderos
Buenaventura
El Sueco
SIERRA DEL NIDO
HERMOSILLO
Kino
Sahuaripa
El Novillo
Madera
Col. Obregón
CHIHUAHUA
Cuauhtemoc
Basaseachic
SIERRA
Guaymas
Empalme
Presa A. Obregón
S. Juanico
Bocoyna
Estacion Creel
Divisaderos
CIUDAD OBREGON
SIERRA TARAHUMARA
Rio Urique
Presa Macuzari
BARRANCA DEL COBRE
Navojoa
Alamos
Etchojoa
Batopilas
California
Presa M. Hidalgo
Guachochic
El Fuerte
MADRE
San Blas
Guadalupe y Calvo
Mochicahui
3150
Los Mochis
Topolobampo
Guasave
Guamúchil
Badiraguato
SIERRA DE LA GIGANTA
1524
El Muerto
Pericos
Presa A. Lopez Mateos
CULIACAN
Altata
Isla Espíritu Santo
Pichilingue
La Paz
El Dorado
La Cruz
2406
Buenavista
Todos Santos
SA. DE S. LAZARO
San José del Cabo
Cabo San Lucas
MAZATLAN
B C D E F

4
Albuquerque
La Cruces
EL PASO
CIUDAD JUAREZ
El Porvenir
Rio Grande
Rio Bravo del Norte
Marfa
Marathon
Presidio
Ojinaga
Boquillas
Boquillas del Carmen
SERRANIAS DEL BURRO
SIERRA DEL NIDO
El Sueco
Col. Obregón
CHIHUAHUA
Cuauhtemoc
Rio Conchos
Delicias
El Reves
Ciudad Camargo
SIERRA TARAHUMARA
Hidalgo del Parral
Jiménez
S. Francisco del Oro
Santa Bárbara
Guachochic
Guadalupe y Calvo
3150
Ocampo
Cuatro Ciénegas
SIERRA DE TLAHUALILO
2164
SIERRA DE LOS ALAMITOS
Tlahualilo
San Pedro de las Colonias
El Zape
El Palmito
Gómez Palacio
TORREON
Ciudad Lerdo
Matamoros
Parras
Tepehuanes
Pedriseña
Santiago Papasquiaro
Cuencamé
MADRE OCCIDENTAL
Canatlán
Juan Aldama
Cerro Huehuento 3150
DURANGO
San Tiburcio
El Salto
Rio Grande
Sombrerete
Sain Alto
Mezquital
3559
MAZATLAN
Rosario
Fresnillo

5
8 9
9 10
A
B
DALLAS
Abilene
20
U . S . A .
35
B
C
Sonora
10
Houston
10
Del Rio
aña
SAN ANTONIO
s Negras
Eagle Pass
37
Pan American Highway
ende
C
D
Sabinas
CORPUS CHRISTI
Nuevo Laredo
Laredo
Anáhuac
2
Monclova
Castaños
85
Presa Falcón
Sabinas Hidalgo
53
Cd. Alemán
Presa del Azúcar
Reynosa
Brownsville
D
E
Grutas García
MONTERREY
40
Rio Bravo
MATAMOROS
China
CANON DE LA HUASTECA
35
47
101
Laguna Madre
LA COLA DE CABALLO
Montemorelos
Galeana
Linares
San Fernando
MADRE
Pan
85
57
101
American
Presa de las Adjuntas
3035
La Pesca
CIUDAD VICTORIA
E
F
Real de Catorce
Matehuala
Jaumave
Highway
7
8 9
9 10
Entronque Huizache
Aldama

6
5 6
6 7
E
F
F
G
G
H
H
I
I
J
5 6
6 7
4
La Cruz
Cerro Huehuento 3150
OCCIDENTAL
DURANGO
Juan Aldama
San Tiburcio
El Salto
Rio Grande
Sombrerete
Sain Alto
Mezquital
3559
MAZATLAN
Rosario
Fresnillo
SIERRA DE LOS HUICHOLES
Valparaíso
ZACATECA
Jerez
CHICOMOZTOC
Acaponeta
Ojo Calien
Novillero
Villanueva
Tuxpan
Mexcaltitán
Santiago Ixcuintla
AGUASCALIENTES
Ojuel de Jali
Los Corchos
Rio Grande de Santiago
Jalpa
San Blas
Tepic
Compostela
Jalostotitlán
Lago Mor
Las Tres Marías
Ixtlán
Ahuacatlán
Tequila
GUADALAJARA
Puerto Vallarta
IRAPUAT
2680
Mascota
Ameca
Ocotlán
Salam
Jocotepec
Laguna de Chapala
La Pi
Sahuayo
Zamora
Autlán
Ciudad Guzmán
Chamela
Uruapan
Bahía Tenacatita
Colima
Barra de Navidad
Apatzingan
Manzanillo
Tecomán
Boca des Pascuales
2764
Playa Azul
Lázaro Cárdenas
Ixtapa
Bahía
OCEANO
PACIFICO
15
45
49
54
15
54
80
90
200
54
80
15
200
37

7
5
8
8
8
9
9
10
8
9
9
10
E
F
F
G
G
H
H
I
I
J
MADRE
ORIENTAL
SIERRA
MADRE DEL SUR
CIUDAD VICTORIA
Presa de las Adjuntas
La Pesca
Real de Catorce
Matehuala
Jaumave
3035
Entronque Huizache
Aldama
Pan American Highway
Ciudad Mante
Ciudad Madero
TAMPICO
Ebano
SAN LUIS POTOSI
Ciudad Valles
Tamuín
Rio Verde
Santa María del Rio
Tempoal
Laguna de Tamiahua
Xichu
Tamazunchale
Jalpan
Huejutla
Molango
Tuxpan
Dolores Hidalgo
QUERETARO
Poza Rica
Tecolutla
Celaya
San Juan del Rio
Ixmiquilpan
EL TAJIN
Nautla
TULA
PACHUCA
Tulancingo
Acámbaro
Teziutlán
CD. DE MEXICO
Ciudad Hidalgo
JALAPA
MORELIA
Zitácuaro
Apizaco
TOLUCA
TLAXCALA
Zacatepec
VERACRUZ
5700
Popocatépetl
5452
PUEBLA
Córdoba
MALINALCO
CUERNAVACA
Atlixco
Orizaba
Tierra Blanca
Izúcar de Matamoros
Tehuacán
Taxco
Iguala
Teotitlán
Tuxtepec
Balsas
Xalitla
Río Balsas
Huajuapan de León
Chiltepec
Valle Nacional
Mexcala
Chilpancingo
Chilapa
Tlapa
Teposcolula
Ixtlán
Juxtlahuaca
3703
Guelatao
Tlaxiaco
OAXACA
Atzompa
Atoyac
MONTE ALBAN
MITLA
Zaachila
Tule
Zimatlán
Laguna de Coyuca
ACAPULCO
Ometepec
Laguna de los Tres Palos
Coajinicuilapa
Miahuatlán
Punta Maldonado
Pinotepa Nacional
Puerto Escondido
Puerto Angel
57
85
101
70
180
15
95
190
130
140
75
200

8
Golfo de Mexico
Tecolutla
Nautla
JALAPA
ZEMPOALA
La Antigua
VERACRUZ
Bahia de Campeche
Isla del Carm
Córdoba
Orizaba
Alvarado
Tlacotalpán
Tierra Blanca
Santiago Tuxtla
Catemaco
Paraíso
Frontera
Comalcalco
Coatzacoalcos
Hueyapán
Acayucan
Teotitlán
Tuxtepec
Chiltepec
Valle Nacional
LA VENTA
Minatitlán
VILLAHERMO
Palen
ISTMO DE TEHUANTEPEC
Simojovel de Allende
Raudales
Ixtlán
Guelatao
Atzompa
OAXACA
Zaachila
Tule
MITLA
Zimatlán
Ciudad Ixtepec
Presa Netzahualcoyotl
Ocozocoautla
Chamula
San Cr de las
TUXTLA GUTIERREZ
Teopisca
Santo Domingo
Tepanatepec
Amatenango
Miahuatlán
Tehuantepec
Juchitán
Arriaga
Tonalá
CHIN
SUR
Salina Cruz
Paredón
Arista
Presa de la Angostura
Ciudad Cuauhtemoc
SIERRA MADRE SUR
Golfo de Tehuantepec
Puerto Angel
Huixtla
Tapachula
Puerto Madero
180
75
185
200
7
9 10 10 11
E F G H I J

9
12
13
14
E
F
G
H
I
J
Rio Lagartos
San Felipe
I. Contoy
S. Clara
Puerto Telchac
Dzilam de Bravo
Punta Sam
I. Mujeres
Puerto Juárez
I. Cancún
Progreso
Tizimin
DZIBILCHALTUN
Motul
180
Puerto Morelos
MERIDA
Dzitas
Valladolid
COBA
Celestún
180
CHICHEN ITZA
Cozumel
Maxcanú
Akumal
Ticul
Mani
UXMAL
LABNA
Peto
Xel-Ha
Becal
TULUM
Dzibalchén
Hecelchakan
KABAH
SAYIL
Calotmul
Bolonchen de Rejón
Punta Allen
Campeche
Hopelchén
Lerma
Felipe Carrillo Puerto
Polyuc
EDZNA
YUCATAN
Champotón
Nohbek
180
Laguna de Bacalar
Bacalar
Banco Chinchorro
Isla Aguada
Chetumal
186
Ciudad del Carmen
Francisco Escárcega
Xpujil
KOHUNLICH
186
Coahuila
Belize
UAXACTUN
Tenosique
TIKAL
Belmopan
BELIZE
LACANDONA
YAXCHILAN
BONAMPAK
Lagunas de Montebello
Puerto Barrios
GUATEMALA
QUIRIGA
Huehuetenango
Los Amates
COPAN
Zacapa
Chichicastenango
Chiquimula
HONDURAS
Quezaltenango
GUATEMALA
Laguna de Atitlán
Amatitlán
EL SALVADOR

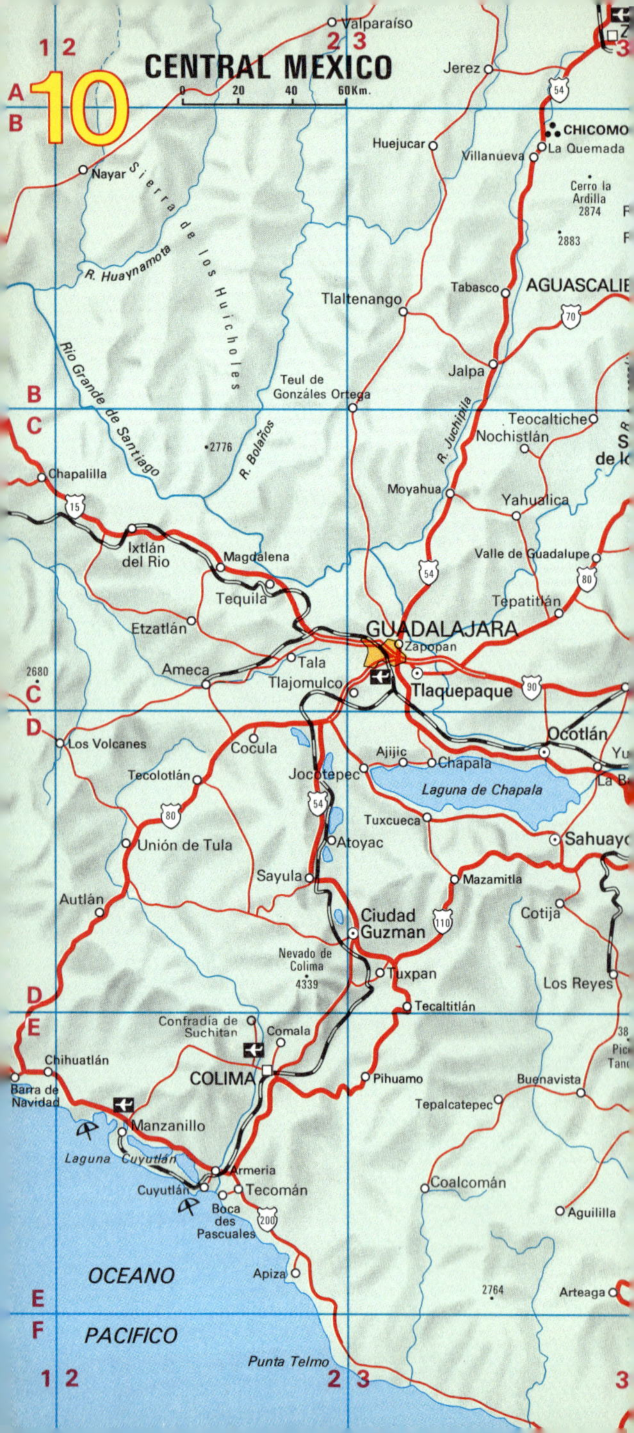

CENTRAL MEXICO
10
0 20 40 60Km.
Valparaíso
Jerez
Huejucar
Villanueva
La Quemada
CHICOMO
Cerro la Ardilla 2874
2883
Nayar
Sierra de los Huicholes
R. Huaynamota
Tabasco
AGUASCALIE
Tlaltenango
Rio Grande de Santiago
Jalpa
Teul de Gonzáles Ortega
R. Juchipila
Teocaltiche
Nochistlán
2776
R. Bolaños
Chapalilla
Moyahua
Yahualica
Ixtlán del Rio
Magdalena
Valle de Guadalupe
Tequila
Tepatitlán
Etzatlán
GUADALAJARA
Zapopan
2680
Ameca
Tala
Tlajomulco
Tlaquepaque
Ocotlán
Los Volcanes
Cocula
Ajijic
Chapala
Tecolotlán
Jocotepec
Laguna de Chapala
Tuxcueca
Unión de Tula
Atoyac
Sahuayo
Sayula
Mazamitla
Autlán
Ciudad Guzman
Cotija
Nevado de Colima 4339
Tuxpan
Los Reyes
Tecaltitlán
Confradía de Suchitan
Comala
Chihuatlán
COLIMA
Pihuamo
Buenavista
Barra de Navidad
Tepalcatepec
Manzanillo
Laguna Cuyutlán
Armeria
Coalcomán
Cuyutlán
Tecomán
Boca des Pascuales
Aguililla
OCEANO
Apiza
2764
Arteaga
PACIFICO
Punta Telmo
15
54
70
80
90
110
200

CATECAS
4
4 5
5 6
11
A
B
C
D
E
F
Moctezuma
Arista
Salinas
Ojo Caliente
Peotillos
49
57
80
Ahualulco
Cerritos
3340
Pinos
SAN LUIS POTOSI
Santa Catarina
Tepetates
TES
Santa María del Río
Ojuelos de Jalisco
Reyes
70
45
80
51
Encarnación
San Felipe
57
Juan Lagos
Lagos de Moreno
Jalostotitlán
San Miguel el Alto
LEON
San Luis de la Paz
Dolores Hidalgo
Comanjilla
San Francisco del Rincón
Cubilete
GUANAJUATO
Atotonilco
Silao
San Miguel de Allende
45
Arandas
Manuel Doblado
Comonfort
Irapuato
otonilco
Rosas
QUERETARO
Cuerámaro
Apaseo
Salamanca
Celaya
Abasolo
Apaseo el Alto
Galindo
Valle de Santiago
La Piedad
Salvatierra
Uriangato
Yuriria
Moroleón
Acámbaro
Zamora
Puruándiro
Cuitzeo
acona
L. de Cuitzeo
Maravatio
Zacapu
Zinapécuaro
Chupicuaro
Paracho
Quiroga
Ciudad Hidalgo
L. Pátzcuaro
MORELIA
Angahuan
Eronguaricaro
Pátzcuaro
ricutín
San José Purua
Uruapan
Villa Escalante (Santa Clara del Cobre)
Zitácuaro
Tzaracuaral
Tacámbaro
Valle de Bravo
Apatzingán
Ario de Rosales
Nueva Italia
Tingambato
Nocupetaro
Tejupilco
134
Presa del Infiernillo
Bejucos
Huetamo
Río Balsas
Ciudad Altamirano
Infiernillo
51
2652
Arcelia del Progreso

12
Ciudad Mante
González
Manuel
El Salto
Antiguo Morelos
Cerritos
Ciudad del Maíz
El Estribo
Las Tablas
Ebano
Santa Catarina
Cárdenas
Ciudad Valles
Tamuin
Tanimul
Río Pánuco
Rio Verde
Rayon
El Higo
Pan American Highway
Pedro Montoya
Aquismon
Tanquián
Tempoa
Xichu
Concá
Río Tamuin
Tancoyol
Xilitla
San Luis de la Paz
Jalpan
Landa
Tilaco
Tamazunchale
Huejutla
Tolimán
Molango
Eloxochitlán
Tianguistengo
QUERETARO
E. Montes
Metztitlán
Tequisquiapan
Ixmiquilpan
Mansión Galindo
San Juan del Río
Huichapan
Atotonilco
Actopan
San Miguel Regla
TULA
PACHUCA
Tulancingo
Maravatio
Jilotepec
Zempoala
Tepeapulco
Atlacomulco
Tepotzotlán
ACOLMAN
Otumba
Apan
TEOTIHUACAN
Ixtlahuaca
Tlalnepantla
Tepexpan
Calpulalpan
CIUDAD DE MEXICO
Texcoco
L. de Texcoco
Villa Victoria
Zitácuaro
CALIXTLAHUACA
Tlaxcala
Valle de Bravo
TOLUCA
Xochimilco
Chalco
Iztaccíhuatl 5286
4577
Capulhuac
Amecameca
Tingambato
Nevado de Toluca
Tenango
Popocatépetl 5452
Ozumba
CHOLULA
Temascaltepec
Tenancingo
Tepoztlán
Acatepec
MALINALCO
Chalma
CUERNAVACA
Ixtapan de la Sal
XOCHICALCO
Yautepec
Cuautla
Atlixco
Tejupilco
Oaxtepec
Amayuca
CHALCATZINGO
Bejucos
Grutas de Cacahuamilpa
Zacatepec
Izucar de Matamoros
Tepalcingo
Taxco
Tequesquitengo
Tehuixtla
Iguala
Chiautla
Arcelia del Progreso
101
80
180
85
70
105
120
57
55
15
190
95
134
51

13
A
B
C
D
E
F
8
9
10
GOLFO DE
MEXICO
Lomas del Real
Altamira
Ciudad Madero
TAMPICO
180
Laguna
de
Tamiahua
Naranjos
Tamiahua
Portrero
del Llano
Tuxpan
Alamo
Castillo
de Teayo
Ixhuatlán
Poza Rica
Tecolutla
Papantla
EL TAJIN
130
Huauchinango
Nautla
Tlapacoyan
Martinez de la Torre
Zacatlán
Cuetzalán
Misantla
Teziutlán
Acuaco
Altotonga
119
Punta Villa Rica
Perote
4282
Cofre
de Perote
JALAPA
ZEMPOALA
Chachalacas
140
Apizaco
Oriental
Zico
La Antigua
Huamantla
Zacatepec
Veracruz
4461
La Malinche
Huatusco
Mocambo
El Seco
Citlaltépetl
5700
Cosomatepec
Soledad
Doblado
Boca del
Rio
Amozoc
Acatzingo
Fortín
de las Flores
Córdoba
Tepeaca
Tecamachalco
Orizaba
La Tinaja
Alvarado
R. Atoyac
Tierra
Blanca
Tehuacán
3719
Psa. Temaxcal
Presa
M. Aleman
Cosamaloapan
Chilac
Coxcatlán
Acatlán
Temaxcal
Teotitlán
Huautla

14
CIUDAD DE MEXICO
0
0·5
1 km
POPOTLA
POLANCO
PLAZA URUGUAY
Museo de Antropologia
Monolito Tlāloc
Museo Rufino Tamayo
Auditorio Nacional
Zoológico
Museo de Arte Moderno
BOSQUE DE CHAPULTEPEC
Castillo de Chapultepec
Museo de Historia
Galeria de Historia
Secretaria de Salubridad Asistencia
CHAPULTEPEC
Los Pinos
PARQUE ESPAÑA
JUANACATLAN
PARQUE LIRA
TACUBAYA
PASEO DE LA REFORMA
AV. CONSTITUYENTES
ANILLO PERIFERICO
AV. RIO SAN JOAQUIN
AV. EJERCITO NACIONAL
AV. HORACIO
PRESIDENTE MASARIK
CAMPOS ELISEOS
RUBEN DARIO
CALZ. MARIANO ESCOBEDO
AV. MARINA NACIONAL
CALZ. MELCHOR OCAMPO
AV. OBSERVATORIO
GRAN AVENIDA
CALZ. DEL REY
CALZ. DEL CERRO

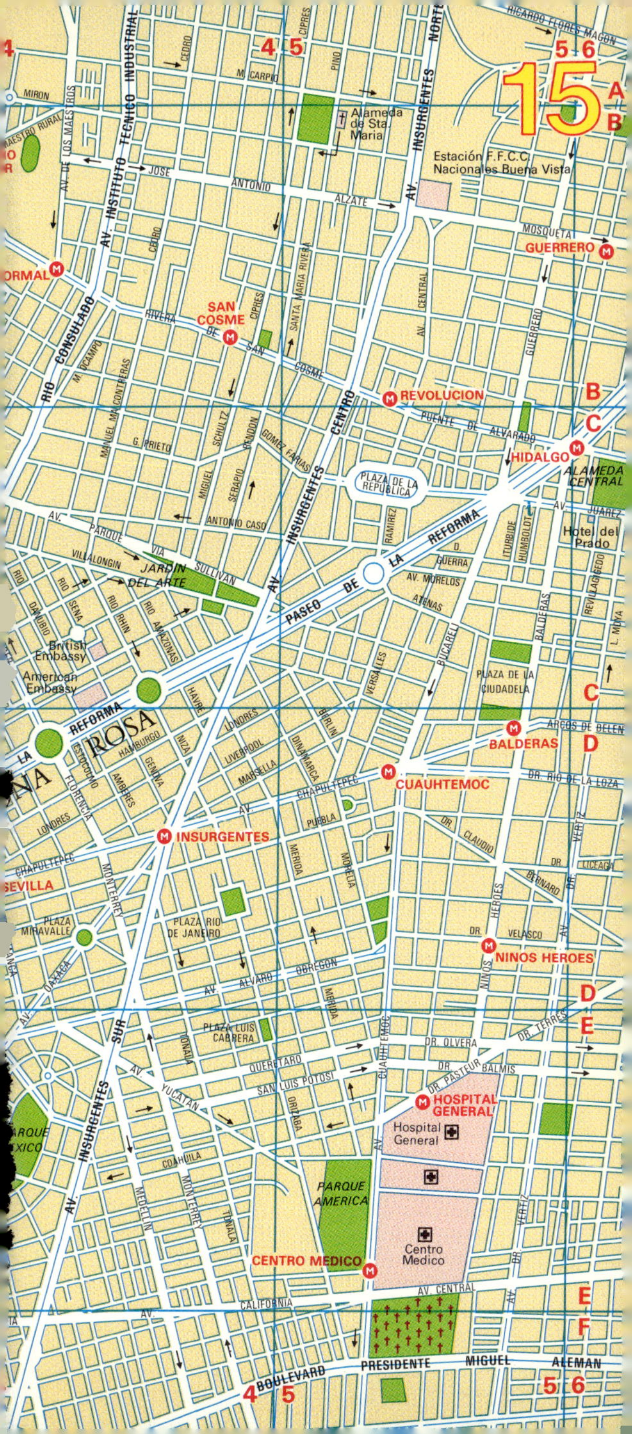
15
A
B
C
D
E
F
4
5
6
Ricardo Flores Magon
Miron
Maestro Rural
Av. de los Maestros
Av. Instituto Tecnico Industrial
Cedro
M. Carpio
Cipres
Pino
Insurgentes Norte
Alameda de Sta. Maria
Estación F.F.C.C. Nacionales Buena Vista
Jose Antonio Alzate
Mosqueta
Guerrero
Normal
Rio Consulado
Rivera
San Cosme
Santa Maria Rivera
Central
M. Ocampo
Manuel M. Contreras
Revolucion
Puente de Alvarado
Hidalgo
Alameda Central
G. Prieto
Miguel Schultz
Serapio Rendon
Gomez Farias
Plaza de la Republica
Av. Juarez
Hotel del Prado
Av. Parque Via
Antonio Caso
Villalongin
Jardin del Arte
Sullivan
Ramirez
Iturbide
Humboldt
D. Guerra
Av. Morelos
Atenas
Revillagigedo
Rio Danubio
Rio Sena
Rio Rhin
Rio Amazonas
Paseo de la Reforma
Av. Insurgentes Centro
British Embassy
American Embassy
Versalles
Bucareli
Balderas
L. Moya
Plaza de la Ciudadela
Havre
Londres
Berlin
Arcos de Belen
Zona Rosa
Hamburgo
Estocolmo
Niza
Liverpool
Dinamarca
Genova
Marsella
Florencia
Amberes
Cuauhtemoc
Dr. Rio de la Loza
Av. Chapultepec
Puebla
Insurgentes
Dr. Claudio Bernard
Dr. Liceaga
Dr. Vertiz
Sevilla
Monterrey
Merida
Morelia
Plaza Miravalle
Plaza Rio de Janeiro
Dr. Velasco
Ninos Heroes
Av. Oaxaca
Av. Alvaro Obregon
Plaza Luis Cabrera
Tonala
Dr. Olvera
Dr. Terres
Dr. Balmis
Dr. Pasteur
Queretaro
San Luis Potosi
Av. Yucatan
Orizaba
Av. Cuauhtemoc
Hospital General
Parque Mexico
Av. Insurgentes Sur
Coahuila
Medellin
Parque America
Centro Medico
Av. Central
Av. California
Boulevard Presidente Miguel Aleman

KEY TO NUMBERED BUILDINGS

1 Catedral Metropolitana
2 Sagrario
3 Museo Benito Juarez
4 Palacio Nacional
5 Suprema Corte de Justicia
6 Ruinas Aztecas y Museo Etnográfico
7 Nacional Monte de Piedad
8 Iglesia de la Enseñanza
9 Iglesia de la Profesa
10 Ex-Palacio de los Condes de Valparaiso
11 Biblioteca Nacional
12 Hospital de Jesus
13 Museo de la Cd. de Mexico
14 Escuela de Artes Plasticas de Sn. Carlos
15 Iglesia La Santisima
16 Iglesia de Santa Teresa
17 Iglesia de Loreto
18 Iglesia de Sta. Catarina
19 Iglesia de Sto. Domingo
20 Camara de Senadores
21 Palacio de Bellas Artes
22 Casa de los Azulejos
23 Torre Latinoamericana
24 Iglesia de San Francisco
25 Palacio de Iturbide
26 Iglesia de Sta. Veracruz
27 Iglesia de San Juan de Díos
28 Museo de Artes e Industrias Populares
29 Colegio de las Vizcaínas
30 Iglesia Regina